FLORIDA FIREARMS
Law, Use & Ownership ™

EIGHTH EDITION
– June 2015 –

by: Jon H. Gutmacher

FREE UPDATING POLICY
Cumulative updates to this book are available
free on our website revised in interim bulletins as
needed throughout the year.

www.FloridaFirearmsLaw.com

Warlord Publishing
a division of
Jon H. Gutmacher, P.A.
1861 South Patrick Drive, #194
Indian Harbour Beach, Fl. 32937
Phone: 407-279-1029

Email: Floridagunlawyer@aol.com

DISCLAIMERS, COPYRIGHTS & TRADEMARKS

Author: *Jon H. Gutmacher*

Warnings & Disclaimers:

Cover photo: Kel Tec Model PF-9 semi-auto handgun
courtesy Kel-Tec Weapons www.keltecweapons.com
Realtree cover background courtesy Jordan Outdoor Enterprises, Ltd.

TABLE OF CONTENTS

ACKNOWLEDGMENTS

The author wishes to gratefully acknowledge all those who have given him support and assistance through the years with special thanks to Greg Hopkins, Stephen F. Shaw, John Monroe, Daniel A. Harris, and Locke T. Clifford, for all the really hard work and time they put into their sections of the book, and also to John Harris for his help trying to get in Tennessee. Likewise, my thanks to all of those who have stuck with me through the years, too numerous to mention. To Bill and Joe at Action Gun Outfitters for their help at the range, my brother Glenn Gutmacher, my webmaster, David Cate at Orlando Web Development, my printing advisor, Mitchell Faine, Derek Kellgren at Kel-Tec, John Booth at FDLE, Joe Snyder for his constant encouragement but overly long telephone calls, my good friends Norm and Gary Belson, Charles Berrane, and Wally at the 911 store. With special remembrance for Larry Anderson at Shoot Straight who passed away during the Seventh edition. A truly great guy I could always call, who deeply believed in the book. To all of you, and so many more – thank you!

INTRODUCTION

For many gun owners, this book has often been referred to as "the bible" on Florida firearm, weapon, and self defense laws. I'm very proud, and awed that anyone would even use that phrase, and totally understand that no offense or comparison was ever made or intended. However, I've put my heart and soul into the book, plus I've put over forty years of experience as a criminal trial attorney and NRA certified firearms instructor with a rather wide range of experience on everything from being a prosecutor, police legal advisor, civil police liability attorney (plaintiff and defense), and criminal defense attorney with over two hundred jury trials under my belt, and hundreds of non-jury trials on top of that. I write, think, eat, sleep, and breathe this stuff 24/7, just about 365 days a year, and try to keep on the cutting edge of not only the law – but the practical side of firearms, weapons, and self defense issues. The book is a matter of personal pride, and although every now and then I've had to rethink prior positions, or admit on rare occasions that I might have been wrong – as a general rule, my opinions have sooner or later been adopted by the courts or the legislature, and have proven to be "spot on".

This "Eighth Edition" marks a new beginning in the book. Not only is the coverage greatly expanded in all areas of the law, but the book was rewritten from top-to-bottom! In depth coverage includes not only Florida and Federal laws – but I was able to add sections on Alabama, Georgia, North Carolina, and South Carolina by enlisting some of the top attorneys in their field from these states to write the sections on their state – two of them having their own books already published. While the out-of-state sections are obviously not as extensive as the Florida and Federal coverage – it should be more than enough information so that you can drive through, or take a vacation in these states while understanding your rights. Likewise, since many of you have been asking me to expand the book with more question-and-answer sections, adding more statutory and case citations and sections, giving more advice on what to do if stopped by the police or arrested – all that has been accomplished in this new version

For those of you not familiar with the book, it's been around since November 1993, went thru seven prior editions, as well as revisions of each edition at least once yearly, and as of the completion of this Eighth Edition (October 2014), has sold over 194,000 copies, almost all of them in Florida. With the addition of Alabama, Georgia, North and South Carolina – that's probably going to change. Likewise, there have been major additions to the book in almost all chapters, and several major corrections were made due to changes in the law – the most important being the substantial revisions to the self defense statutes were passed by the Florida Legislature in 2014!

As I've said in every version before, while this book is not written as legal advice, it has been found to be authoritative by lots of very knowledgeable people including the NRA, Florida Sheriffs Association, Florida Association of State Troopers, and Gun Owners of America. It will clarify most of your questions about some very complicated areas, and will point out the areas of law that appear to remain in controversy. While it's not perfect -- many people – including those in the industry, law enforcement, and the courts – think it's about as good as it can get.

I personally suggest that when reading the book – you highlight the key areas. You need not read it in chapter order – it is written so you can pick whatever chapter you want, in whatever order you want. Plus, once you read it – plan reading the sections again – because every time you pick up the book – you're going to see something you missed, or something you read before will suddenly take on new, or clearer meaning.   Likewise, if you have any questions after reading it feel free to drop me an *email* from the link on my website. Please don't try phoning me – I do **not** respond to legal questions over the telephone – ever!   I use the phone only for actual business – and just in case you missed the update on my website, I recently retired from trial practice, and now only *consult* on actual cases, except with regard to administrative matters dealing with BATFE. After forty years of slugging it out in the courtroom – I finally had enough.

Anyway, I hope you enjoy the book, and more so – hope it keeps you and those you love out of trouble.

Jon H. Gutmacher, Esq.

CHAPTER ONE

THE RIGHT TO BEAR ARMS
& CONSTITUTIONAL UNDERSTANDING

On December 15, 1791, the Congress of the United States ratified the first ten amendments to the Constitution. These Amendments have been become known to us as the "Bill of Rights". Foremost among them, from the standpoint of this book, is the Second Amendment. In a historical context, the Second Amendment covers two clearly distinct concerns of the framers of our Constitution. One was to insure the rights of the People to keep and bear arms. The other was to insure the existence of the popular militia. I will discuss both.

THE BILL OF RIGHTS THE SECOND AMENDMENT

> "A well regulated militia, being necessary to the security of
> a free State, the right of the people to keep and bear arms,
> shall not be infringed."

A WELL REGULATED MILITIA:

At the time of the Constitutional Convention, a loose confederation of thirteen individual colonies had just defeated King George of England in what was basically a citizen's revolution. For the most part, the American Revolution was won by a collection of locally organized militia which had been banded together into larger groups and armies to fight the common enemy, the British. These militia were comprised of freemen from all walks of life, who were locally organized, self-armed, and who trained and drilled under locally elected leaders. This was the choice method of defense -- as regular, or "standing armies" were thought by many of the free populace to be instruments of tyranny -- the means by which despots and kings were able to control their subjects by force, and thereby rule. Thus, the definition of "*well regulated militia*", was simply a well understood reference to an independent group of self-armed freemen, under self-elected leadership, who regularly or occasionally drilled, and were not under government control. In more general terms, it was clearly understood that the phrase "*well regulated militia*" referred to the "body of the people", ie: the free citizens of the land, as a whole.

There was significant argument during the *Constitutional Convention* whether the creation of a central government would tend to foster tyranny, and much of this discussion revolved around the argument as to whether a standing army for this central government should be permitted at all. Many enlightened thinkers of the time believed in the concept that "power tends to corrupt", thus they had a basic fear of any centralized government, and its eventual ability to oppress.

The only counter to this fear was that a well organized militia comprised of the free people of the several states would always be more powerful than any standing army -- and thus the People could overthrow any corruption of government by force of numbers. Moreover, the thinking that also pervaded the times was clearly that the local militia would always be necessary to the national and local defense -- as there was no desire to allow a centralized government to gain such power as to obviate this need. Of course, to guarantee these beliefs, the right for a people's militia had to be ensured. The result of this thinking lies in the first part of the wording in the Second Amendment: "*being necessary to a free state*".

Over time, the well regulated militia has passed-away, and been replaced by the professional soldier, the National Guard, and an organized police force. The National Guard has little to do with what the Framers of the Constitution envisioned as "*a well regulated militia*" as it lacks the localization, freedom from government control, and freedom from government purse strings that would be necessary to this concept. In fact, the ***National Guard*** would have been defined as a "***select militia***" in the late 1700's, that term meaning a militia armed and maintained by the government, and obviously subject to its discipline.

So, don't get thrown off track by media misinformation. A "*well regulated militia*" historically referred to the body of the free citizens of this country, locally organized, and free of government control. While we probably don't need such active militias now, the right to have them is historic, and is guaranteed in the Constitution.

THE RIGHT TO KEEP AND BEAR ARMS:

What phrasing could be any more clear than that of "*the right of the people to keep and bear arms, shall not be infringed.*" Yet, until 2008 hardly anyone except historians, and the Fifth Circuit Court of Appeals [2] understood that it meant exactly what it said. However, on June 26, 2008, the United States Supreme Court, decided the landmark case of *District of Columbia v. Heller*, 128 S.Ct. 2783 (2008), which changed that forever. Let me tell you in very succinct fashion exactly what the Opinion said:

First – the Second Amendment protects an individual's right of firearms ownership for purposes of self defense unconnected with any militia or military purpose. The Court held that the historical purpose of the Amendment was to make sure the federal government would not seize firearms from citizens, and thereby be able to rule over them in a tyrannical fashion. Moreover, it made clear that at the time of its passage the right of free citizens to own and possess firearms for self defense was sacrosanct. Still, the Court recognized that the right to own and possess firearms is not without limitations, and that unusually dangerous weapons, and those used primarily by criminals could be regulated - just as they were in Colonial times. However, the Supreme Court found that handguns are the primary defensive weapon of choice in the modern era, and thus these types of weapons are protected under the *Second Amendment*.

That's the entire essence of the Opinion. There are lots of historical quotes, lots of cases quoted, and lots of facts and figures – but – in the end, it's all that simple. Now true, four Justices weren't real happy with that analysis. Their main argument was that the *Second Amendment* has outlived its usefulness - so we should just ignore it!

The majority of the Justices in the case responded to this argument by stating:

> *"A constitutional guarantee subject to future judges' assessments of its usefulness is no constitutional guarantee at all. Constitutional rights are enshrined with the scope they were understood to have when the people adopted them, whether or not future legislatures or (yes) even future judges think that scope too broad."*

McDONALD v. CITY OF CHICAGO:

The follow-up to the *Heller* case came in *McDonald v. City of Chicago*, 130 S.Ct. 3020 (2009). That case involved a challenge to what amounted to a total ban on handguns in the homes of ordinary citizens by the City of Chicago, and a challenge to that ban by a Chicago resident who believed he had a Constitutional Right, under the *Second Amendment*, to keep a handgun in his home to protect himself from attack in the high crime neighborhood in which he lived. Having lost his challenge in both the federal trial court, and the federal appellate court, the United States Supreme Court reversed the lower court decisions, and held that the *Second Amendment* applied equally to the States under the *Fourteenth Amendment* of the United States Constitution "***Due Process***" clause, which provides that no state may deprive "*any person of life, liberty, or property without due process of law*", and that the Chicago ban was therefore unconstitutional. Of note, is that 38 states joined in arguing for the case on the side of Mr. McDonald, on the grounds that the *Second Amendment* was a fundamental right of the people. While there are lots of great quotes from the case, one of my favorites is the following zinger:

"Chicago Police Department statistics, we are told, reveal that the City's handgun murder rate has actually increased since the ban was enacted and that Chicago residents now face one of the highest murder rates in the country and rates of other violent crimes that exceed the average in comparable cities."

A WARNING ABOUT CONSTITUTIONAL INTERPRETATION:

People should be wary about constitutional changes. Every time the State or Federal Constitution is amended -- you, the ordinary citizen, are giving-up more and more of your "retained", and supposedly "inalienable" rights.

Why?

Because in our country, government derives all of its power from the People. This is in the form of those grants of power embodied in the Constitution. What the Constitution says the government can do -- is all it is authorized to do, nothing more! If it wasn't given to the government in the Constitution -- it is **"retained"** by the People -- and the government cannot legally interfere with any of these "retained" rights.

So, why do we have a *"**Bill of Rights**"*? Aren't these rights retained, anyway?

Basically, whenever a *Bill of Rights* is adopted, it is a precautionary statement of those rights which the People want to make especially sure the government realizes are off limits to legislative or judicial erosion! In other words, it's a statement by a bunch of real nervous people that don't trust the government, in the first place. Or, like Thomas Jefferson said:

"Government is a necessary evil"

In Florida we've gotten into some very bad habits, because we tend to randomly amend the State Constitution on fairly regular basis, instead of recognizing it for what it is. Since a constitution is supposed to be a basic framework for government -- it's not a good idea to go amending it every year. That's what the legislature is for. They pass laws, amend laws, repeal laws -- all within the framework the constitution has set forth.

It may seem like a good idea to amend the Constitution in the heat of the moment, but most of the time, we later realize we'd have been better off if we just left it alone, and let the courts or the legislature deal with it. An example of this are some additions made to the Florida Constitution regarding the right to keep and bear arms:

FLORIDA'S RIGHT TO KEEP AND BEAR ARMS:
Florida Constitution, Article I, Section 8:

a.   The right of the people to keep and bear arms in defense of themselves and of the lawful authority of the state shall not be infringed, except that the manner of bearing arms may be regulated by law.

b.   There shall be a mandatory period of three days,excluding weekends and legal holidays, between the purchase and delivery at retail of any handgun. For the purposes of this section, "purchase" means the transfer of money or other valuable consideration to the retailer and "handgun" means a firearm capable of being carried and used by one hand, such as a pistol or revolver. Holders of a concealed weapon permit as prescribed in Florida law shall not be subject to the provision of this paragraph.

c.   The legislature shall enact legislation implementing subsect ion (b) of this section, effective no later than December 31, 1991, which shall provide that anyone violating the provisions of subsection (b) shall be guilty of a felony.

d.   This restriction shall not apply to a trade in of another handgun.

The restrictions set forth in this section of the Constitution cannot be changed by the Legislature, the Governor, or the Judiciary. The People voted for it, and made it part of the "unchangeable" portion of our basic law. For better or worse, it's there forever -unless the citizens vote to change the Constitution, again.

PREEMPTION LAW:

Florida is a *"**preemption**"* state. That means that the Legislature has decided to keep local government out of firearms regulation, unless it specifically authorizes an exemption. The reason we have a *preemption law* is because of all the problems we had before this law was enacted. Every local government had its own version of the law, and nobody knew what the heck the law was from city-to-city, or county-to-county. In essence, it was politics at its worst — and the citizens paid the price.

The preemption statute, F.S. 790.33, was amended in 2011 by the Legislature with the following provisions:

"(1) PREEMPTION: Except as expressly provided by the State Constitution or general law, the Legislature hereby declares that it is occupying the whole field of regulation of firearms and ammunition, including the purchase, sale, transfer, taxation, manufacture, ownership, possession, storage, and transportation thereof, to the exclusion of all existing and future county, city, town, or municipal ordinances or any administrative regulations or rules adopted by local or state government relating thereto. Any such existing ordinances, rules, or regulations are hereby declared null and void.

(2) POLICY AND INTENT: (a) It is the intent of this section to provide uniform firearms laws in the state; to declare all ordinances and regulations null and void which have been enacted by any jurisdictions other than state and federal, which regulate firearms, ammunition, or components thereof; to prohibit the enactment of any future ordinances or regulations relating to firearms, ammunition, or components thereof unless specifically authorized by this section or general law; and to require local jurisdictions to enforce state firearms laws.

The amendment also added prohibitions and penalties that allow individuals and organizations affected by any violative ordinance or regulation to seek declaratory and injunctive relief in court to declare the ordinance or regulation invalid and void, and penalties against individuals and government that create or enforce such laws or regulations.   Attorney fees, damages, and legal interest are awarded if the citizen or organization wins the case. However, the amendment will not affect the right of a county to create waiting periods and criminal history checks under *Fla. Const ., Article 8, section 5(b).* (ie: purchase of firearms on property the public has a right to access).   —

Exceptions to the amendments in F.S .790.33 include non-discriminatory zoning ordinances, ordinances and regulations that affect government employees while at work; regulations by law enforcement agencies concerning firearms and ammunition used by peace officers while on duty; and regulations by the *Florida Fish and Wildlife Conservation Commission* related to the taking of wildlife, or their managed shooting ranges.

You might note that the preemption statute does not apply to weapons other than firearms and ammunition. F.S . 790.33 However, pursuant to Florida constitutional law, local government is still restricted from regulating other weapons if they pass laws that conflict with Chapter 790 of the Florida Statutes.

STATISTICAL DATA ON USE OF FIREARMS:
In recent years there has been a serious attempt to discredit the private ownership of firearms, and to minimize and distort the meaning of the *Second Amendment.* Media has taken an increasingly active part in this conspiracy, and seems to be a leading proponent in the battle to despoil your right of self-defense. The classic argument is that if by banning firearms we can "save one life" -- it will be worth it all. [5] Of course, that means giving up more of your fast disappearing personal liberty. But more importantly, it distorts the actual truth.

Statistics compiled by the government show that firearm accidents have significantly declined over the years, not just percentage wise -- but also numerically. Moreover, research done by Florida State University professor Gary Kleck has established that 800,000 to 2.5 million people a year use a firearm throughout the United States in lawful self-defense, and in stopping the commission of serious felonies.

In an ideal society, there would be no criminals, no terrorists, no foreign enemies, and no need for self-defense. But that society is a dream, and the reality is that law-abiding citizens need a method to defend themselves, their property, and their families. A firearm furnishes that method, and if a person learns gun safety, and has a basic knowledge of what he or she can lawfully do, all of society benefits by their being armed. That is one of the basic pillars upon which this Great Nation was founded – the media be damned!

THE EXTENSION OF THE POWERS OF CONGRESS:

Earlier in this chapter I briefly mentioned why you need to be cautious about giving away your "***retained rights***", by constitutional amendment. Let me show you how this has run amuck in the federal system -- so you can understand where all these federal regulations are coming from, at least, from a legal standpoint.

Article 1, section 1, of the United States Constitution states that "*all legislative powers herein granted shall be vested in a Congress of the United States . . . .*" That literally means that if the Constitution doesn't grant them the power -- they don't have the power. The *Bill of Rights*, in the *Tenth Amendment* states that "*the powers not delegated to the United States by the Constitution, nor prohibited by it to the States, are reserved to the States respectively, or to the people.*" That section basically means the same thing, but more forcefully. Literally, it means that the powers not granted to Congress, and not withheld from the states (such as the right to make treaties, formulate currency, etc.) are reserved to the several states, or their citizens.

Last but not least, we have the *Ninth Amendment* to the United States Constitution. This states that "*the enumeration in the Constitution of certain rights, shall not be construed to deny or disparage others retained by the people*". This means that those rights which were thought by the framers of the Constitutional to be the "natural" or "inalienable" rights of free citizens -- cannot be infringed upon by the government.

Well, it all sounds good, but in actuality it hasn't been working too well since the time the Civil War began. Let me show you why, by giving you a brief lesson in Constitutional law:

A BRIEF LESSON IN CONSTITUTIONAL LAW:

The *Tenth Amendment* to the United States Constitution reserves all powers not otherwise delegated to Congress, to the individual States, or to the People. However, Congress, with the apathetic assistance of the federal judiciary, has managed to completely usurp the purpose of this Amendment. In essence, the federal judicial system has generally failed in its responsibilities, and lets Congress run amuck by not policing it. Let me give you an example: An extremely important federal appellate decision, *United States v. Lopez*, invalidated a portion of the 1990 "*Gun-Free School Zones Act*". This remarkably dumb federal law made it a federal felony to possess a firearm within **1000 feet** of a school zone. It was dumb because if you happened to be driving within 999.9 feet of a one room wooden kindergarten, even if the kids were home on vacation, even if you didn't know it was there until you went around that blind curve in the road that suddenly revealed it, and even if there's a raging river between the road you're on and the school -you're in deep buffalo chips with the law unless you have a CWL.

Now, you ask: "How can Congress legislate such a law? Isn't this a purely an area of state concern, reserved to the state legislatures?"

Excellent question! I see I've gotten you thinking!

However, and unfortunately, the answer, according to your wonderful federal government, is "no" -- and that's because Congress can presumably pass any law they want under the power of the "*Commerce Clause*", because Congress has the constitutionally granted power to regulate anything that "*substantially affects interstate or foreign commerce*", and in such instances, the *Tenth Amendment* doesn't apply. In other words, the *Tenth Amendment* would restrict the exercise of federal lawmaking jurisdiction only when there are **no other clauses** in the Constitution under which the Congress has power to act! In essence, this would require a process of elimination. Thus, if Congress can't pass legislation under the Commerce Clause – is there **another** clause they could still pass it under? If not -- the law would be outside of its power to act, and therefore "reserved" to the states.

"Is this really the law," you ask?

The unfortunate answer is "yes" -- but that's not the most unfortunate part. You see, the courts are supposed to have the authority to make sure that any power exercised by Congress is exercised legitimately. That's what our

Founding Fathers meant by "*a system of checks and balances*". In other words, if the Congress wants to legislate something under the *Commerce Clause*, then the problem it's attempting to address and rectify should, in actuality "*substantially affect interstate or foreign commerce* ". If it doesn't, then it's an illegitimate use of power that's should be reserved to the individual state legislatures, or the People.

The problem here is that federal courts normally don't do that kind of policing. In actuality, they routinely "defer" to any factual findings made by Congress no matter how unsupported, or outlandish these findings may be! All you need is some Senator or Congressman saying: "We're passing this legislation because gun possession around a school affects interstate commerce" -- and Whoop-de-Doo -- the court usually says : "Fine -- sounds good to us!"

That's basically what *United States v. Lopez* said. In fact, the Opinion of the Court actually said that it was not really its job to second guess Congress -- but, it was *up to the People* to elect representatives who would not pass unconstitutional laws under the guise of constitutional ones. To put it another way: if you elect representatives who don't understand or care about the Constitution, and your rights -- you get what you deserve.

So much for the system of "*checks and balances*" that our Founding Fathers envisioned. Let one part fail, and the result is that Liberty pays the price!

However, the Lopez court still invalidated the law because the federalists in Congress actually forgot to include any statement that commerce "*was affected*" by guns near schools when they passed the Act -- and thus the court was free to determine from a standpoint of common sense (something little used in government) -- that this stupid law really had nothing to do with interstate commerce in the first place, didn't affect it one iota -- and was therefore unconstitutional.

So, for a short time, the citizens lucked out -- only because of a simple oversight. If not, the magic words, "*affecting commerce*" would have been uttered at the right moment in Congress, and another oppressive law would have stayed on the books, unchecked by the one branch of government that the Founding Fathers thought would stop such abuses.

It seems that the federal courts are too political, and too "politically correct". If the Constitution must suffer -- it usually does. However, there is some rare good news in this rather one-sided area. In the last few years we've started to see changes in the cases coming out of the United States Supreme Court. It appears that a small majority of the Supreme Court is beginning to interpret legislation in a more traditional manner, consistent with our basic constitutional precepts. This is a very welcome change. In fact, in the Lopez [7] case that I just discussed, the Supreme Court, by a very narrow margin, sustained the decision of the federal appellate court, and agreed that the "1000 foot law" had no substantial affect on interstate commerce, and was therefore beyond the power of Congress to enact.

Of course, Congress was not to be deterred, and after the Supreme Court made it clear that the law was an unconstitutional intrusion into an area of purely state concern — Congress reenacted the law, once again, with the following findings:

> *"The Congress finds and declares that crime, particularly crime involving drugs and guns, is a pervasive, nationwide problem; crime at the local level is exacerbated by the interstate movement of drugs, guns, and criminal gangs; firearms and ammunition move easily in interstate commerce and have been found in increasing numbers in and around schools, as documented in numerous hearings in both the Committee on the Judiciary of the House of Representatives and the Committee on the Judiciary of the Senate; in fact, even before the sale of a firearm, the gun, its component parts, ammunition, and the raw materials from which they are made have considerably moved in interstate commerce; while criminals freely move from State to State, ordinary citizens and foreign visitors may fear to travel to or through certain parts of the country due to concern about violent crime and gun violence, and parents may decline to send their children to school for the same reason; the occurrence of violent crime in school zones has resulted in a decline in the quality of education in our country; this decline in the quality of education has an adverse impact on interstate commerce and the foreign commerce of the United States; States, localities, and school systems find it almost impossible to handle gun related crime by themselves--even States, localities, and school systems that have made strong efforts to prevent, detect, and punish gun-related crime find their efforts unavailing due in part to the failure or inability of other States or localities to take strong measures; and the Congress has the power, under the interstate commerce clause and other provisions of the Constitution, to enact measures to ensure the integrity and safety of the nation's schools by enactment of this subsection."*

So, we're back where we started — and we've proven what we knew all along -- that many of our representatives don't care about the Constitution when it comes to guns. The question that remains now is what will the Supreme Court do if the issue gets back to them, again? At least two appellate decisions have held the amended statute as constitutional. *Danks v. U.S.*, 221 F.3d 1037 (8th Cir. 1999); *U.S. v. Pierson*, 139 F.3d 501 (5th Cir. 1998). But, a recent Supreme Court decision seems to reassert the invalidity. *U.S. v. Morrison*, 146 L.ed.2d

658 (2000). [8] From a practical standpoint, it's likely the lower appellate decisions will stand, because the Supreme Court rarely accepts jurisdiction, even when a decision is wrong. Just remember, if you have a concealed permit, you don't have a problem with this law because that's one of the law's few exceptions. So — get the CWL!

Obviously, only the Supreme Court should be able to change that interpretation of unconstitutionality. However, federal courts tend to rule in favor of the government almost all the time. They rarely interpret the law to protect the People — instead, they interpret the law to protect the government. Again, a concept that the Founding Fathers might have trouble with. Only time will tell.

Some other recent decisions of the Supreme Court have also been promising. The Court invalidated portions of the **Brady** law [9], and in another case required the government to prove *"willful"* violations of certain firearm laws before a conviction could be obtained.[10] Still, these decisions have been won by a one vote majority -- and are being made by a very divided Court.

Interesting, huh?

WAITING PERIODS ON FIREARMS SALES:
        Florida has multiple laws and constitutional provisions regarding gun sales. The first is **Florida Constitution , Article 1, section 8**, which requires a three (3) day waiting period between the purchase and delivery at retail of any ha ndgun. CWL holders are completely excepted. Likewise, the provision does not apply to a trade of a handgun for another handgun with no cash involved. Weekends and legal holidays are not counted in the waiting period, and you begin counting days on the day following the sale. (ie: sale is Monday – delivery can't be until Friday. Sale is on Sunday – delivery can't be until Thursday). **Florida Statute 790.0655** duplicates this section, with the same exceptions, imposing an almost identical mandatory three (3) day waiting period on the sale of any handgun at retail.

        Fla. Const. , Article 8, section 5(b), is a more recent provision that grants each county the right to pass ordinances that require a criminal history records check, and/or a **3-5 day** waiting period (excluding weekends and lega l holidays) on the sale of **any** type firearm when any part of the transaction is conducted on property *"to which the public has a right of access"*. Holders of a CWL are again exempted from this provision. The phrase *"to which the public has a right of access"*, has not been defined. However, since the entire purpose of the provision was to curb alleged (but almost non-existent) "gun show abuses" at municipally owned facilities – the phrase should mean it applies to non-private property, or, to put it another way – "government owned property". That's because on private property – the general public has no "***right***" to enter, although they usually have a limited "***license***" to enter, which may be revoked at will by the owner. However, since the amendment failed to define the phrase regarding "*right of access*", many counties have been interpreting this as anywhere the public is allowed to go. BATFE has sided with them, for now. In my opinion, totally incorrect – but a test case waiting to happen. Likewise, if a records check is required – you would have to get an **FFL** (ie: federally licensed firearms dealer) to run it, and BATFE has said that is up to the discretion of the individual FFL. Plus, if they agree, they can charge you a fee for doing so, besides the normal fee for the records check.

CHART ON WAITING PERIODS:

	Fla. Const. Art. 1, §8	Fla. Const. Art. 8, §5(b)	Florida Statute 790.0655
wait period	3 days	3-5 days	3 days
don't count	weekends & legal holidays	ibid.	ibid.
records check?	dealer sales only	county decides	dealer sales only
applies to	retail only	any firearm transaction taking place on property public has "right of access" to.	retail only
firearms	only handguns	all	only handguns
excluded from laws	CWL, and trade for trade without cash.	CWL	CWL

CHAPTER TWO

QUALIFICATIONS FOR PURCHASING OR POSSESSION OF FIREARMS

Did you notice the title of this chapter? Did it seem a little unusual? Qualifications for purchasing -- "or" possession of firearms? Surely, it should say qualifications for purchasing, "and" possession of firearms?

However, the answer is a definite no. Anytime a person seeks to purchase, borrow, own, or possess a firearm, a different set of rules probably applies. Moreover, these rules are governed by both State and Federal law. You must comply with both sets of law to be legal. In fact, there are certain qualifications for possession of a firearm, that are dramatically different from those required to purchase a firearm. This chapter will outline those requirements for you, at least as required by Florida and Federal law. In another state, completely different rules could apply.

DEFINITION OF A "FIREARM":

Before we get into the guts of this chapter, you need to know what is, and what is not -- a *firearm*: In its most basic form, a *firearm* is any weapon that discharges a projectile by use of an explosive charge, or is designed or is readily convertible to such a use. Both the federal and Florida definitions include the *frame or receiver* of any such weapon, and any *firearm muffler or silencer*. F.S. 790.001(6). Firearm mufflers and silencers are generally illegal to possess without special pre-qualification from BATFE (ie: *Bureau of Alcohol, Tobacco, Firearms & Explosives*), and will be covered elsewhere in this book. The federal definition also encompasses "*destructive devices*" which include all explosives, poison gas, bombs, grenades, rockets with more than 4 ounces of propellant, missiles with an explosive or incendiary charge of over one quarter ounce, mines, and most devices which are not shotguns that have a inside barrel diameter (bore) of **one half inch** or more, and will fire a projectile. The definition also includes any *"combination of parts"* by which such a device can be *readily assembled*. "*Readily assembled*" is a federal term, and should not be taken literally. I will explain it in a later chapter.

The only exception to the definition is when the item is not generally considered to be a "*weapon*". One such example would be a "*potato cannon* ", which legally, is normally considered to be a "*recreational device*" made of PVC irrigation pipe that is used to fire potatoes or golf balls by use of a propellant such as ignited hair spray or MAPP gas. Since its use is really not as a "*weapon*"

-- it is not considered a "*destructive device*".   However, if you used it as a weapon -- then it should qualify for the definition,   and could get you in some very serious problems with the law. Another example would be legal fireworks, and probably illegal fireworks, to the extent they are not being used as a weapon, but are being used merely as *fireworks*. [11]

ANTIQUE FIREARMS -- AND OTHER EXCEPTIONS:

One of the exceptions to the usual definition of a firearm is the class of weapons known as "*antique firearms*."   An antique firearm is usually, but not always, a black-powder gun of some sort, and is generally classified as a "*weapon*", rather than as a "*firearm*". This is a major distinction in definition, because "weapons" that are not legally defined as "firearms" escape a large number of state and federal regulations that otherwise would apply – especially where someone has a prior felony, or misdemeanor domestic violence conviction.

In order to be an "*antique firearm*" under Florida law, the weapon must have been manufactured during or before **1918**, or be a *"replica"* of such, and it may not use "*fixed ammunition*" unless this "fixed ammunition" is no longer manufactured in the United States, and such ammo is not readily available in ordinary commerce. F.S. 790.001(1).   "*Fixed ammunition*" is defined as self-contained ammunition consisting of a case, primer, explosive charge, and projectile. Likewise, under Florida law, if you use an antique firearm in the commission of a crime -- it legally changes its status back to a "firearm", and loses it's status as an "antique firearm. F.S. 790.001(6).

On the other hand, Federal law defines an antique firearm as any firearm manufactured before **1898**, or a replica thereof. If it's a *replica*, it can't use rimfire or conventional fixed ammunition unless that ammunition is no longer manufactured in the U.S., and is "*not readily available*" for purchase. A 1998 amendment to the federal law [18 USC 921(16)(C)] also expanded the definition of an antique firearm to include any *muzzle-loading firearm* that is designed to use black powder or a black powder substitute, cannot use fixed ammunition, and cannot be converted from a modern firearm, or readily convertible to any firearm that can fire fixed ammunition. [12]

Unfortunately, in *Bostic v. State*, 902 So. 2d 225 (Fla. 5DCA 2005), the Fifth District Court of Appeals, seriously muggled up the Florida definition, and held that the black powder muzzle loading rifle the defendant used for hunting (*Thompson Center Arms Model Black Diamond*) was not an "*antique firearm*", but was instead a "*firearm*" because it was not a **reasonably exact reproduction"** of a muzzle loading firearm produced on or before the year of

1918. Thus, since Mr. Bostic was a *convicted felon* not permitted to own or possess *"firearms"*, he was subject to being found guilty of a second degree felony (15 year maximum prison sentence with three year mandatory minimum prison sentence) as a *"felon in possession"* of a firearm pursuant to F.S. 790.23. The Opinion of the court totally confused Florida law on what was a *"replica"*, by adding this new and totally unexplained requirement that replicas now had to be *"**reasonably exact**"*. Thus, once the decision came out – nobody could figure out what *"reasonably exact"* meant. Did that exclude scopes, finish, alloys? Nobody knew! Likewise, even while the decision was legally correct under Florida law – the legal reasoning was totally incorrect:

Why?

Well, if you trace the history of the definition of *"antique firearms"* you find out that prior to 1969 there was no Florida law that defined an *"antique firearm"*. A convicted felon back in those days, according to Florida law, could legally own any firearm other than a pistol, sawed-off rifle, or sawed-off shotgun. Federal law added some other restrictions, but in essence, a convicted felon could own most long-guns. However, with the assassination of Martin Luther King on April 4, 1968, and Robert F. Kennedy on June 5, 1968, Congress passed the ***Gun Control Act of 1968*** which made sweeping changes in gun laws. The federal law also created a class of firearms known as *"antique firearms"*, and left them as an unregulated category of guns by stating any such gun was not to be defined as a *"firearm"*. The theory was that these firearms were not as powerful or capable as modern firearms, and didn't really pose a criminal threat. Thus, an antique firearm could still be purchased and shipped through the mail, and owned and possessed by convicted felons. In a more modern context – an *"antique firearm"* does not require you to go through a NICS criminal history check to purchase it, nor does such a purchase include any required "waiting period". Well, at least not until the *Bostic* case came along.

The problem in the *Bostic* case came from the lack of clarity in both the federal and Florida statutes as to exactly what is, or is not a *"replica"*. According to Florida law as defined in F.S. 790. 001(1), an "antique firearm' means any firearm manufactured in or before 1918 *(including **any** matchlock, flintlock, percussion cap, or **similar early type of ignition system**) or **replica thereof***, whether actually manufactured before or after the year 1918 . . . ."

The 1968 federal statute [18 USC 921 (16)] has many substantial similarities, and defines an antique firearm as:

A.   Any firearm (including any firearm with a matchlock, flintlock, percussion cap, or similar type of ignition system) manufactured in or before 1898; or

B.   any replica of any firearm described in subparagraph (A) if such replica:

   (i)   is not designed or redesigned for using rimfire or conventional centerfire fixed ammunition, or

   (ii)   uses rimfire or conventional centerfire fixed ammunition which is no longer manufactured in the United States and which is not readily available in the ordinary channels of commercial trade;

Common sense tells you that the Florida law was meant to be given similar meaning to the federal definition. Moreover, in the case of _Modern Muzzleloading, Inc. V. Magaw_, 18 F. Supp. 2d 29 (Dist. Columbia 1998), both the government and the court recognized that the definition of a "_replica_" included "***any matchlock, flintlock, percussion cap, or similar early type of ignition system***" so long as it was "_not designed or redesigned for using rimfire or conventional centerfire fixed ammunition_".   This was in accord with a longstanding interpretation by BATFE, and confirmed in _ATF Industry Circular 98-2_. The only controversy was whether a modern muzzleloader that could use a **modern primer** was still an "_antique firearm_", and whether muzzle loading firearms that used ***interchangeable barrels*** that could also be converted to fire modern ammunition were "antique firearms", or to be more accurate – "_replicas_". Congress solved the problem, and changed the law to add another subsection, as follows:

> _(C) "any muzzle loading rifle, muzzle loading shotgun, or muzzle loading pistol, which is designed to use black powder, or a black powder substitute, and which cannot use fixed ammunition. For purposes of this subparagraph, the term "antique firearm" shall not include any weapon which incorporates a firearm frame or receiver, any firearm which is converted into a muzzle loading weapon, or any muzzle loading weapon which can be readily converted to fire fixed ammunition by replacing the barrel, bolt, breechblock, or any combination thereof."_

This subsection made it **legal** to use ***modern primers*** on muzzleloaders, and still retain the classification of an "_antique firearm_" – but denied this status to those muzzleloaders that had the ***interchangeable barrels***. (ATF Firearms Update, November 18, 2004). But, Florida has made no such change , so assuming you could forget about the _Bostic_ case, and interpret Florida law along federal lines, you'd soon realize that under current Florida law any muzzleloader that can use a ***shotgun primer***, or ***interchangeable barrel*** is not an "antique firearm", not a "replica", and therefore is a "***firearm***" subject to all the restrictions on sale, possession, etc.

So, it looks like the *Bostic* case was right, after all, but not on the basis of the Opinion – because the *Thompson Center Arms Black Diamond* can use a **shotgun primer!** [14]

However, a fairly recent appellate court case from the First District Court of Appeal took a contrary view to *Bostic*. That case is *Weeks v. State*, 39 Fla. L. Weekly D35 (Fla. 1DCA 2013). In *Weeks*, the appellate court held that it is the firing or *ignition mechanism* of a gun that determines whether it qualifies as a *"replica"* regardless of the date of manufacture, or whether it has other more modern features such as a scope. Thus, they held a black powder muzzle loader with a percussion cap firing system qualified as a *"replica"*, and also held that the statute was so uncertain as to what constituted a "replica", that it rendered that portion of the statute as unconstitutional. Conflict with the *Bostic* case was then certified to the Florida Supreme Court. Thus for now, it depends in what part of Florida you live as to what a *"replica"* antique firearm is, or isn't – at least until the Florida Supreme Court settles it.

OTHER EXCLUDED DEVICES:
Also excluded from the definition of a *"firearm"* are **starter pistols** that are not capable of discharging any projectile, air guns, BB guns, and *pyrotechnic devices* that are used for signaling, or throwing safety lines. However, case law makes it clear that a starter gun can be classified as a firearm if it is "*readily convertible*" to the firing of a projectile. On the other hand, *air guns and BB guns* are not considered firearms since they don't expel a projectile by use of an explosive, although they can be defined as a weapon, or even "*deadly weapon*", depending upon their use, or intended use. [15]

AGE ON PURCHASES FROM A FIREARMS DEALER:
Now that you know what a firearm is, you probably want to know some of the requirements for purchasing one. In Florida, the age of majority (ie: not a "minor") is **18 years** unless otherwise specified by the Florida Constitution, or state beverage laws. For our purposes -- that means 18 years of age, or older.

However, under federal law, in order to purchase a *handgun* from a federal licensee (ie: a federally licensed firearms dealer or "*FFL*") -- you need to be at least **21 years** of age. On the other hand, in order to purchase a rifle or shotgun from an FFL -- the lawful age is lowered to 18 years. The same age requirements apply to the purchase of ammunition for these firearms from a federal licensee. In other words, you can't buy .38 caliber ammunition from a federal licensee until you are 21 years of age, because it's not generally used in anything but a handgun. On the other hand, if you were 18 years of age, and wanted to buy .22 caliber ammunition – if you represented it was for a rifle, it would be legal.   If you represented it was for a handgun, it would be illegal. That's because .22 caliber is used in both types of firearms. However, if you misrepresented it's use, and really wanted it for a handgun -- you'd be committing a federal felony.

If you present falsified identification, or lie on the federal form (*Form 4473*) required to purchase a firearm from a licensed dealer – you have just committed a federal crime, as well as a third degree felony in Florida.[16] You could actually be prosecuted in both state and federal court, at the same time. If you are lucky enough to have the feds prosecute you, remember that federal prisons have lots of room. You will stay there for a long time.

JUVENILE FELONY OFFENDER:
You should also know that if you had a conviction or even "*withheld adjudication*" as a juvenile offender on a crime that would otherwise be a felony, F.S .790.23(1)(d) makes it a second degree felony for you to own or possess a firearm, electric weapon, or carry any concealed weapon including chemical sprays until you reach the age of **24 years** old. [17]

AGE FOR NON-DEALER PURCHASE:
Both Florida and Federal laws are primarily aimed at sales made by licensed firearms dealers (ie: "FFL") [18] to private citizens. This leaves a few loopholes when the sale is strictly between private persons, or if the transfer of a firearm is a gift between private individuals, and no licensed dealer is involved. Under Florida and Federal law, any citizen of the age of 18 years, or more, who is not under some other legal disability, may possess or own a handgun, rifle, or shotgun.   A person who has a legal disability is considered a "*prohibited person*".

In other words – even if it would be illegal to purchase a handgun from a licensed firearms dealer because you're not yet 21 – it may still be legal for you to purchase, or receive it privately -- as long as you're at least 18 years of age, or older, and suffer no other legal disqualification.

PURCHASES UNDER 18:
In Florida, it is a first degree misdemeanor to give, lend, or sell a person **under 18 years** of age **any type of weapon** (not just firearms) -- except an

"common pocketknife", unless they are given permission to do so by one of the minor's parents, or by the minor's guardian.[19] If it's a firearm, then it's a felony. This proscription is primarily directed to private persons, since the penalty is greater for federal licensees, and other dealers. [20] Moreover, federally licensed firearms dealers cannot sell a *"firearm"* to anyone unless that person meets the federal age requirements of 18 or 21 years, regardless of whose permission they have.

PURCHASES DISALLOWED, EVEN WITH PERMISSION:

It is also illegal for any person who deals in weapons (any type of weapons – not just federally licensed firearms dealers) to sell a *dirk*, [21] *Bowie knife, brass knuckles,* [22] *electric weapon, or slungshot* (ie: a flexible handled weapon with a weight on the end used for striking) to anyone **UNDER** the age of **18 years** -- even with their parents permission. However, it is legal for the parent to purchase such a weapon, and then give it to the child as a gift.

USE DISALLOWED EXCEPT UNDER ADULT SUPERVISION:

Furthermore, it is illegal for any child under the age of **16 years** of age to "use" any *firearm, BB gun, air rifle, or electric weapon* except under the attending **supervision of an adult**, who is acting with permission of a parent. If an adult who is then responsible for the child knows that the child is using or in possession of an air gun, or electric weapon in violation of this section -- then that adult is guilty of a second degree misdemeanor. A firearm is a felony -- and will probably result in civil liability for any damages caused by the minor, as well. [23] F.S . 790.22

In addition, Florida has made it a felony for an adult who is responsible for the child to knowingly and willfully permit a child **under 18 years** to possess any **firearm** at any place other than **unloaded** at the child's home, unless the following criteria are met:[24]

A.   The child is engaged in lawful hunting, and is at least 16 years of age, or if under the age of 16, is being supervised by an adult while engaged in lawful hunting.

B.   The child is engaged in lawful shooting competition, or practice, or other lawful recreational shooting activity, and is at least 16 years of age, or if under the age of 16, is being supervised by an adult who is acting with the consent of the minor's parent or guardian.

C.   The firearm is unloaded, and is being transported directly to or from the event authorized in either (A) or (B).

However, under federal law, the child can not keep a ***handgun*** in his possession at home, even if unloaded. He could only have a rifle or shotgun. [25] We'll discuss this in the next section.

YOUTH HANDGUN SAFETY AMENDMENT:

Federal statute 18 USC 922(x), adds restrictions for persons **under 18** years, that forbids possession of **handguns**, or ammo suitable only for handgun use except for target practice, hunting, handgun instruction courses, ranching or farming with the consent of the property owner, if such is not prohibited by State law, and the minor has the prior **written consent** of a parent or guardian who is not a "***prohibited person***" on his person at all times, and the handgun is transported unloaded and in a locked case directly to and from any such activity, if being transported by the minor. Remember, the restrictions here apply to ***handguns*** -- not shotguns or rifles.

POSSESSION OF MINOR FOR PURPOSE OF EMPLOYMENT:

Florida does NOT permit a minor to use or possess a firearm (handgun or long gun) in the course of employment, nor during ranching or farming -- whereas the federal statute does. F.S. 790.22. In case you're curious about the apparent conflict, the Florida statute controls because it's more restrictive. Whenever there is a conflict between state and federal firearm restrictions, the more restrictive statute controls. Whether this restriction it's constitutional or not under Florida law, is another question.

SOME QUESTIONS ABOUT AGE:

QUESTION: I wanted to give my nephew a really great gift on his 16th birthday, so I bought him a bow and arrows. I didn't ask his folks if I could do this because I thought they might be mad. Could I get in trouble?

ANSWER: Sure! If Mom and Dad wanted to make an issue of it, you just committed a first degree misdemeanor[26] -- because you didn't have their permission to give it to the kid. On the other hand, if his Dad said it was OK -- and his Mom didn't -- you'd still be legal, although, you probably wouldn't be invited over for dinner anymore. The same thing would apply to an air gun, most knives, sword, electric weapon, mace, etc. If the kid is **under 18 years** of age -- you need the permission of a parent, or guardian.

QUESTION: I am a licensed firearms dealer. An 18 year old wanted to buy ammunition for his rifle, which was of a caliber that could also be used in a handgun. Can I legally sell it to him?

ANSWER: Sure. As long as he represents it's for a longgun (rifle or shotgun), and you have no real reason to doubt he's telling the truth -- you can freely do so. Obviously, the type of ammunition must be typical for the weapon he says it's for -- otherwise you're on notice that the sale could be illegal.

QUESTION: I'm only 19 years old, but I really want a handgun. My father said I could get one if I maintained at least a "B" average in school – and I have. How do I purchase the gun?

ANSWER: As long as you are 18 years of age or older, you may legally purchase a handgun from a private owner. You do not need your parents permission. However, it is illegal to have somebody else buy it for you from a licensed firearms dealer, although you could receive it as a gift. [27] If you pay someone to buy it for you as a "*gift*" (which would be a lie – since you're actually paying him back for it) you both have just participated in what's known as a "*straw purchase*", and is a very serious federal crime. The feds want to know who the ultimate purchaser of a firearm from an FFL is, and any inaccuracy or misleading information provided on the Form 4473 has the potential for serious legal issues.

QUESTION: I am not a licensed firearms dealer, but I have a store, and carry a selection of knives. A juvenile and his uncle came in last week, and the uncle wanted to buy a Bowie knife for his nephew. He gave the nephew the money, who handed it to me. I refused the sale. Was I right?

ANSWER: Absolutely. Otherwise, you would have committed a second degree felony. You could not sell the knife directly to the minor, even if he had been there with a parent, rather than the uncle -- since a direct sale is prohibited. You could have sold it to the uncle, even if you knew he was going to give it to his nephew – although that might not be wise from a civil liability standpoint if there was any hint that it was without parental approval. And, of course, if the uncle then gave it to his nephew without the actual permission of a parent -- he would have committed a first degree misdemeanor, although you should be legally O.K.

RESIDENCE, LOANS, RENTALS & BEQUESTS:

Federal law strictly prohibits the transfer, sale, loan, trade or delivery of any firearm to a non-resident by a non-licensee, and also restricts many transfers by a licensed firearms dealer to a non-licensee. It is therefore a federal crime for an ordinary citizen to sell, transfer, give, or receive a firearm when the person receiving the handgun is not a genuine *"resident"* of the state in which the transfer is made. In such instances, anyone willfully involved would be guilty of a federal felony.[28] There are a few exceptions which we will discuss, shortly. These restriction also apply to transfers made by a federal licensee to a person who does not reside in the dealers state. However, there are again, some exceptions.

One of the exceptions occurs when the transfer is a temporary one, in the sense of a ***loan or rental***[29] of a firearm. However, the loan is restricted to only those instances which are for a lawful *"sporting purpose"*.[30] This exception applies to both dealers, and private individuals. But, don't try to get cute with the "temporary" nature of the transfer. It's not something to play with.

Another exception is where the transfer is the result of a ***bequest or devise***, due to the death of the owner of the firearm. In this case, a non-resident may receive the firearm bequeathed to him, regardless of his state of residence, although he still may not transport it into his residence state, unless it is legal to have it there.[31]

Rifles and shotguns are treated somewhat differently from handguns, and federal law does not prevent a qualified citizen who resides in another state from purchasing a rifle or shotgun in a *face-to-face* transaction with a federally licensed firearms dealer outside his state if: the purchase would be legal in both states, and if the regulatory requirements of both states are complied with. 18 USC 922 (b)(3). It could not be purchased privately, out-of-state unless sent to an FFL in the purchaser's residence state for pick-up.

OUT-OF-STATE PURCHASE OR SHIPMENT BY NON-FFL:

Under federal law, an *FFL* (federal firearms licensee) can purchase a firearm from anyone in any state, dealer or not. Likewise, a private party may purchase a longgun in a face-to-face transaction with an FFL if they are not a *"prohibited person"*, meet the age requirements, and such is lawful in both the sale state, and purchaser's state. The same can't be done with a handgun. Also – a *private individual* may not legally purchase **any firearm** while out of his or her residence state from another *private individual*. However, there still is a legal method to get around all of this. So, assuming you see a firearm you want to buy somewhere other than your residence state, or even online – here's how it works:

Federal law says a firearm is not transferred until *"delivery"*. If the delivery occurs in the buyer's state of residence at an FFL (ie: gun store), if the sale is lawful in the buyer's residence state, and the buyer fills out the *Form 4473*, and obtains the criminal records check approval in his or her residence state – then the *"sale"* is lawful, and for federal purposes – occurs in the *"delivery"* state. Of course, the firearm **cannot** be given to the purchaser directly by an out-of-state seller, even for shipment – as the law says the seller must first have it transported to another FFL in the purchaser's home state. To deliver it directly (except for a legal *face-to-face* sale of a longgun with an FFL) is a federal felony. 27 CFR 478.147.

This procedure would also apply to a *"gift"* of any firearm to an out-of-state resident.[32] So, if you want to make such a gift, you'll have to arrange to have it sent to a federal licensee in his home state. [33] And, if you want to obtain firearms from out-of-state, you'd better make sure you buy them from a federally licensed dealer, or other person, who ships them to a federally licensed dealer in your home state for your eventual pick-up. Almost all gun shops will assist in this process for a small fee. As a strong word of warning, you should know that it is illegal for a third person to purchase a firearm with the intent of transferring it to a non-resident, or to someone who has a legal disqualification. This is known as a **"straw man"** transaction, or a *"straw purchase"*, and is a federal felony for anyone involved, as well a felony under F.S. 790.065. Thus, if the dealer has *reasonable cause* to suspect that this is the intent of the purchaser, he cannot make the sale without committing a federal crime.

For instance. Your nephew from New Jersey comes down to Florida for a visit. He is staying with you, is over 21 years of age, has never been arrested, and is an all-around wonderful person. He knows you have a couple of handguns, and that you even have a Florida Concealed Weapons License. You've taken him out shooting with you at the range -- and he's a better shot than you.

He's always wanted a handgun, but New Jersey law won't let him get one. He asks you if you can buy him one, and he'll pay you back. You say "sure". You've heard it's illegal to purchase a handgun for somebody else who lives out of state, and your gun dealer tells you "no way" will he sell you one -- even if you promise to swear that it was only for you. So, you decide to give your old .38 caliber revolver to the nephew as a gift.

What's the harm?"

The harm is that you just violated the *Gun Control Act of 1968*, and are subject to five years imprisonment in a federal penitentiary, and a fine of up to $5,000.00. Your nephew is also subject to the same penalty. What a great uncle, you are! Won't the family be pleased?

PRIVATE SHIPMENT & RECEIPT OF FIREARMS:
Where shipment of a firearm out of state is lawful – shipment can be a real problem for most private individuals as the post office generally only accepts longguns, and has a ton of regulations. 18 USC 1715. On the other hand, many common carriers refuse shipping firearms from private individuals. My experience is that shipment by *UPS or Fed Ex* can only be accomplished by shipping from their actual local terminal. While the firearm must be declared – the shipping wrapper on the actual item cannot indicate it contains a firearm. I have also been told that these carriers will only deliver to an FFL. An *"FFL"* not only includes gun stores, but includes firearm manufacturers, and licensed gunsmiths.

Interestingly enough, BATFE says you can ship a firearm you lawfully own to "**yourself**" in another state. To do this you must address the package to yourself "**care of**" whoever else it might be delivered to – however, the package cannot be opened by anyone but you! BATFE suggests the package be kept in a safe and secure place until you can personally pick it up.

Last, if you have shipped a firearm for repair or customizing to an FFL – and the same firearm is returned to you, or a replacement of the same kind and type – it can be delivered directly to you without the need for the Form 4473 or a NICS criminal history records check. 18 USC 922(a)(2)(A); 27 CFR 478.124(a).

DUAL RESIDENCE:
It is possible for a person to have a *dual residence*, and thus be able to purchase a rifle, shotgun, or handgun in more than one state legally. This means

that the state you are attempting to purchase the firearm in is not a place that you are merely visiting -- but is one in which you reside at, and maintain as your home. Examples would be a college student living away from home part of the year. Persons who owned permanent homes, or leased apartments in different cities where they regularly lived or worked. And people who kept permanent vacation homes where they resided part of the year. Mere ownership of property does not constitute residence. Of course, to prove residence you are probably going to have to have a Florida driver's license or identification card. You are no longer allowed to have both a Florida and out-of-state driver license due to compliance with the federal *Real ID Act*. Of course, **military on active duty** have legal residence both at their permanent duty station, and actual residence.

PURCHASE BY ALIENS:

Due to changes in the interpretation of federal law[34], an *alien* (ie: citizen from another country -- not from another planet), who is lawfully in the United States, may be able to possess firearms and ammunition, and sometimes even purchase such for private use. Here are the changes:

First, a *"resident alien"* (ie: green card) may purchase a firearm in their state of residence. There is no longer a "90 day" residency requirement.[35] Such a person may possess firearms and ammo in any state, although purchase of a firearm is still limited to their state of residence. As to foreign nationals who enter the U.S. on a *"non-immigrant visa"* – these individuals are generally considered *"prohibited persons"*, and may not even momentarily possess firearms or ammunition unless they have a **valid hunting license** (from **any** State, local, or federally recognized tribal government); were admitted specifically for lawful hunting or sport shooting purposes; have a waiver from the Attorney General; or fit into the other exceptions pertaining to foreign government and law enforcement personnel. However, if they fit within any of these exceptions they still may not **purchase** a firearm for use in the U.S. unless they are also a resident of the state in which the purchase is made. They can purchase for export.

Those aliens who enter the country under the *"Visa Waiver Program"* are **not** considered *"non-immigrant aliens"* , and may possess firearms and ammo anywhere in the United States – but again – may only purchase a firearm if they are also a **resident** of the state of purchase. Therefore, they may legally go to a range, rent a firearm, purchase ammo anywhere, and shoot to their hearts content. Entry is with a passport, and through online ESTA. *ESTA* has replaced the green *Form I-94W.*

On the other hand, most citizens of *Canada and Bermuda* do not need anything beyond a passport to enter the United States. Again, there are some exceptions. However, those who do not require a visa – do not fall within the prohibitions and definition of a *"non-immigrant alien"* under federal firearm laws – and therefore have the same right to possess and purchase as persons within the *Visa Waiver Program*. Of course – they can't get a Florida CWL because a requirement of the CWL includes being a U.S. citizen, or resident alien. On the other hand, they may purchase firearms, but only if they are a resident of a state, and the purchase is made within that state. There is no restriction on purchase of ammunition unless entry was on a visa. However, if your legal status as an alien ever changes or expires so that you're illegally in the U.S.A. – your ownership or possession of a firearm or ammunition will constitute a felony.[36]

LEGAL DISABILITIES PREVENTING PURCHASE:

If you're purchasing from a private individual, you already know that you must be a resident of the same state where the purchase was made (unless the transfer was made through an FFL in the purchaser's *residence* state), and the purchaser must be at least 18 years of age. Another requirement of any purchase or receipt of firearms or ammunition – no matter who you get it from – is that you don't have a *"felony conviction"* where the "possible" imprisonment (imposed or not) was over one year, or a *"misdemeanor conviction"* where the possible imprisonment (imposed or not) was over two years. Most legal disabilities are set out in the federal statute at 18 USC 922(g).

CONVICTIONS & WITHHELDS:

A *"conviction"* means that you were actually convicted of the crime. In Florida this means you must have had an *"adjudication"*. Federal law is supposed to follow the state's interpretation of its own laws. Thus, under Florida law, a "***withheld adjudication*** " should not constitute a "*conviction*" of a felony for firearm purposes. However, due to a mistaken interpretation of Florida law by the federal 11th Circuit – a "*withheld adjudication*" will still disqualify you, and label you as a "*prohibited person*" under federal law if you plead "***guilty***", rather than having plead "***no contest***" to a felony. The case involved is United States v.Chubbuck , 252 F.3d 1300 (11 [th] Cir. 2001).

FLORIDA JUVENILE FELONY OFFENDER:

On the other hand, firearm prohibitions do not apply to a delinquency adjudication for a felony arising from a Florida juvenile court proceeding due to both F.S . 790.23, and F.S. 985.35(7). Under those statutes, even an "*adjudication*" for a crime that would be a felony in adult court disappears as a *"conviction"* in Florida once the individual reaches **24 years** of age. Prior to that age, all the prohibitions apply. Violation is a second degree felony. Federal courts recognize the exception, however, if a juvenile were prosecuted as an "adult" – the exception would not apply. *United States v. Cure,* 996 F.2d 1136 (11th Cir. 1993). The law in other states as applied to a juvenile conviction could be entirely different – as the result depends on the law of state where the juvenile proceedings occurred. .

OUT OF STATE CONVICTIONS:

If you have a federal, or out-of-state conviction, the federal law, or laws of the state of conviction control your legal status to possess a firearm -- not Florida law. On the other hand, if you were "*adjudicated*" with a Florida felony -- you're obviously going to have to read the upcoming chapter on removal of legal disabilities. Tough luck!

OTHER LEGAL DISABILITIES RESULTING IN PROHIBITIONS:

Other additional disabilities which would make it a crime to own, sell, transfer, possess[37], or receive, a firearm include:

a. The purchaser is under Indictment or Information for a felony, or crime punishable by more than a year in jail. However, this would not bar "possession" unless and until an adjudication of guilt is imposed.

b. The purchaser is a fugitive from justice (ie: any person who has deliberately fled another state to avoid prosecution for a crime, or avoid testifying in a criminal proceeding).

c. The purchaser is an unlawful user, or addicted to controlled substances (21 USC 802) The definition includes persons who are current users of illegal drugs, and those who abuse legally prescribed drugs. Even a single joint of marijuana could technically get you a five year federal felony if you possessed firearms around the time of use!

MENTAL HEALTH, DRUG & ALCOHOL COMMITMENTS:

d. The purchaser has been adjudicated a **mental defective**, or has been **committed** to any mental institution, any time. The term is defined in 27 CFR 478.11, and F.S. 790.065(4). The case law interpreting *"commitment"* holds that **involuntary** placement in a mental facility for *"observation"* is not a commitment unless there is a determination by some board or agency or court of mental illness or mental defect and need for (involuntary) treatment. Also included would be a finding of "*not guilty by reason of insanity*" in a criminal case, and would also include an involuntary commitment, inpatient or outpatient, for drug or alcohol use pursuant to the **Marchman Act**. F.S. 790.065(2) [38] To be clear, a "**commitmen**t" does not include a person in a mental institution for *observation*, or where the person is discharged (usually within 48 hours) based upon the initial interview with an examining physician. It also does not include a situation where a person "*voluntary*" checks themself into a hospital or mental institution for treatment.

However, in 2013 the Florida legislature amended F.S. 790.065(2) by prohibiting the purchase of firearms, or obtaining or retaining a Florida CWL, by persons who were admitted for involuntary examination under the **Baker Act**, and then voluntarily agreed to treatment, where there is also a finding by the examining physician that the person is an imminent danger to themself or another, the examining physician certifies that if the patient did not agree a petition for involuntary commitment would be filed, the patient likewise agrees in writing to that finding on an approved form that warns them that their agreement may prohibit the individual from purchasing a firearm or obtaining a CWL, and a judge or magistrate approved of the process. There is a question whether the amendment covers private sales of firearms, or possession of firearms already possessed by the individual, however, because a judge or magistrate would have to approve the process – it is likely that the procedure would be considered a "***commitment***" under federal law – thus making it a crime, and prohibiting the individual from possession of firearms or ammunition. Restoration is accomplished by filing a petition with the court, and serving a copy on the State Attorney, where the individual has the burden of establishing that he or she "*will not be likely to act in a manner that is dangerous to public safety and that granting the relief would not be contrary to the public interest*". A denial of relief allows an appeal to the District Court of Appeal. A denial would also allow re-application for relief one year after the date of the order of denial.

Also, on the federal side,, and pursuant to the **NICS Improvement Amendment Act of 2007,** the term also includes an administrative decision by a board, agency or commission that you are a danger to yourself or to others or are incompetent to manage your own affaires. This stigma and prohibition will be extinguished if the agency that made the decision later: (1) sets the decision aside or expunges it; (2)the person has been fully released or discharged from all mandatory treatment, supervision or monitoring by the agency; or (3) the person was found by the agency to no longer suffer from the mental health adjudication. However, this exception does not apply to anyone found "*not guilty*" or acquitted in a criminal case, or military tribunal due to a lack of mental responsibility, insanity, or incompetence.

FIREARM DISABILITIES – CONTINUED:

e.   The purchaser was dishonorably discharged.

f.   The purchaser renounced his/her U.S. citizenship.

g.   The purchaser is subject to a court order restraining the purchaser from harassing, stalking, or threatening an intimate partner[39], or child of such, or engaging in other conduct that would place the intimate partner in reasonable fear of bodily harm to the partner or child -- so long as such order was issued after a hearing of which the purchaser received actual notice, and had an opportunity to participate -- whether or not the purchaser did participate. And, in such restraining order the court must find that the person represented a credible threat to the physical safety of the other, or alternatively, that the court order expressly prohibits the use, threatened or attempted use of physical force. [40]

h.   The person was convicted of a crime of a "***misdemeanor crime of domestic violence*** ". 18 USC 922(g)(9). A misdemeanor crime of domestic violence means an offense that has, as an element, the use or attempted use of physical force, or the threatened use of a deadly weapon, committed by a current or former spouse, parent, or guardian of the victim, by a person with whom the victim shares a child in common, by a person who is cohabiting with or has cohabited with the victim as a spouse, parent, or guardian, or by a person similarly situated to a spouse, parent, or guardian of the victim.[41] It doesn't apply to casual relationships unless you were living together. Under current federal law it likely includes cases where a "***guilty***" plea was entered versus a " ***no contest*** " plea, or where there was a trial with a " *guilty*" verdict, even if the adjudication was later "*withheld*". It will always include an "*adjudication*". [42]

MORE ON DOMESTIC VIOLENCE CRIMES:

       There are some defenses to these federal firearm prohibitions where the domestic violence conviction occurred when the individual was not represented by an attorney, and where he or she did not "***knowingly and voluntarily***" waive the right to counsel, or when the individual was entitled to a jury trial, and did not *"knowingly or intelligently"* waive that right.   Likewise, an *expunction* or *pardon* is a defense to the prohibition as long as such restores the right to own and possess firearms. All of the foregoing disabilities are imposed by federal law, and violations are taken **very** seriously by your friendly federal government, and ATF agent (ie: Bureau of Alcohol, Tobacco, Firearms, and Explosives). They apply equally to sales by licensed dealers, and private individuals.

Florida has similar laws in F.S. 790.065(2)(c)(1); and F.S .790.233. Moreover, Florida defines *"domestic violence"* somewhat different than federal law in F.S. 741.28. [43] Under that section – *"domestic violence"* is defined as any assault, battery, stalking, kidnaping, false imprisonment, or criminal offense resulting in physical injury or death of one family or household member by another. *"Family or household member"* means spouses, former spouses, persons related by blood or marriage, persons currently or formerly residing as a family, parents of a child in common. However, to be a *"family or household member"*, except for parents of a child in common – the persons must have resided in the same single dwelling unit at some point.

Because some Florida *"domestic violence"* crimes are **not** necessarily federal *"misdemeanor crimes of domestic violence"* – you should know that if you somehow escape the federal prohibition, then Florida violations, even a *"withheld adjudication"* will cause the following minimum problems:

1.   No CWL for a **three year period** after probation and any conditions imposed by the court have expired. F.S. 790.06(2)(k)

2.   Cannot purchase a firearm from a licensed dealer for a **three year period** after probation and any conditions imposed by the court have expired. F.S. 790.065(3).

FLORIDA DOMESTIC VIOLENCE INJUNCTIONS:
You should also know that Florida has a statute, F.S. 741.31(4)(a), that allows law enforcement **seizure** of a person's firearms and ammunition if a judge orders their surrender pursuant to the issuance of an *injunction for protection* against domestic violence. Under these circumstances, it is a *first degree misdemeanor* to refuse turning the guns and ammo over to the police. Once the injunction ends – you are entitled to get them back. Likewise, it is a first degree misdemeanor under Florida law to control or possess firearms or ammunition in violation of a final injunction for protection against domestic violence. F.S. 790.233 These prohibitions do not apply to firearms and

ammunition of a law enforcement officer for use in his or her official duties, although a federally defined *misdemeanor crime of domestic violence* conviction would prohibit even a police officer from owning or possessing firearms or ammunition under federal law. Of course, if you are in violation of the federal definition, the penalties are more substantial. 18 USC 922(g)(8).

SOME DOMESTIC VIOLENCE ISSUES:

If you haven't already figured it out for yourself – sometimes people tend to use domestic violence charges for leverage – usually in a divorce, and even more times when there are custody issues. Sometimes, just to get even. Sometimes, just to make a point. I'm not saying many of these aren't totally legit – the majority are – I'm just saying from experience – that quite a number aren't.

However, the big problem is that when someone reports *domestic violence* to law enforcement – an arrest of someone is almost a certainty – even where the "violence" is just a minor shove. No warrant is required under Florida law – just probable cause. So be forewarned! If you have a volatile situation – get the hell out of there! It isn't worth making a point – only to get arrested, and lose your firearm rights for something you didn't do, or didn't start.

Likewise – if you are served with a *Notice of Hearing* for a temporary injunction or restraining order against domestic violence, repeat violence, dating violence – or anything else that resembles it – **beware**! Substantial rights to possess firearms and other weapons are involved! If you go to the hearing without a lawyer – you are likely gonna get **seriously screwed** – even if you did nothing! Moreover, a lawyer can, and many times should ask for a *continuance* of any such hearing – so you can prepare your evidence, take depositions, and do all the other things you need to do before having an evidentiary hearing in order to give you a fair shot at showing the truth. If you don't ask for it immediately, the right way – you probably have "*waived*" all your rights to a proper hearing. If somehow you can't get a lawyer in time, and it's a "*final hearing*" – you're in big trouble, and you'd better ask for a *continuance,* and also ask for time to hire an attorney – or you'll have waived your rights to all of that, as well. Once the decision is made – it's too late to correct it! Appeals rarely work.

One more warning – if you have any firearms, ammo, or weapons that are illegal – I can almost guarantee that the person who makes the domestic violence complaint to the police is gonna tell them! Or – when police come to seize your firearms pursuant to the temporary injunction – that unregistered M16 in the gun safe is gonna cost you a possible ten years in federal prison. If you don't believe it – I've seen it happen.   Just a word of warning to the wise.

Likewise, one more thing – even though we've discussed it. This stuff is not something you should handle yourself without a lawyer! The judge is probably going to order the seizure of all your firearms at the initial hearing unless you can somehow beat it. I have rarely seen anyone have any success without an attorney involved. And once again – if you can't get the attorney in time – you need to ask the judge for a *"continuance"* so you hire one. Do that at the beginning of the hearing! Don't wait for your turn – ask immediately, but politely.

CHART – FEDERAL MISDEMEANOR DOMESTIC VIOLENCE:

Elements required for federal "misdemeanor crime of domestic violence"		
use or attempted use of physical force . . . or	threatened use of a deadly weapon	
committed by a:		
spouse	former spouse	persons with a mutual child
• Such person cohabitated or currently cohabitates with the victim as a spouse, parent, guardian . . . . . or . . . . . • As a person similarly situated to a spouse, parent, or guardian of the victim		
Any finding of guilt as to a domestic violence criminal charge to be legally considered under federal law as a finding of "domestic violence" must include:		
was represented by an attorney or waived representation	If he or she was entitled to a jury trial, there was such trial, or the person waived jury trial by a plea, or otherwise	
Any prohibition is restored if:		
conviction expunged, pardoned, or set aside	Civil rights were restored or pardon, including restoration of firearm rights	

*Any waiver must be "knowing & intelligent"

*Elements considered: The elements in the statute alleged to be violated .

GUN PURCHASE FROM A PRIVATE INDIVIDUAL:

In Florida there are ordinarily no restrictions regarding the purchase or sale of a firearm to a private individual so long as neither the seller, or the purchaser are "prohibited persons". No ***bill of sale*** is required, although that is sometimes a good idea for both individuals – and could be as simple as a signed handwritten document describing the make, model, serial number, name of purchaser, name of seller, and date of sale. Again – not necessary – just sometimes a good idea.

The purchaser must be at least 18 years of age, and you should make sure the purchaser lives in the State of Florida by checking a driver's license or other official photo i/d. Likewise, the seller should be at least 18 years of age, or the sale could be declared invalid. You have **no responsibility** as a seller to ask the purchaser if he or she is a *"**prohibited person**"* or if he or she has any felony convictions, etc. – however, if the purchaser tells you they do, and you still sell it – you've committed a federal felony. Plus, if that happens at a **gun show** – they're probably working undercover for law enforcement. Likewise, if you have a reasonable basis not to believe the purchaser about being "prohibited" – it could be a federal felony to sell it unless you clarify that with the purchaser. If you somehow sell to a *"prohibited person"* but did not know that, the sale is usually still legal, and the only thing you probably have to worry about is the possibility of being a witness for the prosecution in a federal trial against the purchaser.

The one exception to all of this is due to the change in the Florida Constitution that allows individual counties to make up their own rules on waiting periods, and the need for running a criminal history on a private sale when any part of the sale happens on *"**property to which the public has a right of access**"*. That generally means a **gun show** on public property, in a building owned by the government, or any other public property. However, as I said in the previous chapter – many counties are interpreting that to include gun stores, and anywhere there's a gun show, even if on private property. I think they're dead wrong – but BATFE is going along with them, for now. So, check with your county if you fall into this wonderful black hole, or do the really smart thing, and get your Florida CWL.

By the way, there are no restrictions on the sale of ammo so long as the purchaser is at least 18 years of age, and the ammo is legal. You can even sell ammo to an out of state resident, but not to a foreign visitor unless they have a valid hunting license, are from Canada, or came in on the Visa Waiver Program.

PURCHASE FROM A LICENSED FIREARMS DEALER:

In order to legally sell firearms as a *"**business**"*, a person or corporation must be federally licensed. (ie: FFL) This requirement does not apply to the sale of ammunition [45], although a federal licensee who sells ammunition must comply with certain federal laws that a non-licensee who sells ammunition, does not.

Whatever, anybody who sells firearms as a business with the idea of making a profit vs. enhancing his personal collection – must be licensed by the feds. A failure is a very unpleasant federal prison sentence. This requirement applies to pawnshops, antique dealers, or whoever. Only sales from legitimate private collections are exempt, and sales directly from the executor of an estate -- and these better be very on the level.

Now, purchasing a firearm from a dealer is a very different animal than buying it privately. There are a lot more regulations that you both have to comply with, certain forms, record checks, and you may find that while you could legally buy the same gun from a private person -- you can't legally purchase it from a dealer. Doesn't make much sense, does it?

QUESTION: What are the differences in a private sale?

ANSWER: Normally, no waiting period. Normally, no FDLE background check, or federal *Form 4473* to fill out, no requirement that handgun purchaser be 21 years old. **Eighteen years** old would be sufficient. Same age of eighteen applies to rifles and shotguns. But you still can't sell to someone from out-of-state, a convicted felon, etc.

FLORIDA FIREARMS PURCHASE PROGRAM:
Florida has instituted, amongst other things, a firearms purchase program administered by the *Florida Department of Law Enforcement* (FDLE). This program requires any firearms dealer to run a criminal history records check of any prospective purchaser over the phone on a special line to FDLE. There is an **five dollar** service fee[46] which is charged to the potential purchaser, even if the sale cannot be completed. The record s check is a mandatory requirement to purchase a firearm from a licensed dealer.

The records check searches the person's record for anything that would prevent the person from purchasing or possessing a firearm under both federal and Florida law. If anything is found, the purchase will be disapproved. It can also make mistakes, and could even miss an old battery or assault conviction that now qualifies as a "misdemeanor crime of domestic violence". If it that happens, and you make the purchase -- you are still illegal, and could face prosecution. Reliance on the records check normally does not relieve a "*prohibited person*" from federal criminal responsibility for an unlawful purchase.

ARREST FOR "DANGEROUS" CRIME:

If you are trying to purchase a firearm from a dealer, and have an arrest for what is considered a "***dangerous crime***" as listed in F.S 907.041(4)[47], or for certain other specified felonies, you will get a "***conditional denial***" and not be able to purchase the firearm, until there is proof the case was dropped or you were acquitted of the charge. Hopefully, this will show on the NICS check, but if not, it's **your responsibility** to get the matter corrected. You will also be denied if you have a current domestic violence injunction or repeat violence injunction entered against you, have a conviction for domestic violence, a "*withheld*" for a domestic violence where 3 years hasn't elapsed since the sentence was completed, or where you are formally charged with the commission of any felony. A "***formal charge***" means an *Information or Indictment* has been filed against you in a court of law. The list of arrests that bar your approval from purchasing from a licensed firearms dealer[48] are on the following chart, which also includes those defined as "*dangerous crimes*":

CHART OF ARRESTS PREVENTING FDLE APPROVAL:

arson *#	child abuse *#	aggravated battery *#	sabotage
aggravated assault *#		kidnapping *#	homicide *#
illegal use of explosives *#, other explosive violations		sexual battery *#	robbery *#
indecent assault or act on or in the presence of a child under 16 years. *#		hijacking *#	terrorism *#
		car jacking *#	
sexual activity with child 12-17 by or through custodial or familial authority		criminal anarchy	extortion
any controlled substances violation in C.893		domestic violence #* including "withhelds"	abuse of elder or disabled *#

* includes any ***attempt*** or ***conspiracy*** to commit
\# constitute "***dangerous crimes***"

WARNING ABOUT DOMESTIC VIOLENCE CRIMES :

As I've already explained, federal decisional law is in flux as to whether a "***withheld adjudication***" in Florida can be a "***conviction***" for a misdemeanor crime of domestic violence. The 11th Circuit Court of Appeals in Atlanta currently says if you plead "***guilty***", or were found guilty in a trial — a "***withheld adjudication*** " is still a "***conviction***" for federal purposes— although they admit they may be mistaken on this interpretation.[49] Thus, only a plea of "*no contest*" , together with a " ***withheld adjudication***" are currently safe for federal purposes, unless the case was dropped or you won at trial. Moreover, <u>F.S.</u> 790.065(2)(a)(3), states that a *"withheld adjudication"* on any *felony*, *misdemeanor crime of domestic violence*, or any *misdemeanor crime of violence* will result in a **non-approval** for purchase of a firearm from a federally licensed dealer until **3 years** has elapsed after you've *"completed"* any sentence. Completion would include finishing probation, and paying any fines and court costs.

STATE DISABILITIES RECOGNIZED BY FEDERAL LAW:

Section 922 (b)(2) of the (federal) Gun Control Act of 1968 [18 USC 922(b)(2)] states that it is illegal for a licensed dealer to transfer a firearm to any person whose purchase or possession would be in violation of State law. Florida law does not seem to permit the following additional persons to possess firearms, so they should also be legally excluded from purchasing from a licensed dealer, although this may constitute a loophole for sale from a private individual. Even if this loophole exists, it would be risky, and could subject you to some very costly civil liability if something went amiss. Anyway, here's the additional list:

A.   Person who is a habitual or chronic alcoholic.

B.   Vagrants

C.   Person on Florida probation

PERSON ON FLORIDA PROBATION:

Ah, yes! The great zinger of Florida law! Pursuant to <u>F.S.</u> 948.03(1)(m), a person on any type of Florida probation cannot possess, carry, or even **own** a firearm — unless authorized by the court, and consented to by the probation officer. [50] There is also authority, although mistaken, that this extends to other weapons. [51]

QUESTION: You mean that if I get a lousy DUI, I've got to sell my firearms, when placed on probation?

ANSWER: Yes, amazing, huh? Unless the courts correct this error in interpretation, it applies equally to misdemeanors, felonies, and even criminal traffic offenses where probation is imposed — at least, unless you can get the judge and probation officer to agree otherwise.

QUESTION: How could I own or possess a firearm on felony probation, even with the agreement of the judge and probation officer? Isn't that always illegal? [52]

ANSWER: If you had a *"**withheld adjudication** "*[53] you would not be a *"**convicted felon**"*, and could technically still own firearms if you could get this permission. I assume it would have to be by a written order of the judge to be valid. Same theory applies on a misdemeanor (adjudicated or withheld) except domestic violence.

QUESTION: So, what happens once I'm off probation?

ANSWER: Unless you were *convicted* of a felony, the "probation" restriction disappears.

QUESTION: Any way around this?

ANSWER: My only suggestion is to legally transfer ownership of the firearms to a trust, with the trustee directed to return the firearms only upon the expiration of probation. Hire a lawyer to set up the trust, it's actually pretty simple. Don't get cute, and ask someone to "hold them" for you — because if you do, you still have *"**constructive possession** "* of the firearms, and could face a probation revocation or new prosecution. This can be very serious stuff if the feds decide they want to prosecute you because you're a *"prohibited person "* under federal law.

DENIAL FOR FELONY RECORD:

The criminal history check run by FDLE will also search to see if you have any felony *"convictions"*, or if you received a suspended sentence, or a *"withheld adjudication"* for any felony. If you were actually *"convicted"* of the felony -- you will not be eligible to purchase, own, or possess a firearm under any circumstances -unless the legal disability has been removed. Also, as previously explained, the case of U.S. v. Chubbuck [54] makes it clear that the feds will still prosecute and convict you on a Florida crime if you plead "guilty", or were found guilty after a trial, even if you got a "withheld adjudication", even though they realize they're probably wrong on the law. If you think that's unfair — be warned. The Eleventh Circuit is very conservative, highly pro-government, and technicalities often prevail over justice. In other words – they really don't care.

THREE YEAR WAITING PERIOD:

If you received a suspended sentence, or a "*withheld adjudication*" on a felony -- then you can't get an FDLE approval to purchase from a licensed dealer until you have expunged your record, or three (3) years has passed from the date that your probation was over, and any of the conditions set by the court have elapsed. [55] Once the **3 years** is up, you're eligible to purchase from a dealer again, however, the loophole here is pretty clear -- you can still purchase from a private individual.

One word of caution. Don't get a friend to buy you a firearm from a dealer, or anyone else if you don't qualify under these sections. This is called a "*straw purchase*", and is a state and federal crime. If you do, both you and your friend will be guilty of a felony.[56] Same thing goes for giving false identification. [57]

WAITING PERIOD FOR HANDGUN PURCHASES:

As we discussed in Chapter One,   Florida passed a constitutional amendment that provided a **three (3) business day** waiting period (weekends and legal holidays don't count) for the purchase of a handgun at retail unless you have a concealed weapons license, or it's a trade for another hand gun. *(Fla. Const., Art. 1, section 8)*.   *Florida Statute* 790.0655 is pretty much identical.   In November 1998 another amendment *(Fla. Const ., Art . 8, section 5)* added more red-tape to this, and allows each county to place a waiting period of from **three** to **five (5) days** on any firearm — if any part of the transaction takes place on *"property to which the public has the right of access".* This applies to most gun shows because they are often held in government owned convention centers.[58] It also applies to streets, side walks, parks, etc. It should not apply to a private home, business property, or stores as the public does not have a "*right*" to access private property.   However, many counties have interpreted "*right of access*" to be anywhere the public can generally enter, and BATFE has gone along with them. Test case waiting to happen! Anyway, due to this stupid provision, each county may also require a criminal history records check on private sales conducted on property which the public has a "*right of access*". Again, this is a county-to-county thing.

So, how do you get a criminal history records check when you purchase from a private party where the sale is on property to which the public "*has a right of access?*" Well . . . you'd have to go to an FFL, and hope they would run it for you. BATFE says it's up to the individual dealer to decide if he wants to run it, or not. Likewise, if they do agree to run it, they can charge you a fee, plus the fee it normally costs for running a check. However, neither the statute or the constitutional provisions apply to sales to a CWL holder. A CWL holder can purchase without any of the waiting periods, and in a *private sale* only – a CWL holder can also skip any records check even if the purchase is made on government property.

If all you're doing is a trade, and you don't have a CWL, in order to avoid the *Article 1, section 8,* three day wait provision (which applies only to handguns) you are stuck with a "*straight trade*", handgun-for-handgun without additional money or items allowed. However, the *Article 8, section 5,* county-by-county restrictions would not apply to a "*straight trade*", as that section applies only to "*sales*" on property which the public has a *right of access.* Of course, there is no case law on either of these interpretations. By the way, law enforcement officers are not exempted from either of these requirements unless they have a CWL.

If you think these Constitutional provisions are kind of stupid – you're right. They could have passed either in the legislature by statute, and had it uniform, so we would all know what the law was. To do it by constitutional amendment was absurd. However, almost everybody in Florida voted for it. Score another one for ignorance, and how easily the media can sway people. So, here's my quote for the day:

> *"Experience should teach us to be most on our guard to protect liberty when the Government's purposes are beneficial . . . . The greatest dangers to liberty lurk in insidious encroachment by men of zeal, well-meaning, but without understanding."* Justice Louis Brandeis in <u>Olmstead v. U nited States</u>, 277 US 438 (1928).

QUESTION: So, if I have a CWL, I don't have to wait 3 days to get my handgun?

ANSWER: Correct. However, you will still need to have the federal *Form 4473*, with the **NICS** background check. Your permit is currently issued by the *Department of Agriculture* which is not a "*law enforcement agency*", and therefore cannot do the NICS check required by federal law. Only "*law enforcement agencies*" can access NICS, and therefore the federal exemption that normally applies to concealed weapon permits, does not apply to those issued in Florida.

To make all these disabilities a little easier to remember, I've prepared a chart on the next page to help you. Remember, there will be some exceptions to the chart, as previously discussed.

CHART OF PERMITTED/NON-PERMITTED SALES:

	Handguns		Rifles & Shotguns	
	Private	Dealer sales	Private	Dealer sales
Age	18 years	21 years old	18 years	18 years old
Residence	same state	same state	same state	any state
3 Day Wait	none	yes, except CWP holder	none	none
Felony conviction	not allowed	not allowed	not allowed	not allowed
Felony "withheld"	allowed	after 3 years	allowed	after 3 years
"Dangerous crime" arrest	allowed	not allowed	allowed	not allowed
Indictment or Information for felony	not allowed	not allowed	not allowed	not allowed
fugitive	not allowed	not allowed	not allowed	not allowed
unlawful drug user	not allowed	not allowed	not allowed	not allowed
illegal alien	not allowed	not allowed	not allowed	not allowed
mental defective or was committed	not allowed	not allowed	not allowed	not allowed
dishonorable discharge	not allowed	not allowed	not allowed	not allowed
renounced citizenship	not allowed	not allowed	not allowed	not allowed
conviction of domestic violence, or restraining order	not allowed 18 USC 922(d)(8)	not allowed	not allowed	not allowed
legal aliens if Fla. resident	allowed	allowed	allowed	allowed
on Probation in Florida	not allowed	not allowed 18 USC 922 (b)(2	not allowed	not allowed
chronic or habitual alcoholic	not suggested	not allowed	not suggested	not allowed

CHAPTER THREE

WHAT TO DO
AFTER THEY TURN YOU DOWN

Ah, ha! They turned you down . Those lowly pencil-pushing, dirty so-and-so's had the nerve to turn you, the all-knowing, all seeing, all-perfect one, down! A pox on all of them! What do they know?

Well, that's actually a good question, Oh Knowing One. You've raised an interesting point.

To answer that, let's first see how it actually works in FDLE Land. It may surprise you. And, by the way, these are generally pretty nice people . . . so don't get down too hard on them. If problems arise -- it's usually not their fault.

THE APPROVAL (OR DISAPPROVAL) PROCESS:
In 1989 Florida passed a law requiring licensed firearm dealers to do a telephone records check on non-licensee purchasers with the *FDLE* (ie: *Florida Department of Law Enforcement*) prior to completing any sale. The purpose of the law is to do a statewide and national criminal records check before an approval for purchase is given. Philosophically speaking, this is a pretty good idea. A rare thing in government. It was also pretty good anticipation of the *Brady Bill*. Score one brownie point for Florida!

Anyway, under Florida law, sales of firearms between private individuals from their private collections are normally not covered by these "record checking" regulations, although sales between private individuals are still subject to certain federal and state restrictions, and in certain counties, sales on public property may require a record check, and even up to a **five day** wait on purchases unless you have a CWL. Otherwise, there currently is no FDLE check in a private sale. However, since we're now talking about dealer sales, and not staring into a crystal legislative ball -- let's get back to the subject at hand.

IDENTIFICATION NEEDED TO PURCHASE:
The procedure when purchasing a firearm from a licensed firearms dealer is to have the buyer complete a federal *Form 4473*. This is required by both state and federal law. It is not generally required as to sales between private individuals. The purchaser must also furnish government issued photo identification establishing his or her name, actual residence address, and date of birth.[59] Photo identification is normally done by a drivers license, or state

identification card. Other acceptable photo identification includes a CWL, Military identification card, passport, and immigration card. Production of your Social Security card is also recommended to clear-up any potential misidentification when FDLE does the records check. A five dollar processing fee is then collected, and the dealer calls FDLE at a special toll-free number.

THE COMPUTER CHECK BY FDLE:

At this point the FDLE operator conducts a computerized state and national criminal records check. Based on the findings of that check the operator will provide the dealer with an approval, non-approval, conditional approval, or conditional non-approval number. The operator is not allowed to release any criminal history over the phone, and the dealer may not ordinarily reveal the results of the check with anyone except the buyer. Of course, giving false information to the firearms dealer in order to secure a firearm is also a state and federal crime -- a felony.

HOW THE FDLE CALL-IN SYSTEM OPERATES:

When FDLE gets the call, they have a limited amount of time to make a determination of your eligibility, assuming your record is unclear. The maximum delay is **24 working hours**. "*Working hours*" mean Monday to Friday, from 9:00 a.m. to 5:00 p.m., legal holidays excluded. If the record shows no disability -- the approval is immediate.

If FDLE can't make a determination one way or the other within this time frame, the dealer is given a *conditional approval number*, and you are allowed to purchase the firearm. However, if FDLE receives information at a later time that you were really ineligible, this conditional approval is revoked, the conditional approval number becomes a "*non-approval number*", and local law enforcement is alerted. Obviously, you can't keep the firearm, and that brings up some interesting civil questions on whether the dealer would be obligated to take it back, and give a refund. The answer to that is normally "no".

If you have a pending arrest on any "*dangerous crime*", *domestic violence*, or one of the special enumerated felonies I listed in the last chapter -- you get a *conditional non-approval* until the case is disposed of, and you inform and establish to FDLE that you're now off-the-hook. At that point, if you check-out as OK -- the qualified non-approval number becomes an *approval number*. If an Indictment or Information is filed against you for any felony (not just the "*arrest*" – but the actual filing of the case), then the same rule applies, and you receive a *conditional non-approval* until the case is resolved in your favor. If resolved against you, your *conditional non-approval* becomes a literal non-approval or denial.

Obviously, if the check comes back that you have a felony conviction, are a deserter, were found mentally incompetent, or had some other legal disability, you will be disapproved. Same thing if it comes back with a withheld adjudication on any felony unless **three (3) years** have elapsed from the date all probation and any other conditions set by the court, including restitution, have been completed. If the amount of probation is unknown, then FDLE will use the **three years**, as a rule of thumb, until it can be shown otherwise.

Whatever happens, the dealer writes the approval, nonapproval, conditional approval, or conditional non-approval number on the Form 4473. He retains this in his records, and you do not get a copy -- so don't bother trying. The records are confidential. You can, and should get the *denial number*, ie: – NICS transaction number (ie: **NTN**). You need this for any "appeal".

WHAT HAPPENS IF THE COMPUTERS ARE DOWN:

If computers are down -- FDLE has until end of *next business day* (5:00 pm) to notify the licensed firearms dealer that the purchase is prohibited. Otherwise, they must issue an approval, or conditional approval number, and you can purchase the gun. The "*next business day*" is a Monday thru Friday, holidays excluded. This is true even though FDLE is required to have these phone lines working 7 days a week, 9:00 a.m. to 9:00 p.m. -- except Christmas and New Year's Day.

If telephone service is not working at the licensee's premises due to the fault of the telephone carrier, or because of any natural disaster, act of God, war, invasion, insurrection, riot, other bona fide emergency, or any reason truly beyond the control of the licensee, then the FDLE phone check and approval is not necessary. In that case, all that's done is fill-in, and sign the federal Form 4473, and if everything else is OK -- you can buy the gun, then and there.

PROBLEMS WITH MIS-IDENTIFICATION:

When you apply for the records check, the computer is trying to match you with millions of disqualified people. If somebody has the same name, sex, date of birth, and skin color -- you've got a problem. Same thing if somebody else has been using your name, or identification illegally. Identity theft is rift in America! Since the law of averages says that this is very possible -- problems can occur. A non-approval usually happens like this:

    a.   All identifying data in the inquiry matches.

b.   Where it's for a female, if there's a match on race, date of birth, social security number, and first name.

c.   Regarding possible misspelling matches -- where the first name of the applicant has another common spelling or ending (Bill, Billy, Billie, William, Wil, etc.); or the last name has a common similar spellings or ends in "s" or "z" (Rodrigues, Rodreques, Rodreguez, Rodriguez).

d.   Regarding, possible name matches – where the purchaser gives a full name, and there is a match with a person with the same last name who has a matching initial for the first or middle name.

APPROVAL, OR NON-APPROVAL NUMBERS FROM FDLE:

Once you're approved, the approval number is valid for a total of **thirty (30) days** from issuance, or until the purchase transaction is completed. It expires upon use. If a non-approval number is assigned, the sale cannot be completed, and the dealer is supposed to advise the purchaser of his right to "*appeal*" the non-approval. There is a form for doing this which the dealer is supposed to provide, and he also should complete the "dealer" section. Any appeal must be filed within **21 days**.

If the "*appeal*" is successful, FDLE sends the buyer a letter notifying him that the firearm may be purchased. The buyer may bring the letter to any dealer who can then make a sale without any further FDLE check. The letter will have a cut-off date, after which it becomes invalid. The letter is then kept by the licensed firearms dealer, and attached to the federal Form 4473. This "appeal" procedure is explained in the next section.

APPEAL PROCEDURE & CRIMINAL HISTORY REVIEW:

Actually, this "*appeal*" procedure is not really an appeal, but is a formal "*criminal history records check*", where you provide FDLE with your fingerprints to assist a more in-depth examination of the (hopeful) mix-up. The procedure is outlined in *Section 11C-8.001* of the *Florida Administrative Code*. There is no charge for the records check by FDLE, but you must obtain a set of your fingerprints from a local law enforcement agency on the appropriate fingerprint card (FBI FD-258), or on the fingerprint portion of the appeal form. The local agency may charge you a fee for doing the fingerprinting, although the Sheriff is supposed to do it for free, upon request. Once you have the fingerprinting done, you send the card and the "*Firearm Purchase*

Non-Approval Appeal Form" to FDLE, on the address listed on the form. Make sure the card is in an appropriate envelope, because a bent fingerprint card is not going to do you much good if somebody is trying to compare prints. The address is:

> FDLE – Firearm Purchase Program
> Post Office Box 1489
> Tallahassee, Florida 32302-1489

If a positive fingerprint identification is made against an existing criminal record, then FDLE will return the fingerprint card, appeal form, and a single copy of the record directly to the applicant, unless you submitted it through a law enforcement agency. If you still think there is a mistake, there are additional procedures you may follow, but they get very complicated, and I suggest you hire an attorney to assist you with them. Again, FDLE must receive your *"appeal"* within **21 days** of the denial. You may also appeal thru the FBI, and there is no date restriction to do so. Likewise, you may obtain copies of your own criminal history both from FDLE and the FBI by going on their websites, and requesting such. FDLE charges $24 bucks via credit card, and the entire thing can be done online. If you "appeal" thru the FBI, that is really a more complicated and involved procedure which I recommend an attorney for from the beginning. The procedure, in brief, can be found on the FBI website at [http://www.fbi.gov/hq/cjisd/nics].

A QUICK HINT:

If you get turned down, and think it's a mistake -- you may be right. Sometimes the FDLE operator punches in the wrong information (hey, they're human!), and you get a disapproval. If this happens, don't despair. Try again a day or two later, and it will probably be approved. If not – then, you may have a problem, and will have to get a criminal history records check through the appeal process I've already explained, on your own, or both. Quite frankly, I always advise getting both the FBI and FDLE histories, as well as doing the appeal. Makes things a lot easier to understand during the process.

THE BRADY ACT & NICS:

The *Brady Act's* permanent provisions went into effect on November 30, 1998, and did not substantially affect Florida, since many of its provisions were already operational here. There were some temporary problems due to Federal law requiring background checks through the *NICS* (*National Instant Check System*) system, as that computer system has a wider data-base than what Florida formerly used. The NICS system check includes injunctions against repeat or domestic violence, misdemeanor crimes of domestic violence, involuntary commitments, etc.

Other than that, *Brady*, required sales of multiple handguns (ie: more than one handgun in **five work days** from same dealer) to be reported by dealers on both an BATFE form, as well as to State or local government -- so that your local police, etc., will now have a "track" of purchasers buying more than one handgun in a week's time from the same dealer, and raised the application fee for becoming a federally licensed dealer. Under Florida law, when you purchase a firearm with a CWL, and thereby avoid the waiting period on handgun purchases, your CWL number is copied into the *Form 4473*.

MENTAL HEALTH LAW AMENDMENTS:

In 2013 the Legislature amended F.S. 790.065(2) by prohibiting the purchase of firearms, or obtaining or retaining a Florida CWL, by persons who were admitted for involuntary examination under the *Baker Act*, and then voluntarily agreed to treatment, where there is also a finding by the examining physician that the person is an imminent danger to themself or another, the examining physician certifies that if the patient did not agree a petition for involuntary commitment would be filed, the patient likewise agrees in writing to that finding on an approved form that warns them that their agreement may prohibit the individual from purchasing a firearm or obtaining a CWL, and a judge or magistrate approved of the process. This should also apply to *Marchman Act* proceedings. There is a question whether the amendment covers private sales of firearms, or possession of firearms already possessed by the individual, however, because a judge or magistrate would have to approve the process – there is still a high likelihood that the procedure would be considered a *"commitment"* under federal law – thus prohibiting the individual from possession of firearms or ammunition. Restoration is accomplished by filing a petition with the court, and serving a copy on the State Attorney, where the individual has the burden of establishing that he or she *"will not be likely to act in a manner that is dangerous to public safety and that granting the relief would not be contrary to the public interest"*. A denial of relief allows an appeal to the District Court of Appeal. A denial would also allow re-application for relief one year after the date of the order of denial.

CHAPTER FOUR

REMOVAL OF LEGAL DISABILITIES

Sometimes the computers are right -- and there's really no mistake about it. You've got a felony conviction, or other type of legitimate legal disability. Since the rest of us are now somewhat concerned that you may not be the type of person we really want walking around with a firearm – you may be wondering what your options are. That's what this chapter is all about. Of course, *executive clemency* includes death penalty matters, and many other things you're not really interested in, and therefore I'm going to keep the chapter geared strictly to persons not in prison who are not seeking a reduction of sentence, but just want their firearms rights restored. Hopefully, it will be of some help in explaining the process.

Now, if you've read any of the earlier versions of this book, up to around 2007 – this chapter has undergone a lot of change. That's because the rules relating to executive clemency likewise changed. Anyway, here's how it works today:

EXECUTIVE CLEMENCY:

The *Florida Constitution, Article 4, section 8*, grants the governor, with the approval of two (2) members of the Cabinet, the ability to grant full or conditional pardons, as well as the restoration of the civil rights of most individuals. This is also known as the right to "*executive clemency*". You have no individual right to *executive clemency* -- it is totally in the discretion of the governor and his cabinet. That means if you're denied -- tough luck! There's no appeal, although you can reapply at a later time.

Executive Clemency is granted by the *Board of Executive Clemency* [https://www.fcor.state.fl.us/clemency.shtml], with the investigative assistance of the *Florida Commission on Offender Review* [http://www.dc.state.fl.us/restoration.html]. The *Board of Executive Clemency* literally means the Governor and his Cabinet. Your chance to meet some really important people, who probably will not want to invite you home for dinner. . While there are numerous applications from prisoners for commutation of sentences, the main areas of executive clemency you are likely to be concerned with fall into the following categories:

a. Full Pardon

b. Pardon without firearm authority

c.   Pardon for misdemeanor

d.   Specific authority to own, possess, or use firearms

e.   Restoration of Civil Rights in Florida

Now, you should know that any form of executive clemency can be granted as "*conditional*". That means just what it says, the *Executive Clemency Board* added some type of condition to the relief granted. If you violate the conditions, the executive clemency will likely be rescinded. You should also know that when applying for *executive clemency* the information you provide must be accurate or you are committing a felony, and that your application, if it meets the qualifications — will be investigated by the *Florida Commission on Offender Review*. I understand waiting times for review of an application take **years** to accomplish due to limited staff and funding. If you fail to fully cooperate with the investigation, your application will be denied. Applications can be obtained online at the Board's website, as well as loads of information on the process.

EXPLANATION OF FORMS OF EXECUTIVE CLEMENCY:

O.K., so you know there are several forms of executive clemency, so which is the one for you? Here's the explanation:

A.   Full Pardon   — This is an unconditional release from punishment forgives guilt, and restores all rights including firearms. To be eligible you must have completed all sentences imposed, all conditions of supervision must be completed or expired, for no less than **ten (10) years** , and you may not have any outstanding detainers, pending charges, or unpaid restitution, nor outstanding fines from other criminal or traffic cases that total more than $1,000.00. Figure if you have any fines left over that you'll likely be denied. However, if the sum is too great to pay, you should know there is a separate mechanism for remission of fines and forfeitures which can be sought through executive clemency. You should also know that the ten year period is not written in stone as it is subject to "waiver". Again, waivers are treated later in this chapter.

B.   Pardon without firearm authority   — same as a full pardon, except no firearm rights. Same time limits and conditions. If this happens you are still illegal under state and federal law to own, use, or possess.

C.   Pardon for misdemeanor — This releases a person from punishment and forgives guilt. Useful for domestic violence convictions.

D.   <u>Specific Authority to Own, Possess, or Use Firearms</u> — This restores all your firearms rights **only** where the conviction was from a Florida State court.   If your conviction was from out of state, or in a federal court -- only the other state or feds have jurisdiction! You can apply for the Florida clemency, assuming you qualify, at the same time you are applying for any other form of executive clemency, or you can do it separately if you've already been granted a partial restoration of civil rights, or partial pardon. Application is not less than **8 years.**

Like the pardon, to be eligible you must have completed all sentences imposed, and have all conditions of supervision completed or expired for no less than **eight (8) years** , and no outstanding detainers, or restitution, nor fines from other criminal or traffic cases that total more than $1,000.00. Make sure all fines are paid off on any traffic tickets, etc. — or you may wind-up with a denial.

E.   <u>Restoration of Civil Rights in Florida</u> — This restores all rights of citizenship except right to own, possess, or use firearms. Depending on the crime involved, the period before you can apply is either **5** years or 7 years.   However, if granted, it does not relieve a person from registration and notification requirements imposed upon a sexual offender. You may apply for restoration of firearms rights at the same time you apply for your restoration if the **eight (8) years** has passed, otherwise you need a waiver.

<u>CRIMES THAT CAN DISQUALIFY YOU:</u>

To be eligible you must have completed all sentences imposed including all conditions of supervision.   If convicted in a court other than a Florida state court, then the person must a legal resident of Florida at the time the application is made, and until it is decided. There are a number of *crimes that will disqualify you* from applying unless you have secured a waiver. These are a conviction for a capital or life felony; habitual offender; habitual violent offender; three time violent offender; violent career criminal; or prison release reoffender; any statewide prosecution; any RICO conviction; drug trafficking; any *"dangerous crime"*; accessory after fact to crime of violence; lewd, lascivious, indecent; crime requiring registration under Sexual Predators Act, sexual battery; crimes against law enforcement, DUI related felony; homicide; public corruption; crimes by elected official; shooting into vehicle or dwelling; leaving scene of accident involving death/serious injury; and possession of a firearm by convicted felon. All of these are listed in the rules of the *Board of Executive Clemency* available on their website.

REAPPLICATION:

A person who has been granted or denied executive clemency cannot reapply for at least **two (2) years** from the date the denial became final.

SOME LIMITATIONS ON PARDON POWER:

Although a full pardon would normally be thought to "blot out guilt" — all pardons now granted have a proviso that the pardon "*will not erase or expunge the record of conviction, and it will not indicate innocence*". If you want an expunction — you'll have to apply for that separately, assuming you qualify. [65]

FEDERAL RESTORATION OF CIVIL RIGHTS:

It used to be that a state restoration of civil rights was insufficient to remove legal disabilities for firearms ownership without also going through an additional approval with BATFE in Washington, D.C. Due to a change in federal law, so long as the restoration is "full", including firearms rights, and is from the state of conviction, this is no longer true, (unless it was a federal court conviction, as only federal courts have jurisdiction in such an instance). To understand the change, you need to understand the following:

The federal definition of a "conviction" is set forth in 18 USC 921 (a)(20)(B), and states:

> "*What constitutes a conviction of such crime shall be determined in accordance with the law of the juris diction in which the proceedings were held. Any conviction which has been expunged, or set aside or for which a person has been pardoned or has had civil rights restored shall not be considered a conviction for purposes of this chapter, unless such pardon, expungement, or restoration of civil rights expressly provides that the person may not ship, transport, possess, or receive firearms.*"

Do not read this section literally. The restoration must be total. Thus, until your firearms rights are restored, you do not have a "*full*" restoration, and cannot possess firearms under either Florida or Federal law. As I said before, if you had a federal conviction, you are plum out of luck, as Congress, since 1992, has refused to fund the federal procedure to remove legal disabilities for firearms rights, and the United States Supreme Court upheld it in *United States v. Bean*, 537 US 71 (2002). Thus, the only current method of getting federal rights restored from a conviction is by a Presidential pardon. Start those presidential contributions rolling! (Just kidding!)

RESTORATIONS FROM MENTAL COMMITMENTS:

However, pursuant to the *"NICS Improvement Amendments Act of 2007"* you should know that if your prohibition was due to a commitment to a mental institution for mental illness by a federal court or agency, there is a remedy for restoration where the adjudication or commitment, respectively, has been set aside or expunged; the person has otherwise been fully released or discharged from all mandatory treatment, supervision, or monitoring; has otherwise been found by a court or agency to be rehabilitated from the mental health condition that caused the commitment; or in instances where the commitment or adjudication was based solely on a medical finding of disability, not involving being a *"mental defective"*, where there was no opportunity for hearing . Application is made to the federal agency which made the adjudication – which must make a decision on the application within 365 days. If the application is not resolved within that time it is deemed *"denied without cause"*. Review of the denial of any application may be sought *de novo* , in federal court, and if the court case is successful, attorney fees are awardable. This law applies equally to the states in that they must also provide a remedy for such restorations. *ATF Form 3210.12.*

FLORIDA MENTAL HEALTH RESTORATIONS:

In 2013 the Legislature amended F.S. 790.065(2) by prohibiting the purchase of firearms, or obtaining or retaining a Florida CWP, by persons who were admitted for involuntary examination under the **Baker Act,** and then voluntarily agreed to treatment, where there is also a finding by the examining physician that the person is an imminent danger to themself or another, the examining physician certifies that if the patient did not agree a petition for involuntary commitment would be filed, the patient likewise agrees in writing to that finding on an approved form that warns them that their agreement may prohibit the individual from purchasing a firearm or obtaining a CWL, and a judge or magistrate approved of the process. There is a technical question whether the amendment covers private sales of firearms, or possession of firearms already possessed by the individual, however, because a judge or magistrate would have to approve the process – there is still a very high likelihood that the procedure would be considered a *"commitment"* under federal law – thus prohibiting the individual from possession of firearms or ammunition. Restoration is accomplished by filing a petition with the court, and serving a copy on the State Attorney, where the individual has the burden of establishing that he or she *"**will not be likely to act in a manner that is dangerous to public safety and that granting the relief would not be contrary to the public interest**"*. A denial of relief allows an appeal to the District Court of Appeal. A denial would also allow re-application for relief one year after the date of the order of denial.

This same procedure should apply to *Marchman Act* restorations as involuntary commitments for alcohol abuse are included in the definition of "*committed to a mental institution*" in F.S. 790.065.

EXPUNCTIONS & SEALINGS IN FLORIDA:

While not really related to restoration of civil rights, those citizens who were arrested for a crime in Florida, and had their case dropped, or dismissed can apply for an "*expunction*" of a Florida arrest in most instances pursuant to F.S. 943.0585. To a large extent, the granting of an expunction allows the person to lawfully deny the arrest and any prosecution for   most purposes – just like it never occurred. It's not a lie when you do this -- it's called a "*legal fiction*". There's also something called a "*sealing*" pursuant to F.S. 943.059 which is similar to an expunction, can usually be obtained if the person has no prior record, and received nothing worse than a "*withheld adjudication*" in the current charge, and they had no prior findings of guilt on other charges. However, it is not as far-reaching as an expunction.

To qualify for an *expunction*, you cannot have had a previous criminal offense in which you entered a plea of *guilty* or *no contest* , or suffered a previous conviction, and you may not have had a previous sealing or expunction of your record. Likewise, and most unfair, if you went to trial, and won – you cannot obtain an expunction due to an amendment to the statute in 2006.

If you're seeking an expunction (or sealing), there are other things you need to do and know, but quite frankly, you really need a lawyer to accomplish these – so let them handle that.

EXCEPTIONS TO EXPUNCTION PRIVACY:

Even with an expunction, there are still numerous exceptions on your ability to legally deny the arrest or prosecution.   These include working, volunteering, or apply for a job with: (1) a criminal justice agency; (2) you're a defendant in another criminal prosecution; (3) you're applying for a sealing or expunction in another case; (4) you're applying for admission to The Florida Bar; (5) you're applying for a position or license with the Department of Children and Family Services, the Department of Juvenile Justice, or will be employed or used in a position involving direct contact with children, the developmentally disabled, or the elderly; (6) any position in programs providing care to children, the developmentally disabled, or vulnerable adults; (7) positions with the central abuse hotline; (8) all persons working under contract who have access to abuse records; (9) all mental health personnel working in public or private mental health programs and facilities who have direct contact with unmarried patients under the age of 18 years; (10) persons involved in foster care and substance abuse; (11) child care personnel including schools and day care; (12) care giver of any "vulnerable adult"; (13) those working in delinquency services; (14) those working in nursing homes.

FEDERAL & OUT-OF-STATE CONVICTIONS:

You should know that the State of Florida does not have the power to expunge or seal an out-of-state conviction, nor does it have the power to expunge or seal a federal conviction, even if the federal court was located in Florida. If you have an out-of-state problem – you'll likely need a lawyer in that jurisdiction to handle it. When an expunction is granted most of your judicial and almost all law enforcement agency records are actually shredded, and removed from all computers including the FBI, except for the file and computer records kept by FDLE. Those records are generally confidential except by court order, and for verification purposes through FDLE when you apply or work in a position previously described.

In federal land, the federal courts rarely permit an expunctions, and they have jurisdiction only to expunge judicial records, and not law enforcement records. *U.S. v. Flowers* , 389 F.3d 737 (7 th Cir. 2004). As a practical matter, this is a very uphill battle, would require a showing of actual innocense, and probably not worth the effort.

NEW YORK CERTIFICATES FROM RELIEF OF DISABILITIES:

There seem to be quite a few former New Yorker's who have a problem getting a Florida CWL once they move down here. Since I keep getting questions asking about rectifying the problem, here's the scoop: A New York *Certificate of Relief from Disabilities* immediately restores the full firearm rights of anyone convicted of a felony in New York where either *Box A* or *Box B* is checked. However, before Florida will issue a CWL, an applicant who had a New York conviction must also supply verification from the *N.Y. Division of Criminal Justice Services* that the certificate was filed with them. That's normally done by getting a letter from them verifying that. For contact information, look up their website. On the other hand, if *Box C* was checked – you will also need proof that a "full" restoration was ordered in the certificate that also covers firearm rights.

PROHIBITED EXPUNCTIONS:

Certain crimes cannot be expunged. Here's the list: Violations of F.S . 393.135 & F.S . 394.4593 (sexual misconduct); any predicate offense for a sexual predator as listed in F.S . 775.21; F.S . 787.025 (luring or enticing a child); C.

794 (sexual battery); F.S. 796.03 (procuring minor for prostitution); F.S. 800.04 (lewd or lascivious acts); F.S .810.14 (voyeurism); F.S. 817.034 (communications fraud); F.S. 825.1025 (lewd or lascivious acts in presence of elderly or disabled); F.S . 827.071 (sexual performance by child); C . 839 (offenses by public officials); F.S . 847.0133 (transmit or show minor obscene materials); F.S . 847.0135 (computer pornography); F.S. 847.0145 (offering or allowing minor to be used for sexual conduct or depictions); F.S . 893.135 (drug trafficking); any violation listed in F.S . 907.041 (ie: "dangerous crimes"), F.S. 916.1075 (sexual misconduct), and any crime where registration as a sex offender/predator is required.

You might also be interested in knowing that a *sealed* record can normally be expunged after ten years. F.S . 943.0585(2)(h).

RAP SHEETS, & DATABASE CORRECTIONS:

There are lots of reasons why your record can get confused or screwed up, and you get denied for a firearm purchase. Sometimes the record is correct, sometimes the government data systems have confused you with someone else, sometimes it's just that the systems are missing information that would clarify everything. However – in the end – it's your responsibility – not theirs – to follow thru on any correction, and make it happen. I'll outline some of those procedures here, but if you think you have a problem I strongly recommend you first order your criminal history (ie: "*rap sheet*") both from the FBI, and from FDLE (Florida Department of Law Enforcement). For the FBI, you can do that by sending a written request, including your signature, $18.00 in payment by money order, certified check, or credit card (credit card form is at: www.fbi.gov/hq/cjisd/fprequest.htm), payable to "U.S. Treasury", along with a fingerprint card completed by law enforcement to the address that follows. A **brochure** on how to do this is also available at the website address I just mentioned, and I highly recommend you take a look at it:

FBI – CJIS Division Attention: Record Request
1000 Custer Hollow Road
Clarksburg, W.V. 26306

If all you want is just your Florida criminal history – it's a bit easier since you can do the whole thing online at the FDLE website. (https://www2.fdle.state.fl.us/cchinet) The cost is $24.00, and while it is not as extensive as the FBI database – it occasionally shows things not on the national databases. More information on this is also available at http://www.fdle.state.fl.us. You can also get a better, and more reliable check from FDLE by including a **fingerprint card** done by law enforcement, and sending it with a check or money order for $24.00, and written request to:

Florida Department of Law Enforcement
Attention: Criminal History Services
P.O. Box 1489
Tallahassee, Fl. 32302-1489

HOW TO APPEAL A FIREARM PURCHASE DENIAL:

While Florida and Federal law talk about an "*appeal*" of a firearm purchase denial – it really isn't an "appeal" so much as a formal request for a records check. While you can do this thru either the FBI or FDLE – I generally like doing it thru the FBI, but it's just a personal preference. It's probably easier through FDLE for most folks. However, the FBI is legally responsible for making sure the data on the NICS information system is correct. 28 CFR 25.5 There's a brochure on the FBI website that outlines their procedure at: http://www.fbi.gov/hq/cjisd/nics.htm. It works about the same for both the FBI, or thru FDLE, like this:

Pursuant to 28 CFR 25.10 – any person who was denied a firearm purchase is entitled to request the reason for the denial from the agency that conducted the *NICS* check (FDLE in Florida), or from the NICS Section at the FBI. Your choice. You must have the *NTN* or *STN* number (ie: NICS or State Transaction Number) to do this. This is the transaction number assigned by NICS when the firearms dealer called in your attempted purchase for approval. In appropriate circumstances, I guess you could also call it your "*denial number*". Lucky you! The dealer is required to give this number to you only if you ask for it. Once you have it, you may submit your "*appeal*" to the FBI via facsimile at 1-888-550-6427; by e-mail at: nicsappeals@leo.gov; or by mail to the FBI, Criminal Justice Information Services Division, NICS Section, Appeal Services Team, P.O. Box 4278, Clarksburg, West Virginia 26302-9922. I suggest the correspondence include your name, address, social, date of birth, race and sex, and STN or NTN number , you should title it "*Appeal of Firearms Purchase Denial*" , and should probably say something like this:

> "*On __(date) ___ I attempted to purchase a firearm at (insert dealers store name and address), and the purchase was denied after the NICS check. I wish to appeal the denial. The STN number is: ____. My social security number is _____ , d a t e o f birth is _____ , city of birth is _____ and I am a (white/black/Hispanic/Asian man/woman).*"

You can do the same thing with FDLE, but for FDLE, you need to do it within **21 days** of the firearm purchase denial. As already stated, it works almost the same as the FBI method.

Anyway, once your "*appeal*" is received, the agency has five business days in which to respond by a letter stating the reason – or requesting further documents that are needed to them to be able to furnish an answer. This will often be a request for a fingerprint card, therefore it is probably a better practice to include a fingerprint card with your initial appeal application. When you get the reason back – it will usually come in the form of a "***rap sheet***", or criminal history.

If you still think there's a mistake, and wish to challenge the accuracy of the record upon which the denial is based, or if your firearm rights were restored, you can seek correction by further "appeal" thru FDLE (if it was a Florida denial), or the FBI – again – your choice. If that agency is unable to resolve the appeal, they will notify you, and also provide the name and address of the agency that originated the record upon which the denial was based in the first place. You should then seek correction of the original record directly from the agency from which it originated. If you're beginning to think this process can be time consuming – you're right!

If the record is corrected – you need to furnish proof of that (usually by ***certified copies*** of the government or court records) to either the FBI or FDLE, which will then verify what you've provided – assuming the originating agency hasn't already done that. Once it's verified, the record will be corrected in NICS. If any of that sounded simple – sometimes it is, and sometimes it's not. Plus, there are other more complicated alternate procedures – and, as a last resort – you can also sue in federal court. I've done this procedure several times, and suggest that if hiring an attorney – bring this book with you, and show them this section – because they probably haven't a clue how to handle it.

If you want to know the typical reasons why a denial occurs (other than your being confused with another person), I've found that many times there is a criminal charge in the data system without a "***disposition***". In other words, there's a notation in the system about an old arrest – but no information what happened to the arrest. Likewise, there may be a criminal charge that doesn't make clear if it was a felony or misdemeanor – or in some instances – whether it was or was not a "*misdemeanor crime of domestic violence*". In these instances you (not them) have the responsibility to clear up the confusion – usually by furnishing *certified copies* of the court documents that prove the case was either resolved in your favor – or certified copies of the court documents that conclusively prove the case did not qualify as a felony, nor as a *misdemeanor crime of domestic violence*. Sometimes you'll be able to get this on your own, sometimes things get a bit more complicated – and you 'll need an attorney.

QUESTION: Why would I need an attorney?

ANSWER: Well . . . in certain instances the court records may need clarification. If that happens you may need an attorney to get an *order of clarification* from the court that originally entered the information. There are other instances, but that's the one I've done quite often, or suggested.

VOLUNTARY APPEAL FILE:

Sometimes, no matter how hard you try – things continue to be screwed up record-wise. This is normally because the system is confusing you with another person who is almost identical in name, date of birth, and place of birth – or an identity theft situation. In such instances, it is often a wise move to sign up, and get entered into the FBI's *Voluntary Appeal File* database. By signing up, you allow the FBI to retain the records that show you are not a prohibited person – and thereby allow future firearm purchase approvals to go through without substantial problems. The application, applicant's statement, and other information on how to accomplish this can all be found on the FBI website previously cited: http://www.fbi.gov/hq/cjisd/nics.htm

CHAPTER FIVE

FLORIDA CONCEALED WEAPONS LICENSE

Having a Concealed Weapons License (CWL) is the smartest thing anyone can do if they own or carry any type of weapon, whatsoever! If you only have a pocket knife -- get it! If you have a firearm -- you're nuts not to have it, even if you never take it out of the house! Why? Because it takes the worry out of 90% of the situations that could happen, and generally gives you the "benefit of the doubt" if law enforcement is involved. From a federal standpoint — it means you are not criminally liable for driving through a school zone with a firearm! Plus, the fact that you have the CWL is now confidential, and no longer can be disclosed as a public record. F.S. 790.0601.

It's also the best thing that ever happened to the honest Florida firearms, or weapons owner because prior to the passage of this State law, every single Florida county had its own individual set of standards and regulations – which drove everyone who was trying to be honest totally nuts – and left your ability to legally carry a firearm at the mercy of each particular Board of County Commissioners. Politics at its very worst! Of course, the criminals could care less, one way or the other -- but that's another story.

Today, if you meet certain specified qualifications -- you can legally carry a concealed firearm, or any other concealed weapon, almost anywhere in Florida -- with certain exceptions which I will outline later in this chapter. Although the specific purpose of this legislation was to authorize the carrying of a firearm " *as a means of lawful self-defense*", you should remember that it's still only a license to "*carry*" the firearm (or weapon) in a **concealed** manner -- and does NOT generally include the use or display of such weapons. The "*use*" aspect of having a firearm, or any other weapon, is still governed by the criminal laws, and the law of justification and self-defense. "*Display*", or the unlawfulness of display, is covered by a number of criminal laws.

WEAPONS COVERED BY LICENSE:

Pursuant to F.S. 790.06(1), the license "technically" covers only "*handguns, electric weapons, tear gas guns, knives, and billies*", however, as a practical matter it covers any weapon or firearm other than *destructive devices* and maybe *machine guns*, inasmuch as F.S. 790.01(3) exempts persons with a valid Concealed Weapons License from any of the prohibitions of carrying concealed weapons/firearms. Of course, there are no cases interpreting this facet of F.S. 790.01, and therefore if you want to be completely safe, stick to the weapons listed. On the other hand, it seems somewhat irrational to say a person can carry a concealed firearm, but can't carry something less lethal, and I can't imagine a contrary interpretation that would pass constitutional muster, or make any sense. Still, as absolutely sure as I am, it could be a *test case*.

QUALIFICATIONS FOR THE CONCEALED PERMIT:

Obtaining a Florida Concealed Weapons License (ie: *CWL*) is a fairly reasonable procedure. It takes up to three (3) months, and often less to get it, from the time you send in the application -- and lasts for seven (7) years before it must be renewed. The basic qualifications for obtaining the Concealed Weapons License[1] according to F.S. 790.06(are as follows:

1.   You must be 21 years of age, or older, and a legal resident of the United States, or are in the military, or a veteran discharged under honorable conditions.

2.   You don't suffer from any physical infirmity which prevents the safe handling of a weapon or firearms.

3.   You're not a *convicted felon*, unless your right to own and possess a fire-arm was restored by *executive clemency*.

4.   You have not been *"committed"* for drug abuse within **three (3) years** of the date of your application for the permit, nor have you been found *"**guilty**"* of any drug crime, including misdemeanor possession, within the same time frame. In this sense, "***guilty***" is the equivalent of either a ***conviction***, or a ***withheld adjudication***.

5.   You are not a chronic and habitual user of alcohol to the extent that your normal faculties are impaired. This situation is presumed to be true if you were *committed* for alcohol treatment pursuant to Chapter 396 of the Florida Statutes; were convicted of using a firearm while under the influence of alcohol or a controlled substance; were convicted of DUI two or more times within **3 years** of your application; or have been deemed a habitual offender of the disorderly intoxication laws within **3 years** of your application by three convictions within 12 months.

6.   You have not been adjudicated an incapacitated person under F.S. 744.331, or have waited **five (5) years** after such incapacity was removed by court order.

7.   You have not been *committed* to a mental institution, unless you have a certificate from a psychiatrist licensed in Florida that you have not suffered from any such disability for **five (5) years**.   Of course, if you were *committed*, and the disability is extinguished or removed other than by the procedure in F.S. 790.065 — you will still be a *"prohibited person"* under federal law,   and should still not be able to obtain the CWL.

8.   You have not had a *withheld adjudication* or *suspended sentence* on any *felony*, or any *misdemeanor crime of domestic violence* unless **three (3) years** have passed since you completed probation, and any other conditions set by the court; or unless your record was sealed or expunged. Furthermore, be warned — current Federal law does not permit firearms possession if you plead *"guilty"* vs. *"no contest"* to a felony, or to a federally defined misdemeanor **domestic violence** conviction — *"withheld adjudication"* or not. <u>United States v. Chubbuck</u>, 252 F.3d 1300 (11th Cir. 2001). This also applies to police officers, even on duty. <u>F.O.P. v. United States</u>, 173 F.3d 898 (DCC 1999).

9.   There is no injunction currently in force that restrains you from committing either repeat or domestic violence.

10.   You are not prohibited from purchase or possession of a firearm by **Florida** or **Federal** law. F.S. 790.06(2)(m). Since F.S. 790.065, and federal law affect this subsection, the following additional prohibitions currently would **stop** you from obtaining a permit:

   a.   If you plead *"guilty"* instead of *"no contest"* to any felony, or to any *misdemeanor crime of domestic violence*, or were found guilty of such after a trial — even if adjudication was *"withheld"* because the 11th Circuit Court of Appeals says it's still a "conviction". They also admit they're probably wrong, but will still uphold any federal conviction![2] Hence, Florida would be wise to refuse the CWL, as well.

   b.   Even if you had a *"withheld adjudication"* on any felony, or any misdemeanor crime of *domestic violence*, and even if you plead *"no contest"* — you must still wait until **three (3) years** have elapsed since all conditions of the sentence were fulfilled, including fines, probation, parole, and restitution. F.S. 790.06(2)(k)

c.   If you have a criminal *Indictment or Information* for a felony pending against you — you can't get the CWL until the case is resolved, since **federal law** does not permit you to purchase from a dealer.

d.   If, while your application is pending, you have an **arrest** for any *"**dangerous crime**"* listed in F.S. 907.041; any violation of any firearm/weapons law in Chapter 790 of the Florida statutes; stalking, resisting an officer with violence, drug crimes under Chapter 893; extortion; explosives; assisting suicide; treason; sabotage; or criminal anarchy — you will be denied until the charge is disposed of, assuming the disposition does not disqualify you from firearms ownership or possession. It is your responsibility – not theirs – to supply proof of a favorable disposition once the charge is disposed of.   This is normally done by obtaining a *certified copy* of the *Nolle Prosequi*, or *No Information* filed by the State Attorney in the court clerk's file. F.S. 790.065(2)(c)(1)

e.   You have not had an *adjudication*, or even a *withheld adjudication* on any *"crime of violence constituting a misdemeanor"* unless **three (3) years** have elapsed since all conditions of the sentence have been fulfilled, or the record was sealed or expunged. F.S. 790.06(3)

11.   You are not a resident of the United States, unless you are a consular security official of a friendly foreign government. (Yes -- you can be an out of state resident, and still obtain a CWL. But remember, it's only valid in Florida, and those states that have a reciprocity law with Florida. Likewise, it may not be valid in some other states, even with reciprocity, unless you are a *resident* of Florida, and/or not a *resident* of their state.

There are also training requirements "*to demonstrate competence with a firearm*". These are to assure the State that you have some intelligent idea of what you can legally do with a firearm, and know how to use it. Unfortunately, these standards are woefully inadequate at this time, and need to be upgraded to make sure students understand how to operate their firearm properly. However, as minimal and varied as this qualification may be in application, it seems to be working extremely well. Very few CWL holders are getting in trouble with the law since the program started. The training qualifications can be any one of the following:

1. Completion of any hunter education or safety course approved by the Game & Fresh Water Fish Commission, or similar agency of another state.

2. Completion of any NRA firearms safety or training course.

3. Completion of any firearms safety or training course, or class, available to the general public which is staffed by instructors certified by the NRA, Department of State, or Criminal Justice Standards & Training Commission, and offered by: (a) law enforcement; (b) a college or junior college; (c) a private or public institution, or organization; or (d) a firearms training school.

4. Completion of any law enforcement firearms training or safety course, or class, offered for security guards, investigators, special deputies, or any subdivision of law enforcement or security enforcement.

5. Presents evidence of equivalent experience with a firearm through military service (copy of Honorable Discharge, or *DD214*), or through participation in organized shooting competition.

6. Is licensed, or was licensed to carry a firearm in this state, any county of this state, or any such municipality, unless the license was revoked for cause.

7. Completion of any firearms training or safety course, or class, conducted by a state certified firearms instructor, or an NRA certified firearms instructor.

If your training is under subsection 2, 3, or 7 of the above — and you took your instruction on or after July 1, 1998 — the instructor must also certify you "*safely handled and discharged the firearm*", as part of the course. This can technically be a "**one shot**" requirement. F.S. 790.06(2)(h), although I would certainly hope for more – including loading and unloading. Plus, the *NRA* (ie: *National Rifle Association*) requires its certified instructors to have the student use an actual "*firearm*" with live ammunition – not *AirSoft*, or blanks – which is totally consistent with the language of the statute. Obviously, the more instruction you get — the better off you are from a practical side, even if this is not necessary for the license. There are many excellent instructors in your geographic area, and no matter what your level of expertise, you'll probably learn something.

Once you complete the course, you enclose a photocopy of your completion certificate with the rest of your application form, and you send it to Tallahassee. If you don't have a completion certificate you may substitute an affidavit from the instructor, school, club, group, or organization that conducted or taught the course/or class that attests to your completion -- or participation in firearms competition.

COMPLETING THE APPLICATION PROCESS:

Starting July 1, 2012 the fee for a new CWP will be $70.00 plus $42.00 for hard copy fingerprinting. Renewals will be $60.00, and further fingerprinting is not required. Currently, the initial and renewal permits are five bucks more, each. The Legislature changed the fees in 2012. (P.S. - I highly recommend "*electronic fingerprinting*" through your local sheriff's office, which will speed your application by about 60 days). If you use the paper fingerprint card you must use **Black** ink only! You can also do the entire application/photo/ prints by making an appointment at any regional office of the *Florida Division of Licensing*, and in some instances your county Tax Collector (if they have signed up for the program). F.S. 790.06(5). If you use the *Tax Collector*, they can charge an additional fee of $22.00 for an original application, or twelve bucks for a renewal. These last two should be the absolute fastest method of getting your CWL – but you must have an actual appointment if you go to the regional office of the *Division of Licensing*. You can also obtain the application and other required documents online from the Florida Department of Agriculture at:

> Florida Department of Agriculture
> Division of Licensing — Concealed Weapon Permits
> P.O. Box 6687
> Tallahassee, Florida 32314-6687
> www.freshfromflorida.com/Divisions-Offices/Licensing

Fingerprinting can be done at any law enforcement agency, and cost is $42.00 for a hard copy submission, or $35.00 for electronic digital print submission, plus any fee charged by the law enforcement agency. You will also have to supply a color photograph taken within 30 days of your application which meets a certain required size format. Separate instructions on this come with your application packet, and most passport photos are OK.

If you are currently a law enforcement, corrections, or correctional probation officer, or hold active certification from the **Criminal Justice Standards & Training Commission**, you do not need a background check for the permit, nor do you pay a fee for such. However, you are still stuck with the application or renewal fee.

Furthermore, if you are applying for the permit for the first time and held any such position -- and you retired within the year immediately preceding the date of your application -- all fees are waived, no fingerprinting, and it's a one-time freebie. As stated, this does not apply to renewals, but only to initial applications. Officers retired more than a year pay a $30.00 license fee, plus the $42.00 fingerprint fee. If you are a judge, you still must establish proof of the training requirements - but that's it, no fees.[3]

RECIPROCITY:

A great feature of the permit is that Florida has reciprocal agreements with a number of other states that allow you to carry concealed in their state with your Florida permit. A number of these states also require that you <u>not</u> be a resident of their state to do this, and that you are also an actual resident of Florida if you're using a Florida permit. This varies state-to-state, but is something you must know. There are a few other warnings that must be given: if you carry in a reciprocal state you must carry pursuant to **their laws**, and not those of Florida. Sometimes, these vary greatly from Florida! Another warning repeats what I've already said — a CWL, at least in Florida, covers only **concealed carry**. Anything else, including use or display of the firearm is **NOT** covered. Last, is that in many of these states the concealed license covers only **handguns**, and nothing else! Thus, although your Florida CWL covers knives, tear gas gun, handgun, billie, electric weapons, etc. — carrying anything else but a concealed **handgun** in another state could result in your being arrested.

The answer to these questions is to know the law of concealed carry in each state. I've included some other states in a later chapter to aid in this, and there are some other books out there that can help. However, the *Florida Department of Agriculture* website has links to the laws of each of the reciprocal carry states, and also a summary of important reciprocal state restrictions. If you haven't linked up to the web by now — here's a heck of a good reason to do so. The list of reciprocal states as of the date this chapter was written, October 2014, appear on the next page, and are as follows:

Alabama, Alaska, Arizona, Arkansas, Colorado, Delaware, Georgia, Idaho, Indiana, Iowa, Kansas, Kentucky, Louisiana, Michigan, Missouri, Mississippi, Montana, Nebraska, New Hampshire, New Mexico, North Carolina, North Dakota, Ohio, Oklahoma, Pennsylvania, South Carolina, South Dakota, Tennessee, Texas, Utah, Vermont, Virginia, West Virginia, Wyoming [total of 34 states besides Florida]

Remember that Florida does not recognize an out-of-state license that was issued to a non-resident of the licensing state, or anyone under 21 years of age. F.S. 790.015. Several other states likewise require you to be a "*resident*" of the issuing state for the license to be valid. And, FYI – as of August 31, 2014, the total number of Florida CWL's issued was: 1,316,746.

PROHIBITED PLACES WITH CONCEALED PERMIT:

The issuance of a CWL allows you to carry any type of the listed weapons in a concealed manner. These are handguns, knives, billies, electric weapons that do not shoot a projectile, and tear gas guns. F.S. 790.06(1). Thus, chemical sprays, long guns, nun-chuks, throwing stars, swords, hatchets, brass knuckles, etc. are not technically covered by your license, although they are **still legal** by virtue of F.S. 790.01(3). That's the section of the statutes that makes concealed carry of firearms or other listed weapons a crime. However, the section also *excludes* a CWL holder from its prohibitions. While the CWL does not apply to any automatic firearm (ie: machine gun), it would seem they would likewise be allowed per F.S. 790.01(3) – especially as owning or possessing one is so heavily regulated by the feds. However, that's just my opinion, for now. On the other hand, *open carrying* of weapons and firearms are **not** covered by your CWL, although there was a recent statutory amendment that allows a CWL holder to:

> "*briefly and openly display the firearm to the ordinary sight of another person unless the firearm is intentionally displayed in an angry or threatening manner, not in necessary self defense.*" F.S. 790.053(1).

In other words – you can display a firearm or other weapon openly, even in public, with a CWL – so long as you use common sense, don't flaunt the situation, and are not using it in a manner consistent with an "***improper exhibition***" as prohibited by F.S. 790.10 – which I explain in a later chapter.

There are also some limitations on where you can carrying concealed. Some of these make good sense, some do not. Here's the list of where you can't carry the weapon or firearm under your license:[4]

1.   Any place of nuisance as defined in F.S. 823.05 (house of prostitution, crack house, place of illegal gambling)

2.   Any police station or facility (Sheriff, FHP, local police, etc.)

3.   Any jail, prison, or detention facility.

4.   Any courthouse, unless you're a judge. (*Here come da judge!*)

5.   Any courtroom, unless permitted by the presiding judge.

6.   Any polling place.

7.   Any government meeting involving the governing body of a school board, county commission, city commission, or special district.

8.   Any meeting of the Legislature, or any of its committees.

9.   Any athletic event of a school, or college -- and also for any professional athletic event (Marlins, Dolphins, the Heat, Buccaneers, diving contest, skateboard, etc.) of all types.[5] There is an exception to this prohibition only if the event is one that is related to firearms.

10.   At any elementary or secondary school facility, or administration building. The definition of a "*facility*"[6] normally relates to buildings, and structures -- thus, an entrance road or parking lot should not ordinarily fall within this definition. However, there are no Florida decisions regarding this, and the interpretation, for now, is purely mine.[7] Moreover, I would still advise keeping it "*securely encased*" and out of sight inside your vehicle as F.S. 790.115(2)(a)(3), probably restricts it, anyway. Likewise, because of this statute – keep any firearms or weapons off your person while on any school grounds including colleges (except for *pepper spray* or a *common pocketknife*), including inside your vehicle. Please see the section on schools for a more detailed analysis!

        You should know that F.S. 790.115 has a blanket prohibition on the "**possession**" of any firearm or weapon on the "**property**" of a school,[8] school bus or school bus stop, and further prohibits the "**display**" of a weapon on such areas, as well as within **1000 feet** of a school, **if** the display is done in the presence of others, and in a rude, careless, angry, or threatening manner — and not in lawful self-defense. However, it then exempts CWL holders from the penalties of F.S. 790.115, and refers to their punishment as a *second degree misdemeanor* under the concealed weapons statute, F.S. 790.06(12). That's confusing   – because it leaves four possible interpretations per F.S. 790.06(12)(d): (1) if you are a CWL holder and violate F.S. 790.115, you've committed only a *civil infraction* unless done "*willfully*"; or (2) it's a second degree misdemeanor only if done "*willfully*"; or (3) it's a *second degree misdemeanor* willfully or not; or (4) assuming that F.S. 790.06(12) allows concealed carry on "*grounds*" vs. "*facilities*" with the CWL then it's legal if concealed, and you don't go on or into any structure. Of course, the last interpretation is legally dangerous, and I will never advise it. Just too much of a stretch, although not impossible. Don't chance it!

11.   Any career center – ie – vocational or technical center.

12.   In any portion of a restaurant, bar, nightclub, or other establishment licensed to **serve** alcohol for consumption on the premises (not a liquor store which only sells the packaged stuff vs. serving it) in the **portion** of the premises that is primarily devoted to that purpose.

        In other words, if you go into a restaurant, you can't go in the bar, you can't even walk through the bar -- but you can sit at a dinner table, go to other places within the establishment not within or through the bar area, and even order drinks with your meal, or just order drinks. However, be warned, that in many of the reciprocal states you are totally prohibited from going in any establishment that serves alcohol with a concealed weapon or firearm.

QUESTION: What if I **work in a bar**, or own it?

ANSWER: Well, aside from the fact that I should get at least one free round of drinks out of this – I think that since you could carry even without a CWL pursuant to F.S. 790.25(3)(n), you are legal, and carry would be pursuant to the statute rather than the CWL. The subsection in the CWL law, F.S 790.06(12), doesn't say it "*prohibits*" legal carry pursuant to F.S. 790.25 – it just says the license doesn't "*authorize*" carry in certain places.   So – if it doesn't "*prohibit*" it – and something else "*authorizes*" it – common sense says you should be fine. Thus, if you're legal under F.S. 790.25 – you should be legal even if you have a CWL, because you're not carrying "*pursuant*" to it. Again, this is just my opinion since there's no case law on it, but it's just common sense, and is also in accord with constitutional interpretation. On the other hand, if you're a school teacher don't think you can bring it into the school. That would be an entirely different matter, governed by different statutory sections, and highly illegal. Possession at schools is only allowed to specified persons at specified times.

13. Any college or university facility, however, there is an exception where the CWL holder is also a registered student, faculty member, or employee of the facility, and the weapon is a stun gun or other non-lethal electric weapon that does not fire a dart or projectile, and is designed solely for defensive purposes. Chemical weapons are not permitted, although there is a huge legal loophole for a "*self defense chemical spray*" which I explain in a later chapter. Anyway, the listed persons may carry such electric weapon into buildings and structures on the college and university campus so long as it is **concealed**. If you're wondering about *parking* on college or university grounds. That is now lawful due to recent interpretations by the Florida appellate courts. Again, the firearm or weapon must be "*securely encased*", and not on your person to be legally safe. More on this in a later chapter.

14. Inside the passenger portion of any airline terminal, and the "*sterile area*" of any airport (ie: the X-ray machine checkpoint and possibly its waiting line, and beyond). These are the areas normally reserved for passengers making flight departures, or arrivals.

    However, there is an exception for anyone who is a passenger, is in the terminal (but not the sterile area), and is carrying a firearm for shipment as baggage on an airline so long as that firearm is already unloaded, and encased in a hard-sided, locked container. More on that in the next chapter, especially in light of federal regulations.

15. Any other place a firearm is prohibited by **federal law**, including any federal office or building.[9] This means, amongst other places -- a post office, IRS, social security. It does not mean a *bank*. If you go to a bank, and take out lots of money -- you may need a firearm. If you go to an ATM (automatic teller), and it's after hours, statistics show you'd better have one! Likewise, if you go into a store that sells stamps or has a small post office inside it is defined as a "*contract post office*" pursuant to 39

CFR 241.2. Such a site should not be considered a federal office or building as the regulation defines it as being wholly private.[10] Thus, there should be nothing illegal if you have a valid CWL.

You should know that any violation of any of these subsections is a second degree misdemeanor (maximum 60 days jail, 6 months probation, $500.00 fine) only if done "*knowingly* and *willfully*". Otherwise, it appears a violation is not a crime, and should constitute a defense to a criminal charge.[11]

PROHIBITED AREAS - STUN GUNS & CHEMICAL SPRAYS:

In 2006, *Florida Statutes* 790.01 (concealed carry), and 790.053 (open carry) were amended to allow citizens to carry, open or concealed: "*self-defense chemical sprays, non-lethal stun guns, dart-firing stun guns* (*Taser*), *and other non-lethal electric weapons* and devices designed solely for *defensive purposes*. No prohibited areas or places were listed in these statutes. These statutory changes were obviously meant to **expand** carry privileges of specific non-deadly defensive weapons to the general populace. (Schools, federal buildings, and similar places are usually still **prohibited** by different laws.) However, by adding these specific weapons as a *class of weapons* that can be carried concealed by the general populace without a CWL – the meaning of subsection (3) was unintentionally affected, and placed into a "*grey area*" of the law.

Why?

Because, a "literal reading" of subsection (3) now gives the impression that everybody **but** a CWL holder can carry these particular weapons concealed. Of course, that was not the intention of the amendment, and should not be interpreted that way. In order to understand the confusion, let's take a quick look at F.S. 790.01, subsection by subsection:

1.   "*Except as provided in subsection (4), a person who carries a concealed weapon . . . commits a misdemeanor.*"

2.   "*A person who carries a concealed firearm . . . commits a felony.*"

3.   "*This section does not apply to a person licensed to carry a concealed weapon or a concealed firearm pursuant to the provisions of s. 790.06*"

4.   "*It is not a violation of this section for a person to carry for purposes of lawful self-defense in a concealed manner a . . . self defense chemical spray . . . non-lethal stun gun or dart firing stun gun, or other nonlethal*

electric weapon or device . . . ."

Now, until subsection (4) was added to the law in 2006 – the meaning of subsection (3) was crystal clear! Subsection (3) meant that a CWL holder was **excluded** from the prohibitions of concealed carry set out in the rest of the statute. But, once subsection (4) was added, if you didn't know the **history** of F.S. 790.01, a literal reading would make it look like everybody **but** a CWL holder could carry a defensive stun gun or chemical spray concealed! Of course, that makes no sense, whatsoever, would probably render the statute at least partially unconstitutional, and was something never intended by the addition of subsection (4). Why prohibit CWL holders who have gone thru a criminal records check, and also have the **most training** from carrying these weapons concealed – but let everyone else do it? It makes no sense!

So, if you're asking my opinion on whether this subsection prevents a CWL holder from carrying a *self-defense chemical spray, non-lethal stun gun, dart-firing stun gun (Taser),* or other *non-lethal electric weapon* in a concealed manner any different than anyone else in Florida – my answer is "no". Subsection (3) remained unchanged in the 2006 amendment, and its original meaning should likewise remain unchanged. However, once again – since there's no case law – just my opinion.

Now, you ask me: "Why is any of this important? What does it have to do with me? Don't I have the right to carry a *Taser*, or *self defense chemical spray* concealed per my CWL?

Well, the answer is "no", because per F.S. 790.06(1), the CWL section covers just : *"handguns, electronic weapon or devices, tear gas guns, knife or billies."* Everything else you can carry concealed comes by virtue of F.S. 790.01, by *excluding* you from the prohibitions of that section because you have a CWL!

Moreover, because you have a CWL, it might appear that you are not *"authorized"* to carry any of these exempted *"defensive weapons"* concealed into a bar, organized sporting event, etc., due to the exclusions (actually *"non-authorizations"*) in F.S. 790.06(12). However, due to subsection (4), almost **everybody** else in Florida does! On the other hand, if subsection (3) keeps its original meaning – then you would obviously **escape** any of the restrictions of 790.06(12), because you would be concealed carrying these *"defensive weapons"* not per 790.06 – but per 790.01! So – the interpretation of subsection (3) suddenly gets really important – because even if I can't take a *"firearm"* into some of these places, I still would like some form of protection! At least pepper spray or a self defense stun gun!

Of course, **open carry** of these weapons per <u>F.S.</u> 790.053 is still allowed to CWL holders, regardless of any possible restrictions in <u>F.S.</u> 790.06(12) – because "**open carry**" has nothing to do with the CWL statute! On the other hand – if you open carry this stuff, there are lots of places you'll probably be asked to leave, or prevented entry. That's why concealed carry is so important.

LICENSE VIOLATIONS:
There are certain problems that can arise when you have the CWL. In comparison to what could happen to someone without the license -- these consequences are really mild. One thing you need to know is that if you are carrying a concealed weapon or firearm, you must also have your actual permit on your person.[12] A failure to do so is a noncriminal violation with a $25.00 fine. Same thing goes if a police officer asks to see your permit and other identification while you're carrying -- and you don't have it, or refuse to show it (that would be really stupid). Of course, you may get arrested for a felony if the officer is too lazy to check the CWL database. But, you'll eventually be able to beat that charge, since you do have the CWL somewhere, or get proof through the Dept. of Agriculture. And, you might even have an interesting false arrest case if there was no other legal basis for your arrest. Of course, this will occur long after you are hassled-to-death by the system, as you try to straighten things out.

Another problem is if you violate any of the use restrictions I just outlined in the preceding numbered paragraphs, 1 -12. If you do, and that violation was done "**knowingly**" and "**willfully**" (ie: deliberate violation of the law)[13] -- it's a second degree misdemeanor. Moreover, if you carry into the *sterile area* of an airport -- it's also a federal felony, unless you can establish the defense that you are a total idiot, and really forgot that you had the .357 Magnum in your pocketbook. You'd be surprised how many people do this every year! You should also know that this type of incident is seriously scrutinized since 9/11.

LOST LICENSES, OR CHANGE OF ADDRESS:
You are also required to notify the Department of Agriculture of any change in your permanent address, or if your permit was lost, stolen, or destroyed -- all within a period of **30 days**. A failure is a noncriminal violation, and another big twenty five dollar fine. If you move, the process is real simple. You can do it online or by mail. If you want a replacement license the cost is fifteen bucks. No charge unless you want a replacement license. The procedure is the same if your license was lost or stolen. The address for all of this is, including

the web is:

> Florida Division of Licensing, Concealed Weapons Permit Program
> P.O. Box 6387
> Tallahassee, Florida 32314-6387
> www.freshfromflorida.com/Divisions-Offices/Licensing

QUESTION: I heard if my CWL is lost or stolen, but I still have a copy -- the CWL is invalid until a replacement is issued. Is that true?

ANSWER: Silly, huh? Yeah, that's the way the statute reads. F.S. 790.06(9). From a constitutional standpoint there may be a way around it, but who would want to be in that position? Remember, test cases are only good for lawyers.

SUSPENSION OR REVOCATION OF YOUR PERMIT:
The State is not happy if you suddenly do something you shouldn't have, and still have your CWL. Most of the time this makes good sense. However, if you use your gun for self-defense, get arrested because somebody on the government side is too chicken to stand-up against possible adverse publicity, and temporarily/permanently lose your CWL -- it (pardon the expression) stinks. However, this is not where I am going to lecture you on my personal philosophy of life, so let's get back to the law.

Most of the things that would disqualify you from getting the CWL will also cause you to have it suspended or revoked. F.S. 790.06(3) & (10). If you plea to, or are found guilty of a felony while you hold the CWL, obviously, it's history. Same thing if you get a *"conviction"* or *"withheld"* for any drug crime, even if it's a misdemeanor; or a *"conviction"*, or *"withheld"* on a misdemeanor crime of domestic violence. As to other exciting reasons why your CWL will be revoked, here's the list on revocations:

1. committed as an alcoholic, or deemed a disorderly intoxication habitual offender.

2. convicted of a second DUI within 3 years of any prior one.

3. adjudicated an incapacitated person.

4. committed to a mental institution.

5.   develops or sustains a physical infirmity which prevents the safe handling of a weapon or firearm.

6.   chronically and habitually uses alcoholic beverages to extent that normal faculties are impaired.[14]

7.   May revoke if licensee is found "*guilty*" (ie: an "*adjudication*" or "*withheld adjudication*") of one or more *crimes of violence* within the preceding three years.[15]

8.   Shall suspend the license upon notification by FDLE, a court, or law enforcement agency of the **arrest** or formal charge for a drug crime, a felony, or second DUI within three years – until final disposition of the charge resolves whether a CWL is legally permitted.

9.   Any *conviction* or *withheld* on a felony or misdemeanor crime of domestic violence unless **three years** have passed since all conditions of sentence have been completed.

10.   Is prohibited by Florida or Federal law from possession or purchase of a firearm.

Likewise, your CWL is going to be suspended for a number of other reasons by virtue of F.S. 790.065 – since the law also says that you can't have a CWL whenever your **right to purchase** a firearm from a dealer is prohibited. Thus, the area of suspensions includes all those arrests listed for revocation, plus arrests for criminal anarchy, extortion, explosives violations, controlled substance violations, resisting with violence, any weapon or firearm violation in C. 790, treason, assisting suicide, sabotage, or stalking.

If this list isn't real clear to you, I've included a chart later in the chapter to make it easier. Remember, that if you plead "*guilty*" rather than "*no contest*", or were found "*guilty*" after a trial, you will still be considered as "*convicted*" under current federal interpretation of **federal law**, no matter what Florida law actually is!   This is true regardless of whether you were "*adjudicated*" or received a "*withheld adjudication*".[16]   Florida says the feds are wrong – but the feds don't care. So, be careful. Who would want to be prosecuted by the feds for something you're actually innocent of?

REVOCATION DUE TO PROBATION:

Something people don't often think about is what if you get arrested for a minor crime – a misdemeanor, and are placed on probation? Persons on probation in Florida are not permitted to possess firearms. So, obviously, if the Division of Licensing is on the ball – your CWL is gonna be revoked. Once the probation is over, assuming you don't have a three year waiting period on firearm purchase from a dealer, you should have no problem applying for a new one – however, you will likely have to supply *certified copies* from your court case showing that your sentence has ended, and the nature of the crime of conviction. This is usually done by a certified copy of the Judgment and Sentence, but may also require certified copies of any document showing other charges were dropped (usually called a *"Nolle Prosequi"* or *"No Information"* or *"No Prosecute"*), and perhaps the actual nature of the charge set forth in the charging document – often called an *"Information"*. Non-certified copies are not usable – so don't get cheap, and try to save the price difference. Since getting these documents requires a trip to the courthouse – and a certification of each document you need (or the Clerk can certify all of them as a group) – you might as well get all the ones I listed at once, rather than taking the chance of needing to go back again for one you missed.

HOW YOU CAN CARRY CONCEALED:

Carrying a concealed weapon or firearm under F.S. 790.01 means "*on or about your person*". "*On or about*" your person generally means within your reach or immediate control. Thus, with the CWL you may legally carry your firearm or weapon in a briefcase, bag, etc. -- as well as on your immediate person, so long as it's concealed. Logically, this means you could have it within reach, under a towel in your car - although that's likely not a great idea. And no, it doesn't have to be in a holster!

DEALING WITH POLICE OFFICERS:

Now, just because this is legal, don't think you can't get arrested. The problem is that many police officers have not been trained very well in this area, and have their own idea of what the law is. I personally used to handle at least three or four cases a year where the police arrested someone for something that was totally legal. Unfortunately -- they just didn't know the law. More unfortunately, some innocent slob got arrested for being legal. That's life in the big city. It happens.[17]

The only thing I can tell you is that once you finish reading this book, keep it in your vehicle. Then if a police officer pulls you over, and suddenly announces you're being arrested for something the law says you can do -- you can

politely tell him or her that you're sure he or she knows the law, and you don't want to sound like a "wise guy" -- but you've got this book on firearms in the car that's being used by seven police academies, and over eighty law enforcement agencies -- and it says that it's O.K. Would he/she please *"just take a look?"*

With a little bit of the Irish luck, he'll realize he may be making a slight error, and with even more luck, he'll say something to the effect of:

"I don't care what the book says, I know the law. But, I'm gonna give you a break. Don't do it again."

At this point, **thank him!** Then, shut your mouth, and be thankful you didn't have to go to jail to prove your point. Got the point? Of course, if you are arrested, see a good civil lawyer once the case is dropped, as you've got a great false arrest claim. By the way — don't threaten the officer that you'll sue him if he arrests you — that will only get him angry, and is a sure way to complicate whatever situation you're already in. Even in a tough situation try to be respectful. Most of them really deserve your respect, anyway. In this day and age, it's not the easiest job around.

WHY THE CWL IS THE BEST:
        If you haven't already guessed, I'm the greatest believer in the CWL there is. Well . . . at least, I'm one of them. I think that it takes the edge off situations where you might otherwise get arrested, and normally puts you in a position where a police officer will give you the benefit of a doubt. It also fills in the gaps where you need to carry concealed, or unintentionally do carry concealed. In other words -- it's there.

More importantly, you join the ranks of 1,316,746 (as of 8/31/14) active permit holders. Dems a lot of votes, partner! The more CWL holders there are, the less likely it will be that politicians are going to try to take any of your rights away. And, if you don't think there are forces out there that would love to see you disarmed, and easy prey for everything and everybody -- you better start getting educated, because the battle is raging around you every single day.

A chart that explains when you would get a license suspension or revocation appears on the next page:

CHART ON LICENSE SUSPENSION/REVOCATION:

Suspension or Revocation* of Permit -- 790.06(10) & 790.06(3)
Physical infirmity that renders handling of weapon/firearm unsafe.
Felony conviction.
Found guilty of any drug crime.
Committed as substance abuser.
Three convictions within 12 months for disorderly intoxication.
Two DUI convictions within 3 years.
Adjudicated as an incapacitated person.
Committed to mental institution.
Chronic user of alcohol or other substances.
Convicted of using firearm while under influence. — F.S. 790.151
Withheld adjudication on any felony, or any misdemeanor crime of domestic violence (until 3 years elapsed since completion of sentence & all conditions).
Current injunction against repeat or domestic violence.*
Otherwise prohibited from possession/purchase of firearm by Florida or Federal law — F.S. 790.06(2)(m) – which would be: • felony indictment or information -- pending.* • withheld adjudication on felony, or misdemeanor crime of domestic violence if plead "guilty", or if found "guilty" after trial. • arrest for any "dangerous crime" per F.S. 907.041 — pending.* • arrest for any violation of C.790 — pending.* • arrest for resisting officer with violence, drug crime, extortion, explosives, assisting suicide, treason, sabotage, criminal anarchy — pending.*
Found guilty (or suspended sentence) for any misdemeanor or felony which involves violence (until 3 years elapsed since completion of sentence & all conditions). F.S. 790.06(3)
Upon notification and verification of an arrest, indictment, information, or formal charge for any crime that would disqualify person for license. [same as F.S. 790.06(2)(m)]*

CONCEALED WEAPONS BADGES:

I keep getting asked by people whether they should buy a concealed weapons badge. My answer is a definite "no". It has no statutory basis, no real useful purpose, is not a substitute for the CWL, and is a possible way to get arrested assuming you are taken as pretending to be a law enforcement officer by the way you've used and displayed it. F.S. 843.08 On the other hand, if its just something you want to put on your mantle to impress folks (assuming they're stupid enough to be impressed by something anyone can buy for a few bucks) – it's legal because F.S. 843.085 which made it unlawful to display law enforcement badges by persons who were not law enforcement personnel was declared unconstitutional because the statute did not require an intent to deceive by the possessor.[18]

OPEN/BRIEF DISPLAY & "PRINTING":

F.S. 790.053 was amended in 2011 to allow a CWL holder to *"briefly and openly display the firearm to the ordinary sight of another person unless the firearm is displayed in an angry or threatening manner, not in necessary self defense"*. This section allows a brief, intentional display for a lawful purpose to another, even in public, as well as unintentional display (ie: bending over exposes a belt holster), and printing. Until the courts interpret it, I would caution on how and where you decide to intentionally show your firearm to others – at least, in public places. However, I note the Legislature intentionally eliminated the *"rude"* and *"careless"* language of F.S. 790.10 (ie: *"improper exhibition"*) to expand the application of this new subsection.

ENDNOTE SECTION TO CHAPTER FIVE:

1. (n/a)

2. U.S. v. Chubbuck, 252 F.3d 1300 (11th Cir. 2001).

3. F.S. 790.061

4. F.S. 790.06(12)

5. There is an unanswered question whether the parking lot of a professional (not school or college) arena is "at' a sporting event - especially when you think of tailgating parties. My personal opinion is that it is not – but that is purely an opinion. Otherwise, just watching the game on TV – could be "at" a sporting event – and that's clearly not the case!

6. 18 USC 930(g)(1) defines "federal facility" as a building or part thereof owned or leased by the federal

government, where federal employees are regularly present for the purposes of performing their official duties. F.S. 790.115(1) differentiates between school "grounds" and "facilities" — thus, they obviously relate to different definitions. F.S. 159.27(22) defines "educational facility" in terms similar to the federal statute recited.

7. If the legislature wanted to cover everything, they probably would have included the "grounds" of the school, just as they did in F.S. 790.115(1)(ie: "on the grounds or facilities of any school"), or they would have defined it as "school plant" per F.S. 228.041(7), or "campus" per F.S. 228.091. Research of numerous Florida statutes shows similar definitions. Compare, 18 USC 930(g)(1), as in the prior endnote.

8. Except for "securely encased" per F.S. 790.115(2)(a)(3).

9. 18 USC 930. "The term "Federal facility" means a building or part thereof owned or leased by the Federal government, where federal employees are regularly present . . . ." Postal regulations also forbid dangerous weapons and firearms in a post office. 39 CFR 232.1

10. 18 USC 2115 allows a prosecution for a burglary or robbery committed on such property, but it does not cover CCF or CCW.

11. F.S. 790.115 concerns school related possession of weapons.

12. F.S. 790.06(1)

13. "Willful" under Florida law means: intentionally, knowingly, and purposefully. State v. May, 670 So.2d 374 (Fla. 2DCA 1996). Under federal law it means that the person actually knew his conduct was illegal. Ratzlaf v. U.S., 510 US 135 (1994); U.S. v. Sanchez-Corcino, 85 F.3d 549 (11th Cir. 1996).

"A thing is willfully done when it proceeds from a
conscious motion of the will, intending the result which
actually comes to pass. It must be designed or intentional,
and may be malicious, though not necessarily so.
"Willful" is sometimes used in the sense of intentional, as
distinguished from "accidental," and, when used in a
statute affixing a punishment to acts done willfully, it
may be restricted to such acts as are done with an
unlawful intent." Jersey v. Paper, 658 So. 2d 331
(Fla. 1995)

14. This is a chronic alcoholic whose mental process is
permanently affected — not somebody who got
intoxicated a few times — unless they've been
convicted of two DUI's within 3 years.

15. This particular subsection allows revocation of the
license in the discretion of the Dept. of Agriculture — it
is not mandatory. F.S. 790.06(3).

16. In McFadden v. State, 732 So.2d 412 (Fla. 3DCA
1999), aff'd 772 So.2d 1209 (Fla. 2000), the court
held that a "withheld adjudication" is not a conviction
even on a guilty plea.   The problem is that the
federal appeals court (11th Circuit) refuses to
recognize this even though they are legally bound to
do so.   This may be shocking to many people, but
the 11th Circuit is not known for being a court that is
overly concerned with citizen rights.   They normally
rule as restrictively as possible against the citizen, and
bend over backwards for the government. That's my
opinion.

17. Miami v. Swift, 481 So.2d 26 (Fla. 3DCA 1985),
affirmed a jury award of $50,000 for the false arrest of a
person with a gun in the console.

18. Sult v. State, 30 Fla. L. Weekly S. 470 (Fla. 2005).

CHAPTER SIX

**TRANSPORTATION AND CARRYING OF
WEAPONS AND FIREARMS**

When I do a speaking engagement, the questions I am asked most frequently are those related to the transportation of firearms. In other words: "*Where the heck can I keep it, and how?*" Leading the confusion chart are questions relating to transportation of a gun in your own car while you're in Florida. But what about private boats, private aircraft, public aircraft, in a taxi, while you're camping, going to the range, going to a gun show, or traveling state-to-state in your car, etc.?

If you're a CWL licensee -- you have a much easier problem to contend with since you can keep it anywhere in a vehicle or conveyance as long as it is concealed, however, you still need to understand the concept of "*securely encased*" when you're on school grounds. So, with the number of state and federal laws that govern this area, the legal carrying or transporting of firearms, as well as other weapons, is far from simple -- CWL, or not. That's what I'll try to show you in this chapter. And although the statutory law is not perfectly clear on all points, it has been substantially clarified by the case law. Whatever the circumstances, I'll make it as clear as anybody can. I'll start off with a chart that outlines the concept of "securely encased", and we'll move on from that to a fuller explanation:

CHART OF WHAT CONSTITUTES "SECURELY ENCASED":

in a snapped or strapped holster — anywhere — loaded or unloaded.
in a closed console — loaded or unloaded.
in a closed glove compartment — loaded or unloaded
in a zippered gun case — loaded or unloaded.
in **any** other type of **closed** container which the gun cannot be fired from until withdrawn — loaded or unloaded. Even a cardboard box with a closed lid will suffice.

SUMMARY OF WHERE HANDGUN CAN BE KEPT IN VEHICLE:

Most of the common questions on firearms law concern where a person can legally possess a handgun in a vehicle, with or without a CWL. The answer to that is covered in Florida Statute 790.25, and generally falls under the definition of what is, or is not – "*securely encased*". Firearms that are "*securely encased*" in a vehicle are lawfully possessed so long as you are not a "*prohibited person*", and are at least 18 years of age – as well as some specific exceptions in restricted or prohibited areas. The preceding chart contains the short list, confirmed by appellate case law, on what's definitely "*securely encased*":

So, while the chart was the easy, correct answer, there are still some things that cause confusion, especially with law enforcement officers not trained in this subject. For some reason, a number of law officers are under the mistaken impression that it is illegal to have a firearm under the seat even if otherwise "*securely encased*". The law is clear on this – if it's in a snapped holster, zippered case, or any other type of closed container – it matters not where else it might be. However, because of this sometime confusion – maybe it's not a great idea to keep it under the seat?

Likewise – it seems that a lot of Florida drivers think that having a firearm wedged under the seat, in between the seat and console, or in a door pocket, are legal. However, unless you have a CWL – it's only legal if it's also "*securely encased*". None of these areas qualify. Thus, if caught the charge is the felony of "*carrying a concealed firearm*".

POSSESSION BY CWL LICENSEE IN VEHICLE:
And last – just to make it crystal clear – it is my absolute and firm opinion (again, no case law) that a person with a valid CWL has the option of carrying a firearm either "*securely encased*" – or – **fully concealed "*on or about*"** their immediate person while inside a vehicle. That's not just common sense, but it's because F.S. 790.25(5) is clearly addressed only to non-CWL holders:

> "*it is lawful and not a violation of 790.01 . . . to possess a concealed firearm or other weapon . . . **without a license** . . . .*"

Thus, while I really don't recommend it – if you have a CWL and wanted to put your firearm under a thick towel on the seat next to you within reaching distance – my opinion is that it's covered by your CWL as it is "*concealed*", and is therefore legal. However, make damn sure it's fully concealed – otherwise it's "*open carry*", and a misdemeanor!

THE LEGAL CARRYING OF FIREARMS -- LISTED:
Since Florida generally prohibits open carry of firearms[1], and (without a CWL) concealed carry of almost everything[2], there is a statute, F.S. 790.25,

that gives certain listed exceptions to this — lot's of exceptions which I've listed in the following chart:

Members of the military or National Guard, while on duty.
Carrying out training for emergency management duties pursuant to C. 252
Law enforcement officers of this state; or those of other states, or the federal government while carrying out official duties in Florida.
Florida or federal officials authorized to carry concealed weapons
Guards or messengers of common carriers, express companies, mail carriers, armored car carriers, banks, and other financial institutions while actually employed in and about the transportation or delivery of any money, treasure, bullion, bonds, or other thing of value within this state.
Members of organizations or clubs organized for target, skeet, or trap shooting, while at such practice or event, or going to or from such.
Members of clubs organized for firearms collecting, while such members are at, or going to/fro any gun show, convention, or exhibit.
A person engaged in fishing, camping, or lawful hunting, or going to or from such an expedition.
Any person/employee of a business engaged in the manufacture, repair, or dealing in firearms while engaged in the lawful course of such business.
Legally firing weapons for testing or target practice, under safe conditions, and at a safe place, not prohibited by law, or while going to or from such place,
A person on a <u>public</u> conveyance transporting a securely encased weapon, which is not in his manual possession.[3]
A person who carries a <u>pistol</u> unloaded, and in a secure wrapper, from the place of purchase to his home or business, or to a place of repair, or back therefrom.
A person at his own home or place of business (but this does <u>not</u> pertain to "*common areas*" shared with other individuals in an apartment building or condominium, or a shared parking lot).
A person in a <u>private</u> conveyance (vehicle, aircraft, or boat) where the weapon is "*securely encased*", or *not readily accessible* for immediate use. However, in this circumstance the law says it <u>CANNOT</u> be carried on your person.
An investigator employed full-time by the Public Defender or Capital Collateral Representative, in the course of their official duties, who meet other requirements of statute.

While the statute may seem contradictory in parts, the case interpretations have been extremely consistent, and clearly indicate that these sections allow both **concealed carry** on the person without a CWL (except in *"private conveyances"* – ie – *"vehicles"*), and **open carry.**[4] However, I advise you to use some discretion. Like I've said before, a number of police officers don't know this area of law — others don't care -- and you certainly don't need to be arrested, mistakenly or otherwise. And, a short note of warning – the list isn't as clear as it seems due to the statutory wording, and appellate decisions that have since interpreted it. Thus, some of these areas are totally clear-cut, and yet others need explicit explanation. You may also have noticed that in some of these instances I mentioned weapons **other than** firearms. However, most weapons other than firearms do not fall under the *"preemption law"*, and are **not** regulated by the Florida state statutes unless they are carried concealed. Thus, unless local laws prevent it, with only some exceptions, it is technically legal to carry most weapons, **other than firearms**, in the open -- just about anywhere other than at schools, school bus stops, school buses, *conveyances*, courthouses, and public transportation. However, because they are not covered by the *preemption law* – that would likely allow local authorities to regulate them, unless the regulation is in conflict with other Florida state laws. We covered that somewhat in Chapter One, but I'll also cover that later in a separate chapter.

LEGAL CARRYING IN AUTOMOBILES & PRIVATE VEHICLES:

The most often asked question in the State of Florida related to firearms -- is how can they legally be transported in a private vehicle. By **"vehicle"** I mean a car, truck, motorcycle, or any other type of private conveyance you can think of that normally drives on the road. By the word **"private"**, I mean any vehicle that is not driven by somebody for hire, but is privately owned and driven. By **"conveyance"** I mean a trailer, motor vehicle, ship, railway car, or aircraft.[5] A **bicycle** is <u>not</u> a conveyance.[6]

A vehicle that is driven in a car-pool is private, even if you all chip in on the gas. A non-private vehicle would include a taxi-cab, or rented limo. Any other interpretation of what is or is not private can probably be figured out by common sense. And by the way, these definitions were my interpretations, not the Legislature's -- because the Legislature didn't bother to give us any definition -- and the courts haven't gotten around to interpreting these definitions, either.

So, now that you know what is probably private, and what is not -- you still need to know the definition of the next two phrases: **"securely encased"**, and "***not readily accessible for immediate use***". Each of these phrases apply to very different legal ways of transporting a firearm in your private vehicle. Here's how it works.

<u>SECURELY ENCASED:</u>

"***Securely encased***"[7] means that the weapon or firearm is in some type of holster, bag, enclosure, box, or container that is secured with a clasp, lid, zipper, strap, snap, flap, or other device, so that in order to fire or use the weapon, the device must first be opened, removed, or undone.[8] It does not require a lock. The purpose behind this was to give a person a very brief opportunity to think about it, before actually using it. This includes a closed glove compartment or console; zippered, snapped, or Velcro-closed bag, holster, or case which first must be unclasped in order to fire; any type of box or enclosure with a closed lid; or even a purse -- assuming you can't operate the firing mechanism through the fabric, and there is some physical act required to open the top of the purse and unhook/unclasp/move an obstruction/unzip it. A briefcase or suitcase also falls into this category. A cardboard box with the lid closed also complies. A man's plastic purse with a flap over the opening is also included because the flap must be moved in order to withdraw the weapon. <u>Urquiola v. State</u>, 590 So.2d 497 (Fla. 3DCA 1991). Likewise, in <u>Alexander v. State</u>, 477 So.2d 557 (Fla. 1985), the Florida Supreme Court held that a man's zippered leather pouch containing a firearm was "*securely encased*" even though there were other items in the pouch, and even though the man had opened and zippered the pouch several times in the presence of a police officer.

So, you can see the courts are fairly liberal on what is "*securely encased*". As long as the statutory purpose is met, a firearm can be kept in just about anything in a vehicle if it has a lid, closure, or something must be opened to get it out.

QUESTION: Can the handgun be loaded if I do this?

ANSWER: Absolutely. It won't do you any good, otherwise.

QUESTION: I heard it must be in a holster if I have it in the glove compartment, and the glove compartment must be locked?

ANSWER: Nope. All you need is to have the glove compartment closed.

QUESTION: What if it's in my console, loaded, and ready to go?

ANSWER: Totally legal as long as the lid is closed. If the lid is open wide enough to remove the firearm you are in big trouble.

QUESTION: What if the lid is partially opened?

ANSWER: The courts focus on whether the weapon can be obtained without removing/opening the lid wider to gain access. If you still have to move the flap – the statutory purpose has been met, and it should be *"securely encased"*.   How wide the opening is will be the deciding factor, and is a factual question.

QUESTION: OK, I hear what you're saying, but I really don't understand. How can a firearm be "*securely encased*" if all I have to do is flip open a lid?

ANSWER: Well, it seems clear that the statutory definition of "*securely encased*" does **not** mean that the weapon is "**encased securely**". It just means that the method of carry meets the statutory definition. If it does, it's "*legally*" secure, even if it's not factually secure.

QUESTION: I've heard that keeping a firearm in a car is a *two step rule*, or *three step rule*. What does that mean?

ANSWER: It means that the person who gave you that advice couldn't remember what the statute actually said, so they made up their own definition to substitute for it. Forget it. Just remember the statute.

QUESTION: If a police officer stops me, and the gun is legally in my handbag along with my drivers license -- what do I do when he asks me for my license?

ANSWER: If you're stopped - advise him, and ask what he wants you to do, keeping your hands away from it. Do not take it outside the car without asking. Do not open the bag unless he so directs.   Unless you have a CWL, you are only legally "*securely encased*" **inside** the vehicle. If you carry the purse and firearm outside without his direction -- it could be a felony -- "*carrying a concealed firearm*". If it's another weapon other than two ounce chemical spray, a stun gun, Taser, or common pocketknife, it's a misdemeanor -- "***Carrying a Concealed Weapon***", commonly known as *CCW*.

If you tell him you have a firearm in the purse, and he tells you to hand it to him outside the car – fine. Obviously, <u>don't</u> hand him the firearm, itself! That would be stupid! He'll be nervous, and he also has a gun. Instead, give him the entire purse, and leave it closed, unless he instructs you otherwise. Or, better yet – stand away from the car, and have him take the purse out on his own. You don't want to get shot over a stupid misunderstanding.

QUESTION: If I tell the officer I have a firearm, what can he do?

ANSWER: Usually, he'll ask for its location, ask you to move to an area away from it, take temporary custody of the firearm, empty the cartridges, and when he's done giving you a ticket (unless he's arresting you for something), he should give you back the firearm and cartridges separately, and instruct you not to load it until either you or he leaves. Such a procedure is totally legal, very intelligent, and completely proper.

QUESTION: Can the officer keep the firearm for safety reasons, and refuse to return it to me?

ANSWER: Not legally unless he takes you into custody, or the firearm was reported stolen, or is somehow otherwise illegal such as having the serial number obliterated. Other than that, it should be returned to you at the end of the stop.

QUESTION: I'm a CWL holder. I've been told I cannot carry a firearm concealed on my person while in my vehicle.

ANSWER: Since you have the CWL my opinion is you may carry concealed "*on or about*" your person per the CWL, or "*securely encased*", or "*not readily accessible*" under 790.25. Your choice. However, I warn you that a few untrained police officers don't seem to understand this, and also, there is no case law.

QUESTION: I live in an apartment complex. Can I take it from my car to my apartment?

ANSWER: Not usually. Although you have the right to have it either in your car, or inside your apartment -- you cannot carry it across **"common areas"** -- such as a parking lot, elevators, or hallways -- unless you have the CWL, or fit into one of the exceptions in 790.25. This was a major goof by the legislature.

QUESTION: What about a condominium.   The condo documents say I "own" all the areas in common with the rest of the owners.

ANSWER: I cannot advise it as the case law on "*common areas*" has been almost universal that such are not considered your "*home*" per 790.25(n). On the other hand, none of these cases involved a **condominium**, and all of them involved apartment units. So, a "*test case*" might find differently since you are an "*owner*". I could argue the case from either side with no problem, and haven't the slightest idea which side the courts would rule on.

QUESTION: What if I'm in the car, and I put it in a paper bag, but I twist the top of the bag really well?

ANSWER: Technically, I think you have a problem since the bag is easy to rip, and you may be able to pull the trigger through it. It certainly isn't a zipper, snap, or anything similar. It's also pushing the "flap" example in the *Urquiola* case. Although it's an argument – I wouldn't want to try it. Same thing for a cloth **"Crown Royal"** bag, which I used to see somewhat often when I was practicing. From a legal standpoint the issue will be whether it can be fired without opening the bag, and what steps need to be taken to get the bag open. *Test case* time, again.

QUESTION: What if I have it in an unsnapped or unstrapped holster?

ANSWER: If the gun is in a concealed area of the car, it's the third degree felony of *carrying a concealed firearm.* (ie: *"CCF"*) If the gun is in the open -- it's a second degree misdemeanor of *"open carrying of weapons."* If the unsnapped holster is in the glove compartment, closed purse or briefcase, or closed console -- you're OK.

QUESTION: Why?

ANSWER: Because you're still legal under another part of the same section of the statute which says it is *"securely encased"*. (ie: in a glove compartment, or other closed container).

QUESTION: What if it becomes unsnapped, or unstraps without my knowledge?

ANSWER: Assuming it unsnaps without your knowledge - you have a defense of *"lack of scienter"*, or *"lack of guilty knowledge"*. The terms are synonymous. Unfortunately, if the officer doesn't believe you it becomes an issue of proof.

QUESTION: What if I have it on my person in a snapped shoulder holster, but the holster can be detached intact from the shoulder harness?

ANSWER: Remember what I said before? Without a CWL, it can't be on your person **unless** you have a CWL! Only a CWL holder may have a firearm or other weapon concealed on their person within a vehicle.

QUESTION: Is there any special place the firearm or weapon must be kept, if I have it in a securely encased bag or holster?

ANSWER: Nope. Anywhere you want except on your person. It can even be under the seat -- as long as it's *securely encased* in a container or box with a closed lid; or a zippered, snapped, or Velcro-closed pouch, holster, or gun case. Likewise, a *steering wheel holster* is legal and *securely encased* as long as there is a strapping device that must be undone before the firearm can be withdrawn.

QUESTION: What about weapons other than a handgun?

ANSWER: F.S. 790.25 applies to any legal weapon, including rifles and
            shotguns. Thus, any weapon that is *"securely encased"*, or
            "not readily accessible for immediate use" is legal in a private
            conveyance. However, there is also case law and statutory
            authority that *rifles and shotguns* may be **openly carried** in a
            vehicle if being transported for lawful purposes. Still, my
            recommendation is that they be transported in a closed case or
            gun rug *"securely encased"*, simply to avoid a situation where
            you know more about the law than the police officer.

QUESTION: What about a motorcycle?

ANSWER: What about a motorcycle? It has the same rules as a car. It
            must be *securely encased*, and cannot be on your person unless
            you have a CWL. Otherwise, it must be in a closed container
            such as a saddlebag actually **attached** to the bike –not you.
            Of course, no case law on this.

NOT READILY ACCESSIBLE FOR IMMEDIATE USE:

There's another legal way to transport a firearm in a *private
conveyance* (ie: *"vehicle"*) called **"not readily accessible for immediate
use"**.[9]   Under the law, you can transport a firearm in a vehicle *"securely
encased"*, *"not readily accessible for immediate use"*, or both.   Any
combination is legal.   Likewise, if you have a CWL, you can have the
additional method of carrying concealed on or about your person. Your
choice. Nobody should really care because legally it doesn't matter – if
you're legal, you're legal.

However, while *"not readily accessible for immediate use"* may
sound like *"securely encased"*, and to some extent there may be an overlap,
it's a separate concept entirely. *"Not readily accessible for immediate use"*
means that the firearm or weapon cannot be used without some type of
difficulty that <u>significantly</u> hinders it's immediate use. Court cases establish
that this should include a loaded firearm with a **trigger lock**; or an empty
firearm without any ammunition in *"close proximity"*, although recent case
law has held that if the ammo is *"securely encased"* separate from the
firearm, the firearm is not *"readily accessible"*. *Strikertaylor v. State*, 997
So.2d 488 (Fla. 2DCA 2008); *State v. Weyant*, 990 So.2d 675 (Fla. 2DCA

2008), Likewise, if the ammo was in the trunk it would be fine. Same thing if the ammo were in a locked box. If you have a weapon in the trunk, and can access the trunk by folding down the rear seat – it should meet the definition of both *securely encased* and *not readily accessible for immediate use*. Seems like a no-brainer to me.

Another example of *"not readily accessible for immediate use"* occurs with a weapon that just can't be used inside the vehicle, as a practical matter. Thus, in the case of <u>*Boswink v. State*</u>, 636 So.2d 584 (Fla. 2DCA 1994), the appellate court held that a loaded shotgun and rifle in the back of a small pick-up truck was not *"readily accessible"* because the cab was too small to use the weapons from the inside without difficulty, and the occupant would normally have to exit the truck in order to retrieve, and use them effectively. Thus, they were not subject to retrieval *"as easily and quickly as if carried on the person."* Again, I wouldn't suggest relying on this case, too much. It left out too much, and guns and trucks come in different sizes.

UNCONCEALED SHOTGUNS AND RIFLES:

An interesting point not raised by the <u>*Boswink*</u> case is whether it's illegal to have an unconcealed, but loaded shotgun, or rifle in a private conveyance, at all. This question arises because <u>F.S.</u> 790.25(5), states that:

> "Nothing herein contained prohibits the carrying of a legal firearm other than a **handgun** anywhere in a private conveyance when such firearm is being carried for a lawful use."

Thus, if *"legal firearm"* means any legally possessed long gun not being carried for the commission of a crime -- it"s legal. This seems clear because the statutory language would otherwise be meaningless. Moreover, in <u>*Mitchell v. State*</u>, 494 So.2d 498 (Fla. 2DCA 1986), the appellate court found that a rifle on the back seat of a vehicle did not furnish probable cause for an arrest. Likewise, a <u>*Dept. of Hwy Safety Legal Bulletin*</u> 88-02, reviewed the 1982 enactment of this section and confirms my definition.

On the other hand, I've never seen this issue come up, or be raised in court before, so it could wind-up as a *"test case"* in some of our more populated areas. Get rural -- it should be an entirely different story. Under any circumstance, you could legally have a loaded rifle or shotgun in a **locked gun rack**, as it would **not** be *"readily accessible for immediate use"*! Still, I personally would not have an exposed shotgun or rifle on the back seat in an urban setting. I just think too many police officers would make the wrong legal decision in this situation. I'm not saying it's illegal – because I believe the law is absolutely clear on this -- I'm just saying it's probably smarter keeping your rifle or shotgun in a case unless you're in an area where hunting or ranching are common.

THE WAY IT USED TO BE:

I thought I'd get off the track here for a moment, and give you a little historical insight from our not too distant past. I get a perverse kick out of how some liberal legislators, and other *"anti-gunners"* think that permitting a firearm in a car is a recent, and overly generous gift to the citizens of Florida. If you look back into Florida's history, not all that far -- you'll find it wasn't originally thought of as a gift -- but was thought to be pretty much a **basic right** -- part of the right of an individual to self preservation. So, just in case you'd like to see how it used to be viewed by the majority, let me give you a quote from the 1941 Florida Supreme Court case of *Watson v. Stone*, 4 So.2d 700, 702-703 (Fla. 1941):

> *"The business men, tourists, commercial travelers, professional man on night calls, unprotected women and children in cars on the highways day and night, State and County officials, and all law-abiding citizens fully appreciate the sense of security afforded by the knowledge of the existence of a pistol in the pocket of an automobile in which they are traveling. It cannot be said that it is placed in the car or automobile for unlawful purposes, but on the other hand it was placed therein exclusively for defensive or protective purposes. These people, in the opinion of this writer, should not be branded criminals in their effort of self preservation and protection, but should be recognized and accorded the full rights of free and independent American citizens."*

INTER-STATE TRANSPORTATION OF FIREARMS:

If you are traveling from state to state in a vehicle, the transportation of firearms and other weapons is governed by each state's law that you pass through. In Florida -- you know how you can transport it. But what happens when you get to the Georgia border, or beyond?

Federal law says that if you are traveling state to state, you can legally carry a firearm if such is for a lawful purpose, and it would be legal for you to possess and carry it in your final destination state. However, to qualify for this -- the firearm must be unloaded, and neither the firearm or ammunition can be readily or directly accessible from the passenger compartment of the transporting vehicle -- which means it should be locked in the trunk, unloaded. If your vehicle has no separate compartment from the drivers compartment, then the firearm or ammunition must be kept in a *locked container* that is neither the glove compartment or the console. This section usually applies to trucks.   18 USC 926A.

If you follow federal law, you may legally transport your firearms state to state, even if some of the intervening states would not otherwise permit it. Of course, don't take the gun out of this protected area until you arrive at your destination, unless you know that such would be lawful in whatever other state you are traveling in.

Federal law also states that if there's a more liberal way of transporting the firearm in the state you're traveling in – you can do it that way while you're in that particular state – without losing your federal state to state protection during the rest of your trip. So, check out the website of the *Florida Division of Licensing* that has links to the reciprocal states where many of them list a summary of their firearm laws on their respective web sites, or get a summary of each state you're passing thru from the NRA-ILA. There are also books written by some very fine attorneys in some states which you can find on the web. Of course, there's also a brief section in this book on a smaller selection of states close to Florida.

SPECIAL PROBLEM WITH NEW YORK CITY AREA:

While the previous section of this book explained how federal law allows you to transport a firearm one state to another if your possession is legal in both states – that does not mean problems can't arise. If your point of destination or embarkation is the New York City area – you need to read the following:

Under federal law your possession is legal only during the transportation of the firearm from the originating state to the destination state (and back) – and your possession must be legal in both states! New York/New Jersey Transportation police have taken the position that how the heck are they supposed to know whether you're legal in both states? In fact – unless you're getting off a direct flight – how the heck are they supposed to know what state you began transporting the firearm from? So – rather than picking up the phone and making a few calls to find out, or looking up the statutes of each state – they just arrest you – and let the courts sort it out! Lucky you!

Now – I hear you saying: "You gotta be kidding? Are they serious? How can they get away with that?"

Well, the answer is supplied in a recent Second Circuit federal appellate court case entitled *Torraco v. Port Authority of New York and New Jersey* decided on June 30, 2010. *Torraco* is a case involving three different plaintiffs – two of whom were arrested in New York, and the other who was not permitted to board his flight until days later. One was a resident of Florida who had briefly stayed at his second home in New Jersey, and was about to fly back home to Florida from LaGuardia Airport. Another was a New York resident with a New York gun permit who was traveling to Arizona by air from JFK International Airport, and had a valid Florida CWL (concealed weapons permit) which was reciprocal in Arizona. (he was not arrested - but was denied boarding) The third was a defense contractor from Ohio who'd been staying in New Jersey, waiting for deployment to Iraq until a family emergency required him to travel back home by air from Long Island MacArthur Airport.

In each of the cases, the traveler fully complied with *TSA* (*Transportation Security Administration*) regulations by having the firearm packed in a locked box, unloaded, in non- carry-on baggage, separate from any ammo, and declaring it. Furthermore, in the first case, a *TSA* supervisor had even advised the **New York Port of Authority Police** that the traveler was properly transporting the firearm per federal law. Despite all of this – New York Port Authority Police either denied boarding, or made arrests – based on the reasoning that the police were under no obligation to take the traveler's word for the legality of firearm's possession – and that before possession could be considered lawful – the traveler (not the police) had the responsibility to affirmatively prove: (1) their possession of the firearm was legal in the place they had just come from, (2) their possession of the firearm was also legal in the place they were going to. Thus, the police were under no requirement to check databases, or statutes of other states to make any determinations – because that was up to the traveler. Only the traveler from New York was *"legal"* in New York – so he couldn't be arrested. All the same, he was still denied passage – until he was able to prove, days later, that he was legal in Arizona. The other two were not so lucky – and were arrested. In other words – around New York City and New Jersey – they're gonna hassle you just for the hell of it!

Each sued the police and Port Authorities for violations of their civil rights under federal law, and in two instances – false arrest. However, the federal appellate court sided with the police, and held that all 18 USC 926A did was to provide a "defense to a criminal charge". It did not establish an independent right to travel with a firearm unless the traveler was able to satisfy the authorities of his or her right to possess the firearm, nor did it create a federal cause of action where police correctly or incorrectly made arrests, or denied passage due to a belief that the passenger did not have sufficient proof of lawful possession at all points. Likewise, I've heard some horror stories of flights that got diverted to New York where the cops also screwed with the passenger because they discovered his checked baggage (being transferred to another flight) had an unloaded gun it in. Welcome to the Big Apple!

So – the moral of the story – if you want to be safe on this – is the following:

1.   If you are legal in the State of departure – you also need proof of legality in the State of destination. To prove departure/destination – you need a ticket showing it. To prove legality - if you have a CWL recognized in the State where the police are checking it – and the destination state is reciprocal to their State – then police should be on notice that you'd be legal in both, and you should be safe.

2.   If you are in a departure State where your firearm possession is legal – you technically should not be arrested if you've complied with *TSA* regulations. However, you could be denied boarding if you could not prove you're legal in the destination State. This shouldn't happen in most States that allow firearm ownership without a permit – but I'd beware if I were in a city that had a reputation for being anti-gun. Still, it might be wise to have a current copy of the statute of the destination State that shows an out of state resident may possess without a CWL, and shows the statute is current.

3.   Of course, if you somehow have a permit or CWL from the State of departure, and also the State of destination – you should be good to go. It seems that only New York, and the Port of Newark will raise the additional idiotic question of whether you were legal in any intermediary stop-over.

Have a great trip! If you stop off in New York, order a 64 oz. Diet Coke or other soft drink, just to piss off ex-Mayor Bloomberg. For now, that's the only way to get back at them!

PRIVATE BOATS:

Private boats that qualify as a "*conveyance*" are just like motor vehicles,[10] and the same state and federal laws apply with slight variation. The variation is that once you're outside the ***three mile limit*** on the east coast, or the western edge of the Gulf Stream (whichever is greater), or the ***nine mile limit*** (three leagues) on the Gulf Coast, you're in international waters -- and you can do most anything you want short of piracy, shooting at other people, boats, protected marine life, or carrying automatic weapons. Of course, once you come back into the jurisdictional limit -- make sure you're "Florida legal". *Fla. Const. Art. 2, section 1.*

THE BAHAMAS & FOREIGN PORTS:

If you are thinking of traveling to the Bahamas -- I contacted their Customs agency and was advised that any firearms other than fully automatic weapons are permitted to be kept on board. Under any circumstance, you will have to declare your firearms and ammunition with Customs when you come into port, or are checked by any Customs vessel, and must leave them on board in some type of secure enclosure. Bahama firearm laws on the internet state that possession of firearms on a non-Bahamian vessel by persons who are not Bahamian residents is legal so long as the firearms and ammunition do not leave the ship, are not used in Bahamian waters, and are declared to Bahamian Customs within 48 hours of arrival. However, keep them under lock and key, as well. Federal law requires, and U.S. Customs also advises that you must **list all firearms** being taken out of the United States on a ***Form 4457***, and keep a copy with you at all times. The form can be obtained and approved at any ***U.S. Custom & Border Patrol*** reporting location, and remains valid for the weapons listed, without renewal. You can get these locations, and the form on the U.S. Customs website: www.cbp.gov. I have also heard that a failure to have this form on international trips by sea or air can result in ***serious problems*** with certain foreign governments - especially Mexico. Please note that Mexico is experiencing serious crime problems with guns, and you should make specific inquiry as to their laws before having firearms in their territorial waters, or airspace.

If you are within the territorial waters of any other nation, or use their airspace you must normally comply with that nation's laws. What those laws are is outside the scope of this book, however, I understand that our jails are pleasure palaces next to those of nations south of the border.

WEAPONS IN AIRPORTS, AND COMMERCIAL AIRCRAFT:

Since 9/11 things have changed somewhat, and the *Transportation Security Administration* (*TSA*) is now in charge of airport security instead of the *F.A.A.* Things are also beginning to be taken more seriously, and as a passenger you need to know what you can and can't do. Even if not prosecuted criminally — the TSA is beginning to levy civil fines up to $10,000.00 for baggage and carry-on violations involving weapons pursuant to 49 USC 46303. Even if not prosecuted, you will be paying the TSA some money, normally around *twenty-five hundred bucks* from the feedback I'm getting on a first offense.

Both Florida and Federal law permit you, assuming you are at an airport as a passenger on a commercial aircraft, to take an <u>unloaded</u> firearm with you if it is checked-in as baggage, and declared with the carrier at the ticket counter. You must have any firearm placed unloaded, in a locked, hard-sided container, in which you are the **only** person on the aircraft with the key or combination. 49 CFR 1540.111. Moreover, any ammunition must now be securely packed in a fiber, wood, or metal package/box *specifically designed* to carry ammunition. That can be packed inside the same container as the firearm, but must still be separately boxed. 49 CFR 175.10. You should declare this, as well. Call the airline ahead of time to find out exactly what their policy is, and make damn sure your possession will be legal in your destination airport. If you have a layover in the *New York City* or *Newark* area – beware! They do not like firearms, and issues have occurred if baggage has to be transferred to another flight! Last, but not least — do not mark the outside of any container to show it contains any weapons or ammunition. That is unlawful under federal law.

As a passenger, you may also transport one *self-defense chemical spray* not exceeding 4 ounces with less than 2% active ingredient, so long as the spray has "a positive means to prevent accidental discharge". According to the SabreRed.com website – most civilian and police pepper spray will be less, and the most common civilian pepper spray comes in 1/2 ounce size. So – other than "*bear sprays*" it should be OK – but only be in *checked baggage*! Carry on is a serious violation! Again, make sure it's legal at your destination airport, and declare it at the main concourse ticket counter before you try checking it into any baggage. Likewise, you can check in with baggage other weapons that are not firearms. This includes knives, box cutters, air guns, starter guns, replicas, etc. Again, this is *check-in baggage* only, and I once again warn you to declare it, and call the airline ahead of time. If you're unsure – all this information is on the TSA website:

www.tsa.gov.

You must also check into baggage any *"dual-use items"* which are those that have a practical function, but could also be used as a weapon. This includes a hammer, crowbar, screwdriver, drill, ax, box-cutter, baseball bat, hockey stick, billie club, etc. Same thing for most pointed scissors, although rounded edge scissors are permitted for carry-on . No explosives anywhere — so fireworks are out completely. Same thing for micro-torches, and the like. Anything that can explode is usually completely illegal to transport as a *hazardous material* with the exception of *small arms ammunition*. And by the way – some airlines have a maximum weight allowed for ammo.

Another thing they only permit in checked baggage is a *"realistic replica"* of a firearm. So, if your toy gun looks real — it needs to be in your checked in baggage. The screeners have *full discretion* on any item. If you don't like their decision — try walking to Vermont. *Arguing* with a screener is actually a federal crime. Generally, if your mistake was innocent, and doesn't involve a firearm, or obvious weapon — you'll have the choice of putting the rejected item in checked in baggage, or returning it to your vehicle. If that's not an option, your only other option is to "abandon" the property to the screener, and if so, the property is automatically transferred to the federal government. If you need more information, check the web site of the *Transportation Security Administration* (*TSA*) at www.tsa.gov.

Anyway,   the real bad news is that intentionally attempting to carry a *dangerous weapon* on a commercial aircraft is punishable by up to ten years in a federal prison. 49 USC 46505 *"Dangerous weapons"* under federal law are just about anything in the weapon department. Same thing for placing a loaded firearm in checked-in baggage, or not declaring it. If you forgot you had such a weapon with you, then the federal standard of knowledge is *"should have known"*. This is a fairly easy standard to prove, and prosecution will likely depend on the discretion of the TSA. If you were prosecuted under state law, it would be a slightly more liberal defense on the level of knowledge required because Florida would require that you had *"actual knowledge"* the forbidden item was on your person or carry-on baggage. This is called *"lack of scienter"* in the law. For that reason, many Florida prosecutors are not filing criminal charges on these cases, or are allowing them to go directly into a *"diversion"* program. However, even if that's the situation, it will still be a very unpleasant experience.

Conversations with the *TSA* indicate that they will generally not prosecute federally if they really believe you carried the weapon on by pure accident. In these instances, it is probably **not** a great idea to claim your Fifth Amendment *"right to silence"*, and I would be as frank, humble, and horrified as possible! Don't take it casually, as people who seem to take it casually are usually the ones they prosecute. Moreover, this is one of the few instances in which I would definitely **not** insist on speaking to an attorney before speaking to them. Failure to make instantly clear that this was one big, stupid mistake for which you are *terribly embarrassed* can often lead to prosecution. Be humble! Be apologetic! Make sure they understand it was a mistake, and you forgot – or didn't realize it was there!

Furthermore, don't wait and try to declare any of these items at the gate, because once you enter the *"sterile area"* you have technically committed a federal crime. If you don't remember what the *sterile area* is, it's the area from the X-ray machine or security checkpoint, on. It's the portion of the passenger terminal usually reserved for the arrival and departure of passengers on scheduled flights. This rule applies equally to persons holding a CWL. Current penalties are pursuant to 49 USC 46505, which are up to ten years for a dangerous weapon, explosive, or incendiary device, or if done *"willfully"* and with reckless disregard to human life — up to twenty years, or if a death occurs, up to life. Moreover, you will receive a civil fine up to $10,000.00, even if they don't decide to prosecute you. [49 USC 46303].

Please remember that if you are in a hurry, and usually carry a gun in a bag, briefcase, or on your person (especially a derringer or small pistol) — you are **likely** to forget it's still there as you rush from your car to the gate! When that happens — you are going to have a rude interruption of your travel plans! You will be delayed! You will miss your flight! You will be paying a hefty fine! And, worse could occur! Therefore, make a *pre-departure checklist* to put the gun or weapon somewhere else! There are numerous examples of this happening in a federal criminal prosecution, and so far the federal courts have varied between a standard of *"actual knowledge"* or *"should have known"*. Most of these people wind-up being convicted if the government decides to prosecute!

Last, but not least, your CWL does not permit you to carry anywhere inside the terminal – including the baggage area unless it is a completely separate building from the terminal. You can carry in most *airport parking garages* since they're separate from the terminal building.

PRIVATE AIRCRAFT:

As a general rule, when it comes to a private aircraft not being used for commercial purposes with less than twenty (20) passenger seats, you may carry firearms and ammunition according to State law, so long as it's done with the permission of the pilot. 14 CFR 119.1. Ammunition should be limited to amounts that do not exceed a reasonable amount for personal use. The *F.A.A.* strongly recommends that ammunition be boxed in suitable containers. Of course, if you land at an airport that handles commercial flights, you may have certain issues.

Security operations at airports are generally reserved for operations involving the transportation of passengers or property for compensation, or for furtherance of a business or vocation, or where turbojet aircraft capable of carrying 30 passengers or more are involved, or any aircraft weighing more than 12,500 pounds. 49 USC 40102. Firearms and other weapons are subject to *TSA* restrictions in any "*air operations area*" which is the portion of the airport where "*security measures*" are required. Where commercial flights are involved, this normally includes taxi areas, aircraft parking areas, loading ramps, safety areas, and any adjacent areas that are not separated by security systems or procedures. That generally means access is controlled by a secured gate or monitored checkpoint. Thus, a "*general aviation area*" may be included within any airport where *security measures* are required. If this is the situation, a *private aircraft* should request specific instructions on what runway and taxiways to use so not to enter a *restricted area*, assuming you have on-board any firearms, ammo, or other restricted *TSA* items. The "*secured area*" is that portion of the airport used by carriers for baggage handling, and loading and unloading passengers, and any adjacent areas not separated by adequate security measures. 49 CFR 1540. Thus, if you are a pilot or passenger on a private aircraft less than twenty passengers – you need to stay out of these areas if you have firearms, ammo, etc.

QUESTION: I often go to air shows. Am I allowed to carry with my CWL?

ANSWER: Many air shows are in non-secured, general aviation areas. In such an area only Florida state law controls. However, stay out of any commercial areas for ticketed passenger or commercial aircraft operations. If there's a fence around the area you enter with a gate – it's probably prohibited.

TRAINS, BUSES, AND OTHER PUBLIC TRANSPORTATION:

If you are traveling interstate -- federal law controls, and you should deliver the firearm unloaded, in a *locked container* to the carrier for transportation, after declaring it as such. I suggest you follow the same guidelines as commercial aircraft passengers, and I suggest calling the carrier before so you know their regulations. There is also a question whether this applies if you are traveling just in your state, but the bus or train you are on is traveling on an interstate run. If it is, I think the better advise is to follow federal law on this issue, as similar questions have come up on commuter aircraft flights, and it was determined against the passenger.

If you are traveling by public transportation that operates solely within Florida -- F.S. 790.25(3)(L) says the firearm or weapon must be "*securely encased*", and not in your *manual possession.* Since "***manual possession***" normally means that the weapon is actually in your hand -- my best guess is that this subsection means something a bit more secure than the normal definition in a private conveyance.

Obviously, if you were holding it in a holster, it's probably in your *manual possession.* If it were in a zippered gun case, I am again unsure, as "*not in your manual possession*" might be interpreted as requiring more than being in just a gun case. From a conservative standpoint I would want to have any firearm or weapon "*securely encased*" inside a **locked bag** or **locked briefcase**, or in a holster or gun rug **inside** my luggage, bag, or briefcase. If I wanted to be extra careful — it would be unloaded, and checked as baggage.

Naturally, there is no case law interpreting this section, and there are just too many stories of law enforcement officials going on buses, and pressuring people into random searches -- and then seizing their firearms, whether they're legal or not. I wouldn't want you to be the *test case* if you were pushing this interpretation to the limit, so my advise is that it's better to be safe -- than sorry. Or — just get a CWL!

AMTRAK PASSENGERS:

Whatever I just said in the last section – forget as to ***Amtrak***. Amtrak is a special category because it is controlled by federal statutes. Passengers who intend to transport firearms and/or ammunition on Amtrak have special rules to follow. First – you cannot carry on your person. All weapons are supposed to be in checked baggage. Likewise, any firearm being transported must be unloaded, and in a hard-sided locked case. Ammunition cannot exceed 11 pounds, and must be packed in the original ammo boxes, or in packaging specifically designed to carry ammunition. No black powder ammo or caps are permitted. Ammo must be stored separate from any firearms.

In order to transport firearms on Amtrak you must called ahead not less than 24 hours, and have each firearm entered into a *"reservation record"* for your trip. If you don't – you will not be allowed to bring it. Likewise, you may only transport firearms from a station that has a *live ticket agent*. If they have passed away before you get there – I guess you're out of luck! (*Yeah – that was supposed to be a joke*). You should arrive ahead of time as you are required to fill out a ***"Firearms Declaration Form"*** for each firearm being transported. The ticket agent at the station will supply these. Any bag in which handguns are transported cannot exceed a total weight of 50 lbs. All bags having firearms will be checked, and cannot be carry-on. The agent at the ticket counter, after verifying you have first made a reservation for the firearm, will place a copy of the ***Firearms Declaration Form*** into the hard sided case, and then have it loaded on the train. Have a great trip! Thank the feds for another great set of rules – and believe it or not – getting Congress and Amtrak to allow this was like pulling teeth.

COMMERCIAL DRIVERS:

There are no federal regulations that prevent a driver of a commercial vehicle from carrying a firearm or other weapon for protection, and therefore the laws of the individual states you are driving in will control. In Florida, there is likewise no legal restriction that applies specifically to commercial drivers, and the law you must follow is the same as any other person in Florida.

CARRYING IN YOUR HOME OR PLACE OF BUSINESS:

Now that we've beaten-to-death the subject of how you can carry a firearm (and any other weapon) in any type of vehicle or other transportation -- the next most important area is your home, or business. The good news is that you can carry or possess a firearm, or any other legal weapon, anywhere in your home or business, concealed or in the open -- your choice. No CWL necessary! This area of the law is very well settled.

Why?

Well, F.S. 790.25(3)(n) makes it lawful for persons to possess a firearm or other weapon on their home or place of business, either concealed or in the open. Despite several challenges in the courts, this law stands stronger than ever. From the standpoint of your home – we're talking about an apartment, house, or condo. If you're inside the unit, you're totally legal. Once you step outside – it changes a bit. If it's a single family type dwelling – all the surrounding property that is actually deeded to the home is exempt. That's what the Florida Supreme Court pretty much held in *Peoples v. State*, 287 So. 2d 63 (Fla. 1973). This was expanded on in several other appellate court cases that followed the *Peoples* decision. For instance:

> "It is not unlawful for a person to possess firearms at his home or place of business, including surrounding property, as well as buildings and structures situated thereon." State v. Anton, 700 So. 2d 743 (Fla. 2DCA 1997).

> "(The) home exemption applied to the defendant's driveway and yard." Sherrod v. State, 484 So. 2d 1279 (Fla. 4DCA 1986)

On the other hand, if you live in a condo or apartment building – the *Sherrod* case held that the exemption afforded by F.S. 790.25(3)(n) would not apply to "***common areas***" used by all residents such as the parking lot, pool area, garage, and walkways. Whether the walkway area immediately in front of your apartment is considered "part of your home" is unresolved – but there is a fair likelihood that it isn't, so I wouldn't take the chance. On the other hand, none of these cases involved a ***condominium*** owner who normally owns a share of the "*undivided whole*" of the complex, as well as his or her unit. So, I guess there is a *test case* for whether this would be an exception to the general rule. Quite frankly, I could argue it from either side with no problem. So – once again – a CWL is the best answer.

On the other hand, you also have an exemption for your "***place of business***". Similar to the home exemption the *Anton* case held that "*place of business*" includes surrounding property owned by the business, and buildings situated thereon. It likely includes an adjacent sidewalk, according to the case of *Collins v. State*, 475 So.2d 968 (Fla. 4DCA 1985). The safe way of interpreting this is that the property must be the portion where your duties actually take you, or usually take you. And, similarly to the home exemption – areas *common* to other businesses such as common parking lots, walkways, etc. – are likely not protected by this exemption.

However, on the good side of the business exemption, the cases interpreting this section have made it very clear that you don't need your employer's permission to carry.[11] *State v. Commons*, 592 So. 2d 317 (Fla. 3DCA 1991). On the other hand – if you disobey a company directive and get caught – you can usually get fired for it, although there is a limited exception that we will discuss later for employee parking lots when the employee also has a CWL. Likewise, cases say even if you're an employee on the premises during off hours for purely personal reasons – you are legal even without a CWL.

Still, in any of those instances where you decide to *open carry* on home or business premises – you need to steer clear of F.S. 790.10 – "*improper exhibition*". In those situations, open carry in the presence of others should not be done in a "*rude, angry, careless, or threatening manner*".

PROBLEMS WITH CONDO'S & APARTMENTS:

Like I already discussed – unless you have a CWL, you may have a problem getting from the car to your business or home without crossing the new "*No Man's Land*" of Florida – "*common areas*". This is an area the Legislature goofed-up real good, and needs revision. In many other states the issue was resolved by allowing a non-CWL holder to go "*directly*" from their vehicle to the business or residence with a concealed weapon or firearm. But in Florida – not so lucky! So, what are the problems?

Well . . . Florida courts don't think property you share with other owners constitutes "your" home or "your" business. It's everyones! So, if you park in a common parking lot,[12] go through common hallways, use common elevators, or use common facilities – it's not "your property". I realize we could argue this – but that's what the case law says. So, unless you have a CWL, or you're coming to/from a hunting, fishing, or camping trip, sport shooting -- or one of the other interesting exceptions I mentioned before in F.S. 790.25 -- you can't legally carry while you're on or in any of these "*common areas*", concealed or otherwise.

QUESTION: So how the heck am I supposed to get my firearm from my car to my apartment?

ANSWER: Ah, ha! You got it! You're not! Go get a CWL, or tell your state legislator that the law is *stupid* as written, and you want it changed. Heck, it certainly is!

QUESTION: What if it's my own home, a duplex, and I'm renting the other half?

ANSWER: No problem for you, and no problem for your renter as long as you don't share any common areas. Technically, since you're the sole owner, and the other guy is only a renter -- he can't use the *common areas* for carrying a firearm, but you can. Again – stupid!

QUESTION: What if I hear a noise on the stairway outside my apartment, and I think it's a burglar?

ANSWER: Interesting example! Legally, you have no right to go out with a firearm on a *common area*. However, since you do have a constitutional, and statutory right to *self-defense*, and defense of property -- my opinion is you have an exception to the general rule. Get a good lawyer. Possible *test case* time unless there is an actual break-in in progress. At that point – you would be legal as long as you don't use *excessive force*.

As you can see from these questions and answers -- there are certain restrictions on carrying if you don't live in a private residence. If you do live in a private residence, even if you <u>rent</u> it -- you have a right to carry and possess firearms anywhere on the property, not just inside the dwelling. *Caban v. State*, 475 So.2d 968 (Fla. 4DCA 1985)   Same thing if you're renting a room in a motel, as far as the room itself goes. During the rental period it's considered as your "***residence***", although only temporary. Since your property normally includes the driveway -- no problem getting the gun from the car to the house. This applies to every member of your family.

QUESTION: I'm a construction worker, and I'll be working on a project at one location for the next six months. Does that qualify as "***business premises***"?

ANSWER: In many other states – yes. In Florida – I'm not sure, although there's a good argument for it thanks to the case of *Little v. State*, 104 So. 3d 1263 (Fla. 4DCA 2013), which held that "*place of business*" is "*simply a location where business is transacted*". However, at a minimum, the *construction trailer* of the company you work for should qualify. *Test case* time.

QUESTION: I heard that you couldn't shoot anyone except if you were in your house. So, how can I legally carry a gun outside my home, even if it's on my property?

ANSWER: You are confusing two different areas of the law. You're thinking about the old "***retreat rule***" or "***castle doctrine***" which really concerned the *use* of a firearm, rather than when and where you can carry it. "***Carrying***" a weapon or firearm is an entirely separate matter. The law says you can *carry* a firearm, concealed or in the open, anywhere on your property. In the house, in your business, or on the premises, outside. It doesn't matter. On the other hand, **how** you *use* it, point it, or handle it, does!

QUESTION: You say I can get fired if I carry a gun against my employers directions. Isn't Florida a *"preemption"* state?

ANSWER: The ***preemption law*** only covers government — not private entities or persons. The ***parking lot law*** modifies this somewhat, and is covered elsewhere in this book – however, it only applies to firearms ***securely encased*** in a parked vehicle.

WHEN YOU STILL CAN'T HAVE IT:

There are always exceptions to the exceptions of legal possession and carrying. One big exception is when you're about to commit, or are committing a crime. That's a felony. Another concerns school grounds and school sponsored events – although there are some exceptions for parking I'll discuss later. These laws generally apply to all persons, whether you have a CWL or not. There are still other instances which could penalize otherwise legal possession, but let's just cover the areas I've mentioned, for now:

SCHOOLS, COLLEGES, UNIVERSITIES:

Rather than go over the rules that pertain to schools, and colleges -- let me tell you that this is gone over extensively in the chapter about children -- Chapter Eight. It's a really important area, and I highly suggest that you read it. Whether you have kids, or not, you'll find that it applies to you in some way. However, since one of the questions I get all the time is whether a *private* school or college can authorize teachers or administrators to carry weapons – the answer is "absolutely not" – with the exception of colleges/universities as to students, faculty, and employees who have a valid

CWL, and carry a **stun gun**, or other non-lethal electric weapon that does not fire a projectile. (ie: no *Tasers*) Personally, I think the law should be changed to allow any specially designated and trained administrators and teachers to be allowed to carry concealed firearms, and at an absolute minimum to amend the CWL statute, F.S. 790.06(12) to also allow the carry of a *Taser* at the post-secondary school level – if for no other reason, where there is an imminent threat of death or great bodily harm to students or faculty. One thing you should know – you can now have a *"securely encased"* firearm or weapon in a vehicle on *college or university premises* thanks to recent case law. More on this in Chapter Eight.

CHURCH & OTHER RELIGIOUS INSTITUTIONS:

There are no laws in Florida that forbid carry on the grounds of, or inside any religious institution. Thus, concealed carry with a CWL is not illegal. And, since the real nut cases tend to go on the rampage at churches, schools, and former places of employ – my question to you is – why not carry at religious services? I do! However, the question I seem to get most from religious institutions is whether they can arm some of their congregation to do *security duty*?

The answer is that Chapter 493 of the Florida Statutes permits only law enforcement, and properly licensed individuals (ie: "G" license) to carry firearms in security work – even as a volunteer. Still, a *volunteer* could be armed with a *Taser*, or other weapon that was not a firearm. Not a great defense against a nut case with a firearm – which is why I strongly advocate CWL carry at services. On the other hand, if you want to just encourage members of your congregation who have a CWL to carry to services – no problem! (except in portions that may constitute a *"church school"*)

NATIONAL FORESTS:

Unlike National Parks, **National Forests** follow state law. Under current Florida regulations [Rule 62d-2.014] a CWL holder can carry concealed on their person in a National Forest. Without the CWL, you can carry only if you are engaged in lawful fishing, hunting, or camping, and the weapon or firearm must be concealed. That's right – even without the CWL – it must be **concealed**. However, you can also keep a weapon or firearm in a vehicle or tent if it is **"secured from minors"**. This goes for CWL holders, as well, if *not on your person* that's been defined being in a **locked container** of some sort. If you ask me, this is completely illegal and contrary to the *preemption law* – but that is something that would have to be tested in court for a definitive answer.

NATIONAL PARKS & WILDLIFE REFUGES:

Federal law permits *concealed carry* in *National Parks* [36 CFR 2.4], *National Wildlife Refuges* [50 CFR 27.42], and reclamation lands and water bodies [43 CFR 423.30], except inside any *"federally owned building"* on such premises normally used by federal employees. 18 USC 930. That does not include separately located public bathroom facilities. Any building where firearms or weapons are prohibited will have signs **posted** at all public entrances so stating. For any if you who associate with trolls – a *"cave"* is considered a *"building"* by the *U.S. Park Service*. Of course, *open carry* of firearms in permitted areas for hunting during season, with the proper firearm and a valid hunting license, are unaffected. However, weapons are not permitted at *Kennedy Space Center,* or *NASA restricted areas* which are considered *"national security areas"*. Buildings on park property owned and run by private enterprises are regulated by state law, not federal.

ARMY CORPS OF ENGINEERS:

I'm not sure if we have any property or waterways controlled by the *U.S. Army Corps of Engineers* in Florida – but if we do – no loaded firearms, and absolutely no ammunition are permitted on their properties or waterways, nor any other weapons except when and where permitted for hunting and fishing with such being unloaded until hunting or fishing begins, at authorized shooting ranges, or with permission of the District Commander. 36 CFR 327.13

STATE FORESTS AND PARKS:

In 2006 the Legislature did away with firearms restrictions in national forests and state parks by repealing Florida Statutes 790.11; 790.12; and 790.14 [HB 1029]. Since *National Forests* follow state legislative restrictions on weapons (don't confuse this with *"National Parks"*), that basically put legal carry in *National Forests* and state parks in Florida under Florida Statute 790.25. The Legislature then left it to the *Florida Department of Environmental Protection* to pass a rule implementing this. That rule, 62D-2.014 states:

> *"weapons shall at all times be in the possession of a responsible party or properly secured within or to a vehicle or temporary housing . . . while in state parks. "Properly secured" means the weapon shall be locked away and not accessible to minors , and if in a tent, the weapon shall be secured in a locked container. No person shall use or openly display in any state park weapons . . . Except when such are used for resource management purposes as authorized in this subsection."*

Obviously, the Rule doesn't follow all that 790.25, and other Florida Statutes allow, and should run afoul of the 2011 amendment to Florida's **preemption statute**, F.S. 790.33. How that will work out in the future will probably fall on those "*test cases*" where the courts will hopefully uphold what the Legislature directed, rather than the more restrictive version of what the Florida DEP enacted. Although I've already covered it in the previous section on National Forests, the **safe side** of what the rule means is that anyone with a CWL can carry weapons and firearms concealed, upon their person (including any bag or knapsack you personally carry), in a state park or national forest in Florida. It also means that if you don't have the CWL – and so long as you are engaged in "lawful" fishing, hunting, or camping a weapon or firearm can be carried on your person, so long as it is carried *concealed*. "*Lawful*" generally means with a valid hunting or fishing license, in season if hunting, and for hunting or fishing, in a place where being there is not otherwise unlawful. However, any individual (CWL or not) may keep a weapon or firearm in their tent or vehicle if it is in a *locked container*. Under a literal reading of the Rule, a minor could not carry any type of weapon, nor could an adult carry a partially or fully exposed weapon on a belt, or for that matter, any electronic or chemical weapon that wasn't fully concealed. A holster or sheath that fully covers the entire weapon, including the handle, should be considered "*concealed*" even though the content is obvious. However, if any part of the weapon is visible - it is likely not "*concealed*" under the law. The fact that this agency has not changed its rule for more than two years since the preemption law was amended is absolutely incredulous!

You should know that many counties and municipalities have restrictions on carry in county and city parks. These restrictions should likewise be illegal due to the 2011 **preemption law**, and be **presumed** unconstitutional. While previously, such ordinances and regulations would be "*presumed*" legal – the change in F.S. 790.33 should mean these ordinances and regulations are now presumed to be "*null and void*", and enforcement should expose government to liability. Personally, I think the *Attorney General* should go after the *Florida Department of Environmental Protection*, and the individuals responsible!

MAILING & SENDING FIREARMS:

As a general rule, it is illegal to send any handgun or ammunition through the **U.S. Mail**, [18 USC 1715 & 1716] although the restriction on ammunition is because it is a "*hazardous material*", rather than it's transport being prohibited. You can send a rifle or shotgun thru the mail if you declare it as such -- but not a handgun. Send the handgun by a *commercial carrier* such as UPS, but you must declare any firearm to the carrier in writing, and it must be unloaded and securely encased. If you use UPS or FedX, and you do not have a daily business pick-up account – it has to be dropped off at a mailing center,   sent by overnight air, and federal law requires a signature. Remember, you may only send a firearm *out-of-state* if it's for repair, return to a federal licensee (ie: firearms manufacturer, dealer, importer, or gunsmith – all being *"FFL's"*), or shipment to such a licensee for any other lawful purpose – otherwise it is a federal crime. 18 USC 922(a)(2)(A), although you can legally ship a firearm to **yourself** in another state by a commercial carrier if your possession in that state is lawful. Of course, most carriers will only deliver to an FFL from a private party – so if you ship to yourself – good luck in finding a carrier that will accept it. Likewise, if you ship it to yourself in care of someone else – BATFE says the package should be addressed to you *"in care of"* that other person, the package should **not** be opened by anyone but yourself, and until you pick it up, it should be kept unopened in a secure location.

QUESTION: What if I need to get a firearm repaired, or have to ship it to a FFL out-of-state?

ANSWER: You can mail it if it's a long gun, or UPS it if it's a handgun. However, the preferred method is never to send a firearm by the mail. By the way, Federal Express, or any other common carrier or trucker, can qualify for your shipment. I just know that UPS does a lot of these. However, remember to declare it in writing to the carrier or it's a felony.   Oral is not sufficient. 18 USC 922(e)   Likewise, any firearm so transported across state lines requires the carrier to obtain a signature of receipt from the licensee or whoever it is delivered to. 18 USC 922(f)(2). This will cost you a bit extra to obtain – but it is a federal requirement! Also, don't mark the package showing that the contents are a firearm. That's also a federal "no no", even if it's otherwise obvious.

QUESTION: If I send a firearm to an FFL for repair or replacement – can they send it back to me directly, and not through another FFL?

ANSWER: Yes. 18 U.S.C. § 922(a)(2)(A), allows an FFL to return the same firearm or its same kind replacement to the non-FFL who sent it to them.

QUESTION: What about mailing a "handgun" to a relative within Florida?

ANSWER: Buy a toothbrush, and meet your new cellmate, Guido. This is a violation of federal statutes. However, you may legally UPS it (not the U.S. Mail) so long as it's within the same state you sent it from, and the person receiving it is not legally disqualified – assuming you can find a common carrier willing to handle it.

QUESTION: So, how the heck does my firearms dealer get his stuff, with all these regulations?

ANSWER: Try to remember that he's a federal licensee, and can receive or ship to or from any other federal licensee. He can also receive from an unlicensed individual. The rules are different because of his qualifications.

LEGAL WAYS TO SHIP TO NON-LICENSEES:

If you need to ship a firearm to somebody in another state, and that person can legally possess it there, you might consider having a federally licensed gun dealer in your home state do it for you, or you could make arrangements to send it direct to an FFL in the state you are sending it to. He'd charge you a fee, and send it to a dealer in the other state. The person you're sending it to would be able to pick it up from the dealer in the other state after complying with the law there — which is usually a short waiting period plus the NICS criminal history check, and paying the dealer in the receiving state a fee for his services.

QUESTION: So, I can sell or transfer my firearm to an out-of-state resident, after?

ANSWER: Yes, according to BATFE this is perfectly legal so long as the delivery to the out-of-state resident is to and thru an FFL in the state of receipt, or thru an FFL in your home state who does the actual shipping to another FFL in the buyer's home state. The legal theory on this is that the sale or transfer is not complete until "*delivery*", and the "*delivery*" is being made by the out-of-state FFL, who is also doing the transfer paperwork. [ie: *NICS* check and Form 4473].

QUESTION: How about a ***bequest or inheritance***?

ANSWER: Well, that's an exception to the usual rule, and does not require
            an FFL intermediary. This is per 27 CFR 478.30, although I
            would advise that only the executor or administrator of the estate
            can legally send it (UPS), and he or she make darn sure the person
            receiving it is legal in the state of receipt. However, if it's an
            NFA weapon (machine guns, etc.) the executor can only transfer
            it to a beneficiary **after** approval by ATF on a Form 5. Also, if
            the machine gun was a "***dealer sample***" (ie: manufacture/import
            after May 19, 1986) it can only be transferred to an FFL Class III
            dealer via a pre-approved Form 4.

            An interesting aside on ***machine guns*** — if you transfer it
            contrary to law – it becomes "***contraband***", and is illegal to
            possess. The recipient can't legally send it back to you to "undo"
            the mistake, because once screwed-up it becomes "*contraband*"
            forever, and cannot be made legal. Thus, it's a very serious
            federal crime to keep it in your possession.

INDIAN RESERVATIONS:

Indian land, including any ***gambling casino*** on such property, is
protected under 18 USC 1165. It is a crime for anyone to go on Indian lands to
hunt or fish without the permission of the tribal authorities. Quechan Tribe v.
Rowe, 531 F.2d 408 (9th Cir. 1976). Likewise, it is a felony to have any
switchblade knife on Indian land. [15 USC 1241-1245] Otherwise, everyday
Florida law and statutes control what you can or can't do. F.S. 285.16. Thus,
it is not "technically" illegal to have a firearm in a casino with a CWL – although
it is highly likely that such is not permitted by the casino, and thus could possibly
result in a *trespass warning*, and maybe even an arrest.

SEAPORT RESTRICTED ZONES:

F.S. 311.12(7), enacted in 2006 states it's a first degree misdemeanor
to have a "*concealed*" weapon inside any designated "*restricted*" area in a
seaport, even if *securely encased* in a vehicle. In my opinion – another
stupid law, especially when you're taking an evening gambling cruise, and
then need to traverse back home in the middle-of-the-night without any
protection!

While seaports are generally open to the public, the legislation makes clear that any unauthorized person in a marked (ie: posted) *"restricted area"* or *"restricted zone"* is subject to a arrest. I assume that means that if the area or entrance to the area is **conspicuously posted** – you could get arrested. Likewise, I assume the defense to any such arrest would be you didn't see the signs because they were not conspicuously located, or the signs weren't posted where you entered the restricted area. It would be likely up to you to prove this defense. Take plenty of photos, and hope the sign isn't in one of them!

The loophole in this statute is the word *"concealed"* because only *"concealed"* weapons and firearms get you in trouble under this section of the law. So, I guess you could have a *"**securely encased**"* handgun in plain view in a holster. Probably the same for some other weapons. On the other hand, I would think that the statutes (likely with the same defenses) are still going to apply. Unfortunately, if a charge was brought – it might be prosecuted as an armed trespass, which is a felony. Not a fun charge to face, or defend.

If you want to get around the statute legally – you can. However, you need the *written permission* from the seaport director to possess. Still, law enforcement officers are permitted to have them, although there is no requirement in the statute that they need be on duty. *Security guards* working in these areas should obtain written permission, or a blanket written OK for the entire security service would probably be fine, as well.

HOSPITALS & MENTAL FACILITIES:

F.S. 394.458 states that *"except as authorized by law"* it is a third degree felony for any person to bring, carry, possess, or transport a *"firearm or other dangerous weapon"* (or alcoholic beverage) upon the grounds of any "hospital (or mental health facility) providing *mental health services"*. As a practical matter, almost every hospital and hospital emergency room provides mental health services – so, from a technical standpoint, the statute seems to prohibit firearms or weapons anywhere on its grounds, with some important exceptions.

What are the exceptions? Well, the answer lies in the phrase *"except as authorized by law"*. F.S.790.25 authorizes *"securely encased"* weapons in vehicles. Hence, a securely encased weapon or firearm in a vehicle should be considered *"authorized by law"*. Likewise, for all you CWL holders, F.S. 790.06(12) lists all the places you can't go with a CWL – and *"hospitals or mental health facilities"* are not on the list. Thus, logic holds that carrying in those situations are also "*authorized by law*". Since the Legislature has refused to change the law despite it being brought up several times in various bills attempting to put it off limits to CWL holders – it's a good bet my interpretation is correct. Of course, there are no court decisions on this area for now, so I urge caution. Possible *test case* time!

MEDICAL PRIVACY & INSURANCE DISCRIMINATION:

F.S. 790.338 allegedly prevents any medical facility or personnel from inquiring about, or entering information on firearms ownership into a patient's medical records unless, in good faith, it is believed to be relevant to the patient's medical care, safety, or safety of others. Inquiry may also be made by emergency personnel if the possession of a firearm would pose an "*imminent danger*". However, a patient may refuse to answer such inquiry, without penalty. Violations are grounds for administrative disciplinary action. Subsection (7) of the same statute prevents insurance companies from raising rates or denying coverage because of ownership of firearms, ammo, or their storage. The law was upheld recently by the 11th Circuit federal appeals court.

PARKING LOT LAW:

F.S. 790.251, also known as the "***parking lot law***", passed in 2008 allegedly made it illegal for a business or employer to prohibit the use of parking areas to customers or employees who keep a lawful firearm and/or ammo in their locked vehicle, forbade retaliation against the employee or customer for doing so, forbade questioning of the employee or customer to determine if he or she had such a stored firearm, and forbade searches of vehicles to determine such.   Unfortunately, the bill suffered from severe drafting problems, and a federal district court [*Florida Retail Assoc v. Attorney General*, 576 F.Supp. 2d 1281 (N.D. Fla. 2008)] held the statute **only** protects employees who have a CWL, and that the provisions applying to customers and other invitees were unconstitutional, as written.   (better drafting would have resulted in a different result).

Likewise, the statute granted several overbroad exceptions to various business interests so that it doesn't apply to:

> "*Company provided vehicles, any property involving school grounds, correctional institutions, property used for national defense, aerospace, domestic security, manufacture/storage/or transport of combustible or explosive materials, or any other property prohibited by state or federal law.*"

That phrasing arguably eliminated all theme parks that use *fireworks,*[13] service stations, etc. Plus, as a practical matter, the enforcement provisions of the statute for private individuals are worse than dismal, and strongly favor business and large corporations. Should the Legislature ever get around to re-writing it properly – it would easily pass constitutional muster as a similar statute did in another federal appeal, *Ramsey Winch, Inc. v. Henry*, 2009 WL 388050 (10th Cir. 2009).

More unfortunately, *Disney*, *Universal*, and the rest of the attractions rat pack have interpreted the "*fireworks*" portion as applying to **all** their property – even those portions that have nothing to do with fireworks. Since *Disney* owns *forty square miles* for *Disney World*, you get a rough idea how unfair and outlandish this interpretation really is! Our past Attorney General, Bill McCollum, slinked away from fighting this interpretation – and unless some organization with bucks enough to challenge it takes it on – that's the way it's being interpreted, for now. Obviously, I don't agree.

DISNEY AND THE ATTRACTIONS:

Give me an "M"! Give me an "I"! Give me a "C" . . . etc. What does it spell?

It spells: "We don't give a damn about the *Second Amendment*! Keep your firearms and weapons off our property!"

Since the Legislature seems to cower to these entities – your rights on their property are somewhat non-existent. If they find out you have any firearms or weapons in your room, on your person, or in your vehicle – count on being booted off the property, and likely getting a *trespass warning* on top of it! They don't care if it's midnight, and you're sleeping soundly in your two hundred dollar a night room with your kids – you, and them are out! Dat's life! I hear about these situations all the time!

Unless the Legislature decides to "*man up*", and at least make it mandatory to allow "*securely encased*" firearms and weapons in a *parked vehicle* on their property – this sad state of affairs will continue. Heck – it can take hours or days to drive there, and hours or days back! It can be a hundred miles or a thousand – and I gotta leave my protection home because some damn Mouse is anti-gun? Who the hell is in the Legislature?

As for carry within the parks – that makes some sense to me since the parks are normally heavily patrolled, weapons have a tendency to fall out of some rides, there are a million kids around, and how anybody can stand in line for an hour waiting for a ride without totally losing it – beats me! So, for now – be warned! No firearms or weapons in Mickey Land!

ENDNOTE SECTION FOR CHAPTER SIX:
1. F.S. 790.053

2. F.S. 790.01

3. The term "manual possession" came from former F.S. 790.05, and means that the weapon is actually in your hand.

4. In Peoples v. State, 287 So. 2d 63 (Fla. 1973), the Florida Supreme Court interpreted F.S. 790.25 as including concealed carry on residential or business premises.

5. Dozier v. State, 662 So.2d 382 (Fla. 4DCA 1995). Also, the term "ship" should be synonymous with the term "boat" in the sense of a motor boat, and a sail boat with a cabin. Since a "bicycle" has been excluded as a conveyance — I assume a canoe or similar type craft would also be excluded, but there is no case law.

6. A.M. v. State, 678 So.2d 914 (Fla. 1DCA 1996)

7. F.S. 790.001(16)

8. Urquiola v. State, 590 So.2d 497 (Fla. 3DCA 1991)

9. F.S. 790.001(15) states: "readily accessible for immediate use' means that a firearm or other weapon is carried on the person or within such close proximity and in such a manner that it can be retrieved and used as easily and quickly as if carried on the person."

10. Again, I remind you that a "bicycle" is not a conveyance - and I doubt that a canoe, single man sailboat, or a rowboat would qualify, either because they would probably be considered purely "pleasure craft", and not really a functional conveyance.

However, there are no court cases defining this.

11. In <u>Brook v. State</u>, 999 So.2d 1093 (Fla. 5DCA 2009), the court held that an employee may legally carry at his place of business even after hours when the business was closed – purely for social reasons.

12. <u>See</u>, <u>Sherrod v. State</u>, 484 So.2d 912 (Fla. 3DCA 1986), where a conviction for carrying a concealed firearm was sustained because the defendant was on his apartment unit's parking lot when arrested -- a "common area".

13. Then Attorney General McCollum cut a deal with Disney whereby the Attorney General agreed that basically all 47 square miles of Disney's property were excluded from the law even though only a very small portion of the property was used for fireworks.

CHAPTER SEVEN

COMMON WEAPON VIOLATIONS
AND RELATED CRIMES

The only people who don't have to worry about weapons violations are criminals, and juveniles who are becoming criminals. They don't care -- so whatever regulatory laws we pass aren't going to stop them. The only thing that will stop them is a jail sentence, and except for juveniles, we already have more than enough laws to accomplish that, if anybody would bother to enforce them. The rest of us who are just trying to defend ourselves, and stay out of trouble -- have all the problems obeying this stuff. Since you are hopefully in this later category of the population, God bless you, you need all the help you can get.

CARRYING CONCEALED WEAPONS AND FIREARMS:
By this time you should all know, with certain limited exceptions, you can't carry a *concealed* weapon or firearm without a CWL unless you're at your home or business premises. If you don't understand that by now -- you need a remedial reading course.

Carrying a *concealed firearm* without a CWL is a third degree felony (except at home or business premises). Carrying a *concealed weapon*, which is not a firearm, is a first degree misdemeanor, unless you have a CWL. F.S. 790.01. Of course, there are the exceptions that we've already discussed in a previous chapter, and a few more I'm going to update you on in a moment.

LAW ENFORCEMENT OFFICERS OFF DUTY CARRY:
If you're an off-duty law enforcement or corrections officer, you can carry a concealed weapon or firearm under several different regulations when off duty. One would be the CWL. Another would be pursuant to the federal *Law Enforcement Officers Safety Act* discussed later in Chapter Ten. A third would be with the permission of your superior to do so while off duty, for professional purposes, or if your department has a written policy that you're always "*on duty*", even when not in uniform -- you're legal per F.S. 790.052. However, the real zinger is that as long as you have an active law officers certification from the *Criminal Justice Standards and Training Commission*, you can carry concealed just like a private citizen with a CWL pursuant to F.S. 790.052 and F.S. 790.06(5)(b). This last one applies to full and part time (auxiliary) officers, and even those no longer working for an agency, so long as their certification is current and not suspended. *Stumpff v. State*, 998 So.2d 1186 (Fla. 4DCA

2009).   So, I guess the only real benefit of the CWL would be avoiding the waiting period for firearm purchase.

DEFENSE OF LACK OF SCIENTER:
      Sometimes, people forget they are carrying a concealed weapon. This normally happens when they're in a rush, are preoccupied, and are legally transporting the weapon in a bag, or briefcase with other things – and then forget it's there. If you wander into a courthouse or airport, even if you have a CWL – you're gonna be in big trouble when the metal detector suddenly goes off![1] And, if you're thinking that this could never happen – I can assure you that it happens all the time. Remember – we're all just human!

      "So", you ask. *"Are there any defenses?"*

      Well, if you remember, we already discussed that in Chapter Six, and the answer is "*yes*".   Under Florida law there is a defense which I like to term: "*complete and utter stupidity*". The court definition is a bit more legally precise, and is blandly referred to as a *lack of knowledge, mistake of fact,* or **lack of scienter.**[2]   Since you were caught voluntarily placing a heavy metal object directly into a metal detector -- most people will probably come to realize that you did it innocently, and by mistake, rather than with a *criminal intent.* In other words, if you honestly forgot it was there, and can convince your friendly local prosecutor, or jury of that -- you will likely get out of it, assuming they want to bother with the charge, in the first place. In many circuits – it's just so obvious it's not worth the trouble.

COMMON POCKETKNIVES:
      A **common pocketknife**, according to Florida law, is not a "**weapon**", unless it is used as a "**deadly weapon**". Thus, anyone may carry a concealed "*common pocketknife*" without a CWL. In some respects, this was a very confused area. The cases that interpreted the statute couldn't decide what the word "*common*" meant — and you took your chances whenever you had something even slightly unusual.[3]   Federal law has been fairly clear-cut,[4] and does not consider a "*pocketknife*" with a blade **less than 2 ½ inches** to be a "**dangerous weapon**".[5] 18 USC 930(g)(2) However, under federal law you still can't take these into any "*sterile area*" at an airport.   In 1997 the confusion in Florida law was momentarily changed by an opinion by the Florida Supreme Court in <u>L.B. v. State</u>, 700 So.2d 370 (Fla. 1997).

      Adopting a close version of the Attorney General's definition, and somewhat expanding on it, the Florida Supreme Court held that a *common pocketknife* is not a *"weapon"* when it is a *folding knife* with a blade **four inches or less**. In fact, the Court noted there might be some instances where a *pocketknife* might still qualify as a *"common"* pocketknife if it had a blade length over four inches. In making the decision the Court stated:

> *"Webster's defines "pocketknife" as "a knife with a blade folding into the handle to fit it for being carried in the pocket." From these definitions, we can infer that the legislature's intended definition of "common pocketknife" was: "A type of knife occurring frequently in the community which has a blade that folds into the handle and that can be carried in one's pocket." We believe that in the vast majority of cases, it will be evident to citizens and fact-finders whether one's pocketknife is a "common" pocketknife under any intended definition of that term. We need not be concerned with odd scenarios construing smaller but more expensive knives as "uncommon".*

This definition should still exclude **butterfly knives**, **switchblade** and probably other **automatic knives**, or knives that do not fold in the traditional manner. Likewise, for some untold reason, Florida appellate courts have found that if kept concealed on the person they must be in the fully closed position, or a jury issue arises, and they could actually be found to be a *"weapon"*. While **"spring assisted knives"** have been the most common selling pocketknife in the last five years, I wouldn't carry one without a CWL, and will discuss that shortly. However, you should know a 1997 case out of the Third District Court of Appeal muddied up the water by holding that a **3 ½ inch** bladed folding knife with a large finger guard, and notched "combat-style" grip still qualified as a *"deadly weapon"* because of its features. *J.D.L.R. v. State*, 701 So.2d 626 (Fla. 3DCA 1997). Anybody who knows anything about knives knows this, for the most part, was ridiculous – but, that's what they found. Thus, if a pocketknife has significant features normally reserved to a *combat type* fighting knife — it may be considered a *"weapon"*. My personal interpretation of that decision is that a *finger guard* is an excellent safety feature for protection of your hand – not combat – unless unusually large, or where edged or having outward sharp points. Likewise, a *"notched grip"* is also normally a *safety feature* where the finger notching is not a major feature. However – BEWARE! My lowly interpretation is not the law, and it is obvious that few appellate judges in the Third District have much experience with them.

On the other hand, the Fourth District gave us some real relief in the case of *C.R. v. State*, 73 So. 3d 825 (Fla. 4DCA 2011), where the court held that a folding pocketknife with a blade less than **4 inches** was still a *"common pocketknife"* even though it had a belt clip, blade knob that made the blade easier to open, locking mechanism, and textured handle. All features which anyone who goes to a gun show, Lowe's, Wal-Mart, or Home Depot knows are extremely common features in most small folding knives today.

Another important thing to know is that it's not illegal to possess a *common pocketknife* in a **concealed** manner at a school, school grounds, school bus stop, or school bus. F.S.790.115(2), although **open carry** in a *rude, angry, careless, or threatening display* is still a felony. Thus, open carry of a *common pocketknife* in these school areas could be legally dangerous, as carry in the open position is more likely considered a "*weapon*" than a tool.

ELECTRIC , TASER & CHEMICAL WEAPONS:

Most **pepper sprays** have a maximum effective range of about ten feet. If the wind is blowing — make the proper adjustments, and make sure you aren't firing into a strong wind, or it may blow back on you. **Oleoresin Capsicum** (ie: OC) is the active ingredient, and is normally measured by it's pre-diluted strength in heat units. Most pepper sprays will have either the pre-diluted content measured in SHU's, or diluted OC content as "*Scoville Content*". The "hot" stuff is around 2,000,000 SHU's, which translates into 200,000 SC's. Make sure you buy something with at least 1.5 million SHU heat units — or it may be ineffective. Forget about percentages — because they don't tell you the SHU's of the concentrate it was taken from.

In 1997 and 2006 the Legislature amended some of the carrying restrictions concerning chemical and electronic weapons -- in favor of the ordinary citizen. You may now carry, for lawful self defense purposes, concealed or in the open, any "**self-defense chemical spray**". A "**self-defense chemical spray**" is a device carried solely for lawful self-defense, that is compact in size, is designed to be carried on or about a person, and contains no more than **two (2) ounces** of chemical.[6] "*Chemical*" does not refer to the propellant portion.

You may also carry openly or concealed, for lawful self-defense, any "**nonlethal electric weapon or device**", including a **stun gun**, and *Taser* type weapons (ie: "**dart firing stun guns**"). The necessity for having a CWL to carry a *Taser* ended in June 2006. (C. 2006-298). F.S. 790.001(15); 790.01; 790.053

Of course, you still can't have most of these weapons at schools, school buses, and school bus stops. I'll discuss these restrictions in Chapter Eight. It is also a felony to take them into any state prison, county jail, or juvenile detention facility. F.S. 944.47; F.S. 951.22; F.S. 985.4046 .[7] Technically, there doesn't appear to be any current criminal prohibition against taking either a *nonlethal stun gun* or *self defense chemical spray* into a city jail facility or state courthouse (except maybe if you have a CWL, are carrying a *nonlethal stun gun*, and you do so "*willfully*").[8] On the other hand I would ***strongly recommend*** you don't try it as there's <u>no way</u> you're getting in if they find out, it will likely get you arrested, and they'll probably close this loophole at some point, anyway.

There is an issue whether subsection (3) of <u>F.S.</u> 790.01 precludes a CWL holder from carrying these excepted weapons in a concealed manner in places prohibited by <u>F.S.</u> 790.06(12) – such as a bar, sporting event, etc., when carrying under 790.01 vs. 790.06. I've already gone over that earlier. As I said, my personal opinion is that it is not illegal as to *Tasers* and "*self defense chemical sprays*" as neither of those are listed in 790.06(1), and therefore they should not be regulated by <u>F.S.</u> 790.06. However, that is a "*test case*" area – as there is no case law on it at this time.[9]

QUESTION: Do you mean I can take a *non-lethal stun gun, dart firing stun gun, or self defense chemical spray* into a bar, concealed or in the open?

ANSWER: Yes, unless maybe if you have a CWL , as there is an open question whether a CWL holder is prohibited by <u>F.S.</u> 790.06(12)[10]. Still, even if you don't have the CWL I wouldn't recommend you "*open carry*" as it will probably upset the world. Moreover, the establishment can request that you get rid of it, and if you chose to ignore this request you have probably committed a misdemeanor ***trespass***,[11] and if it's another weapon that qualifies as a "***dangerous weapon***" or *firearm,* it becomes a felony. <u>F.S.</u> 810.08(2)(c).

One warning about these exciting exceptions to concealed and open carry laws — *knowing* and *willful* use of such weapons against a law enforcement officer engaged in the performance of his/her duties is a third degree felony. Moreover, unless the weapon is initially being carried for purposes of lawful self-defense — it's not covered under the statutory exception. Last, but not least, if you misuse the weapon for something other than lawful self-defense, you may still be prosecuted.

Before we get into the next section, let me add one point for general reference. Pepper spray, mace, tear gas, similar sprays, and most nonlethal electric weapons, including the Taser, are <u>not</u> generally considered "***dangerous***" weapons under Florida law, (but usually are under federal).[12] This is because they are designed to temporarily incapacitate an opponent, rather than cause any permanent harm. If they do, it would normally be unintended. Thus, the use of mace, tear gas, pepper spray, stun gun, etc., should not constitute the use of *"deadly force"*, although it would certainly constitute the use of *"non-deadly force"*.[13] This will suddenly become enlightening when you get to Chapter Twelve, which concerns your right to self-defense. Likewise, while unlikely – if their use is disproportionate to the harm involved – their use might constitute *"excessive force"*. A good example of *excessive force* would likely be repeated stuns from a stun gun, or repeated sprays of pepper spray – when a culprit had been subdued, suffered an obvious medical emergency, or was no longer a viable threat.

OPEN CARRYING OF WEAPONS OTHER THAN FIREARMS:

Florida does not generally prohibit the *open carrying* of weapons (other than firearms, and lethal or non-defensive electric weapons) although such is prohibited on a school bus, at a school bus stop, or within *1000 feet* of the real property that comprises a public or private elementary, middle, or secondary school, etc.[14] More on this in Chapter Eight. The crime of *"open carrying"* of weapons is covered in F.S. 790.053, and that section prohibits only firearms, and certain electric weapons from open carry. Moreover, 790.053(2) also specifies it is legal for a person to *"openly carry"* (for lawful self-defense) any *"self-defense chemical spray"*, and any *nonlethal stun gun* or other *non-lethal electric weapon*, including *Taser* type weapons. (ie: *"dart firing stun gun"*). A subsection also permits a CWL holder to briefly expose a firearm to another person as long as not done in a threatening, or angry manner. F.S. 790.053(1).

By *"openly carry"* I mean that the weapon is not concealed from ordinary view, and that anyone with moderate intelligence can see you have a weapon, if they bothered to take a look.[15]

Technically, this means you could carry a knife, machete, bow, cross-bow, sword, spear, nun-chuks, and almost anything else with you -- almost anywhere -- totally legal -- so long as they are not concealed. Amazing, huh?

QUESTION: You mean I can walk down the streets armed with a crossbow, or spear?

ANSWER: Yes, unless prohibited by local ordinance.[16] Although I don't suggest you try it with the more obvious of these weapons. Somehow, I don't think most people or police officers would appreciate you doing your personal impression of William Tell, or Attila the Hun -- no matter what the law says.

QUESTION: How about a Taser type weapon, or stun gun?

ANSWER: Sure, as long as it's designed to be nonlethal, and is for defensive purposes -- even a Taser type weapon now complies due to a change in the law in 2006. However, it's a felony to use them against law enforcement officers in the performance of their duties.

QUESTION: Any place I couldn't open carry a weapon, other than a firearm, for sure?

ANSWER: Yes, schools, school buses, school bus stops. Read Chapter Eight for the low-down. Also, you're not getting in the courthouse with one, open or concealed. The same applies to police stations, jails, prisons, and federal offices and facilities.

IMPROPER EXHIBITION OF FIREARMS & WEAPONS:

The crime of ***improper exhibition*** of a firearm or other weapon [F.S. 790.10] is a first degree misdemeanor in Florida. It occurs when any person carrying a knife, sword cane, firearm, electric weapon, or any other weapon exhibits it to others in a rude, careless, angry, or threatening manner -- unless in necessary self-defense.[17] This does not mean that all you're doing is carrying it. Self-defense is a very involved topic, and is covered in detail in its own chapter. Therefore, I suggest you try not to figure it out until you get there. However, the normal framework of this particular crime is that you can't go threatening, frightening, or endangering people with the display of a weapon. If you do -- you've got problems, and will probably need the services of an attorney. If you want to try a more detailed analysis of the statute, let's give it a go, because it really is terribly drafted, and my personal opinion is that it is *unconstitutionally vague*. F.S. 790.10 states:

> *"If any person having or carrying any dirk, sword, sword cane, firearm, electric weapon or device, or other weapon, shall, in the presence of one or more persons, exhibit the same in a rude, careless, angry, or threatening manner, not in necessary self defense"* the person shall be guilty of a misdemeanor of the first degree.

From reading this statute, which is not a model of clarity, we find that the elements of the crime are as follows:

1. The offender must have or carry a weapon,
2. The weapon is being exhibited,

3. The exhibition is being done in a rude, careless, angry or threatening manner,
4. The exhibition is not in necessary self defense
5. The exhibition is in the presence of one or more other persons

The big problems with the statute are:

A. What is meant by "***exhibited***"? Does that mean that an unintentional display, or displayed where the exhibitor was unaware others were watching? While I doubt it, still a very good question — without any current answer. I'll guess on the side of caution, and so should you.

B. What constitutes "*rude, careless, angry or threatening manner*"? Is that from the standpoint of any onlooker, no matter how unreasonable, or is it judged from what a "reasonable person" would judge? The only likely response to this issue is that the "***reasonable person***" standard must be used.

C. The next issue is what if the person with the weapon is angry or rude — but doesn't use the weapon to further his or her anger/rudeness/threat? The statute says the "*weapon*", not the person, must be exhibited in such a manner. That means some *purposeful or careless use* of the weapon should be a required element. Just being angry and having a weapon on you shouldn't be a violation. Otherwise, just going to the range to blow off a little steam, against something you're angry about would be a violation. Obviously, not an interpretation any court would likely allow.

D. Last issue — what the heck is "*in the presence*" of others? Is that ten feet, twenty feet, a hundred feet away? What if you don't even realize somebody else is watching you? Again, a real problem with clarity. My personal guess is that "***in the presence***" means the other person or persons are in *close enough proximity* that you should *reasonably know* they are there, and are close enough that if your exhibition somehow went amiss — there would be a *reasonable possibility* they could be injured. Is this the law? Darn if I know! The statute is so poorly written that nobody really knows. The only appellate case that ever discussed it was <u>M.C.M. v. State</u>, 754 So.2d 844 (Fla. 2DCA 2000), where the appellate court held that the careful transfer of a rifle from one car to another was not a violation of the statute, could not be considered "*careless*" even where certain onlookers were concerned it might cause an accident. Other than this single case, almost all other appellate decisions involve aggravated assaults, where the issue was whether *improper exhibition* was a lesser possible charge.

So, now that you realize the problems with the statute, you should also know that since the statute concerns a misdemeanor you can only be *"legally"* arrested if the police officer observes all the elements of the alleged violation occur in his presence. He can't legally arrest you on what somebody else said you did unless he has an arrest warrant. I say *"legally"*, because a number of police officers lack the training to realize the limits of their authority. Thus, you can get *"falsely arrested"* for almost anything. The remedy for this is a good lawyer, because if you resist a false arrest with any force – it's a crime *regardless* of the legality of the arrest. Only a charge of **"resisting without violence"** raises the defense that the arrest was unlawful.

In summary — you do have the right to openly display a firearm or other weapon on your own property or place of business, and if done in a careful (ie: not careless), or non-threatening manner — it is perfectly legal. If done in *"necessary self defense"* — it can be rude, angry, or whatever — but that is a separate self defense question, especially with the 2014 revisions to Chapter 776 of the statutes. On the other hand, totally innocent people are getting shot if a police officer thinks they might be going for a weapon to use against the officer. I think there are some serious training issues that law enforcement needs to address in these situations, but likewise, you must be aware that there are too many "crazy" people out there these days who don't think twice in using deadly force against law officers, and because of this it seems there is a tendency for law officers to overreact, rather than take a chance. With modern training to shoot until the "bad guy" drops – and weapons capable of firing multiple rounds in less than a second – you need to be very careful with your own legal weapon if you think a law enforcement officer is approaching, or is involved. You don't want to get shot over a stupid mistake – yours or his!

In 1994 the Legislature made *improper exhibition* a third degree felony when done on any school bus, school bus stop, or within **1000 feet** of the real property on which any school (excluded are nursery schools, colleges, and vocational schools) is located.[18] [F.S. 790.115] The law does not apply to *private property* within 1000 feet of a school, when the offender is there with permission.

There are also some other tricky quirks to this statute that are covered in Chapter Eight. I suggest you read that chapter so you fully understand it.

ISSUES WITH INTENTIONAL DISPLAY:

Last, but not least, there is no Florida case law on whether the mere *display* of a firearm in some type of defensive position (not pointed at anyone) is an *aggravated assault* or possible *"improper exhibition"*, although the case law makes it clear these situations are a *"question of fact"* normally appropriate for resolution by a jury.[19] Thus, except in a clear cut case you may face an arrest, and a decision by a prosecutor, judge, or jury as to what your intent was, whether a *reasonable person* might also have been in fear of *imminent death or great bodily harm*, whether your actions were meant as a *threat*, a *conditional threat*, *"being ready"*, or something more casual just in case things got worse, and last but not least – whether it was in *lawful self defense*?

Moreover, with the 2014 changes in *Chapter 776* of the statutes making *intentional display* only appropriate in responding to a *forcible felony*, or *imminent deadly force* situation (ie: *reasonable fear of imminent death or great bodily harm*) – *intentional display* for self defense, or defense of property, is usually not a legitimate option except in very limited circumstances! Since the difference between an *"aggravated assault"*, or a charge of *"improper exhibition"* is a felony with a *mandatory minimum* prison sentence versus a misdemeanor charge[20] – this becomes a very critical issue, and is why I advise *never* to display a firearm in a *road rage* situation (*"But officer, it was only pointed at the ceiling!"*) unless there's no other way to escape or terminate the situation, and you also *"reasonably"* and *"objectively"* believe any other alternative will wind-up with your getting killed, or in a hospital. More on that in the self-defense chapters.

DISCHARGING FIREARMS IN PUBLIC, OR ZONED FOR DWELLINGS:

It is a first degree misdemeanor to discharge a firearm in any public place, from the right-of-way on any paved public road, or knowingly across any road or occupied premises. However, this would not apply if you were acting in *lawful defense* of self or property, if you were performing official duties requiring the discharge of a firearm, or if the public place or road was expressly approved for hunting by the State. However, if you fire from a vehicle, and you know there's a person within **1000 feet** of you -- hunting or not -- it's a second degree felony. Moreover, if you're the owner or driver of a vehicle, and you direct somebody else to fire from the vehicle -- it's a third degree felony.[21] It is also a first degree misdemeanor to *negligently or recklessly* discharge a firearm on property used primarily as a dwelling, or zoned exclusively for residential use. F.S. 790.15

If you're wondering what all this means -- it means you can't fire a gun from inside, or on a vehicle unless in necessary self-defense. Likewise, if you have a *backyard range* – careless operation would be a crime.

DISCHARGING MACHINE GUNS:

First of all -- you can't have one without a special federal approval. Otherwise, you're looking at a possible ten year federal prison sentence, and a very hefty fine. But assuming you're otherwise legal -- I don't suggest you fire any automatic weapon[22] unless it's at a range. Firing it almost anywhere else with the intent to injure persons or property is a first degree felony punishable by life imprisonment -- whether you hit anything or not. You also cannot shoot one in any "public park" or "public place". F.S. 790.16. I assume you could shoot one at an actual shooting range located in a public park – but that's not what the statute says. An obvious oversight, but still a possible *test case*, as ridiculous as that sounds.

On the other hand, if you have the right to use deadly force -- your use of a machine gun is, with certain reservations, legal.[23] Again, it's not advised, especially as use of a firearm *in the commission* of certain felonies, where the firearm is capable of automatic or semi-automatic fire, and has a magazine capable of holding *twenty or more center fire rounds* requires very strict sentencing pursuant to F.S. 775.087. This requires a *mandatory minimum* sentence of fifteen years if unfired, and 20 years if discharged. Likewise, unloading a twenty round clip into a single perpetrator might catch more than a few raised eyebrows when a prosecutor is deciding whether or not to charge you.

MACHINE GUNS, UNDERSIZED FIREARMS, AND OTHER NFA WEAPONS:

Federal law prohibits the ownership or possession of certain weapons pursuant to the *National Firearms Act*, hence the term "*NFA*" weapons. These include destructive devices, firearms capable of firing more than one shot with a single pull of the trigger (ie: "*automatic*" firearms), shotguns and rifles that have been altered in certain ways usually to make them *shorter* than legal, anything that qualifies as a *silencer* or any of its parts, and certain exotic weapons. That's not a complete list, but it gives you a good idea.

Possession of any automatic firearm (*machine gun*); or a rifle with a barrel length of less than 16 inches (*short-barreled rifle*), or shotgun with a barrel length of less than 18 inches (*short-barreled shotgun*) is illegal under both State and Federal law, unless you have first obtained the tax stamp and transfer necessary under federal law.[24] Moreover, both rifles and shotguns must have an **overall length** of at least 26 inches, or the firearm is classified as *"any other weapon"* under the NFA. *"Any other weapon"* could also apply to other descriptions, as well. If you have a *folding stock*, length is measured from the tip of the barrel to the very end of the folding stock in its extended position, even if it can be fired without extension.[25] It is a second degree felony, as well as a federal crime to have such a firearm unless you are a federally licensed dealer with a Class III approval, or a private citizen, trust, or corporation which has been pre-approved by BATFE, and has already received the special NFA *tax stamp* on an approved Form 4, or if by bequest, via a Form 5.[26] When I talk about *"NFA"* weapons, I am speaking of those weapons regulated by the *National Firearms Act*, which falls under Internal Revenue Code jurisdiction, and can be found beginning at 26 USC 5801.

The most basic definition of a *machine gun* is under Florida law. In that sense, a machine gun is any firearm that shoots, or is designed to shoot more than one shot, automatically, by a single pull of the trigger.[27] If you're wondering why a "*Hell Fire*" equipped weapon is OK -- the "*Hell Fire*" causes multiple pulls of the trigger in extremely rapid succession -- thus although it mimics an automatic, it is "*semi-automatic*" because the trigger is being separately moved to accomplish the firing of each round. In essence, the mechanism allows the gun to "slam fire" in succession. Not so for the *Akins Accelerator* due to a change in BATFE rulings which only BATFE truly understands.

Federal law is a lot tougher on what constitutes a *machine gun* because the federal definition includes the *frames* or *receivers* of machine guns, any parts designed to **convert** a weapon into machine gun (usually the *auto sear*), and any "*combination of parts*" from which a *machine gun* can be assembled. Federal law also controls a number of other weapons and accessories under the *National Firearms Act*. If you're thinking about buying an "*auto sear*" – remember – it's considered a machine gun by itself! If it wasn't registered prior to 1986 – it's already *contraband*, and illegal to possess. There's a supposed exception as to AR-15 drop-in auto sears manufactured prior to November 1, 1981, per *ATF Ruling 81-4*. Assuming you have such an auto sear, and can prove it was manufactured prior to the 1981 date, the ruling says you may possess it without registering it, although you would still be subject to pre-registration and the tax stamp if you have the AR-15 firearm, or even the parts for the AR-15, together with the auto sear – otherwise you have committed a federal felony. On the other hand, some federal courts have made it clear that any transfer of an AR-15 *auto sear* still needs to be pre-registered and approved, although there would be no transfer tax collected by ATF. <u>United States v. Cash</u>, 149 F.3d 706 (7th Cir. 1998).[28] Therefore, I would strongly suggest that before you obtain and take possession of a pre-1981 AR-15 auto sear, you get the transfer pre-approved by BATFE. If you take possession before – you have committed a federal crime!

Some of the weapons and accessories that are a federal crime to possess under the *NFA* (unless you are a dealer or manufacturer of this type weapon or have obtained a *tax stamp* and approval after completing the *Form 4* application for transfer) include: **silencers** and parts intended to fabricate a silencer, undersized firearms, destructive devices, cane guns, pen guns, wallet guns, and any pistol that is fitted for or with a *shoulder stock* -- unless the barrel length is over 16 inches, or the weapon with stock has been placed on the "***curio and relic***" list by the Secretary of Treasury and is not a machine gun or destructive device.[29] Also made illegal are certain **revolving cylinder shotguns** that were ruled as "**non-sporting**" by the Secretary of Treasury. which will be covered later in this book under "***destructive devices***".

If you want to know how to **measure the length of your barrel** to see if it's legal -- place a metal rod in the gun with the action closed, and mark where the rod exits the barrel. Measure that distance, and you have the official barrel length. 27 CFR 479.11

"ANY OTHER WEAPON":

There are some areas of the law that are difficult to understand. One of these is the area under the *National Firearms Act* (ie: *NFA*) concerning firearms defined as "***any other weapon***" (ie: "*AOW*"). Under federal law, any such firearm must be registered prior to taking possession, or you have committed a felony.

> "*Any other weapon*" *means any weapon or device capable of being concealed on the person from which a shot can be discharged through the energy of an explosive . . . . Such term shall not include a pistol or revolver having a rifled bore. . . .*" 26 USC 5845 (e)

> *Pistol: A weapon having* "*(b) a short stock designed to be gripped by one hand and at an angle to and extending below the line of the bore(s).*" 27 CFR 478.11

PISTOL GRIP FIREARMS:

Those of you really into firearms, and *NFA* are probably wondering how a pistol grip shotgun can be non-*NFA*. In explaining, you will soon understand why *NFA* is so damn complicated, and non-intuitive. Hold on to your hats!

"*Any other weapon*" (ie: "*AOW*"), according to BATFE interpretations only pertains to weapons that are "*concealable*" on the person – and they say that normally means an overall length of *less than 26 inches*. Since the *Mossberg 500* pistol grip shotgun length is just over that, it does not fit into *AOW* category since it was originally manufactured with a pistol grip versus having a stock replaced or altered. If it had started with a stock – it would be a "*shotgun*", and *NFA* because once a "shotgun" – always a "shotgun", even if *NFA* – and a shotgun is always designed to be fired from the shoulder. So – the *Mossberg 500* having a pistol grip – is neither a "pistol" or a "shotgun", and according to BATFE is a "*pistol grip firearm*". <u>FFL Newsletter</u>, *March 2013, Volume 2.* If you want to see the letters from BATFE explaining this you can find them on the web. As for me – were it not for the letters and *Newsletter* – I'd have said it was an *AOW* because if you read the definition of *AOW* in the statute – the *Mossberg* appears to be a smoothbore pistol. Shows you how easy it is to screw this stuff up!

PEN GUNS & PISTOLS:

If you read these two sections together you see that any weapon capable of being concealed is an "*NFA*" "*any other weapon*", unless **excepted** from the definition. One of the exceptions is if the weapon constitutes a "*pistol*" with a *rifled bore*. A pistol, to be a "*pistol*" under federal law, must also have a *handle* ("short stock") set at an *angle to the barrel*, and *below the barrel*. Therefore, the law currently does not define a *pen gun* as an *NFA* weapon because the gun is hinged, and the hinged portion is designed to be bent away from the barrel before it can fire. Thus, the hinged portion becomes the "*handle*" which is set below, and at an angle to the barrel.

Sorry, if I confused you on this "*any other weapon*" stuff. This area is complicated. To make it simpler, if you have any weapon that discharges a shell by use of an explosive, the weapon can be concealed on your person, and that weapon does not have the normal configuration of a pistol or revolver -- it probably is "*any other weapon*" under federal law.

WALLET GUN:

Similarly, a *derringer* that can be fired from within a *concealing* holster becomes "*any other weapon*" only when placed in such a holster, and only if the *angled grip* extending from the barrel is no longer visible. Thus, some wallets designed for derringers are legal – and some – only when the gun is placed *inside* the holster – are not. Same thing with a gun rigged to be discharged from inside a briefcase. It doesn't have the configuration required so it becomes "*any other weapon*". Also, there's a single shot pistol built into the handle of a knife which

I've seen at some gun shows — which is currently legal because the handle is set at an angle slightly below the barrel. Even that slight angled grip to the barrel brought it within the definition of a pistol, according an ATF ruling. However, if the definition ever changes – it's *"any other weapon"*.

QUESTION: You mean if I have a derringer with a special wallet holster, I am illegal?

ANSWER: Maybe. Once you put the two together BATFE says you consider them as a "unit". If the unit has now lost the *"angled grip"* it needs to have to be a pistol, you now have *"any other weapon"*, and a potential ten year federal felony! 26 USC 5871

QUESTION: Isn't this a *"combination of parts"* like a machine gun?

ANSWER: It would if *"combination of parts"* included anything but *machine guns,* and *destructive devices*. *"Any other weapon"* does not use the *"combination of parts"* language used for machine guns and silencers.

QUESTION: Can I fit a *shoulder-stock* to a regular pistol?

ANSWER: Absolutely not! It is no longer a "regular pistol" once you do. It falls under another *NFA* definition, a *"short barreled rifle"*, as now it's a pistol designed to be fired from the shoulder, rather than by one hand. Another ten year federal *"NFA"* felony, unless it's exempted on the *curio and relic list* by the Secretary. Same problem when you add a *fore grip* to a pistol – since now it's configured to *fire from the shoulder*, or two hands – and becomes *"any other weapon"* while so assembled.

QUESTION: What if I cut-down my shotgun, and I'm a sixteenth of an inch too short?

ANSWER: Federal crime, and possible jail sentence. Mistakes are just your tough luck, and a possible reason to ask the judge for a more lenient sentence. On the other hand, you may have a shot at a defense that it was not *"knowingly"* or *"willfully"* done. Get a good lawyer – you'll need one!

QUESTION: Can I transport my legal machine gun in Florida just like any other firearm?

ANSWER: Yes, per F.S. 790.25. However, it is an open question whether it is covered for concealed carry per F.S. 790.01(3) if you have a CWL. I think it is – but like I said – possible *test case*. Still, it could be transported *securely encased* per 790.25(5), and maybe even in the open under that section since it isn't a "hand gun". All the same – I'd go for *"securely encased"* to be safe.

QUESTION: What else do I watch out for?

ANSWER: Well, anything unusual should be questioned, and anything too exotic looking might be something to stay away from unless you're really knowledgeable. It's just a really complicated area that is easy to screw up on.

QUESTION: I've heard it's legal to manufacture a *machine gun*. What are the procedures I must follow?

ANSWER: For a start, pack your bags, and kiss your family goodbye for ten years while you're in federal prison. It is totally illegal to manufacture a machine gun unless you are a licensed Class III manufacturer making an approved firearm for the military or law enforcement. Only machine guns legally registered prior to **May 19, 1986**, may be possessed by ordinary citizens, and that's only after receiving formal BATFE pre-approval. [30] The case law that said otherwise was vacated in *United States v. Stewart,* 125 S.Ct. 2899. Because of this, on June 30, 2006, the 9th Circuit reversed its decision in the *Stewart* case, and held that a private citizen who manufactures an *NFA* firearm without prior ATF approval commits a felony. Since BATFE will never allow this, the question is closed forever! [31]

SILENCERS:

Silencers are regulated by the *NFA*, require a tax stamp and pre-approval, and include the *tubes* and the *wipes*. You can't have any of the parts before you have the approval from BATFE. If you get the tube ahead of time it becomes **contraband** (assuming it isn't already), and you've committed a felony even if you get the approval later on. Once contraband – always contraband. Good show! Same thing with the **baffles** (ie: *"wipes"*). You can't have them, even for repairs, because only an *NFA* approved manufacturer can legally have them separate from the entire silencer. Also – don't put a motorcycle muffler on your firearm, or even cut a silencer-like part off the barrel of an air rifle! If you do – it becomes a *"silencer"* under federal law!

If you see any of these great deals on the internet where you can import tubes or wipes from Germany or Sweden for a great price – don't! First of all, you'd need the BATFE pre-approval before you could even ship the stuff. Second of all, it's illegal to import them. Third of all, there are numerous regulations to comply with before you can import any military type item, so you've probably added another felony by importing without the proper documents, and approvals.

CHART ON LEGAL GUN & BARREL LENGTH:

Legal rifle length		Legal shotgun length	
barrel	overall	barrel	overall
16"	26"	18"	26"

USING A FIREARM WHILE UNDER THE INFLUENCE:

If you're under the influence of alcohol, or any other harmful or illegal chemical substance, to the extent your ***normal faculties are impaired***, it is unlawful to have a **loaded** firearm **in hand**, or to fire it. If you do, it's a second degree misdemeanor, unless you're acting in lawful self-defense, or defense of your property. F.S. 790.151. It will also cause the loss of your CWL, if you have one. Of course, if the firearm doesn't have ammunition in it — you're still legal — but definitely stupid.

"Normal faculties" doesn't mean you're "drunk". Normal faculties is a lesser standard normally associated with *DUI*, and means that your coordination, ability to see, speak, judge distances, perform ordinary tasks, or make decisions is affected to an extent that these functions are noticeably interfered with. If you have a "buzz", you are certainly under the influence, and maybe drunk, as well. If you need to try harder to concentrate -- same thing. If you've just had a couple, and it has relaxed you, but nothing more -- you're likely not under the influence in the legal sense, because although all alcohol has had some effect -- it hasn't yet affected your *"normal faculties"*.

If a law enforcement officer has probable cause to believe you were using a firearm while under the influence, he can require you to take a breath test for alcohol, and a urine test for drugs. If you caused death or serious injury to anyone -- he may take blood, and take it by force if you refuse.

A blood alcohol reading of .10 percent or greater is evidence of being under the influence of alcohol to the extent your *normal faculties* are impaired. Less than .05 percent means you're presumed to be fine. Anywhere in between means "it depends". Although the DUI standard has changed to .08 percent as the presumed level of intoxication since January 1, 1994 -- a .10 will still apply for this firearms offense.[32]

Personally, I don't think you should be walking around with a loaded firearm if you are anything other than stone cold sober, unless somebody or something is coming at you. Otherwise, it's too damn risky.[33]   On the other hand, the statute is more than fair, and does not penalize carry — only actual use, or **in-hand** possession.

SHOOTING AT VEHICLES, VESSELS & STRUCTURES:

The deliberate or reckless shooting, or throwing of any projectile or other hard object which could produce *great bodily harm,* at or into any building, whether **occupied or not**, or at any boat, train, aircraft, bus, or any other vehicle which is occupied or being used by any person -- is a second degree felony if done *wantonly* or *maliciously*. F.S. 790.19. "*Wantonly*" means consciously and intentionally, with reckless indifference to consequences and with the knowledge that damage is likely to be done to some person. "*Maliciously*" means wrongfully, intentionally, without legal justification or excuse, and with the knowledge that injury or damage will or may be caused to another person. *Shelden v. State*, 38 So.3d 214 (Fla. 2DCA 2010).

This is the statute that juveniles are usually charged with when they throw rocks from bridges, and overpasses – -- and miss. If they hit anybody, add ***aggravated battery*** and possibly *homicide* to the list. Anything that can produce serious injury qualifies. A rock, piece of debris, shooting with a firearm or bow, etc. Very dangerous stuff -- especially if the vehicle is moving, as it adds velocity to the impact.

In *Juarez v. State,* 892 So.2d 1158 (Fla. 5DCA 2005), a woman threw a concrete irrigation donut into an unoccupied garage which she knew was unoccupied. In what can only be described as a terrible decision, the appellate court affirmed her conviction because the house to which the garage was attached was occupied. How this *"could produce great bodily harm"* under the facts is a complete mystery to all, but she was still convicted of a very serious felony charge. Be warned!

SELF-PROPELLED KNIVES:

It is a first degree misdemeanor to manufacture, sell, or possess any *"spring knife"*, *"ballistic knife"* or *"self-propelled"* knife -- which are three names for the same thing: a device that propels a knifelike blade, generally by use of a coiled spring, compressed gas, or elastic. F.S. 790.225. Bows, cross-bows, and spear guns are excluded from this definition if they discharge a bolt, dart, or arrow. Federal law defines these knives as a *"ballistic knife"*, and it is a ten year felony to knowingly possess, manufacture, sell, or import such a knife. [15 USC 1245] The definition has been around for a long time, and has nothing to do with a *switchblade* or *automatic knife*.

POSSESSION BY CONVICTED FELON:

Under Florida law any person convicted of a felony in this, or any other state, or of a crime that would be considered a felony in Florida[34], or a federal felony, is considered a *"convicted felon"*, and such a person cannot possess, own, or have in his/her care or custody any firearm, ammunition, or electric weapon, without first having his right to own and possess such being restored by *executive clemency*. A convicted felon is also forbidden from carrying **concealed**, any *"weapon"*, including chemical sprays. Violation is a second degree felony, with 3 year mandatory sentence,[35] 10 years if you had a prior armed violent felony , and a first degree felony with a *mandatory minimum* 15 year sentence (F.S. 790.23 & F.S. 790.235) if you qualify as a *"violent career criminal"*. Even juveniles may qualify as violent career criminals, and are subject to the mandatory sentence if prosecuted in *adult court* rather than juvenile court.

Juveniles who do not qualify as *"violent career criminals"* under F.S. 790.235, get a break when they become an adult. Any *"convicted felon"* status disability expires, unless the prior conviction was in adult court vs. juvenile court.[36] However, their prior juvenile adjudications can still be counted to later qualify them for *"violent career criminal"* status if they don't clean-up their act. Moreover, any juvenile conviction or even a *"withheld adjudication"* on a charge that would have been a felony if prosecuted in adult court prohibits that person from owning, possessing, or carrying these items in exactly the same way as it prohibits a convicted felon – until the juvenile offender reaches the age of **24 years**. At that time, if they have no other legal disability, the prohibition on firearms and weapons disappears. F.S. 790.23(1)(d).

I seem to get at least a dozen emails every year from folks who live with convicted felons wondering if they (the non-felon) can own and possess firearms. The answer is you can – and can't get in trouble over it – however, the **convicted felon** might. This is where the *convicted felon* has access and ability to obtain the firearm or ammunition. This concept is known as "***constructive possession***", and is a factual question normally left to a jury.

If you want a safe way of keeping firearms and ammo so your "*convicted felon*" partner doesn't get in trouble – I can't give you one. There is always the element of factual truth involved.   However, if you keep your firearms and ammo in a safe that only you have the combination to, the safe is one that normally is secure, it is in a room the felon does not go into, and there are no fingerprints on the firearms or ammo or room interior that are his or hers – your friend is "*probably*" OK. "Probably" is the best I can do. In such a situation it is likely best to get an order from the court defining where keeping of the firearm and ammo will not violate any probation, or such, since **you** have a *Second Amendment* right to keep firearms, independent of your friend or spouses restrictions.   However, if the *convicted felon* ever gets to it – even in an emergency – you can likely bet on a felony prosecution against him or her.

On the other hand, say you are being placed on probation, or are about to receive a felony conviction. What do you do with your firearms and weapons? You can't own or possess them on probation. With a felony conviction – you then become a *prohibited person,* and certainly can't own or possess them. What do you do?

The answer is that you must sell or *transfer ownership* to someone before your status changes! Give them as gifts. Sell them to a gun store. Sell them to someone else. Or, go see a lawyer and have them placed in a "***non-revocable trust***" until such time as your probation ends. A *trustee* will have to be appointed who holds the firearms for you, and the trust can be made to end when your probation ends – assuming you are not a prohibited person at that point. It will need a federal tax i/d number! During the term of the trust you cannot have **any** control over the firearms, whatsoever. Either it's real – or it's a fraud. If it's a fraud – it's "***constructive possession***", because the law says if you maintain the "ability" to control the firearms – even if you don't – you still legally "*possess*" them. So – see a lawyer if you decide to go this route, otherwise you're in for real trouble. And, whatever you do – don't have the firearms you use to own in the same home or business you're living or working in! That is the classic where the feds will come after you!

AMMUNITION & PROHIBITED PERSONS:

Federal law on *convicted felons*, like Florida law, forbids a convicted felon, as well as other *"prohibited persons"* from possession or ownership of *ammunition*. Since ammunition includes any *component* (ie: a single dummy shell would do, or even an *empty casing*) — it can be a real trap for the unwary. Moreover, the feds are very pro-active on prosecuting felons in possession, and other prohibited persons.

QUESTION: My boyfriend, and I live together. He is a convicted felon, and wants a gun in the house. Can I buy it for him, if I keep it.

ANSWER: No. If you're buying it "for him", it's a second degree felony for him to have it, and you're violating State and Federal law by making a *"straw purchase"*. Very serious stuff.

QUESTION: How about if I really just want it for me, and not for him.

ANSWER: As I previously described: First, he should not have access to the firearm. You should keep it on your person, and when not on your person, it should be kept locked in a safe or strong box that he does not have either the key, or combination to. This is technically legal, but very risky as the feds really like to prosecute this type of case. Remember, even if it's yours -- your convicted felon live-in could still be charged with "*constructive possession*". That means that he has knowledge of where the firearm is located, and has the ability to control it, as well. This is a factual issue for the jury, and in my opinion is not worth the risk. Also, don't leave any ammunition lying around -- as this is just as serious for a felon to possess as a firearm, and the feds will prosecute it if given the chance. *Ammunition* includes *any part* of a cartridge, even if empty, and even if it's on one of those cool key chains!

QUESTION: How about an *antique firearm*?

ANSWER: An *"antique firearm"* is not considered a firearm by either Florida or the feds unless used in the commission of a crime, therefore it is legal for a convicted felon to have such a weapon (when not on probation/parole) so long as it is **not concealed**. F.S. 790.001(6). However, make sure you've read the section in the book on what constitutes an *"antique firearm"*, and understand its definition is in flux due to two appellate districts not agreeing. It is something the Florida Supreme Court will be resolving in the future.

Federal law is very different, and well established, but since we're talking about Florida – Florida law controls. Thus, most *modern muzzleloaders* are currently unsafe, and even if you have plastic grips, or a modern sight added to a fairly accurate replica – until the Bostic case is settled, the area is somewhat uncertain. Of course, the Legislature could easily cure it by adopting the federal definitions, which was the intent of the original Florida statute, anyway.

QUESTION: What if I received a felony conviction in another country?

ANSWER: Both Florida and Federal law require the conviction occurs within the United States or its possessions to be recognized. *Small v. United States*, 125 S.Ct. 1752 (2005).

FIREARMS INVOLVED IN THE COMMISSION OF A FELONY:

The mere carrying of a firearm during the commission of a felony, is a separate felony of the third degree under Florida law. F.S. 790.07 That means that nobody even needs to see it -- only that you have it. If you display it, use it, or threaten its use -- it's a second degree felony. F.S. 790.07 Moreover, whatever felony you were involved with is generally increased one degree, and certain felonies, including most defined as a *"forcible felony"* receive at least a *"mandatory minimum"* sentence of three (3) years -- which means that the judge must impose that sentence, as the absolute minimum of prison time, even if he doesn't want to. F.S. 775.087 You will see how this has a very "chilling" effect on your right to self-defense later when we discuss *aggravated assault*. And, if you committed the crime while being armed with a semi-automatic with a *high capacity magazine*, which is a *box magazine capable of holding more than 20 centerfire cartridges*, or if you were armed with a *machine gun* -- make it an fifteen (15) year mandatory minimum.[37]

USE OF BULLET PROOF VESTS:

Any person who, while possessing a firearm, commits or attempts to commit a murder, sexual battery, robbery, burglary, kidnaping, arson, aggravated battery, aggravated assault, escape, or aircraft piracy -- and has the nerve to wear a bulletproof vest in furtherance of the crime -- is guilty of a third degree felony. F.S. 775.0846. It is also a federal felony for any *convicted felon* to purchase or possess body armor. 18 USC 931. The federal statute has a limited exception when such is certified by an employer as being necessary for work purposes, and it is only used for work purposes.

ARMOR PIERCING OR SPECIALITY AMMUNITION:

F.S. 790.31 governs the "Florida version" of what is, and what is not allowed in most ammunition for firearms. Under the Florida statute an "***armor-piercing bullet***" is one with an inner core of steel or other metal of equivalent hardness (not lead), and a ***truncated cone*** (ie: a cut-off tip) which is designed for use in a **handgun** as an armor or metal piercing bullet. If it isn't designed for a handgun — it doesn't meet the definition.

Other Florida "no-no's" under F.S. 790.31 include the following list of exotics:

a.   "**Exploding bullet**" — is one that is designed to detonate by use of an explosive or deflagrant (ie: burning agent) contained or attached to the bullet, and can be fired from any firearm.

b.   "**Dragon's breath shotgun shell**" which is one that is solely designed to spew a flame or fireball (not a tracer — but simulates a flamethrower), and contains exothermic pyrophoric misch metal as the projectile. Please be aware – *Tracer ammo* is not generally illegal. Just be careful where you use it so you don't start a forest fire.

c.   "**Bolo shell**" which is any shell that expels two or more metal balls connected by a solid metal wire, and can be fired **in** a firearm.

d.   "**Flechette shell**" means any shell with two or more pieces of fin-stabilized metal wires or solid dart-type projectiles, that can be fired **in** a firearm.

Under the Florida statute it is a third degree felony to sell, offer for sale, or deliver any of these five types of ammunition. Also, if you merely possess armor piercing ammo when it is ***loaded*** into a handgun, you are also guilty of a third degree felony. Same thing for the other four types of exotics — except they can't be loaded into **any** type firearm, not just a handgun. If you possess any with the intent to use it in the commission of a crime, loaded or not, it's a second degree felony — 15 years! Of course, the statute excepts law enforcement use, and sale to law enforcement agencies.

Federal law is a bit different because it only covers ***armor piercing ammunition***, and in that instance, doesn't cover purchase, possession, use, or sale by **private** individuals — unless used in the commission of a crime.[38] In that situation, it's a five year mandatory prison sentence on top of the crime committed. On the other hand, federal licensees (legal gun dealers or "FFL") are strictly controlled on what they can sell, and cannot sell armor piercing ammo to civilians. To find out how the definitions work in federal land — here we go:

    a.   "**Armor piercing**" is any projectile or its core which <u>may be used in a handgun</u> which is made entirely of steel, iron, brass, bronze, beryllium copper, depleted uranium, or a combination of tungsten alloys, or

            A full jacketed projectile larger than .22 caliber which is <u>designed and intended </u>for use in a handgun, and whose jacket weighs more than 25% of the total weight of the projectile.

            Excluded from the definition of ***armor piercing*** are shotgun shot required by game regulations for hunting, ***frangible projectiles*** designed for target shooting (ie: breaks up upon hitting target), and projectiles which are determined by BATF to be used for ***sporting purposes***, or industrial purposes.

If you noticed, **lead** is not one of the prohibited metals under Florida or Federal law. Also, you need not worry about federal law unless you are an *FFL*, or intend to use the ammunition in the commission of a felony.

QUESTION: I have some old ***7:62 x 39*** steel core ammo for my ***SKS***. I heard it was illegal to shoot it?

ANSWER: Nope. It's fine unless loaded into a handgun. However, a dealer couldn't sell it to you.

QUESTION: I've got some handgun ammo that is supposed to "explode" like a shotgun shell when it hits someone. Isn't that an illegal exploding bullet?

ANSWER: Nope. An *"**exploding bullet**"* must actually have some chemical or such to make it explode or incinerate upon contact. The type of round your talking about is quite common, and works purely from the force of impact. Normally, you're talking about something like *"**safety shot**"* which contains a number of small pellets that <u>disburse</u> upon impact. Other bullets may be designed to fragment upon impact, with the idea of creating a greater wound channel — thus stopping the assailant before he stops you.

QUESTION: Why call it "safety shot"?

ANSWER: Since these rounds fragment, or disburse -- they lose momentum quicker, and therefore won't generally penetrate walls if you miss. Thus, you don't hit something or someone you didn't intend to. Lots of pros and cons — buy a book on ammunition.

ALTERED OR REMOVED SERIAL NUMBERS:

It is a state and federal felony to **knowingly** remove or alter a serial number on any firearm, or otherwise attempt to disguise it's identification. <u>F.S. 790.27 & 18 USC 922(k)</u>. It is also a felony to **knowingly** possess, sell, or deliver such a firearm, and if you find a firearm with the serial numbers missing, or partially or completely filed, you should call your local police department, and turn it in. First, because it's a crime to have it, and it's considered *"**contraband**"*. Second, because you are on notice that the gun is probably stolen -- and it's also a state and federal felony to possess or sell a stolen firearm. <u>F.S. 790.27</u>

Assuming the firearm was stolen from you, and was recovered but somebody tried rubbing off the serial numbers – you have a possibly remedy by getting in touch with your local BATFE office, and asking the *agent-in-charge* if BATFE will permit the serial number to be re-engraved. If they allow it – and you'll get a letter stating that – fine. Otherwise, the firearm will likely be surrendered by the police agency that recovered it to BATFE. It shouldn't be returned to you unless BATFE has OK'd the re-engraving ahead of time. Of course, if the firearm never had a serial number – which is not uncommon with some older firearms, and homemade guns – it is normally not a crime to possess them as the serial number was never "obliterated" or "altered". And "no" – even an underground WWII curio where the French resistance filed off the serial numbers – is *contraband*. Stupid – but the law. You'd first need a written waiver from BATFE to take possession, and your chances are the same as that snowball you saw during your last visit to you-know-where.

DESTRUCTIVE DEVICES:

A "***destructive device***" under Florida law encompasses both the state and federal definitions.[39] These are many. In its most basic definition it is any bomb, grenade, mine, rocket, missile, or similar device that contains an explosive, incendiary, or poison gas which is designed or constructed to explode, and is capable of causing bodily harm or property damage. It also includes any breakable container filled with an explosive, incendiary, explosive or expanding gas designed or constructed to explode due to its content, and capable of causing bodily harm or property damage. This is usually a "***Molotov cocktail***".

It also includes any weapon with a ***barrel diameter over one half inch*** capable of expelling a projectile by means of an explosive -- other than a ***legal sized shotgun***[40], *line-throwing device* (rescue), or a *signaling device* such as a "*flare gun*". Ammunition for destructive devices are included in the definition of a "*destructive device*". A 1994 treasury ruling outlawed three shotguns, the *Striker, USAS-12, and Streetsweeper* -- unless they are registered under the *National Firearms Act*, just like a machine gun. The reason is that the federal definition of ***destructive device*** includes any "weapon" that expels a projectile by means of an explosive having a barrel bore of more than one half inch, *except a shotgun or shotgun shell the Secretary of Treasury finds is generally recognized as particularly "suitable for sporting purposes"*. The Secretary found that these particular guns had no legitimate sporting purpose, and were really riot and combat weapons.

I also note that the federal statute makes the definition of ***destructive device*** a bit clearer than the Florida statute. That's because:

> "The term 'destructive device' shall not include any device which is neither designed or redesigned for use as a weapon; any device, although originally designed for use as a weapon, which is redesigned for use as a signaling, pyrotechnic, line throwing, safety, or similar device . . . or any other device which the Secretary finds is not likely to be used as a weapon, or is an antique . . . ."

Thus, you now can understand why a ***potato cannon*** is not normally a destructive device. Why? Because it is not something "***designed***" as a "***weapon***". Of course, under the Florida definition — if you use it as a *weapon* — it becomes a *destructive device* under Florida law.

FLARE GUNS:

Now, you know a ***flare gun*** is not an *NFA* weapon because it is not "*designed*" as a weapon, nor is the flare itself used as a *destructive device* because it's a *signaling device*. But, what happens if you purchase or build an insert that will accept a shotgun shell, or even try using a shotgun shell? You guessed it – you've just created a *"destructive device"*.

Why?

Because it is now a weapon designed to be fired with one hand (ie: a *"pistol"*) that does not have a *rifled barrel*, and may also have an inside *bore greater than one half inch*. But, BATFE has also considered and approved inserts for a .22 caliber *rifled* barrel. And, as you can guess – the reason these are legal is that the weapon now meets all the requirements of a *"pistol"*, and obviously has a bore less than one half inch. However, if the insert were not *"rifled"* – NFA! Also – when the insert exceeds .22 caliber – they have a tendency to explode in your hand as a flare gun is normally not designed for that type of pressure.

SWITCHBLADE KNIFE & SPRING ASSISTED KNIVES:
It is not illegal to possess a ***switchblade*** or *"**automatic knife**"* in Florida. It was for a couple of years when one of our appellate courts royally screwed up the definition by confusing it with a *"spring knife"* (ie: *"ballistic knife"*)[41], however, the Legislature corrected this mistake in 2003 in F.S. 790.225(2)(a), by clarifying what had been obvious to anyone familiar with knives or the federal statute, that a *"**spring knife**"* did not include *"any device from which a knifelike blade opens, where such blade remains physically integrated with the device when open"*. A recent federal law also excluded certain *"automatic knives"* from the definition of *"switchblades"* and thereby created a **new category** of automatic knives labeled as *"**spring assisted knives**"*. These knives contain a spring, detent, or other mechanism designed to create a *"bias toward closure"* of the blade, and that requires exertion applied to the blade by hand, wrist, or arm to overcome the bias toward closure to assist in opening the knife. 15 USC 1244(5). Because of the removal of federal restrictions these have become the most common, and most popular small knives being sold, and can be purchased anywhere from Wal-Mart to Home Depot.

You should know that it is a federal felony for anyone to sell, transport interstate, or distribute a *"**switchblade**"* knife, unless they were manufactured in the state of sale, or were manufactured and possessed for the U.S. Armed Forces under contract. Furthermore, it is a federal felony for an individual to transport them into another state, possess them on any federal waters outside of a state's jurisdiction, or on Indian land. The only exceptions to these prohibitions are if the person in possession has only one arm, and the blade is **three inches** or less, or the person is a member of the armed forces in the performance of duty. So, keep them off your person if you go gambling on the *Seminole reservation*, on an ocean voyage, or if you travel state-to-state. Otherwise, it's a five year federal felony! 15 USC 1241-1245.

Likewise, try to remember you need a CWL to carry these anywhere off your property or business. The same thing is true for a "***spring assisted knife***" because until a Florida appellate court catches up with the times – lots of folks who are not familiar with knives, do not consider these as a "*common pocketknife*". Thus, for now, the only safe way to possess these off your home or business premises is with a CWL.

However, to clarify – it is not illegal under federal law or Florida law to own a switchblade knife manufactured out-of-state, and acquired in Florida. On the other hand, under federal law, it is illegal to bring them into the State, or transport out of the State. It would also be illegal to sell or give someone such a knife **if** it were manufactured out of state. And yes – it's a really stupid law!

Just as an aside, you might like to know that switchblades were extensively used as a utility knife by women in the 1800's, and early 1900's -- because their long fingernails would break when opening ordinary pocket knives. They also served as a "*safety*" knife, as they could be opened with one hand. Thus, if one hand was trapped, or pinned -- the knife could still be opened to help cut you loose. Even today, automatic knifes are in extensive use with EMS personnel and police due to this important ability.

ASSAULT WEAPONS:
After a bitter fight, Congress incorporated the Assault Weapons Ban into the 1994 Crime Bill. 18 USC 922(v) & (w). This totally unnecessary piece of legislation finally ended on September 13, 2004. Firearms and magazines that were manufactured or imported during the ban that have the stamp "***RESTRICTED LAW ENFORCEMENT/GOVERNMENT USE ONLY***"; or "***FOR EXPORT ONLY***" are now legal to purchase, as are any other firearms that the ban previously labeled as an "***assault weapon***" or "***large capacity magazine***".

Why did we need the ban?

No reason whatsoever – it was just "pure politics". The firearms were randomly selected based on cosmetic features – and even the FBI admitted they didn't pose a problem based on statistical crime records.

So, you ask: "Why would anybody need such a firearm?"

Aside from looking really cool, being the primary firearm the *Second Amendment* would recognize over others, being the most popular non-hunting sport shooting longgun of today, and being just about the most fun firearm around to shoot – I don't know. Why do some people have cars with big engines? Why do people buy new clothes when the old ones are still good? Why own a big screen TV? Get the idea? And, by the way – in the industry, these rifles are known as "***modern sporting rifles***", and as of the writing of this chapter, **8.5 million** of them are owned by citizens of this Great Country according to the *National Sports Shooting Association*.

USE OF BANGSTICKS:

The use of a ***bangstick*** or ***powerhead*** for self-protection in the salt water areas within State jurisdiction is generally permitted, although the taking of any marine life thereby is strictly prohibited.[42] In other words, unless one of our finny friends has definite plans on having you for lunch, don't use it. Moreover, you should make sure that the *powerhead* is permanently attached to a shaft with an overall length of not less than **four feet**, so you don't fall within the definition of "*any other weapon*" under federal law -- which, as we just discussed a few sections ago, is very illegal.[43] If you're asking why it's not **26 inches** – I don't have a clue other than the *Revenue Ruling* is really old, and maybe BATFE would have a different answer today?

Use of powerheads within National and State Parks is another matter, and will not generally be permitted.

QUESTION: How could a *bangstick* become "*any other weapon*" under the *NFA*?

ANSWER: Well, it's only real purpose is a "*weapon*" — against sharks. If it can be concealed on the person it then qualifies as "*any other weapon*" since it's not otherwise excepted. The Revenue Ruling in the last endnote said if it's **four foot long** with a permanent shaft — it's fine because it really can't be concealed at that length. So, if you want to play it safe — do it the way they tell you.

ARMED TRESPASS:

Trespassing on the property of another while in possession of a firearm, loaded or not --is a third degree felony under F.S. 810.09. Basically, a ***trespass*** occurs if you deliberately go uninvited onto enclosed or posted lands; if you enter or remain in a structure or conveyance without having any express or implied invitation to do so; or if having been ***warned*** to leave, you refuse to do so, or decide to argue the point.[44] It is also an ***armed trespass*** if, while hunting, your shot, bolt, or arrow crosses private land without the permission of the owner.

While I have found no Florida cases on the subject, there are many instances in which you go into a store, or shopping center -- and they have a sign posted saying "***No Firearms Permitted***". The next question you must face is whether you commit a trespass by going in the store. If so, then you've also committed an "*armed trespass*", which is a third degree felony.

My personal opinion is that your going into such a store or shopping mall is ***not a trespass*** just because they post a sign saying "***No Firearms***" because you are still an "*invitee*", and they still want your business -- just without the weapon. It would be like posting a sign "*No red underwear allowed*". Again, that's a personal interpretation. A court could call me wrong, and if you want to play it safe — obey the sign. This is possible "*test case*" time, again. On the other hand, most of the other states covered in this book would agree with my interpretation.

Of course, if you do follow my interpretation, and they asked you to leave, and you refused, or started to argue with them -- that would be another story, and you'd be in serious trouble because they've now made it clear they want you off the property, and the law says you have only a ***reasonable time*** to leave -- not to argue or have a debate with them. Likewise, if they had a guard posted at the mall entrance, and asked you if you were armed -- and you lied -- again, I think you have a problem. But, in essence, they really are only posting these things to protect themselves from a liability standpoint in case something happens. That way, you get sued -- they don't!

Since the offense of *trespass* by an invitee would first require a *warning*, <u>and</u> a refusal to depart my opinion is that you can't legally "***refuse***" until someone asks you to leave. Then, it's time to swallow your pride, and exit very quickly, and very politely. If the wife, and kids are somewhere else in the mall -- ask security if you can locate them before you leave, or, if not -- ask if they'll make an announcement. Don't push your luck if they're reluctant or refuse. You have no legal right to argue with them. Just get the hell out of there, pronto! If the wife or kids will be confused -- try bribing some honest-looking passerby outside the mall to notify them. All this is a lot better than an arrest, and a third degree felony on your record!

LICENSED PRIVATE SECURITY GUARDS:
Chapter 493, Florida Statutes, governs the use of firearms by private investigative, security, and repossession services. The regulations pertaining to this Chapter would take a separate book, so I'll be brief. First, you cannot carry a firearm or weapon as part of your duties without a **"G" license**. If you do, and get caught -- you'll probably lose your license for at least five years. You'll also be committing a first degree misdemeanor.[45]

Security personnel with a CWL may be able to legally carry a firearm without committing a crime in their private lives, but professionally, unless they have also have a **"G" license**, are *required* to carry a firearm as part of their duties, and are doing so *in connection* with their duties -- they will be in serious trouble with the Licensing Division of the Department of Agriculture, will be committing a misdemeanor, and will be a walking civil liability case, if anything happens. This is because there are very stringent training requirements to obtain and maintain a "G" license, and those who don't meet these requirements are deemed to be "*unqualified*" to carry a weapon while on duty.

PERMITTED FIREARMS FOR G LICENSEE:
The type of firearm which can be carried when required for, and in connection with your duties is set forth in F.S. 493.6115(6), and includes .38 and .357 caliber revolvers, and 9mm and .380 caliber semi-autos. You must be pre-qualified for the firearms carried. Do not load .357 ammo! Use factory ammo only. A *waiver* may be obtained from the Department for non-listed firearms.

Holstered and non-concealed carry is required except for Class "C"; "CC" and "D", who may carry *concealed* if they are at least 21 years of age, and hold the "G" license, although the "D" licensee must also be on temporary special assignment where the client requires this type of service. F.S. 493.6305

PROHIBITED AMMO FOR SECURITY GUARDS:
a.   Glasser, Mag-Safe, etc. pre-fragmented type bullets
b.   exploding bullets
c.   full metal jacket
d.   teflon coated (KTW) or other armor-piercing
e.   full wadcutters & reloads (except for range use)
f.   .357 — (use .38 instead)

DECLARED EMERGENCIES:
There are two entirely separate sections in the statutes concerning firearms possession during *hurricanes* and other *emergencies*. The first covers

the power of the Governor, and is found in F.S. 14.021 and F.S. 252.36. In these situations the Governor issues a "*proclamation*" as to what the emergency is, and what measures he's authorized to deal with it. Each proclamation is individual in its scope, and must be read to determine what is prohibited or restricted. The statute limits his power in that firearms that are lawfully possessed may not be seized unless the person is engaged in the commission of a crime. Similar in operation are "***declared emergencies***" by local authorities under F.S. 870.044. That statute is directed more to situations involving public rioting, or such when there is:

> *"reason to believe that there exists a clear and present danger of a riot or other general public disorder, widespread disobedience of the law, and substantial injury to persons or to property."*

In those instances the sheriff, chief of police, or mayor may declare a "***state of emergency***", and take such measures as are necessary to protect the public welfare. When such is declared the statute automatically prohibits the sale or offer to sell any firearms or ammunition; the intentional display of firearms or ammunition at any store; or the intentional possession of a firearm in any *public place*. However, an amendment to F.S. 790.01 passed in 2015 now permits concealed carry during the first 48 hours of any mandatory evacuation while actually evacuating an area. Otherwise, carrying of firearms is prohibited on public roads and property during any "state of emergency". Likewise, under current law, the government may not seize lawfully possessed firearms so long as the possessor is not engaged in the commission of a crime.

Federal law is similar to its Florida counterparts, and is found at 42 USC 5207. The federal law does not permit the seizure of firearms by federal authorities unless the possession is contrary to state law. Under the federal statute, the government may require temporary surrender of a firearm only as a condition for voluntary rescue or evacuation being provided for by the government, with the firearm being returned after the transportation is completed. A violation allows the person to seek redress in federal court for injunctive relief and attorney fees to obtain return of the firearm.

LASERS:

Interestingly enough, the statute that controls pointing of lasers, F.S. 784.062 – doesn't cover all you think it would, and has one really strange aspect. The first section makes it a non-criminal infraction (ie: up to $500.00 fine) to *willfully* point a laser beam *not mounted* on a firearm at any law enforcement officer in the performance of his or her duties where a reasonable person would believe a firearm was pointed at them. So – I guess the worst that happens in that case is a fine. Of course – you'll also get shot by the officer. However, if it's mounted on a firearm – it's not covered by the statute – so no fine – but this time you'll get shot multiple times by several police officers.

On the other hand, if you *willfully* point **any** laser beam at **anyone** who is operating a vessel, vehicle, or aircraft – it's a third degree felony. If that also results in any type of personal injury, it's now a second degree felony. If you just point it at someone in a movie theater – you probably won't get shot – but a punch in the nose seems only fair.

ENDNOTE SECTION FOR CHAPTER SEVEN:

1. If you have a concealed permit, it's a second degree misdemeanor pursuant to F.S. 790.06(12). Otherwise, it's a first degree misdemeanor for a weapon, or a third degree felony for a firearm.

2. The primary case on this issue was Wilson v. State, 344 So.2d 1315 (Fla. 2DCA 1977), reh. denied, 353 So.2d 679 (Fla. 1977); which held that it was reversible error for the judge not to instruct the jury that "knowledge of the presence of the firearm" was essential to a conviction. Accord, L.J. v. State, 553 So.2d 286 (Fla. 3DCA 1989); V.B.L. v. State, 408 So.2d 855 (Fla. 3DCA 1982). In essence, you don't want to make a criminal out of someone who merely made a mistake, and carried it unwittingly. See, Cole v. State, 353 So.2d 952 (Fla. 2DCA 1978).

3. In L.B. v. State, supra, the court held the statute to be vague, and a violation of due process of law.

4. 18 USC 930(g) excludes a pocket knife from the definition of a "dangerous weapon" where the blade length is less than 2 ½ inches.

5. 18 USC 930(g)(2) says a pocket knife with a blade less than two and a half inches is not a dangerous weapon, thus in U.S. v. Hendrick, 207 F. Supp. 2d 710 (S.D. Ohio 2002), the federal court upheld a conviction, and found a three inch blade was a dangerous weapon.

6. F.S. 790.01;   F.S. 790.053

7. Actually, F.S. 951.22 uses the term "dangerous weapon" which should eliminate a "self defense chemical spray" from any criminal liability if brought into a county jail facility for your own use, rather than to aid an escape, etc.   Still, even if not prosecuted, I guarantee you can't get it in if they know about it, nor should you try. The other two statues apply to any "weapon".

8. Since chemical sprays do not fall under F.S. 790.06(1), they are excluded under F.S. 790.06(12). On the other hand, electric weapons are covered under the permit — so "willful" carry into a courthouse or jail is a second degree misdemeanor.   Under any circumstance, the courts have the right to set regulations on citizen access — so, a requirement of "no weapons" is totally legal.

9. Until the 2006 amendment the sole purpose of F.S. 790.01(3) was to allow CWP holders to legally carry all weapons in a concealed manner – thus expanding the practical applications of the CWP beyond the weapons mentioned in F.S. 790.06. The 2006 amendment was meant to "expand" the use of the enumerated non-lethal weapons – not "restrict" them. It would make no sense to allow non-licensees to carry these weapons concealed in all but prohibited areas - but not allow CWP holders to do the same.   This is buttressed by the same 2006 amendment to F.S. 790.053 that likewise extended open carry of these weapons to everyone. Of course, this interpretation is based on my opinion that a CWP holder has the option to legally carry per his CWP, per 790.25, per 790.01, per 790.053, and/or per 790.115(2). Otherwise, the statutes punish the CWP holder for obtaining the extra training and criminal history clearance, defy the purpose for the CWP, and defy common sense. Naturally, no case law on the issue at this time, and it would be a "test case".

10. Since a self defense chemical spray is not regulated by the Concealed Permit law, a licensee would have more legal leeway with the spray. Likewise, there's an untested and common sense argument that if it's allowed under F.S. 790.25 – you should be able to do it as a CWP holder, as you wouldn't be carrying "per your permit", but instead, would be carrying per F.S. 790.25, just like any Florida citizen can do. Test case time!

11. Whether it's a misdemeanor trespass, or a felony depends on whether a self defense pepper spray or nonlethal electric weapon is considered a "dangerous weapon" under F.S. 810.08 & 09. Since a dangerous weapon is one that, taking into account the manner in which it is used, is likely to produce death or great bodily harm — it should be only a misdemeanor. See, Houck v. State, 634 So.2d 180 (Fla. 5DCA 1994).

12. Opinion of Attorney General, 068-103 (1968)

13. In Chaungocnguyen v. State, 28 FLW 2640 (Fla. 1DCA 11/03), the appellate court held that a stun gun would not ordinarily be classified as a "deadly weapon".

14. F.S. 790.115(1)

15. Ensor v. State, 403 So.2d 349 (Fla. 1981).
Goodman v. State, 689 So.2d 428 (Fla. 1DCA 1997).

16. As previously noted, the preemption law covers only firearms and ammunition. Whether local laws concerning weapons other than firearms, ammunition, nonlethal stun guns, and self defense chemical sprays would run afoul of the Florida Constitution (ordinances may not be in conflict with general law) is an undecided question. See, Fla. Const., Art. 8, section 1(f).

17. F.S. 790.10

18. F.S. 790.115(1)

19. In an aggravated assault case mere pointing the firearm at someone else is generally going to qualify as sufficient to create an "imminent" fear of harm – although the "intent" issue would still be for the jury since it is the intent of the person with the firearm that counts – not the subjective reaction of the alleged victim (although reasonable fear is an additional element). Benitez v. State, 901 So.2d 935 (Fla. 4DCA 2005).

20. Improper display is a "lesser included" of aggravated assault. Konrath v. State, 997 So.2d 1281 (Fla. 5DCA 2009).

21. F.S. 790.15

22. An automatic firearm is one which can fire a series of "bursts" (ie: "select fire"), or can fire continuously (automatic mode) -- from a single pull of the trigger. Such firearms normally have the additional ability to fire single shots in a semi-automatic mode, as well. The mode on such firearms is controlled by a manually operated switch located on the firearm. A "semi-automatic" weapon is one which is able to reset itself for each succeeding shot, but still requires the trigger to be pulled before each individual shot can be fired.

23. See, Rinzler v. Carson, 262 So.2d 661 (Fla. 1972), where the use of a registered submachine gun was condoned in a self-defense situation.

24. F.S. 790.221; 18 USC 5801-5872

25. The definition of a firearm in 27 CFR 479.11 states:

> "The overall length of a weapon made from a shotgun or a rifle is the distance between the extreme ends of the weapon . . . ."

26. Yeah, I know some people insist you can manufacture your own machine gun, and be legal.   In 2003in United States v. Stewart, the Ninth Circuit said that possession was not illegal where the defendant manufactured the machine gun at his home, and it was not for resale or transfer. However, the U.S. Supreme Court reversed the decision at 545 US 1112 (2005), and the Ninth Circuit then reinstated the conviction. United States v. Stewart, 451 F.3d 1071 (9th Cir. 2006)

27. F.S. 790.001(9)

28. Since the sole justification for the registration is to pay the tax, it's hard to understand why you would still have to register if there was no tax to pay.

29. An "NFA" firearm (but never a "machinegun" or "destructive device") may be placed on the list per 26 USC 5845(a). This is "Section III" of the published list, which then removes the weapon from NFA requirements. However, a machinegun that is a curio, relic, or antique — still needs the Form 4, and tax stamp. Same thing on destructive devices.

30. The Ninth Circuit, in United States v. Stewart, Docket Number 02-10318 (9th Cir. 11/13/03), held it was not illegal for an individual to manufacture a firearm for his personal use when most of the parts were fabricated by himself in his own home, and the machine gun was not for transfer or sale. This decision is no longer the law, and has been reversed. Therefore, manufacture of any machine gun by an individual will result in serious legal consequences.

31. In United States v. Burgert, 116 Fed. Appx. 124 (9th Cir. 2004), the court found using a conversion kit to construct a machine gun was a felony.

32. F.S. 790.157(2)(c) makes it "prima facie" that a person is under the influence at 0.10 per cent blood alcohol level. Between 0.05% and 0.10% is a gray area. Below 0.05% — you're presumed to be OK.

33. You might also remember that if you're not sober, you may be too intoxicated to realize you're gun is not really unloaded. Certainly, a sobering thought (no pun intended) to ponder.

34. A "felony" under Florida law is a crime that could be punished by more than a year imprisonment, regardless of the sentence imposed.

35. F.S. 775.087(2)(r). Mandatory is only if actual possession proven. Johnson v. State, 855 So.2d 218 (Fla. 5DCA 2003). 18 USC 924(a)(2).

36. F.S. 790.23

37. F.S. 775.087(3)

38. 18 USC 929

39. F.S. 790.001(4); 26 USC 5845 (f)

40. A 12 gauge shotgun has a bore more than one half inch.

41. State v. Darynani, 774 So.2d 855 (Fla. 4DCA 2000). The case, and opinion by the court showed an incredible lack of understanding, and lack of legal research as to a century old definition that was clear in both federal law, and in numerous other states. The result was legally "sloppy", and below the standard of a Florida appellate court.

42. F.S. 370.08; and Fla. Admin. Code 46-4.012(1).

43. IRS Rev. Rul. 55-569.

44. F.S. 810.08 & 810.09

45. F.S. 493.6120

CHAPTER EIGHT

LAWS CONCERNING CHILDREN

Whenever I mention children, the first thing I think of is air guns, fireworks, and where the heck should I put my gun to make sure they don't get hold of it. Children, the younger the more common, have a bad habit of playing with things they shouldn't. If they get hold of a loaded firearm -- the results can be devastating. More importantly, when it happens, it happens so quickly that there are only seconds to counter the potential disaster. School shootings don't help much, either. To counter this tragic situation, the Florida legislature has gone a bit too far -- and the federal government, as usual -- has gone off the wall. Whatever the merits or demerits of these laws -- the first part of this chapter should educate you on what to be aware of in this area.

LAWFUL AGE TO POSSESS FIREARMS OR AMMUNITION:

The passage of the Youth Handgun Safety Amendment to the 1994 federal Crime Bill[1] made it a federal crime for anyone to sell, deliver, or otherwise transfer to a juvenile (ie: person **under 18 years** of age) a **handgun**, or ammunition suitable only for use in a handgun. This means loaded, or unloaded. This means a gift, a sale, just loaning the darn thing, or temporarily handing it over for a "look-see". This applies to parents, uncles, aunts, friends, relatives, scout masters, and any almost every other form of life on the planet, except for firearms dealers. For firearms dealers -- it's still **21 years** of age. Again, we are just talking only about "*handguns*", as *longguns* (ie: rifle or shotgun) have some different rules. The exceptions under the federal statute are a "temporary transfer" for use during:

a.   In the course of ranching, or farming at the residence of the juvenile, or

b.   In the course of ranching, or farming at a location where the juvenile has the permission of the property owner or lessee, or

c.   during target practice, hunting, or a course of instruction on the safe and lawful use of firearms, or

d.   in the course of employment.

On top of these restrictions, there are additional requirements. The additional requirements that must be met while the permitted activities are being performed. These additional restrictions are as follows:

a.   The juvenile must have the prior ***written consent*** of a parent or guardian. The written consent must be kept on the juveniles person at all times he is in possession of the handgun or ammunition (during the permitted activity), and the parent or guardian who gave permission, must not have a legal disability that would make it illegal for that parent or guardian to possess a firearm.

b.   The handgun must be transported unloaded, in a locked container, directly to and from the permitted activity. It must thereafter be returned to an adult.

c.   If the activity is ranching or farming, then such must be done at the direction of an adult who does not have a legal disability that would make it illegal for that person to possess a firearm.

        Anyway, since we're all sick of federal law by now, let's get into Florida law. Don't get too excited -- we've still got some more federal law to go over later in this chapter. It never ends.

FLORIDA LAWS PERTAINING TO MINORS:
        Florida is actually somewhat more restrictive with age limitations than the feds, except where it comes to handguns. Since the "*most restrictive*" laws will control – you must understand both to understand the law. At the end of the chapter I've included some charts that should help explain things.

        In Florida, it is unlawful for anyone to sell, lend, or give a person **under the age of 18** years **any** weapon, whatsoever, except an ordinary ("common") pocketknife -- **unless** a parent (guardian) gives permission. A violation is a first degree misdemeanor for weapons, and a third degree felony for firearms. F.S. 790.17. A "***dealer in arms***" cannot sell to a person **under 18 years of age** -- even with permission, although he can legally sell to an adult, who may then transfer it to the child, with permission from a parent. F.S. 790.18.

        A 1996 amendment to F.S. 790.22 makes it illegal for a minor **under 16 years** to possess a BB gun, air or gas operated gun, or electric weapon unless such is in the presence of, **and *under the supervision of an adult*** who acts with consent of one of the minor's parents. It is a second degree misdemeanor for the adult to *knowingly and willfully* permit such possession. Since a "*BB*" technically meets the definition of ***Airsoft*** – it includes these totally non-weapons, as well! Just plain stupid! Change the statute to exclude ***Airsoft***! At worst, they sting, and leave a little red mark (unless you shoot someone in the eye). Likewise, *paint ball* guns.

If it's any type **firearm**, then it's illegal for a minor **under 18 years** to possess it unless:

a. Engaged in lawful hunting, and is
   1. At least 16 years old, or
   2. Under 16, and is supervised by adult

b. Engaged in lawful recreational shooting or marksmanship, and is
   1. At least 16 years, or
   2. Under 16 and supervised by adult acting with consent of minor's parent or guardian.

c. Firearm is **unloaded**, and being transported by minor directly to or from an event authorized by this statute.

d. Firearm is **unloaded**, and possessed at child's home.

In case you're wondering how this applies to your kid taking a *martial arts class* with weapons training – as long as you have given **permission** for them to use weapons (*other than firearms*) it's OK.

CHART OF PENALTIES FOR CHILD VIOLATIONS:

Any parent, guardian, or other adult who is responsible for the minor who *knowingly and willfully* permits the minor to have a firearm in violation of this section — commits a third degree felony! The other possible penalty for minors and parents are in the following chart:

WITH FIREARM	Type offense	Sentence to jail	community service	weapon	driver license
first offense	misd.	up to 3 days	minimum 100 hours	forfeit	up to 1 year loss
second offense	3d felony	up to 15 days	100 -250 hours	forfeit	up to 2 year loss
1st offense & a crime	1st misd.	15 days minimum	minimum 100 hours	forfeit	up to 1 year loss

2d offense & a crime	3d felony	21 days minimum	100 - 250 hours	forfeit	up to 2 year loss
adult in charge	knowingly and willfully permits child to possess firearm in violation of law is third degree felony.				
parent or guardian	same as above, except may also be required to attend parenting classes, and do community service with child.				
VIOLATIONS WHERE AIRGUN OR ELECTRIC WEAPON ONLY					
child	possible delinquency proceeding under F.S. 985				
adult in charge	second degree misdemeanor				

OTHER PENALTIES:

Other recent additions to the statute (F.S. 790.22) permit a child who is taken into custody for possession of a firearm on school property to be detained for up to 21 days for psychological, drug, and medical examination in the discretion of the court. A further addition is that when the violation involves underage possession of a firearm, and a separate violation of another criminal statute — community control can be imposed, and the court may also order the parents or guardians of the child to pay restitution for any damage caused, unless the parents/guardians can show they made a diligent and good faith effort to prevent such conduct.

In closing, what this law doesn't say, is it's obvious that a number of weapons can be possessed by a child **under sixteen (16)** without supervision -- if they have permission to have the weapon in the first place. Those would include everything **but** firearms, BB & air guns, and electric weapons.
Why?

Because only F.S. 790.22 has any age restrictions relating to weapons or firearms, and the only weapons that have restrictions as far as possession by minors go – are *"BB gun, air or gas-operated gun, electric weapon or device, or firearm"*. Thus, knives, hatchets, machetes, bows, etc. -- are otherwise legal if obtained with permission of the parent, and are not possessed by the child at a school, school grounds, school bus, school bus stops, or otherwise in violation of any other laws, including those pertaining to schools, school sponsored events, school bus stops, and school buses.

QUESTION: So, can I buy my kid an *air rifle* if he is 12 years old?

ANSWER: Sure. But if you let him use it or possess it when you or another adult is not around (until the age of 16 years) -- you're guilty of a misdemeanor.

QUESTION: What if he's 16 years old.

ANSWER: That changes things a little. Now he can possess and use the airgun without supervision.

QUESTION: What about a real rifle -- a .22 caliber?

ANSWER: Well, from 16 until 18 years — he can have it unloaded at home. If he's taking it anywhere, it must be kept unloaded, and be in transport directly to or from lawful recreational shooting, or lawful hunting. Nowhere else! If you let him do otherwise — you've committed a felony!

QUESTION: What if my wife and I disagree? She says "no" -- I say "yes".

ANSWER: Your kid can have the weapon or firearm, but your wife will make both your lives miserable.

QUESTION: So, if I can buy it -- can he keep it in his room?

ANSWER: Yes, if it is unloaded, and is not a handgun.

QUESTION: What about a hunting knife, or bow and arrows?

ANSWER: If a parent, or guardian allows the child to have it -- the child may have it at any age: 3, 5, 10, 14 years old -- whatever age they allow. Once the child reaches 18 years of age -- the "child" is no longer a "minor", and can purchase any type of weapon, on his own, including handguns -- but cannot purchase the handgun from a federally licensed dealer until 21.

QUESTION: What if the kid wants a weapon, and the wife and I refuse to give permission.

ANSWER: If a parent or guardian doesn't give permission, then the child cannot legally obtain any weapon, other than a *common pocketknife*, until he reaches 18 years of age.

QUESTION: What happens at **18 years of age**?

ANSWER: The "child" becomes an "*adult*", for most purposes, and may legally buy any weapon, including a handgun, although he cannot buy a handgun from a federally licensed dealer.

QUESTION: What if his grandfather **bequeathed** him an antique handgun?

ANSWER: Interesting question. It appears that this was an inadvertent loophole left by both Florida and Federal legislators. An "*antique firearm*" is not a "*firearm*" unless being used in the commission of a crime. Even the definition of a "*handgun*" under federal law must still be a "firearm", thus excluding antique firearms. It's obviously not a BB gun or air gun. It's not a "*firearm*". I guess it's OK for the kid to have it until somebody gets around to changing the law, so long as it's given to the child with the permission of a parent. Still, you could become a "*test case*" on this one. I'd hold it for him until 18.

STORAGE OF LOADED FIREARMS:

In this day and age, it should be easy to keep firearms away from children, but anyone who has been around kids can testify that they can get into anything– sometimes so fast, it's scary. In order to cut your losses, the Legislature has enacted laws making it a crime to leave a <u>loaded</u> gun accessible to children **under the age of 16 years** except under certain circumstances. F.S. 790.174(3). If it's unloaded -- you don't have to worry about these statutes.[2] Thus, the storing of a <u>loaded</u> firearm within the reach or easy access of a minor child under the age of sixteen, where the person knows, or should know, the minor is <u>likely</u> to gain access to it without lawful permission or supervision is a felony of the third degree if the minor obtains the loaded firearm and uses it to inflict injury or death upon himself or any other person.[3] If no injury occurs, but the minor still gains access to the loaded firearm -- it's a second degree misdemeanor -- **only** if the minor unlawfully possesses it in a public place, or displays it anywhere, in a "*rude, careless, angry, or threatening manner*". Of course, if the child was in presence and under the supervision of an adult, at the time (and it's one of our wonderful federally permitted activities), it's also fine, unless the adult was otherwise *culpably negligent* under F.S. 784.05

You should know that this law would not impose criminal liability when the firearm was stored in a securely locked box/container, or in a location which a *reasonable person* would believe to be secure, or if the firearm had a trigger lock, or mounted firearm combination lock. It also would not apply if the person who left the firearm should not have *reasonably known* that a minor was likely to gain access to the firearm without the permission or supervision of a parent or person having charge of the minor, or if it resulted from an *unlawful entry* by any person. (ie: a theft). And, if the firearm is being carried by an adult on his body, or within such proximity to his person that he could retrieve, and use it as easily and quickly as if he carried it on his body (*"readily accessible for immediate use"*) -- it's also legal. Of course, the **big loophole** here (probably done intentionally) is: if the child doesn't take possession of the firearm – it's not a crime, at all.

QUESTION: What if my sister's kids come over, and I'm a bachelor. I always keep my gun in a bureau by my bed?

ANSWER: Assuming they don't sneak in the back door, and you have time to take some security precautions, it may be reasonable to contemplate that the kids may go searching around. Thus, unloading the weapon, putting on a trigger lock, or locking it in a container -- instantly take you off the hook. If you want to be a bit riskier it becomes a jury question of whether you acted reasonably, or not. Obviously, if they get hold of the gun -- you have a potential legal problem.

QUESTION: What if I'm driving my kids in the car, and I've got my loaded gun in a closed console next to me.

ANSWER: In my opinion, you're legal as long as you're in the vehicle, you're in the driver's seat, and the console is closed. That's because the statute exempts situations where you are carrying the firearm on your body, *"or within such close proximity thereto that he can retrieve and use it as easily and quickly as if he carried it on his body."* F.S. 790.174(1).

CIVIL LIABILITY IF THE KIDS GET TO IT:

If a child under the age of 18 years *willfully or recklessly* destroys or injures the property of another -- the parent or parents he lives with are legally responsible for the actual amount of damages the child causes. This is pursuant to F.S. 741.24. If you were also found negligent in leaving the firearm in a place where a child could reasonably have been anticipated to get hold of it -- you are probably going to be held civilly liable for any damages caused by that child's use of the firearm -- including the death or injury of somebody else. Conceivably, you might even be subject to a *manslaughter* or *culpable negligence* prosecution.

Obviously, the way to get around this is to buy one of the many devices available to keep a loaded gun ready for use -- but safe. There are a number of small gun boxes or safes that have a keypad lock that opens electronically by pushing a combination of push buttons. Since it can be opened by "feeling" the buttons -- it can be accessed in total darkness, right next to your bed. If you have kids -- this is really what you need. I've seen these for forty to ninety bucks in catalogs, on the internet at *Harbor Freight Tools*, at gun stores, and even some office supply stores. I own them, and think they're great.

If you want a full size gun locker -- they're available at almost any sporting goods store, gun shops, gun shows, locksmiths, and even at Wal-Mart. Prices range from really cheap -- to really expensive, and fit all purposes and pocketbooks. Not a bad idea since the majority of illegal guns are stolen by teenagers during burglaries from honest owners just like you. Then the guns are used against the rest of us. Be responsible -- make sure your guns are safe from kids -- and safe from theft.

As far as **trigger locks** go — I am not a great believer in them, as I think a lock box, or gun safe is far superior. To me, a trigger lock is solely a "storage solution", and not a very good one. A stored gun doesn't have to be loaded — and shouldn't be. Moreover, if you have a trigger lock on a self-defense gun — you are going to be dead before you get it unlocked. There are some recent improvements on *"electronically keyed"*, and other push-button mechanisms installed directly on the gun such a *"Safe-T-Lock"* mechanism — but if that's your answer to keeping the gun where it can be found — I think you need a better solution.

GUN FREE SCHOOL ZONES ACT -- PART TWO:

Well, just as I promised, we're back in federal land. Congress has a bad habit of passing laws that should really be reserved for the decision of the individual states. I already described in the first chapter how the United States Supreme Court decided that this law was unconstitutional, but Congress didn't really care about such minor problems, and reenacted it, again. The reenacted law, 18 USC 922(q), has been upheld by at least two federal appellate courts. *U.S. v. Pierson,* 139 F.3d 501 (5th Cir. 1998); *U.S. v. Danks*, 221 F.3d 1037 (8th Cir. 1999). A later Supreme Court case seems to reassert the invalidity of the law, but the federal appeal courts seem to be ignoring it. *U.S. v. Morrison*, 146 L.ed.2d 658 (2000).[4] Anyway, here's how this law works:

In brief, the law [18 USC 922(q)] makes it a federal crime punishable by up to five years imprisonment to ***knowingly possess*** a firearm in a "***school zone***" unless you meet certain exceptions. A "***school zone***" is defined as the *grounds* of any public, private, or parochial elementary or secondary school — or **within 1000 feet** of such. The exceptions are any of the following:

1. You've got a CWL
2. The gun is not loaded, and is in a locked container , or locked firearm rack in a motor vehicle
3. You're on private property, not part of the school
4. It's for use in a program approved by a school in the school zone (not necessarily at the school)
5. You're a security guard under contract with a school in the school zone
6. You're a law enforcement officer acting as such
7. The gun is unloaded, and you're traversing school grounds for the purpose of legal access to hunting land, if the school authority has authorized such.

Great reason to have a CWP, isn't it?

FLORIDA SCHOOL ZONE LAWS:
In 1997 the legislature passed another law[5] affecting school type situations which amended F.S. 790.115. It sounds something like the federal law we just discussed, but has very few similarities when you fully examine it. You should be aware that it has two key sections that are very dissimilar -- one devoted to unlawful "***display***" of firearms and other weapons, and another devoted to mere "***possession***". A violation of either is a third degree felony unless you are a CWL holder. There is a third section that deals with ***unlawful discharge*** of weapons which is a second degree felony. Anyway — here's how it works:

The first subsection (1) deals with **unlawful exhibition** of weapons and firearms, and does not pertain to mere possession. It makes it illegal to **display** any sword, sword cane, firearm, electric weapon, destructive device, or other weapon including a razor blade, box cutter, or any knife, including "*common pocketknife*" in a "rude, careless, angry, or threatening manner, not in lawful self-defense, and in the presence of one or more persons:

1.   On the grounds or facilities of any school
2.   On any school bus stop
3.   On any school bus
4.   At any school sponsored event (even off school property)
5.   Or, within <u>1000 feet</u> of the grounds of any elementary, middle, or
      secondary school

where such occurs: (a) during school hours, or (b) during the time a school
sanctioned school activity takes place. This section does not apply to exhibition
of a firearm or weapon on *private property* within 1000 feet of school grounds
if such is done by the owner, or by a person who has been authorized, licensed,
or invited by the owner to his property.

Subsection (2) of this statute deals with *mere possession*, and forbids a
person from *"willfully and knowingly"* possessing any firearm, electric weapon,
destructive device, or other weapon, including a razor blade, box cutter, or knife
(*but – excluding common pocketknives*), except as authorized in support of
school sanctioned activities, **on the property** of any school, school bus stop,
school sponsored event, or school bus. The definition of a school is expanded to
include **preschool**, elementary, middle, junior high, secondary, post secondary,
and vocational schools -- public or private -- which means **everything**! In fact,
a *"preschool"* even includes *daycare*[6] – although there is a Florida statute that
might limit that to *daycare* involving over five children.[7] There is also no
restriction as to time of day. In other words, it doesn't matter whether the school
is in session, or not.   Fortunately, this subsection does **not** include the "1000
foot" prohibition. Therefore, so long as you're at least one inch off the school
grounds, and you've merely got a weapon on you -- this section of the statute
does not apply.

<u>EXCEPTIONS – WHICH ALLOW POSSESSION:</u>
As to the exceptions to subsection (2) which would still permit lawful
possession of a firearm or a weapon (not unlawfully display), here they are:

1.   To a firearms program, class, or function that has been approved in
      advance by the principal or chief administrative officer of the school

2.   To a vocational school having a firearms training range

3.   In a vehicle pursuant to <u>F.S.</u> 790.25(5) — ie: securely encased, or not
      readily accessible. However, you should know that the Legislature made
      a very bad mistake here, and receded somewhat from our *"preemption*

law"[8] by permitting a *"school district"* to adopt written and published policies that waive this exemption for purposes of student and campus parking privileges. But, in *Florida Carry, Inc. v. Univ. of North Florida*, 133 So.3d 966(Fla. 1DCA 2013), the appellate court held that only a *"school district"* may prohibit a securely encased firearm in a conveyance, and neither a college or university qualifies as a *"school district"*. Thus, this case firmly establishes that it is lawful to have a **securely encased** firearm in your vehicle on any college or university campus in Florida despite any conflicting rule. Obviously, this should also apply to any other type *"school"* not run by and in a *"school district"*. Likewise, for secondary schools, a waiver should not affect a vehicle that was merely dropping off a person vs. actually *"parking"*, and there is an unresolved legal question whether temporary parking by persons other than students, faculty, and campus employees legally falls within the ambit of such a waiver. *Test case* time!

4.   The penalties of this subsection do not apply to CWL holders (although the prohibitions do). Instead, CWL holders are punished as provided in F.S. 790.06(12), which makes a violation of that particular subsection of 790.06 a second degree misdemeanor -- except that a license holder who unlawfully discharges a weapon or firearm on school property as prohibited by this subsection commits a second degree felony. As I stated in the chapter on concealed licenses — a possible but not suggested interpretation would allow concealed carry by a CWL holder on school *"grounds"* but not school buildings or structures inasmuch as *"facility"* is normally defined as a building or structure.[9] Still, this definition is probably pushing the legal envelope, and I think a court would likely interpret this differently. I therefore **strongly advise** against using this interpretation, as it isn't worth being a *"test case"*.

The third section of this statute deals with the discharge of a weapon or firearm while in violation of the possession prohibitions of this section, unless discharged in lawful self defense, or for other lawful purpose. As previously stated, such is a second degree felony.

A fourth section of the statute deals with safe storage of firearms, and really is a duplication of F.S. 790.174 with some gloss. We already covered it when we discussed that statute. A subsection of F.S. 790.22 also provides that a child who possesses a firearm on school property may be held for up to 21 days for observation and treatment

QUESTION: OK, I'm a law-abiding citizen walking down the street with my *Taser* legally in my hand because it's a "bad area". I suddenly see a school, 999 feet away. I had no idea it was there before this. Am I now guilty of a felony?

ANSWER: No. Only if the display is rude, careless, angry, or threatening — and done in the presence of another person. Still, you can now see why this is such a bad law. If you were moving the *Taser* around, and someone saw you -- and told a police officer -- would he think this was "*careless*"? If he did, maybe you could be arrested for a felony! You'd more than likely win your case -- but who would want to be in that kind of predicament? This is a really dangerous law, and I suggest you write your state legislators to remove it.

QUESTION: I am a teacher. I have always kept my firearm locked in my car so I have it available when I leave. I drive through some dangerous areas. Can this now be forbidden?

ANSWER: Yes. If the **school district** (not the principal) actually passes, adopts, and publishes a written policy forbidding you to park on school property — you commit a felony by doing so, so long as you did so "*knowingly and willfully*".

QUESTION: What if my wife drops me off in the school parking lot, and such a published policy exists? Can we still have a firearm or weapon in the car securely encased, or not readily accessible?

ANSWER: My opinion is it is OK, but only if "*securely encased*", even with a CWL. That's based on my opinion that the school district may not restrict anything but actual parking privileges in the sense of leaving a vehicle unattended vs. waiting for someone in your vehicle while parked. But still, that last one could be argued differently, has no case law, and is a pure *test case*. Of course, if the parking lot is not posted – you have a defense unless you had actual knowledge of the policy.

QUESTION: What about the federal restrictions? Doesn't this forbid mere possession of any firearm within **1000 feet** of any *school zone*?

ANSWER: Very perceptive question. The answer is "yes". Only a CWL holder, school security guard, or police officer is permitted to *"knowingly"* get within **1000 feet** of an elementary or secondary school, unless the gun is unloaded and in a locked container or locked gun rack. However, since only a federal officer is normally going to think about making an arrest for something as stupid as this — I wouldn't worry too much unless you are dealing drugs, robbing a bank, or blowing something up. Better yet, get a CWL as it exempts you from the federal law.

QUESTION: I take my child to his bus stop. This is not a great section of town. I carry pepper spray for protection. What can I do to protect myself?

ANSWER: See my opinion about *"pepper sprays"* later in this chapter. They are not *"weapons"* under Florida law if used/kept for self defense purposes. If you don't trust my opinion, then stay at least "one foot" away from the school bus stop — assuming you can figure out the boundaries of it.

CHURCH SCHOOLS:

A Sunday school, and religious classes at a church or temple should **not** ordinarily be considered as *"schools"* pursuant to F.S. 790.115 **unless** they involve preschool aged children. If so, then they do qualify because F.S. 790.115(2)(a)(3), includes a *"preschool"* in the definition, and *preschools* are usually defined as follows:

> *"Preschools are defined as any enterprise ... which provides for the care and protection of infants or preschool children outside their own homes during any portion of a 24-hour day.... This includes day care centers, nursery schools, [and] kindergartens." Reich v. Miss Paula's Day Care Center, Inc., 37 F.3d 1191 (6th Cir. 1994).*

Otherwise, a *"school"* normally begins at first grade. State v. Edwards, 581 So.2d 232 (Fla. 4DCA 1991), although I'm sure there is also a really good argument that it starts at the "K" level, in *kindergarten*. In these situations, the question becomes whether a building used for both church and class purposes is entirely a *"school"*, or just the areas used for such are a "school". Another issue is whether the "school" areas then include hallways normally used by the students, bathrooms, etc.

My best guess on an interpretation (since there currently is none) is that there is a good possibility that any building used for such regular classes, in its entirety, will be defined as a "*school*" even if the other parts of the building are regularly and equally used for other unrelated purposes. However, I do not believe other buildings would be included – especially a building used primarily or exclusively for religious services. Purely a guess. *Test case* time!

PRIVATE SCHOOLS:

If you're wondering if the same rules apply to **private schools** as public schools – the answer is "yes". If you're wondering if a private school can authorize its teachers or select personnel to carry weapons – the current answer is "no". If you're asking me if this is a good law – the answer (in my lowly opinion) is "hell, no!" I am an advocate of allowing select teachers and administrators (with special training, and approval) to carry at least a *Taser*, if not a firearm. If some nut case gets into school, and starts shooting – at least the kids will have a chance. It only takes a couple of minutes for a multiple tragedy to happen – and the police just won't get there in time to save everybody! Passing laws that prevent responsible adults from having protection only encourages those who commit crimes. No law banning firearms or weapons will ever stop a shooter from killing people – if that's what they've set out to do. Only a firearm in the hand of a responsible person who has the necessary skills, will! History has taught that lesson again, and again.

Also – since F.S. 790.115 prohibits "*possession*" of weapons on school grounds, and since a preschool is defined as a "school" under this section – and since even a "*daycare*" comes under the current federal definition of a "preschool" – you likely can't carry even at someone's home who has a "daycare". You can still park in the driveway under Florida law if the firearm is securely encased, or if you don't have a CWL, and are really concerned about federal law – then locked up and unloaded. The only possible exception is likely where there are less than six children being taken care of. F.S. 402.302. However, this whole area is confusing because there is no definition of "*preschool*" in the Florida statutes – and thus I guess you've just gotta "play it safe".

TRAINING CHILDREN TO BE SAFE:

Most accidents happen due to either ignorance, carelessness, or a combination of both factors. The way to counter these dangers is to train children what to do when they see a firearm. The approved method by the NRA is to teach a child who sees a firearm to do the following:

a.		Don't touch the firearm.
b.		Leave the area.

c.   Immediately tell an adult

This is a great rule, and should also apply to ammunition, and to any toy guns that look real. I don't like the idea of a toy gun that looks real being anywhere near my house -- because the guns I own are real -- and some of the smaller calibers, especially a derringer, <u>look</u> like a toy! I wouldn't want anyone to play with something that might be a gun, or could be confused with a toy. Guns are for adults who have been trained in their handling, and for responsible "young adults" who have adult supervision, and training. Guns are dangerous. Only training prevents accidents. Think about it. Maybe you'll stop a disaster!

SCHOOL TRESPASS WITH FIREARM:

You should know that trespass on school property with a firearm or other weapon is a third degree felony. <u>F.S.</u> 810.095. In this particular statute a "*school*" is also defined as including the **grounds** of any school from kindergarten, up, including a career center, college, or university. Trespass at a school generally entails being there without any legitimate lawful purpose or invitation, or after warning/direction to leave, or an expelled or suspended student. So, you can better understand when you can, and can't possess near schools, a chart follows at the end of the chapter.

POSSESSION OF PEPPER SPRAYS ON SCHOOL GROUNDS:

It is my firm opinion that the carrying of a **concealed** "*self defense chemical spray*" on school grounds is currently not illegal, and is permitted by statute, much the same as a "*common pocketknife*". I caution – this has not been tested in any case, and that *open carry* of such spray would be **unlawful** unless used in necessary self defense.

My reasoning is that <u>F.S.</u> 790.01 allows carrying a "*self defense chemical spray*" concealed without a CWL. Then, <u>F.S.</u> 790.001(3)(b) – **excludes** a "*self defense chemical spray*" from inclusion in the definition of either a "*tear gas gun*" or a "*chemical weapon or device*". And then, <u>F.S.</u> 790.001(13) – does not mention a "*self defense chemical spray*" by itself, or within the definition of a "*weapon*", and therefore excludes it. Furthermore, <u>F.S.</u> 790.115 – forbids the *exhibition* of any "**weapon**" and certain other specifically named devices at schools, and further forbids possession of all such weapons on school property. The section does not mention or include "*self defense chemical sprays*", and thus – much like "common pocket knives" – it appears it is not unlawful to be in possession of such on school property – including colleges. There is no age limit.

Of course, a *"self defense chemical spray"* is defined as:

"a device carried solely for purposes of lawful self defense that is compact in size, designed to be carried on or about the person, and contains not more than two ounces of chemical". F.S. 790.001(3)(b).

And, to be clear – this is only my opinion at this point, as there is no case law.

CHART RELATED TO POSSESSION NEAR SCHOOL:

POSSESSION IN SCHOOL AREA UNDER FLORIDA LAW — F.S. 790.115			
type of conduct that is prohibited:	where prohibited	weapons prohibited	when such conduct is prohibited
any "improper exhibition" within presence of at least one other person vs. mere possession	school grounds/building school sponsored event school bus school bus stop 1000 feet of grounds	any weapon/gun any knife any razor blade any box cutter	school hours or during any school sanctioned activity
mere possession – whether open or concealed – any "weapon"	school grounds school bus school bus stop school sponsored event	same as above except common pocketknife; or self defense chemical spray ***	any time – 24/7
exceptions to any of above prohibitions:			
lawful self defense	on private property if owner or invitee	mere possession with principal's pre-approval to class where firearms allowed, or vocational school with gun range	securely encased or not readily accessible in vehicle *where parking not prohibited by school district published policy.
SAFE SCHOOL ZONE ACT — 18 USC 922 (q)			
knowing possession	1000 feet of school grounds	any firearm	24/7
exceptions:			
concealed permit	on private property not part of school grounds	firearm unloaded in locked container or locked firearms rack in vehicle	law enforcement in official capacity
unloaded & OK'd to cross grounds to get access to hunting area open to public	for use in program pre-approved by the school.	security guard or other person acting pursuant to contract with school	

CHART ON AGE RESTRICTIONS FOR WEAPONS:

FLORIDA LAW – progressive chart on age restrictions *ie: All restrictions of older age categories apply to lower ages*		
Age	other weapons	firearms
21 or older	no age restrictions	no age restrictions
under 21 but 18 or older	no age restrictions	purchase longgun from FFL
		purchase any gun privately
		no other age restrictions
under 18 but 16 or older	cannot purchase any weapon without parents OK, and dealer can't sell whatsoever, except *"common pocketknife"*. May possess any weapons except firearms with parents OK	cannot purchase firearms778
		may possess unloaded longgun at home – not handguns.
		no handgun possession unless hunting or sport shooting with parents written OK on person. (*federal law*)
16 exactly	same as above	hunting or lawful sport shooting allowed without supervision.
		may possess unloaded longgun at home – not handguns.
under 16	Cannot possess air guns, Airsoft, BB, or electric weapons ***except*** under adult supervision	hunting only under adult supervision
		sport shooting only with supervision & parental consent.
		may possess unloaded longgun at home – not handguns.

ENDNOTES FOR CHAPTER EIGHT:

1. 18 USC 922 (x)

2. F.S. 790.174; & the 1997 amendment (C.97-234) to 790.115(2)(c)(2). See also, F.S. 790.175

3. This particular section is governed under the culpable negligence statute, Florida Statute 784.05(3), rather than Chapter 790.

4. As stated in previous footnotes the Ninth Circuit would likely continue to hold the amended act as unconstitutional. United States v. Stewart, Docket Number 02-10318 (9th Cir. 11/13/03).

5. Chapter 97-72, Florida Statutes (1997), and 99-284 in 1999.

6. Reich v. Miss Paula's Day Care Center, Inc., 37 F.3d 1191 (6th Cir. 1994).

7. F.S. 402.302.

8. F.S. 790.33 wisely preempted firearms and ammunition laws (not other weapons) from local governments. However, local government is still restricted on weapons if they pass laws that conflict with C. 790. See, Rinzler v. Carson, 262 So.2d 661,668 (Fla. 1972).

9. 18 USC 930(g)(1) defines "federal facility" as a building or part thereof. F.S. 159.27(22) defines "educational facility" in similar terms. And, F.S. 790.115(1) differentiates between school "grounds" and "facilities" making it obvious that the Legislature recognizes the terms mean different things.

CHAPTER NINE

DEALERS, FFL'S & INSTRUCTORS

I'm sure there are lots of things that licensed firearms dealers, and other weapons dealers should know. I'm also sure they probably know most of them by heart. On the other hand, since I've handled more than my share of BATFE licensing and regulatory issues, I know they can obviously make mistakes, too. Since that's happened more than once, I think it might be a good idea to cover some of the issues and questions that seem to come up, over and over again. As a general rule this chapter is devoted primarily to licensed firearms dealers, rather than collectors, manufacturers, and importers -- but I'll make some exceptions from time to time. Plus, I guarantee that some of the answers will prove very interesting to everyone.

Before getting into details, if you are an *FFL* (*Federal Firearms Licensee*) or are thinking about it — you really should have computer access to the web, and regularly visit the BATFE and *NSSF* websites, and the FBI's website section on *NICS*. The NSSF site has great resources (www.nssf.org/retailers), and has some really great training videos for employees. Moreover, anyone who works in the firearms trade needs to download or order the ***Federal Firearms Regulations Reference Guide***. This is the "bible" of firearms dealers and their employees. It should be read and outlined at least twice a year by every FFL, and their employees. If you don't — you may be needing my legal services, sooner or later. Anyway, back to the book:

WHO MUST SECURE A FEDERAL LICENSE:
Any person or business entity (corporation or partnership) that has as its principal objective, from the sale or transfer of firearms, the goal of livelihood and profit -- needs to be federally licensed. The main question in defining this profit motive is predominantly one of obtaining pecuniary gain and livelihood, as opposed to other interests such as improving or liquidating a personal collection. If all you're doing is making an occasional sale to thin your collection, or make room for some other purchases, or even to liquidate your entire collection, you don't need a federal license. If it's as a business -- you better have an *FFL*, or you are in deep buffalo chips.

The main problem area here is not dealers, it's when people set-up tables at gun shows who are not licensed dealers. I've also seen it where dealer's are dealing out of their *"private collections"*. If this becomes a "business" – be forewarned – BATFE is watching!

WHAT DOES THE LICENSE COVER:

Well, in a nutshell, it allows you to purchase and ship firearms, and ammunition to and fro to any other FFL, no matter where they are located -- and otherwise engage in the business of buying and selling firearms, as a business. It also allows you to rent or loan firearms for temporary lawful sporting purposes, although you technically don't need an FFL for just onsite rentals, such as a *shooting range*. It does not allow you to sell/transfer out-of-state to a non-licensee, unless the firearm is delivered from your actual business location to another FFL in the receiving state, or the sale is a rifle or shotgun sold in a face-to-face transaction where the sale is legal in both states. If you are at a *gun show*, I've covered that in the upcoming "question and answer" section, since it's somewhat complicated. Anyway, since it's easier explaining most of this in a question-and-answer format, here goes:

QUESTION: As an FFL, can I purchase from a non-licensee in another state when I'm not at a gun show?

ANSWER: Yes, so long as the purchase is transported back to your business premises in your home state, and logged into your records.[1]

QUESTION: Likewise, as an FFL – can I accept firearms transferred to me from a non-FFL from another state?

ANSWER: Usually, "yes". It is not a violation of Florida or federal law for an out-of-state resident within the U.S.A. to ship (by commercial carrier) to an FFL in another state although an *NFA* firearm would have to have the proper transfers to a properly authorized FFL. Thus, an FFL may purchase over the internet from an out-of-state individual, so long as the firearm is shipped to the FFL's licensed location, and such is shipped per federal requirements.

QUESTION: What about a sale to a non-resident from my business premises?

ANSWER: You may sell any non-NFA firearm to a non-resident so long as the firearm is shipped from your licensed premises to another FFL in the purchaser's home state, where the purchaser will take delivery. If it's a rifle or shotgun in a *face-to-face* sale made in your state either at your licensed premises or a gun show — then you may also sell and deliver the firearm in your home state so long as the sale complies with the law of both your state, and the purchaser's state, and federal law.

QUESTION: What about at a *gun show*?

ANSWER: If you're selling at a show <u>outside of your state of licensure</u> to a non-resident, even if an FFL, you can only take orders and money, but then you must **ship from your licensed premises** to an FFL in the purchaser's state, assuming it's legal in the purchaser's state. You cannot transfer the firearm at the out-of-state gun show, even to an FFL. The one exception is that you may sell and deliver a *curio or relic* to any FFL, anywhere. 27 CFR 178.50. You may purchase from anyone.

If the gun show is <u>in your state</u>, then you may sell and deliver to any FFL, even if the FFL is from out-of-state. You may obviously sell to any resident who is not a prohibited person. You may sell and deliver a shotgun or rifle to any out-of- state resident where the sale is legal in both states (plus any applicable waiting period). You may take orders and money from any out-of-state resident on a handgun, but may only deliver it to an FFL in the purchaser's state. You may purchase from anyone. However, remember that a *flea market* is never a "*gun show*", and selling there would be a violation of your license.

QUESTION: What about a purchase by an FFL from a private individual who lives out-of-state from a listing on an online website?

ANSWER: A non-FFL who is not a "*prohibited person*" is lawfully permitted to sell to anyone, including an FFL, anywhere in the United States – so long as it is shipped to an FFL for delivery and pick-up. 18 USC 922(A)(2)(A)

QUESTION: Can I carry a firearm pursuant to my FFL?

ANSWER: This is not covered by federal law, and is completely a state law issue. In Florida, this is covered by <u>F.S.</u> 790.25(3)(i), which permits a dealer, or employee, to carry while engaged in the "*lawful course of such business*." This would **not permit** an employee **under the age of 18 years** to carry or even possess firearms in such a business pursuit due to the prohibitions in <u>F.S.</u> 790.22.

CONFUSION WITH CORPORATE OWNERSHIP:

If you have taken your *FFL* as a corporation — the "*corporation*" is the FFL — not you. You are simply an employee, officer, or whatever. If this is the situation, you cannot treat the inventory as your personal property, because it's not — it's the corporation's. Thus, any firearm obtained must be logged into the acquisition portion of the bound book, and if taken home by you, it better be logged out to you on the disposition portion of the bound book, with a 4473 — or you have violated federal criminal and administrative law. There is an exception when the firearm is being taken off the premises for a **legitimate business purpose** by an employee. This is usually to show to a potential customer – although any sale must still take place at the licensed premises, and must be delivered there, as well.

If you have *personal firearms* on display at the store, they must be tagged "**not for sale**", should probably also be tagged as your personal property, and be segregated from the rest of the corporate inventory so there is no confusion. They actually have to be logged into the bound book because they are considered a "**loan**" of the firearm to the FFL, and when you take them back — must be logged out, and do the NICS check with a *Form 4473* – because it is a "private" transaction. A multiple disposition form is unnecessary as it is not a "sale", but merely "**return**" of property — somewhat similar to a gun at a *pawn shop*.

Remember, that if you take a gun out of inventory, and you are not the actual FFL because the corporation is the FFL, you are a mere private citizen in the eye's of the law as far as transfer and purchase of firearms goes. I strongly recommend that both you, and any employee be required to obtain and read the "*Federal Firearms Reference Guide*" which is available free from BATFE in book form, or can be downloaded from their website at *www.atf.gov.* This publication is a review of the statutes, regulations, and questions **most asked** by dealers about the business.

LICENSED COLLECTORS:

The only reason anyone would want to be a licensed collector is if you want to buy, sell, and transport *curios and relics*, out of your residence state. Other than as to curios and relics -- you are treated exactly as a non-licensee.

A **relic** is a firearm manufactured at least 50 years previous, and it cannot be a replica, but must be the real thing. A **curio** must be certified by BATF as curio due to it being novel, rare, bizarre, or connected to a historical event. Before it becomes a "**curio**", a specified procedure must be followed. A *Form 4* is needed for *NFA*.

OBTAINING THE FFL:

If you want to become a dealer, assuming you are 21 years of age, and otherwise qualify, you can get the application from your local office of the Bureau of Alcohol, Tobacco, Firearms, and Explosives -- usually referred to as "ATF" or "BATFE" – or you can download it from their website at www.atf.gov/firearms. Before your application will be accepted you should have a *"place of business"* to operate as an FFL (ie: Federal Firearms Licensee). The location must be a permitted use under state and local law -- which means that if for some reason you want to use your home, and you're zoned only for residential -- you better find another location if you want a license. Since your home is probably not zoned for firearms sale or storage -- it is doubtful it would qualify unless you are applying as a *gunsmith*. Moreover, unless you are licensed as a **gunsmith**, the portion of the premises used for your business must be "*open to the public*" -- and I doubt you want people walking in and out of your home during regular business hours, or have ATF agents nosing around while adminis- trative and records searches are conducted there. Last, do not use one address for your license, and then work from your home or somewhere else, as your license wouldn't cover the transaction. *U.S. v. Bailey*, 123 F.3d 1381 (11th Cir. 1997). Thus, in the *Bailey* case, the 11th Circuit held that where the sale was made from the FFL's home, rather than the actual business address listed on the FFL, he committed the crime of *"dealing without a license"* as the FFL only covered the business address, not the home. A federal felony!

DENIALS AND DISCIPLINARY ACTIONS:

Licensing, disciplinary and revocation procedures for FFL's are set forth in *Subpart E* of 27 *CFR*, *sections* 478.71 - 478.78, and are largely identical. In essence, if your application for FFL or renewal is denied, you will be mailed *a **Notice of Denial.*** At that point you have **15 days** from the date of receipt to request a hearing to review the denial. A failure to make a written request for the hearing is a waiver. The request can also be done by fax, with BATFE permission. Once received, the ***Director of Industry Operations*** (ie: "DIO")will set a hearing date, time, and place. You may request it occur at any BATFE office that is convenient to you. Such should be done at the time you ask for the review hearing. The same procedure and time limitations apply if you receive a ***Notice of Revocation*** if you willfully failed to follow any of the statutes or regulations, or you could receive a similar notice for suspension, revocation, or imposition of a civil fine for other "*knowing*" violations.

An informal hearing is then scheduled within **30 days** of the assignment of the hearing officer, normally to be heard within **90 days** of his or her assignment (although it can be continued for good cause), and you may be represented by yourself, an attorney, accountant, or another person approved by BATFE. A hearing officer has the government put on its evidence first, and then you can put in your evidence. All of this is recorded by tape or digital machine by the hearing officer, although you can also hire your own stenographer. A written report is then generated by the hearing officer within **30 days** of the conclusion of the hearing, and sent to the *DIO* who makes a final decision, and issues a ***Final Notice*** if charges are sustained. You get a copy. If it is against you, you have a right to appeal *de novo* to the *Federal District Court* within **60 days**. 18 U.S.C. 923(f)(3). If it's for you – you'll get a letter saying so. However, where there are problems with BATFE, a compromise or other agreement can often be made to avoid a revocation. This should normally be done at the earliest opportunity by an attorney familiar with these procedures, although I have heard of several instances where the FFL was able to work it out themself. However, trying to do it yourself is not always a great idea, because if negotiations with BATFE go south – it usually makes it impossible for an attorney to rectify from that point on. Therefore, I always suggest early involvement of an attorney who knows this area. Unfortunately, not many do.

If you are unlucky enough to be indicted for a felony, or crime punishable by more than two years imprisonment, or have had a criminal Information filed against you for such, you may continue to operate until any conviction becomes final. If you are ***convicted*** of the felony, you may still file for removal of disability to operate as an FFL due to said conviction. If so, you are allowed to operate for thirty (30) days after the date of which conviction becomes final. If you don't file for this relief you must stop operating once the thirty (30) days after the date of the conviction runs. If you were acquitted of the felony charges, or they are otherwise terminated by dismissal, BATFE may not try to revoke your FFL for same reasons.

ADMINISTRATIVE REVIEW OF RECORDS AND INVENTORY:
Any licensee is subject to administrative audit of your books, records, and inventory. Unless it is pursuant to a search warrant, it will be done during normal business hours. You have no right to interfere, and should keep out of the agents way. If you think something is improper, mentally note it for review with your attorney at a later date. Do not play "big shot". It will only cause you trouble. Here is the way it works:

BATFE may have a judicial magistrate issue a warrant upon "reasonable cause" to believe violation of the firearms law has occurred, and that evidence of such may be on business premises or other storage area. The warrant allows inspection of all records required to be kept, and all firearms & ammo kept on premises.

ATF agents may also inspect <u>without</u> reasonable cause, and <u>without</u> a warrant where:

1. Such is done in the course of reasonable inquiry during a criminal investigation of someone other than the FFL.

2. To ensure compliance with record   keeping requirements, but not more than once in any 12 month period. However, the licensee may elect to conduct this inquiry at the local ATF office, rather than on the business premises.

3. To determine the disposition of one or more particular firearms in course of bona fide criminal investigation.

If any records are seized, the BATF officer may seize only those records that constitute evidence of a violation, and copies must be provided within a reasonable time to licensee.

<u>SALE OF FIREARMS TO ALIENS:</u>
I have placed extensive information on sale of firearms and ammunition in Chapter Two, and suggest you read those sections as they fully explain this area. A *"resident alien"* is someone with *permanent residency status*, and used to be called a *"green card"*. They are treated exactly as a citizen. Aliens who come in through the *Visa Waiver Program* can also shoot, rent, and buy ammo anywhere in the United States, but can only purchase if they are an actual resident of the state of purchase. Most citizens of Canada and Bermuda who don't require a visa, also have the same restrictions as the Visa Waiver. Everyone else who come in on a visa are considered *"**non-immigrant aliens**"* and are *prohibited persons* unless they have a valid hunting license, or fall within the other exceptions. There is no "90" day residency requirement.

<u>SALES OR DISPOSITIONS FROM PERSONAL COLLECTION:</u>
First, I repeat my previous words of warning about an issue that seems to get confused far too many times -- if you are selling firearms as a business, and the business is in the form of corporate ownership -- no individual is the "FFL" -- instead, the *"**corporation**"* is the FFL. Thus, any firearm you obtain from the business inventory that goes off-premises must be logged out to you in the *disposition book* just like any other disposition, together with a *Form 4473*, and NICS check. This applies equally to any employee, manager, corporate officer, or stockholder. On the other hand, if the business really is in your personal

name, then you (and only you) may take firearms out of the business inventory, and off-premises without doing NICS or the Form 4473, and even add them to your *"personal collection"* so long as you have marked them into your FFL disposition book.   On the other hand, if an employee of an FFL is taking a firearm temporarily off premises purely for temporary demonstration purposes – such is lawful, and need not be entered into your disposition book. *BATFE Ruling 2010-1.*

If you are then selling or transferring a firearm from your *"personal collection"* that you obtained from your business inventory as the FFL, and **one year** (ie: 365 days) has passed since taking possession -- you may sell or transfer the firearm as if it was your personal property without doing the *Form 4473* or NICS check. However, you must log the disposition into a personal *bound book*, which you must keep for BATFE. On the other hand, if the sale or disposition is prior to the year's time, then the firearm is treated, for federal record-keeping purposes, as still being the property of the licensed business (ie: FFL), must be re-entered into the acquisition portion of your business records, and then into the disposition portion to record the transfer — plus, you need the *Form 4473* and NICS.

If you purchased the firearm as a personal gun from anyone other than your own FFL, then you may sell it just like an individual, and there is no need to enter it into your personal book. Only firearms obtained from the business inventory fall into this **"one year"** period.

MULTIPLE HANDGUN SALES TO SINGLE INDIVIDUAL:
If you sell two or more **handguns** of any type to the same individual within **five (5)** consecutive business days, you must report it on a *Form 3310.4* -- not later than close of business date of each such transaction. In other words, if the non-licensee buys two handguns on Monday -- you must file on Monday. If he buys another on Thursday, you must file another one, because it's now "three handguns" within five business days. The *Brady* law also requires reporting it to the state, or local law enforcement. 18 USC 923(3)(A).

If you somehow screwed-up by not reporting it when you should — you should still report it as soon as possible, and make sure the dates are accurate, even if that may cause some consternation with BATFE. My advise to any client is that *"better late than never"* is a rule that must be followed in all instances where you missed something. Otherwise, your friends at ATF may feel that your mistake was *"knowing and willful"* rather than just oversight or stupidity. *"Knowing and willful"* is a very bad place to be with the feds. It makes for the creation of serious felony charges, or at least a revocation of licensing issue! And by the way – this particular violation is one of the easier ones to screw up if you're not careful, and one of the ones most likely to get you in trouble with BATFE.

LOST, MISPLACED, OR STOLEN FIREARMS:

If any firearm is stolen or lost from your inventory or collection, it must be reported to ATF, and to local police within **48 hours** on a *Form 3310.4*. Likewise, just having a firearm "*missing*" from inventory qualifies – even if you're sure you're gonna find it. Assuming you somehow screw-up the 48 hour reporting period, I strongly suggest you file the form, and report it, even if late. Filing the form is necessary because federal law has made theft of firearms from a federal licensee, a federal offense. [18 USC 922(u)] If you think you can find the firearm, and that it's only "*misplaced*" — you still only have the 48 hour period to find it, or report it. I guess you could call it a "47 hour" period. If you're unsure whether the firearm was "misplaced" vs. "stolen" -- report it as "*lost*", and not as stolen. That way if you or an employee made an innocent mistake, or if it was legally sold, and the paperwork was misplaced -- the police won't arrest someone found with the firearm. This will save you a *very big lawsuit* for negligence once your legal, but very ticked-off customer gets out of jail. ATF has determined that many times a "*misplaced*" gun was actually legally sold by the FFL, and there was a paperwork mix-up.

PAWNBROKERS:

Pawnbrokers who buy, sell, transfer, or hold firearms as security for a loan must be federally licensed. While filling out the Form 4473 is not needed when the firearm is pledged for security, the receipt of such must still be entered into your **bound book**. However, the Form 4473 must be completed when the firearm is redeemed -- as that is considered a "*disposition*" of the firearm. The NICS check must also be done.

On the other hand, if the disposition is to the same person who pledged the firearms with you, and more than one firearm is involved -- it need not be reported as a multiple sale on the *Form 3310.4*, because it's not a "*sale*" – it's a "*return*". That's not my opinion – that's BATFE's.

Even if the person who pledged the firearm is the same person seeking to redeem it -- it cannot be returned to an under-aged person, or any other *prohibited person*, and should only be returned to person who pawned the firearm, or the ticket holder. If it's a **handgun**, you could not legally return it to an *out-of-state resident*, even if he was previously a Florida resident at the time of the pawn.

Nor could you return it to him if he was under 21 years of age -- even if he was the person who legally pawned it.

SECONDHAND DEALERS:
          In Florida any business that purchases, handles consignments, or trades in second-hand guns or weapons is included within the definition of a "***secondhand dealer***" pursuant to Chapter 538 of the Florida Statutes. Such dealers must register with the Department of Revenue as a secondhand dealer, and keep records on the "*Secondhand Dealer's Property Form*" as approved by FDLE, in all incoming transactions for one year on the premises, and not less than a total of three years. Thus, records may be kept off premises after a year of the transaction. The records include obtaining a right thumbprint, copy of government issued photo identification or all information therefrom, and a signed statement verifying the seller is the owner of the merchandise, or an authorized person. If a copy of the photo identification is made – it must be kept for the same periods as the transaction form. Pawnbrokers follow the same rules under C. 539, Florida Statutes. Acquisitions must be reported within 24 hours.

          The transaction records, and any such goods are subject to examination by law enforcement during normal business hours. For firearms, this does **not** include federal *Form 4473's*, just the records required under *Chapter 538* of the statutes.   Furthermore, any such merchandise cannot be sold for **fifteen (15) days**, except where being returned to the person who actually sold them to the dealer, and a hold may be placed on any such goods by law enforcement where there is reason to believe they may be stolen property. The dealer's registration certificate must be conspicuously displayed on the premises, and a dealer may not acquire from: any individual under the age of 18, any individual who appears to be under the influence of drugs or alcohol, or acquired between the hours of ten in the evening to eight in the morning. Local ordinances may be more restrictive than the state statute. Violations of the statute are a crime. Only the Secondhand Dealers Property Form may be electronically (ie: computer) forwarded to police departments regarding firearms, and any electronic records concerning firearms (except photo i/d)[2] must be deleted from the dealer's system after 30 days – but the hard copy forms must be kept. F.S. 790.335(3)(f)

SELLING TO PERSONS WITH OBVIOUS IMPAIRMENTS:
          Several years ago K-Mart was ordered to pay $12.5 million dollars for selling a rifle to an intoxicated person, who then went out, and shot someone. Technically, this sale violated no law, although it came awful close. The problem was that the jury felt it was negligent to sell a firearm to an obviously intoxicated person, and most juries would probably agree.[3] This should warn you that if you

sell to someone who appears mentally imbalanced, appears to be using illegal drugs (even marijuana), or appears to have had too much to drink -- don't make the sale unless you have a spare twelve-and-a-half million!   Likewise, F.S. 790.17 makes it unlawful to sell any weapon or firearm (other than an *"ordinary" pocketknife*) to someone of *"unsound mind"*.

Florida law doesn't allow an *intoxicated person* to use a **loaded** firearm except in necessary self-defense. That means there's a loophole if it's unloaded. The loophole applies only to the criminal violation -- negligence and recklessness are still civilly actionable, and that's where the money is -- or will go.   In sustaining that 12.5 million dollar verdict, here's what the Florida Supreme Court said:

> *"One who knowingly sells an article to a person incompetent in its use, with reasonable foreseeability that injury to others may occur as a result of such use, can be held accountable in tort to others for the injuries sustained thereby."*

If the guy gets drunk, or shoots cocaine <u>after</u> he buys the firearm, you should be off the legal hook -- unless you knew, or reasonably should have known that he was an alcoholic, incompetent, illegal drug user, or was planning to do something criminal. If you do -- you're in for lots of problems. So, be forewarned.

SELLING TO KIDS:
I know, we've been over this several times. It's easy when you talk about firearms -- 21 for a handgun -- 18 for a rifle or shotgun. But, what about other weapons?

Well, if the kid is **18 years old** he can buy anything he wants from a dealer except a handgun, and illegal weapons. No permission needed. If the kid is **under 18 years** of age -- you can't sell anything but a *common pocketknife.* You could sell to the parents, uncle, or whoever – but unless the kid is at least 18 years of age – it's a crime for you to sell or deliver to the kid any weapon or firearm other than a *common pocketknife*!

If you sell to the parent or uncle or whoever – don't be cute, and hand junior the purchase! Give it to Dad, and let him hand it to junior. Likewise, don't take any payment from junior! Only from someone 18 years of age, or older. If you don't take my warning, and you deliver a *firearm, bowie knife, dirk, brass knuckles, or electronic weapon* -- it's a *second degree felony.*[4] F.S. 790.18. Any other weapon is a first degree misdemeanor. F.S. 790.17. An *airgun* may be considered a weapon. Generally, that depends on its use, or intended use. I would say a *bow and arrow* is always a weapon, because that's what it was traditionally used for. But, why take the chance? Just sell the darn thing direct to Dad, and skip all the possible legal hassles.

Another quirk is that although you can sell a person under 21 years, but at least 18 years of age a shotgun or rifle — a *shotgun with a pistol grip* in lieu of a shoulder stock does not qualify as a "*shotgun*" because a shotgun, pursuant to 18 USC 921(a)(5) is a weapon "*intended to be fired from the shoulder.*" When the shoulder stock is missing, it is no longer intended to be "fired from the shoulder", hence — it's not a "*shotgun*", and according to BATFE is a "*pistol grip firearm*" *(PGF)*. Thus, only a person aged **21 years or older** may purchase it.

SALE OF AMMUNITION TO MINOR:
Florida law does not make it a crime for a non-federal licensee to sell ammunition to a minor. A federal licensee could not. However, the loophole has been somewhat covered in the 1994 Crime Bill by making it illegal for **anyone** to sell or transfer *handgun ammunition* to a juvenile under the age of 18 years, except under very precise exceptions. Thus, a federal licensee can't sell **handgun** ammunition to anyone under 21 years of age, and a *private citizen* can't sell it to anyone under 18 years of age.

As I already pointed out in a footnote, Wal-Mart got socked with a substantial civil jury verdict for causing the death of an individual because they sold handgun ammunition to an under-aged youth who then used it to shoot the decedent. The appellate court held that this was exactly the conduct that the federal statute tried to prevent, thus a violation of the statute was negligence, and the cause of the misfortune.

A warning to the wise is sufficient!

CHART – DEALER PERMITTED WEAPON SALES TO MINOR:

under 18	No weapons or firearms **except** a *common pocketknife* – sell anything else to guardian or parent only!
18	shotgun, rifle, any legal weapon **except** NFA or handgun.
21	any legal weapon or firearm

REQUIRED FLORIDA WARNING NOTICES UPON SALE:

It is a second degree misdemeanor for any retailer to fail to provide the following written warning in letters no less than 1/4 inch in height to the transferee when you sell or deliver a firearm.

> IT IS UNLAWFUL, AND PUNISHABLE BY IMPRISONMENT AND FINE, FOR ANY ADULT TO STORE OR LEAVE A FIREARM IN ANY PLACE WITHIN THE REACH OR EASY ACCESS OF A MINOR UNDER 18 YEARS OF AGE OR TO KNOWINGLY SELL OR OTHERWISE TRANSFER OWNERSHIP OR POSSESSION OF A FIREARM TO A MINOR OR A PERSON OF UNSOUND MIND.

A similar warning must be posted at **each** purchase counter (including gun shows) in block letters at least 1" inch in height. This *written warning* must be given to the purchaser, even if he is 70 years old, has no kids, doesn't know any kids, and has no desire to. It must be in block letters at least one quarter inch high. If you think this is no big deal -- remember the verdict in K-Mart. What do you think a jury will do if some kid gets hold of the firearm, and the jerk who bought it from you says he didn't know he had to keep it in a safe place away from the child? I bet you can guess!

> IT IS UNLAWFUL TO STORE OR LEAVE A FIREARM IN ANY PLACE WITHIN THE REACH OR EASY ACCESS OF A MINOR UNDER 18 YEARS OF AGE OR TO KNOWINGLY SELL OR OTHERWISE TRANSFER OWNERSHIP OR POSSESSION OF A FIREARM TO A MINOR OR PERSON OF UNSOUND MIND.

This means at gun shows, and at your place of business. True, it's only a second degree misdemeanor. But then, there's that silly verdict in K-Mart popping-up again. Get the point?

REQUIRED FEDERAL WARNINGS :

Federal law also requires a posted notice both on the licensed premises, and at gun shows regarding the requirements of the *Youth Safety Handgun Act*. These posters are available through ATF, and repeat the restrictions set forth on ATF Form I 5300.2. You may order this through the ATF Distribution Center at (703) 455-7801, or download it through the web site. You must also deliver a copy of the form with **every handgun** delivered to any non-FFL. The form may be included *within a brochure* supplied by the manufacturer or importer, or any document. 27 CFR 478.103.

STUFF YOU GOTTA SELL:

The Omnibus Appropriations Act of 1999 requires that all FFL's now sell, and have in stock, secure gun storage devices. As of 2005, 18 USC 922(z), also makes it unlawful for an FFL to transfer or sell any **handgun** to a non-FFL unless the handgun is delivered with a secure gun storage or safety device. It does not apply to a longgun, or a curio or relic. It does not apply to a rental or loan that is kept on the FFL's business premises for the duration of the rental/loan. Other exceptions are transfers FFL's, to law enforcement officers or rail security officers for on duty or off duty use in their profession; to government purchasers. This means trigger locks, gun locking devices which render the firearm unable to discharge, lock boxes with locks, or gun safes. If such a device is temporarily not available – it must be delivered to the purchaser within ten (10) days. Mailing it is OK, if it comes to that.

If a firearm is consigned to the FFL, or pawned – a device must be included at the point of return unless the owner supplied one of his own. The law does not apply to *estate sales* conducted by the executor or auctioneer on the estate's behalf - as it only applies to FFL's. If multiple handguns are sold, a lock box that fits all the handguns would be OK.

STUFF YOU JUST CAN'T SELL IN FLORIDA:

It's illegal to manufacture, sell, or try to sell any weapon commonly known as **brass knuckles**, or a **slungshot** to anyone, even an adult. Under F.S. 790.09, this would be a second degree misdemeanor. On the other hand, it's not illegal to own them. Now, you know what *brass knuckles* are (calling them a "paper weight" is bull) , but a "*slungshot*" , "*billie*", or "*slapshot*" -- is a weighted material fixed on the end of a flexible handle or strap, to be used as a weapon. By the way, calling a slungshot a "*tire tester*" is not going to work -- it's still a slungshot. While a telescoping "*tactical baton*" (ie: "*ASP baton*") may act in a similar fashion, it's not the same animal, and in my opinion is perfectly legal.

Another problem is "*hoax bombs*". Under federal law a dummy shell or grenade is not a destructive device or weapon -- it's just a dummy grenade. They make great paper weights! Many of my friends have one. The problem is that under Florida law -- they appear to be illegal due to some really crummy drafting of a statute, F.S. 790.165. If you want to be on the safe side, as silly as it may sound, you should not sell, transfer, or possess these little gems.

Since I'm sure you'd like to know what a "*hoax bomb*" is -- it's "*any device or object that by its design, construction, content, or characteristics appears to be, or to contain, a destructive device or explosive.*" So much for "*dummy dynamite*" clocks in those nifty gag catalogs! People just can't have any fun with these stupid laws!

Anyway, the real bad news is that it's a third degree felony to make these things, sell them, possess them, or deliver them unless you're a member of a theatrical company utilizing them as a prop -- or if you're a security person in an airport using them within your duties as you try to sneak them past detectors to see if anyone notices. Of course, we all know that this law makes no sense, as written.   On the other hand, I think the statute would have a hard time withstanding a constitutional attack, unless the "*hoax bomb*" was being used with criminal intent. *Test case* time, again.

SELF-PROPELLED, BALLISTIC, OR "SPRING" KNIVES:

Lastly, you can't own, sell, possess, or transfer a *self-propelled, ballistic, or "spring knife"*. Violation under Florida law is a first degree misdemeanor .[5] A *self-propelled*, or *ballistic knife*, or "*spring knife*", is a device that propels a knifelike blade as a projectile by means of a coiled spring, elastic, or compressed gas. They use to make them as belt buckles. In Florida, it's a no no. In Federal land it's a lot more serious — it's a ten year felony. [15 USC 1245]

GUN SHOWS:

We've gone over them already, but I've got a paragraph or two I need to kill, so here's the unofficial addendum. **Gun shows** have come under great criticism, primarily by people who don't want you to own guns.   For the most part, the criticism is totally unwarranted. However, there is one thing about gun shows that poses a potential problem -- and that's non-FFL's having tables where they sell firearms out of their "*private collections*". These "private" sales are often being conducted as a regular weekend business by persons who are not following the law, and are hurting the industry as a whole by doing so. BATFE has already sent warnings to some of these people, and has cracked down on others. I have handled some of these cases. I think you should think seriously about it if you are a non-FFL, and are basically conducting a weekend business in firearms. ATF is watching!

Moreover, if you're a private citizen selling firearms from your collection – my personal opinion is that unless a firearm is in your ownership for at least **one year**, you could have a problem if you were regularly selling as a non-FFL. The reason I give a "***one year***" as the magic number is because that is the same period for an FFL who places a firearm from inventory into his own personal collection. Thus, if you really just like to buy and sell so you can try out various firearms, or play around with your collection rather than try to "make money" –

this is the relatively safer way to do it. For good measure, make sure you keep records that document the date you purchased any firearm you're selling. Likewise, if you're selling at a gun show, you may be required to run a records check, and even have a waiting period to sell the gun legally depending on county ordinances in the county the show is held. And, as I've said before, a *private individual* cannot purchase any firearm from another *private individual* out of state unless the firearm is delivered to an FFL in the purchaser's residence state for pick up.

RELOADING AS A BUSINESS:

The same warning applies to reloaders who do not have an FFL. Since they are reloading as a business, they are *"manufacturers"*, and need to be federally licensed under 18 USC 923. If all you are doing is *"selling"* legal ammo, even reloads, and not personally reloading the stuff for resale — don't worry about it, you don't have a problem.

FIREARM INSTRUCTORS:

Firearm instructors don't have much to worry about other than those who certify students for CWL's, as you must now maintain records which certify that he or she observed the student *"safely handle and discharge"* the firearm. F.S. 790.06(2)(h)(7). That should mean using a real firearm with live ammo – not blanks, and certainly not an Airsoft! The *NRA* requires that of its *certified instructors* – and some instructors have actually been prosecuted because they certified students for the CWL application without using real guns or ammo. Likewise, the *NRA* will revoke the credentials of any *NRA* certified instructor who they find conducts a non-*NRA* course unless both the advertising and all documentation including the completion certificate prominently note it is *"Not an NRA approved course!"* If conducting an NRA course – it must be done exactly as the book requires, and the required handbooks to students must be included. Plus, if you want your students to stay out of jail – please sell them a copy of this book, as well.

As far as record keeping goes for your *"student list"* – this may be as simple as a list of the students names, and date observed., but you keep the records for two (2) years. You should also remember that any certificate you send up to Tallahassee should have your *NRA* identification number, or K license number.

As a personal note, you're gonna be asked *legal questions* by students. Beyond the most basic of them – I think you should try to steer away from giving legal advice. Remember, you're not an attorney, and if you give the wrong legal advice you're opening yourself to a lawsuit. That's one of the reasons the book was written, plus it's something everyone who owns a gun really should have. So, instead of giving the wrong advice, or incomplete advice — do your students a favor, and just sell them this book, and let the students find out for themselves, so they also remember it. The law is far too complicated to cover in a class, and quite frankly -- you're really not qualified to do it. Spend your time on safety, firearms handling, proper ammunition, and emergency situations. Push advance classes for students, such as stress-fire situations, combat and cover, low light, and the myriad of other situations that students really should be trained in. It <u>can't</u> be covered in one class! Make sure your students understand that, and understand the importance of furthering their training and knowledge. That's part of being a good instructor!

FFL OPERATING OUT OF HOME:

I know! We've already covered this, however, let me once again emphasize that an FFL can't sell and deliver from a location not on their license other than an actual *gun show* in their home state. A violation is a definite federal no-no. Such was the case in <u>*U.S.v. Bailey*</u>, 123 F.3 1381 (11ᵗʰ Cir. 1997), where Mr. Bailey got convicted of the federal offense of "dealing without a license" because the license covers only specified business premises, and Mr. Bailey was actually working out of his home. Be warned! Serious stuff! Also remember that assuming your home is going to be listed as your licensed premises – it must be zoned for such use. ATF won't issue the FFL unless you are complying with "*all state and local laws*". 27 CFR 478.47

In closing, please remember that being an FFL dealer is not the easiest task in the world. Moreover, just because you may know what you're doing -- there's a very good chance that your employees don't have a clue – especially those working only part-time. You need to train them, and you need the personal knowledge to be able to access if they are operating properly. If they screw up – it's your license that will be lost, irregardless. You can't leave it up to somebody else -- and if you can't figure out exactly what you're supposed to do, call up BATFE, and ask! Or, you could even hire an attorney, assuming you can find one who knows anything about this area besides me. Remember that you must take this stuff seriously, otherwise you can get hit with criminal, as well as civil penalties.

ABBREVIATIONS & BOUND BOOK:

ATF has made clear that they don't particularly care for abbreviations on the Form 4473 except for approved postal abbreviations for the state's, and d/l for driver's license. Also, if you're using a computerized bound book – back the damn thing up regularly, and print out the entire inventory twice yearly. This is an area where I see lots of problems. These systems crash and lose info – and now it's your butt on the line. ATF doesn't like the excuse that "it was the computer's fault".

RESPONSIBLE PERSON:

The Safe Explosives Act defined the phrase *"responsible person"*, and in the March 2006 edition of the FFL Newsletter, BATFE adopted this definition across the board to apply to all FFL's. I therefore reprint that portion of the Newsletter, as I could not do it any better:

"A "responsible person" is defined as an individual who has the power to direct the management and policies of the business entity for which the Federal firearms license is being applied. Neither the Gun Control Act (GCA) nor its implementing regulations define the term "responsible person." However, historically the term "responsible person" was deemed to have the same definition in the firearms context as Congress has now incorporated into the Safe Explosives Act (SEA): a person who has the power to direct the management and policies of the firearms activity. Now that Congress has specifically defined the term in the explosives context, ATF will interpret the SEA definition to also apply in the firearms context. A determination of whether an individual is a responsible person may depend on his or her ownership interest in the business, the management structure of the business, and their ability and authority to direct the management and policies of the firearms business.

"Some examples of different types of business organizations include sole proprietorships, partnerships, corporations, and associations. The owner of a sole proprietorship would be a responsible person. In a partnership, each partner would be a responsible person. In a corporation or association, only the directors and officers who direct the management and policies of the corporation or association with respect to firearms would be responsible persons. In most firearms businesses, the store manager would be a responsible person. Each business entity may have a different business structure, so determining who is a responsible person must be made by referring back to the statutory definition: the individuals who direct the management and policies of the entity pertaining to firearms. It should be noted that not every individual at the management level is a responsible person for the purposes of Federal firearms laws. For example, a human resources manager who does not otherwise direct management and policies relating to firearms would not be a responsible person.

"Finally, every applicant for a license or permit must designate at least one local responsible person for the business. Applications alleging there is no person in the organization responsible for the firearms business will be returned for additional information. Clearly, one or more individuals must be responsible for keeping track of inventory and records. Without denoting a responsible person on the application, a license will not be issued."

In the FFL Newsletter of September 2013, volume 2, BATFE clarified that any new or additional *"responsible persons"* must be added by request to the BATFE licensing center. Since a *responsible person* is simply someone who has the power to direct management and policies of the business – it's more than likely you may have more than one in your operation.

SALE OF UNFINISHED RECEIVERS:

At one point BATFE was threatening prosecution in some sales of unfinished AR-15 type aluminum *lower receivers* as being the sale of an actual *"firearm"*. I know there's ongoing litigation on this. The letter was dated January 29, 2004, and stated that when the machining accomplished a magazine well, trigger slot; cavity for the trigger/hammer/disconnector/safety selector; initial opening for the buffer tube; slot for magazine catch; slot for bolt carrier; right hand and center relief cuts for forward takedown pin – it had reached *"the stage of manufacturing whereby they are identifiable as the frame or receiver."* BATFE advised a solid AR–15 type receiver casting was fine, but with a machined magazine well and central area for fire control components – the machining had gone too far, and it had become a "firearm" because a *"receiver"* is defined as a *"firearm"*. Obviously, in these instances, you need to be an FFL if you're in the *"business"* of selling it, and you need the 4473 for the purchaser unless he or she is another FFL. Just a word of caution.

EMPLOYEES; AND SHOOTERS AT RANGE UNDER 18 YEARS:

If you read Chapter Eight carefully, you would have realized there are three Florida statutes that deal with transfers of firearms or weapons to minors: F.S. 790.17; 790.18; 790.22. Only F.S. 790.22, and federal law apply to a possible *"minor"* (ie: under 18 years old) employee, or a *minor* shooting at a range.

F.S. 790.22 states that anyone **under 18** years **cannot possess any firearm** away from home, except for hunting or sport shooting purposes. Working in a gun store, or gun range is neither! Yes – federal law would allow it with parental written consent. Likewise, both Florida and federal law would allow a minor to shoot at a *shooting range* with *parental written consent,* and for those children **under 16 years** – *adult supervision* is also required. However, on a person note, I think you'd be nuts to allow anyone under 18 to shoot unless with a responsible adult. In such case – I would highly recommend that unless a *parent* actually accompanies a child under 18 years, and can sign the *Waiver of Liability* form – you are probably in for a really big lawsuit if something bad happens. Likewise, although an 18 year old is of lawful age to sign the waiver without a parent – you still have the discretion to require more, if you don't feel comfortable about it. In case you didn't know, any *"on premises"* rental is not a *"disposition, transfer, or delivery"* per *FFL Newsletter* of March 2013, volume 2.

SHOOTING RANGE PROTECTION:

Florida Statute 790.333 is aimed at curtailing government interference with pre-existing non-residential type shooting ranges, and preempts all government control over *shooting ranges* solely to the State, such that local governments may not pass regulations, change zoning laws, or otherwise act in any manner to regulate any type of firearm or airgun shooting range. **Only** the *Department of Environmental Protection* may bring an action against a range where there is evidence of contamination, although a local government may enforce current zoning laws that **pre-existed** creation of the range. However, in order to avoid local government interference, and have *immunity* against any such law suit, all such ranges are required to have made a *good faith effort* to follow environmental management practices pursuant to the "*Best Management Practices for Environmental Stewardship of Florida Shooting Ranges*" published by that Department. Ranges may request technical assistance from the Department for such.

Florida Statute 823.16 is another statute that protects both commercial and residential shooting ranges, but this time – in order for this statute to apply the range owner or operator must "*conform to current NRA gun safety and shooting range standards.*" This is likely an unconstitutional delegation of legislative power, and has other legal defenses attached – so whether it is an absolute requirement is a *test case* waiting to happen. However, what the statute does is prevent any government entity from changing the law related to an "existing" shooting range. Thus, if a *shooting range* was legal when it was first constructed or began operation, any subsequent local laws or regulations that effected it would be void and unlawful. This also applies to "noise violations" and complaints. Thus, if a shooting range was in compliance with existing *noise ordinances* when it first began operating – a subsequent noise complaint is not actionable by government or private individuals. However, legal action could be taken for acts of negligence or recklessness.

BACKYARD SHOOTING RANGE:

Backyard shooting ranges are normally governed by F.S. 823.16. Make sure you get hold of the NRA materials you need – and follow them. Anything else isn't worth the *test case*. You also have a problem with F.S. 790.15, which makes it a crime to *knowingly* discharge a firearm over any public road, street, or occupied premises – and further makes it a crime to discharge a firearm outdoors in a reckless or negligent manner on any property used primarily as the site for a dwelling, or zoned exclusively for residential use.

QUESTION: What about building my own backyard range?

ANSWER: While I've found no case law, my opinion is that it is perfectly legal to have a backyard range pursuant to F.S. 790.25(3)(j), and F.S. 823.16 if such was lawful when the operation of your range first began. However, such should ideally have a high, thick dirt berm – as the area must provide a safe place and conditions. If any bullet passes on to someone else's property or across a public road – big problems! Obviously, you must also follow NRA guidelines if you want to keep away from new local regulations and noise complaints.

GETTING INSURANCE:

Last in this chapter is my strong advice to make sure you have liability insurance. That goes for whether you are an FFL, gunsmith, range, or just a firearms instructor. The NRA has reasonably priced plans for all of these, and there is other insurance out there. A civil lawsuit will bankrupt you unless you have this protection! It isn't worth the chance, even with all the waivers you likely have customers or students sign!

ENDNOTES FOR CHAPTER NINE:

1. Authority to support an FFL receiving/purchasing (not selling) firearms out of state can be found in 27 CFR 478.29 & 478.29a. 18 USC 922(a)(3).

2. There is a conflict between F.S. 538.04(7) & F.S. 790.335(3)(f) on what electronic records are to be destroyed. Common sense dictates that if an electric copy of the photo i/d was taken – it should be preserved for three years per C. 538 – although this is purely my best guess, and the statutes appear to be totally in conflict on this point. Test case time.

3. K-Mart v. Kitchen, 662 So.2d 977 (Fla. 4DCA 1995) was reversed by the Florida Supreme Court on July 17, 1997 in Kitchen v. K-Mart 697 So.2d 1200 (Fla. 1997), which reinstated the jury verdict. Also, in Wal-Mart v. Coker, 742 So.2d 257 (Fla. 1DCA 1997), Wal-Mart was found liable for the death of a person when it sold handgun ammo to a minor who then used it to

shoot the decedent. Big bucks!

4. <u>F.S.</u> 790.18

5. <u>F.S.</u> 790.225. The real bad news is that federal law can make possession, manufacture, distribution a ten year felony per 15 USC 1245:

> "Whoever in or affecting interstate commerce, within any Territory or possession of the United States, within Indian country (as defined in section 1151 of title 18), or within the special maritime and territorial jurisdiction of the United States (as defined in section 7 of title 18), knowingly possesses, manufactures, sells, or imports a ballistic knife shall be . . .imprisoned not more than ten years. . . ."

CHAPTER TEN

MISCELLANEOUS PROVISIONS

THE ASSAULT WEAPONS BAN:

In 1994 the Congress bowed to media pressure, and anti-gun advocates, and passed certain portions of the Crime Bill that redefined what an "*assault rifle*" was, and made the manufacture, import, and possession of such firearms, as well as "*large capacity ammunition feeding devices*" (ie: magazine capable of holding over ten cartridges) manufactured or imported after that date illegal. That law **ended** on September 13, 2004, and hopefully is now and forever, only history. In case you don't already know, these firearms were never a real problem, and are rarely used in crimes. Even the FBI admitted that in its statistics. However, the newest B.S. reason anti-gun politicians are using is that guns are being run across our border to Mexican drug cartels. While it's true some guns are getting there BATFE records show that illegal arms sales from the United States account for only 17% of illegal firearms brought into Mexico.[1]

Most, and the more serious, of these weapons are coming from China, Russia, and South Korea thru Guatemala, and the ones from the U.S. don't include any automatic weapons - which are the ones the cartels really like. Likewise – it's already a very serious crime to run guns across the border – so don't expect any of these criminals to be deterred by reinstatement of the assault weapons law – as usual, it will just prevent honest citizens from getting them. In the meantime, the "*AR*" platform has become the most popular firearm type in the United States for both sport shooting and self defense. In the industry they are referred to as "*modern sporting rifles*" (*MSR's*) . So, when remembering back on the defunct and totally b.s. "*assault weapons ban*", maybe this quote from *Thomas Jefferson* will put it in perspective:

> "Those who would sacrifice a little freedom for a little order, will lose both, and deserve neither."

MODIFICATIONS TO NON-SPORTING RIFLES:

Before you go modifying your *SKS* , *AK, Norinco*, or other semi-auto that could fall into an "assault" type, or more appropriately be termed a "*modern sporting rifle*", let me warn you that this is one confusing area of law! I have read this stuff over and over — and still had to call the Firearms Technology Branch of ATF to explain it to me. The law does not mean what it says unless you studied at "Alice In Wonderland University". Were it not for some letters from BATFE published in the *American Rifleman* in 1994 in response to some questions from the NRA, and some great insight from the Firearms Technology Branch of BATFE — I would never have included this section.[2]

To begin, you start with 18 USC 922 (r), which states:

"It shall be unlawful for any person to <u>assemble</u> from <u>imported parts</u> any semiautomatic rifle or shotgun <u>prohibited from importation under section 925(d)(3)</u> of this chapter as not being particularly suitable for or readily adaptable to sporting purposes . . . ."

18 USC 925(d)(3) pertains to those firearms and types of ammunition which the Secretary of Treasury allows to be imported -- they are on a list which includes most SKS and AK type firearms.   Thus, subsection (d)(3) allows importation:

*"of a type that does not fall within the definition of a firearm as defined in section 5845(a) of the Internal Revenue Code of 1954 (ie: any NFA weapon), and is generally recognized as particularly suitable for or readily adaptable to **sporting purposes** . . . ."*

In conjunction with all this, you need to know the federal regulation that implements the law, and deals with the modification or "assembly of semiautomatic rifles or shotguns", to wit: 27 CFR 478.39. The pertinent parts of that regulation read as follows:

(a)   No person shall assemble a semiautomatic rifle or any shotgun using more than **10 of the imported parts** listed in paragraph (c) of this section if the assembled firearm is prohibited from importation under section 925(d)(3) as not being particularly suitable for or readily adaptable to sporting purposes.

(b)   The provisions of this section shall not apply to:

(3)   The repair of any rifle or shotgun which had been imported into or assembled in the United States prior to November 30, 1990, or the replacement of any part of such firearm.

(c).   For purposes of this section, the term imported parts are:

(1) Frames, receivers, receiver castings, forgings or stampings
(2) Barrels
(3) Barrel extensions
(4) Mounting blocks (trunions)
(5) Muzzle attachments
(6) Bolts
(7) Bolt carriers

 (8) Operating rods
 (9) Gas pistons
 (10) Trigger housings
 (11) Triggers
 (12) Hammers
 (13) Sears
 (14) Disconnectors
 (15) Buttstocks
 (16) Pistol grips
 (17) Forearms, handguards
 (18) Magazine bodies
 (19) Followers
 (20) Floorplates

So, what the heck does all this mean? Well, you still need to read 58 Federal Register 40587 (July 29, 1993). That somewhat explains the application of 27 CFR 479 and 18 USC 922 (r). It states that it was to implement the *Crime Control Act of 1990* by prohibiting the circumvention of the ban of *nonsporting* rifles and shotguns on domestically manufactured weapons thereby preventing the assembly of what are essentially foreign made firearms that would otherwise not be importable. So, if a rifle has **more than half** of the twenty (20) essential parts listed in the regulation made from imported parts (ie: more than **ten**) — it is banned from assembly or further modification in the United States.

Now, remember — the unlawful part here is "assembly". To you, we mean "*modification*". Or, to put it another way — sale, possession, and purchase of these weapons, even if illegally modified, is not illegal! Only ***making*** of the modification is illegal! Also, if you hired someone to make the illegal modifications for you — you're just as guilty as he is under the law as a principal or accessory.

So, back to the question of what you can legally do to modify your *SKS*? Here's the safe list:

1. Replace the existing stock and handguard with a non-folding wooden or synthetic stock having either a Monte Carlo or thumbhole design.

2. Attach a muzzle-mounted recoil compensator that is <u>not</u> also designed as a flash suppressor.

3. Replace the fixed magazine with a detachable magazine — so long as you also replace the standard stock with a Monte Carlo or thumbhole design, and remove the bayonet mount completely from the firearm.

4.   Replace the existing ten round fixed magazine with a five round fixed magazine, or install a block in the well of the ten round magazine limiting it to five rounds.

5.   Replace the existing receiver cover with a cover having telescopic sight bases or rings.

6.   Replace the front and/or rear sights.

7.   Install an ambidextrous safety.

Adding a *folding stock, bipod, flash hider*, is not allowed, nor is adding a detachable magazine (unless you also have the Monte Carlo or thumbhole stock without a bayonet lug), because your federal government says that this renders it as "***non-sporting***", and thus would be banned from import pursuant to 18 USC 925(d)(3). Same thing about the bayonet on those imported after 1989, unless they are the **Russian SKS** on the curio and relic list.

QUESTION: Why can you have a bayonet mount on the Russian SKS?

ANSWER: Because it's on the ***curio and relic list*** issued by the Secretary of Treasury, and thus can be imported with the bayonet under 18 USC 925 (e)(1), since it already had it.

> *"Notwithstanding any other provision of this title, the Secretary shall authorize the importation of, by any licensed importer, the following: (1) All rifles and shotguns listed as curios or relics by the Secretary . . ." 18 USC 925(e)(1)*

I hope this has been of some help to you. It is not the final word on modifications, and I didn't intend it to be. This is not my area of expertise, and I don't want to give you any bad advise. If you decide to modify your SKS, or anything else — good luck!

MANUFACTURE OF FIREARM BY PRIVATE INDIVIDUAL:

There is no federal or Florida law that prohibits you from making a firearm for your own use, unless it's *NFA*, or an otherwise prohibited firearm. On the other hand, you're not supposed to resell it, as it's supposed to be just for personal use. Still, BATFE has said that if you ever transfer it you should add serial numbers, etc. per 27 CFR 478.92. I don't see where that is required by CFR or the statutes – but that's what they're telling me. Again, this is not my area of expertise, and any time I get a question related to it – it takes hours of research to answer.

<u>LAW ENFORCEMENT OFFICERS SAFETY ACT:</u>

In July 2004 Congress passed the " **Law Enforcement Officers Safety Act** of 2004". This Act permits a current, or retired law enforcement officer to carry a concealed firearm in any state or U.S. territory under certain conditions. The Act is found in 18 USC 926B & C, and was amended in October 2010, in the *Law Enforcement Officers Safety Improvement Act*. Here's how it works – and 2010 amendments are added in *"italics"*:

Pursuant to 18 USC 926B, a currently qualified law enforcement officer employed by a state or any of its political subdivisions (county or municipality) who is carrying his government issued photographic law enforcement identification may carry a concealed firearm off duty anywhere in the United States, except this does not apply to a machine gun, silencer, or destructive device. However, it does not limit or restrict any State law that:

1. Allows a private person or entity to restrict or prohibit such possession on the private property of that entity or person, or
2. restricts or prohibits possession on government property

The term "qualified law enforcement officer" means an employee of a governmental agency who:

1. Is authorized by law to engage in or supervise the prevention, detection, investigation, or prosecution of, or the incarceration of any person for, any violation of law, and has statutory powers of arrest;
2. Is authorized by the agency to carry a firearm;
3. Is not the subject of any disciplinary action by the agency, *which could result in suspension or loss of police powers;*
4. Meets standards, if any, established by the agency which require the employee to regularly qualify in the use of a firearm;
5. Is not under the influence of alcohol or another intoxicating or hallucinatory drug or substance; and
6. Is not prohibited by Federal law from receiving a firearm.

If **all** the conditions are met – concealed carry is legal. Open carry would still be illegal, as would all other laws prohibiting firearms carry to a CWL. Thus, carry into a police department or jail would not be covered by this Act.   Likewise, any federal restrictions anywhere – still apply. Thus, the **3 day** wait for purchase of a firearm would still apply in Florida unless you had the CWL.   Furthermore, you could not carry concealed on private property where the owner/person in authority did not permit it; or other places banned by Florida law from concealed carry unless permissible under some other statute.

Likewise, 18 USC 926C , permits the carrying of a concealed firearm by a law enforcement officer who has retired *or separated in good standing* from one or more law enforcement agencies after an accumulated total of *ten (10) years* under the same conditions except:

1.   Said person *must have left (ie: separated)* in good standing from service with a public agency as a law enforcement officer,

2.   Before such separation/retirement, he or she was authorized by law to engage in or supervise the prevention, detection, investigation, or prosecution of, or the incarceration of any person for, any violation of law, and had statutory powers of arrest;

3.   A.   before such separation/retirement, he or she was regularly employed as a law enforcement officer for an aggregate of *10 years* or more; or

       B.   He or she separated/retired from service with such agency, after completing any applicable probationary period of such service, due to a service-connected disability, as determined by such agency;

4.   During the most recent 12-month period, has met, at the expense of the individual, the standards for qualifications in firearms training for active law enforcement officers *as determined by the former agency, the State of residency, or those standards used by a certified firearms instructor qualified to conduct firearm qualification tests for active duty officers within that State, and*

5.   *Has not been officially found by a qualified medical professional employed by the agency to be unqualified for reasons relating to mental health; or has not entered into an agreement with the agency from which the individual is separating from service in which that individual acknowledges he or she is not qualified under this section for reasons relating to mental health;*

6.   Is not under the influence of alcohol or another intoxicating or hallucinatory drug or substance, and

7.   Is not prohibited by Federal law from receiving a firearm.

The identification required by this subsection is:

(1)   a photographic identification issued by the agency from which the individual separated/retired from service as a law enforcement officer that indicates that the individual has, not less recently than one year before the date the individual is carrying the concealed firearm, been tested or otherwise found by the agency; or

(2)   (A) a photographic identification issued by the agency from which the individual separated/retired from service as a law enforcement officer; and

(B) a certification issued by the State in which the individual resides or by a certified firearms instructor that is qualified to conduct a firearms qualification test for active duty officers within that State that indicates that the individual has, not less than 1 year before the date the individual is carrying the concealed firearm, been tested or otherwise found by the State or a certified firearms instructor that is qualified to conduct a firearms qualification test for active duty officers within that State to have met `(I) the active duty standards for qualification in firearms training, as established by the State, to carry a firearm of the same type as the concealed firearm; or (II) if the State has not established such standards, standards set by any law enforcement agency within that State to carry a firearm of the same type as the concealed firearm.

As of March 3, 2008, Florida has implemented this Act thru Florida Statute 943.132, and *Florida Administrative Code 11B*-27.014. Thus, retired law enforcement officers who are qualified under the federal law may now be issued a ***Florida identification card*** once they pass the range requirements. The requirements are per the *Florida Administrative Code* section, and the range requirement "course of fire" (ie: proficiency test) must be given by a firearms instructor certified by the ***Criminal Justice Standards Training Commission***. (minimum score of 80% – ie – 32 of 40 rounds in the scoring area on B-21E target). Cards are valid for one year (actually 365 days), and are consecutively numbered, and are therefore unique to the holder. If lost - the card cannot be replaced. The retired officer must be retested. Likewise, since federal law requires proficiency testing on a yearly (every 365 days) basis as a prerequisite for issuance and validity – so does Florida law. Thus, as a practical matter – a retired officer will have to arrange for retesting and reissuance before the year expires so that his or her authority does not lapse.

The cost of obtaining the testing and certification is purely upon the retired officer. Likewise, since federal law requires a photographic identification from the retired officer's agency be carried – both the *Florida Firearms Proficiency Verification Card* (Form CJSTC-600), and the retired officer's agency photographic identification card should be carried.

The instructor giving the test must keep the test information for a period of two years, which is subject to review and inspection by the *Criminal Justice Standards Training Commission*. Documentation should include the following information on the person tested: name, address, type firearms used, proficiency score, Verification Card number that was issued, date of testing, location of testing, range requirements for test.

As a footnote, federal law still forbids you to carry in the airport *sterile area*, on aircraft, etc., unless it's in your jurisdiction, and part of your duties. And, the law does not permit carrying machine guns, silencers, or destructive devices.

GETTING A SEIZED FIREARM BACK:

Let's assume your firearm was seized by the police. How do you get it back? The starting point is F.S. 705.105, which deals with the "procedure regarding unclaimed evidence". According to this statute, assuming the seizure was legal, title automatically vests to the seizing agency **60 days** after the conclusion of the criminal proceeding, assuming you haven't taken affirmative steps to get it back. There is also F.S. 790.08, which concerns seizure of weapons. That section states that any weapons seized are forfeit if the person used them in a crime, and they are "*convicted*" of the offense. Whether a "*withheld adjudication*" would constitute a "*conviction*" for purposes of this subsection is undecided by any case law, although in every instance I was involved with the firearms were returned if a "*withheld adjudication*" was entered – although there would be obvious complications if you were placed on probation as you could not possess during that period, and likewise, there would be federal issues if you plead "*guilty*" to a felony vs. "*no contest*". On the other hand, if the charges are dismissed or there is an acquittal, the citizen again has **sixty (60) days** to "call for" the weapon. After that, the weapon is supposed to be delivered to the **Sheriff,** and if the weapon remains unclaimed for an **additional six months** it's forfeit — but this time to the State. The Sheriff then may then use the weapons, loan the weapons to other law enforcement, sell the weapons, or destroy them.

The usual way of getting a seized firearm back is by a ***Motion to Return Property*** before the case has ended, and an order from the judge. Assuming charges were never brought, you can try calling the *evidence room* at the agency which seized the weapons, and ask their procedure to get them back. Sometimes, it's as easy as just making a call. If that doesn't work, try calling the "legal advisor" of the agency involved. If all of the above fails, assuming the property is worth an attorney fee — you may want to engage the services of an attorney.

NFA TRUSTS:

Since an individual must obtain a "*chief law enforcement officer*" approval (ie: "sign-off) on the application form to purchase an *NFA* weapon, and since these approvals are very difficult, if not impossible, to obtain in many places – creating a trust where the *NFA* firearm is held has become very popular in the last five or so years, because a trust, like a corporation – is not required to obtain the sign-off. In essence, an *NFA trust* is a simple revocable trust where you name yourself as the trustee so that you have possession of all *NFA* firearms placed in the trust. The trust owns them – you don't – but you control the trust. Since it's a revocable trust, it doesn't have to do a yearly return to the IRS for tax purposes other than you must have paid the "tax stamp" for each NFA weapon in order to get an approval.

While I have heard of people creating the trust on their own with *Quicken Will Maker* – there are important legal formalities that must be followed if a trust is to be valid, and there are numerous considerations that a non-attorney will not be aware of – that you can't find in a computer program. Since we're talking about a possible federal crime, or forfeiture of the weapon if you screw up – I really feel hiring an attorney is not only a smarter option – but the only option. Create the trust only for *NFA* firearms – nothing else. Keep it very simple. If you do that, you should only be paying for a couple of hours or less of attorney time. Any attorney who does real estate, probate, wills, trusts, or corporations – should have no problem doing them, although I highly recommend you find an attorney who's done them before, or advertises on the web for such as "*NFA attorney*", or "*NFA trust*". The guys who advertise normally do lots of them, and do them cheaply as long as they're simple. For complex trusts, you want a lawyer who primarily handles estates, and estate planning. Don't call me – I don't do them.

FREE UPDATING SERVICE & BOOK REVISIONS:
Updates are posted **free** on our website at least twice yearly — **www.FloridaFirearmsLaw.com**. You've gotta be totally lazy, or completely nuts not to download them! One usually appears at the very end of January, and another usually at the very end of August . . . unless in rare situations, nothing happens. Interim updates are also published on the web when I feel they're needed, and much sooner on my blog. You can only get the updates off the web, and I don't keep, or republish past updates. They stay on the web at least six months – and are then replaced by a new one.

On the other hand, updates *do not include* any new materials in the reprinting of the book – and books are reprinted at least once yearly! Updates only show *major corrections* to the current book, new laws, and recent decisions of such importance that they would change the book. Furthermore, updates are written in a very brief summary form. It's not that I want your money for a new book – it's just that this stuff really does change yearly. I'm always adding new stuff to the book, and my opinions can also change, especially when new cases come along. Think of it this way – if you went to your accountant to do your taxes, and he told you he was **two years behind** on the changes to the IRS Code, but he would give you a *really great price break* on doing your taxes – would you hire him? Hell, no!

Well, it's the same thing with a book about law – especially one that covers both Florida, federal, four other states, and regulatory agencies. Stuff changes!!! An update can only do so much. But, as a general rule – as long as you check the website every four months, and download whatever is there, your book should be up-to-date for a period of two years! After that, if you're serious about keeping up with the law – burn it – and buy a new one.

MY BLOG:
          There is a link at the top of my website, or use: *orlandocriminallawyer.blogspot.com* to get to my blog. The blog responds to some of the more interesting email questions I get, and also posts important matters of recent interest for firearm and weapon owners on a much more rapid and extensive basis than the updates. Likewise, interim updates hit the blog weeks before they hit the website. I strongly suggest you check the blog at least every three months for new material. On the other hand, if there's nothing new – it's because nothing that important has happened that you need to know to legally survive. I tend not to post or write anything unless I feel it is important.

QUESTIONS AND THE WEBSITE:
          My website has lots of information, and is constantly undergoing change. Updates to the book can be downloaded free off the website. I always welcome **emails** on weapon and self-defense related questions from the website link, located on the left side of my homepage, and many times I use these questions for blog articles, or in book revisions. I do try to reply to all emails, even if I am not in a position to fully answer it. I try to reply within 48 hours, however, if I have a busy schedule going on, it can be several days. Likewise, if a question is too "fact intensive" or complicated, such that you're really asking for a formal legal opinion on an individualized case that requires research time – that's something I probably won't be able to answer other than acknowledging it, and letting you know I would have to charge you a fee to respond to it. Furthermore, I will **not answer legal questions over the telephone!** I need an email coming in, and my email going out so there is an **exact record** of what was asked, and what was answered. *No exceptions*!

ENDNOTE SECTION:

The endnote sections of the book contain references to the citations, statutes, cases, and other sources from which the information in this book is derived, plus some more intricate legal definitions. While I've placed more of these directly into the chapters because of requests from readers – an endnote section for several chapters still seemed to be unavoidable. However, it contains only a small fraction of the research that went into this book. If I put in all the research – I'd have to write another book to fit it.

LIST OF PRO-SECOND AMENDMENT ORGANIZATIONS:

The following is a very short list of some of the more prominent pro-gun organizations out there. I know I'm leaving out many important ones, and I apologize for that:

National Rifle Association: The most influential of all firearm groups with extensive publications, activities, and political lobbying. Has some of the best magazine publications out there. Well worth the membership for the subscription, alone. Great website, and great organization. For all information phone: 1-800-672-3888. (dues $35.00 yearly). Join on the web at **www.nra.org**.

Gun Owners of America: Not as large as the NRA, but extremely active and influential politically in Congress. Takes a very aggressive stand on firearms issues. Newsletter, e-mail updates, automatic contact with Congress through its Web site, and other programs. Like the NRA, it's essential to belong to. E-mails will keep you advised of everything going on in Congress like nobody else can. To sign-up for membership with credit card phone: 1-800-886-8852. Join on the web at **www.gunowners.org**

Second Amendment Foundation: Another fine organization, active in pro-gun litigation across the country. Suggested dues are $15.00 or $30.00 -- whichever you can spare. It's well worth supporting. www.saf.org

Unified Sportsmen of Florida: This is the NRA's Florida arm headed by Marion Hammer, and critical for passing pro-gun bills in the legislature, and more importantly – stopping the bad ones. Address is: 110 S Monroe St, Tallahassee, FL 32301, Phone: (850) 222-9518. I think it's thirty five bucks a year for regular membership, and you get important notices on proposed laws, and lots of other stuff. No current website.

Florida Carry, Inc.: A very active pro-gun organization that initiates frequent, and successful litigation in the courts related to Florida firearm issues. Very worthy of your support and membership even if you don't agree with their being a strong proponent of open carry. Memberships are anything from free to fifty bucks. So – no reason not to join, especially at the free level. https://www.floridacarry.org

ENDNOTE SECTION FOR CHAPTER TEN:

1. It was established that 90% of "traceable" firearms came from the United States – but since most of the firearms being smuggled into Mexico weren't traceable – the overall total was 17% of total firearms.

2. American Rifleman, "You, Your SKS & The Law", by Michael R. Irwin, May 1994.

CHAPTER ELEVEN

ALABAMA, GEORGIA, NORTH CAROLINA, SOUTH CAROLINA

This next section covers the laws of four additional states, Alabama, Georgia, North Carolina, and South Carolina. Each section was written by one or more attorneys who are considered either the top, or amongst the top in the area of firearms law in their state. There was significant collaboration between myself and these attorneys in getting the answers as thorough and clear as possible. While I did all the editing, I admit having very little knowledge on the laws of these other states other than through the materials and conversations with these other experts. If you have legal issues in these other states – these are the guys to get in touch with! Please understand that the materials in each section are limited, and do not constitute "full coverage" of the entire field of firearms, weapons, and self defense for each state. They only cover exactly what they say they cover. A separate book would be necessary for anything more. On the other hand, this should give you more than sufficient advice to be able to drive through, or vacation in these states. Each state is first covered on the laws of transportation and carry, followed by a section on self defense, and finally a short bio and contact information on the attorney(s) responsible for the section.

THE STATE OF ALABAMA:
by Greg Hopkins, with Jon H. Gutmacher

QUESTION: In what manner (if any) is it legal to carry a firearm in a vehicle for the following persons?
ANSWER: <u>Persons without a CWL</u> may not carry a *handgun* in a vehicle passenger compartment unless it is unloaded and in a locked container or compartment of the vehicle. <u>Persons with a CWL</u> may carry loaded handguns, concealed or unconcealed anywhere in the passenger compartment.

QUESTION: Is the law different regarding other weapons in a vehicle, including Taser, pepper spray stun guns, knives?

ANSWER: All of these may be carried openly or concealed in a vehicle. Alabama law does not regulate them in vehicles.

QUESTION: Without a CWL, are there any places I cannot have a firearm or weapon in a vehicle?
ANSWER: Anywhere firearms are prohibited, to wit:
1. federal property, federal military reservations, military bases, and nuclear plants.
2. A parking lot at a private workplace where possession of firearms is forbidden.
3. The parking lot of any inpatient or custodial care facility for those with psychiatric, mental, or emotional disorders.
4. Any parking lot of a prison, jail, youth detention center, or work release (community corrections) facility.
5. The parking lot of any private or public K-12 school.
6. Exception: As long as firearms are locked in a vehicle and out of sight, the vehicle may be parked in any of the above areas.
7. There are no restrictions for bus stations or airport parking lots.

QUESTION: With a CWL, are there any places I might be driving through or parking where I could not have a firearm or weapon in the vehicle?
ANSWER: Even with a CWL, you cannot have a firearm or weapon in a vehicle anywhere that firearms are prohibited, to wit: federal property, federal military reservations, military bases, and nuclear plants. However, you may have both firearms and other weapons in any other locations. No restrictions in bus or train stations or airport parking lots.

QUESTION: What is the law about carrying on local transportation such as a city bus, train, or subway?
ANSWER: Without a CWL - Firearms may be carried openly, however, with a CWL you may carry either openly or concealed. Alabama law does not address this issue. Therefore, all legal means of carry on city conveyances are allowed with a CWL.

QUESTION: How about transport or carry on a commercial aircraft, train or bus (such as airline terminal and parking, bus terminal and parking, train station and parking)?

ANSWER: Carry in a non-city train, bus, or commercial aircraft or in the "sterile" passenger areas are subject to federal law and, if so prohibited, are not allowed in Alabama. However, there are no restriction on possession or storage of firearms in the parking lots of bus stations, train stations, or airports.

QUESTION: Do you have to tell a police officer you have a firearm/weapon if stopped?

ANSWER: Only if the police officer asks. You are not required to volunteer the information.

QUESTION: Where and how can I transport a firearm when **outside** of my vehicle?

ANSWER: **For a Non-CWL** you may transport your firearm to and from your vehicle to your hotel room or other place you are spending the night (camper, boat, etc), including your apartment even if the apartment has a "No Firearms in Common Areas" policy. Carry is *open carry* only. You may carry openly in any business that does not have a "No Firearms" sign. You may carry openly in public places: streets, parks, etc. However, the places you cannot carry are:

1. You cannot openly carry a firearm in a K-12 public or private school or to a sporting event held there.
2. You cannot openly carry a firearm into a professional sporting event.

For a CWL holder:

3. You may carry *concealed* anywhere that does not have a "No Firearms" sign, including public streets.
4. You may carry *concealed* in any K-12 public or private school and to any sporting event held there, so long as you have no intent to do illegal harm.
5. You may carry *concealed* on college campuses and at all sporting events held there.
6. You may carry *concealed* at any professional sporting events.

7. However, carrying concealed is prohibited if you carry into a business that has a "<u>No Firearms</u>" sign **and** has at entrances guards, metal detectors, key car entry, turnstiles, or other physical barriers during business hours. But Note: Where there are no barriers accompanying the "<u>No Firearms</u>" sign, the sign has NO legal effect except if the business finds out you are carrying, they can require you to leave.

QUESTION: Are there places prohibited for both Non-CWL and CWL:

ANSWER: It is a Class C Misdemeanor to carry any firearm in any of the following places:

1. Anywhere carry is restricted by federal law.
2. Inside any building housing a law enforcement agency
3. Inside a building housing inpatient or custodial care facility for those with psychiatric, mental, or emotional disorders.
4. Inside a courthouse or its annex, or a district attorney's office.
5. Inside any building where a city council or a county commission is currently meeting.
6. Inside the premises (not parking lot) of a prison, jail, youth detention facility. Or work release (community corrections) center.

QUESTION: Can firearms be banned by private businesses, and if so, what is the law?

ANSWER: **For Non-CWL** – A business may ban open carry with "No Open Carry" signs, and subject violators to criminal trespass, **for CWL holders** – a business must post "<u>No Firearms</u>" signs at **every** entrance. However, unless the business finds out you are carrying concealed, the signs alone have NO legal effect, except they can require you to leave or it is a "trespass".

QUESTION: Do you need a CWL for hunting or fishing?

ANSWER: Only if you want to carry concealed during those activities. While a CWL holder may carry concealed, anyone else must carry a firearm openly.

SELF DEFENSE IN THE STATE OF ALABAMA:

QUESTION: Under what circumstances may you actually use non-deadly force to defend yourself?

ANSWER:
1. To defend mere property: trespass, theft, criminal damage, and so forth.
2. When an attacker is committing a misdemeanor assault (non-serious physical injury).

QUESTION: Under what circumstances may you actually *display* a firearm , or use *deadly force* to defend yourself?
ANSWER: When you or a third party is in immediate danger of death or permanent maiming injury from someone about to commit or committing the crimes previously listed following: Any degree of burglary; Any degree of robbery; Attempted murder; Attempted first or second degree assault (causing serious physical injury) armed or unarmed; Forcible rape or sodomy; Kidnaping; Sexual assault or a child under 12 years old; Carjacking; Arson of an occupied/ likely occupied building.

However, in any assault where the assailant is using "a deadly weapon or dangerous instrument" that would reasonably cause even "physical injury" (the impairment of physical condition or substantial pain) or "serious physical injury"(physical injury which creates a substantial risk of death, or which causes serious or protracted disfigurement, protracted impairment of health, or protracted loss or impairment of any bodily organ)-then *deadly force* can be threatened or used.

Whereas, with unarmed attackers it becomes tricky, and before the use of any *deadly force* you would have to show some extreme savagery of the attack, superior numbers, or a martial artist or those kind of techniques employed, etc. the whole "disparity of force" defense. Thus, the fact that a *forcible type felony* is being committed does not automatically allow the use of deadly force unless there is also a reasonable basis to believe that unless deadly force is used, imminent death or great bodily harm will result.

QUESTION: Is there ever a duty to retreat?
ANSWER: Alabama is a "Stand Your Ground" state. You *do not* have a duty to retreat as long as you are: Legally in a place you have a right to be; Not using illegal force; Not committing a crime; Not the initial illegal aggressor; Not involved in a combat by agreement. However, you *must retreat* if you are: Not

legally where you have a right to be; Using illegal force; Committing a crime; The initial aggressor; or involved in mutual combat.

> **_Greg Hopkins, Esq._**, received his first firearms training as an auxiliary police officer in his hometown of Waverly, OH, where he served on the city council. He earned his law degree at The Cumberland School of Law in Birmingham, AL, where he also served as a City Magistrate. After graduation, he clerked at the Alabama Court of Criminal Appeals and was admitted to the bar in 1989. He served as City Prosecutor for Huntsville, AL, where he trained the Huntsville Police Department and its detention officers in legal use-of-force. He received training for police advisors at the FBI Academy in Quantico, VA, and completed Level One of Massad Ayoob's Lethal Force Institute in Pearl, MS. After leaving the City Attorney's office, he practiced criminal defense law, served as a City Court Judge, and became a court certified expert witness in firearms and self-defense law. He regularly consults on self-defense and firearms cases to analyze and reconstruct crime scenes, and works with the Alabama appellate court system, and is therefore unable to accept clients in court cases. His book, "A Time to Kill", is an exhaustively researched study of the moral and legal justifications for self defense taken from the Old and New Testaments. It has some amazing insights (yeah – I read it), is a fast read, and well worth having – especially if you have any interest in the bible. You can purchase it on Amazon, or directly from Greg at his website: www.bibleselfdefense.com. He says he'll sign it if you purchase it direct from his website. Cost is $19.95 plus shipping.

THE LAW OF THE STATE OF GEORGIA:
By: John R. Monroe, with Jon H. Gutmacher

QUESTION: Without a CWL -- where and how can I transport a firearm (rifles, shotguns, and handguns) if I am somewhere *outside* of my vehicle ?
ANSWER: Any way you wish at your home, residence, or business. However, a handgun, or knife with a blade over five inches – must be carried in a closed case and unloaded.   It need not be locked, but must enclose the entire gun or knife. A holster would be insufficient. However, all firearms and weapons are *prohibited* inside the following places: jails; prisons; government buildings, courthouses, places of worship; polling places; state mental health facilities, nuclear power plants, although parking areas on their grounds would be lawful.

QUESTION: Any places a **CWL holder** cannot carry a handgun or knife over 5 inches, or other firearms or weapons?
ANSWER: The following places are prohibited to everyone, including a CWL holder:

1.   inside government buildings
2.   inside courthouses
3.   inside jails or prisons
4.   inside places of worship
5.   inside state mental health facilities
6.   on the grounds of nuclear power facilities
7.   within 150 feet of a polling place
8.   possibly when outside your vehicle on the grounds or in buildings of a   school or college unless picking up or dropping off a student. You are legal in your vehicle even if on school grounds. You are legal carrying a firearm open or concealed when dropping off or picking up a student.   There is current litigation to test whether you have a more extensive right to carry on school grounds with a CWL.

QUESTION: May a **CWL holder** carry a handgun open, as well as concealed?
ANSWER: Yes, but the CWL applies only to handguns and knives over 5 inches. No license is required for other weapons, including rifles and shotguns, and weapons fall under Georgia's preemption law.

QUESTION: How can I lawfully transport or carry a firearm or other weapon *in a vehicle* other than a handgun or knife with a blade over five inches?:
ANSWER:

a.   **Under 21**: Anywhere in a vehicle you personally own, concealed or unconcealed. Rental, loaner, or family vehicles would not qualify. You must be the title holder to qualify.

b.   **21 and over, but no CWL** (*but must be eligible for one* – ie – *no prohibitions*):   Anywhere in vehicle, concealed or unconcealed. Rentals would qualify.

c.   **With CWL**:   Anywhere in vehicle, concealed or unconcealed. Rentals would qualify. Plus, handguns and knives over 5 inch blade also allowed.

QUESTION: **Without a CWL** – are there any places I could **not** have a firearm or weapon in a vehicle?

ANSWER: If you do not have a CWL it is unlawful to have firearms and other weapons on the grounds or premises of an airport, bus terminal, rail terminal, school or college grounds, nuclear power plant, or within close proximity to any bus stop. However, there is an **exception** for *passengers* at bus, rail, and airports who are checking firearms/weapons on their trip like federal law. Proceed *directly* to the check in counter, and follow federal law explained in the Florida section.

QUESTION: How about carrying on local transportation such as a city bus, train, or subway?

ANSWER: Without a CWL firearms must be unloaded, and in a closed container. With a CWL you may carry a handgun or knife with blade over 5 inches either open or concealed legally.

QUESTION: Do you have to tell a police officer you have a handgun or other weapon if stopped?

ANSWER: No. However, I would follow the suggestions in the Florida section on this issue.

QUESTION: How and where can I carry a Taser, a knife with a blade under 5", or pepper spray without a CWL?

ANSWER: Anywhere except school or college grounds. Otherwise, Georgia normally does not regulate the carrying of weapons except for firearms, and knives with blades over 5".

QUESTION: Can firearms or weapons be banned by private business?

ANSWER: Yes, but only as a trespass. You would first have to be asked to leave, and refuse as *"actual notice"* is required. However, if you see a sign saying **"No Firearms"** that might be considered *"notice"*. If you did not see the sign – entry would not be a trespass unless you were first asked to leave.

QUESTION: Do you need a CWL for having a loaded handgun while hunting, fishing?

ANSWER: No, it is lawful. However, if you did not have a CWL, you would have to have your handgun in a case until you began to hunt, or fish. Rifles, shotguns, and other weapons are not regulated and could be carried either concealed or open.

QUESTION: Must the case be locked, or fastened closed?
ANSWER: No, it need not be locked or fastened. However, the case must fully enclosed the handgun.

QUESTION: Anything else important about carry or transportation of a handgun, rifle, or shotgun?
ANSWER: Yes. All federal prohibitions apply. Likewise, many water and camping areas are controlled by the *Army Corps of Engineers*, and federal law prohibits ammunition or loaded firearms on such property, except in limited circumstances such as when permitted during hunting season while lawfully hunting.

SELF DEFENSE IN THE STATE OF GEORGIA:

QUESTION: Under what circumstances could you lawfully *display* (without firing) a firearm if you reasonably believed you might have to use it in self defense?
ANSWER: The law on this question concerns "*threats*", and is as follows:

A.   When you reasonably believe that such *threat* is necessary to defend yourself against another person's imminent use of unlawful force;

B.   When you reasonably believe that such *threat* is necessary to prevent or terminate another's unlawful entry into or attack upon a *habitation* (ie: dwelling, residence, place of business, or motor vehicle);

C.   When you reasonably believe that such *threat* is necessary to prevent or terminate another's trespass on or other tortious or criminal interference with property other than "*habitation*".

Anyone may defend *habitation* – not just a resident.

QUESTION: Could a "threat" made to stop or prevent unlawful conduct ever be unlawful?

ANSWER: Yes, if it is excessive to the point of being unreasonable.

QUESTION: Under what circumstances may you actually use ***non-deadly force*** to defend yourself?

ANSWER: You may use any ***non-deadly force*** as appears reasonable and necessary to stop the *imminent commission* of an unlawful attack, or imminent criminal interference with your property. Likewise, in Georgia *"threats"* are considered completely separately from the actual *"use"* of force. A ***threat*** is lawful to stop or prevent ***imminent unlawful conduct*** as long as it reasonably appears necessary. Thus, the threat of using *deadly force* in a *non-deadly force* situation would be lawful if reasonable. However, if your actions appear ***"unreasonable"*** – it could be an ***aggravated assault*** if a firearm were involved. This is a ***twenty year*** felony.

QUESTION: Same question as to the use of ***deadly force***?

ANSWER: The use of ***deadly force*** is lawful under the following circumstances:

1.   You reasonably believe that such force is necessary to defend yourself against another person's *imminent* use of unlawful force that will cause ***death or great bodily injury*** to you or a third person; or to prevent commission of a *forcible felony*;

2.   Defense of Habitation: You reasonably believe that ***deadly force*** is necessary to prevent or terminate another's unlawful entry into or attack upon a *habitation*, and the entry, or attempt to enter, is made or attempted in a *violent and tumultuous* manner, and you reasonably believe that the entry is attempted or made for the purpose of assaulting or offering personal violence to any person in the dwelling or vehicle, and that such deadly force is *necessary* to prevent the assault or offer of personal violence (*"habitation" is a dwelling or residence, not a business*);

3. <u>Defense of Habitation</u>: Your use of deadly force is against another person who is not a member of the family or household who unlawfully and forcibly enters, and you knew or had reason to believe that an unlawful and forcible entry has occurred or was occurring;

4. <u>Defense of Habitation</u>: You reasonably believe that the entry or attempt to enter is made for the purpose of committing a felony and deadly force is necessary to prevent the commission of the felony,

5. It is lawful to use ***deadly force*** to stop or prevent the imminent commission of ***a forcible felony*** where it is reasonable to believe that the use of such force is necessary. A *"forcible felony"* includes the following crimes: murder, felony murder, burglary, robbery, armed robbery, kidnapping, hijacking of an aircraft or motor vehicle, aggravated stalking, rape, aggravated child molestation, aggravated sexual battery, first degree arson, manufacturing, transporting, distributing or possessing explosives with intend to kill, injure, or intimidate individuals or destroy a public building, terroristic threats, or acts of treason or insurrection, or any other felony which involves the use or threat of physical violence against any person.

QUESTION: Is there ever a duty to retreat?
ANSWER: In a way. A person who is an *aggressor* or who engages in *mutual combat* has a duty to make clear his intentions to withdraw, and stop the aggression. After he does so, if the other person continues to fight, then all self-defense provisions apply.

John R. Monroe, Esq., is considered the preeminent litigator and authority in Georgia on firearm and Second Amendment issues, both civil and criminal. He has been in the practice of law for over twenty years, is vice-president and director of Georgia Carry, an NRA certified firearms instructor, and former law enforcement officer. He has litigated cases throughout the entire State of Georgia, and secured a number of *critical* victories involving Second Amendment causes. He is a key defender of the Second Amendment in that State. You may contact him through the following: John Monroe Law, P.C., 9640 Coleman Road, Roswell, Ga. 30075, Phone: 678-362-7650, email: jrm@johnmonroelaw.com.

THE LAW OF THE STATE OF NORTH CAROLINA:
By: Locke T. Clifford and Daniel A. Harris, with Jon H. Gutmacher

QUESTION: In what manner is it lawful to transport a *firearm* (handgun, rifle, shotgun) in a vehicle without a valid concealed handgun permit, and are there any restrictions as to places you could not drive to, or park at?

ANSWER: **Without a CWL** – North Carolina is primarily an "open carry" State. Thus, any type firearm, and all other type weapons, must be transported in the open and clearly visible. Alternatively, they can be concealed so long as not "*readily accessible.*" North Carolina law does not give a clear answer as to what constitutes "*readily accessible*" but if one wishes to conceal the weapon without a CWL, the best practice is to have it locked in the trunk or in a locked compartment within the trunk (or luggage area in a SUV or hatchback) – so long as not in a prohibited area or place. However, only a CWL holder may have a concealed *handgun* on his person within a vehicle.

With a CWL – a *handgun* may be transported open or concealed, however, all other weapons and longguns must be transported the same as if you did not have a CWL – fully open and not concealed. If you are stopped by a law enforcement officer, in your vehicle or otherwise, you must **volunteer** that you have a CWL and a firearm.

QUESTION: Any places you could not drive with a *firearm* in the vehicle *without* a CWL?

ANSWER: You may not possess or store any type of firearm or any other "dangerous weapon" in your vehicle while on the *grounds* of any State government building; courthouse; parades; funeral processions; picket lines; demonstrations at public places; demonstrations at private health care facilities; upon any school grounds or at any school sponsored activity thru and including the university level.

QUESTION: Is there a difference if you have a valid CWL?

ANSWER: Yes. As for parking – it is legal for a **handgun** stored in a closed compartment in a locked vehicle, including parking on the grounds of State government and courthouses, and educational property. Also lawful to carry concealed at a parade or funeral procession. Otherwise, the same rules as person without a CWL.

QUESTION: In each of the previous questions – can the firearm be loaded?
ANSWER: Yes the firearm may be loaded. North Carolina law is generally only concerned with the concealed nature of the firearm and makes no distinction as to whether it is loaded or unloaded.

QUESTION: Would your answers to the three previous questions apply equally to other weapons, and/or ammunition – or is the law different?
ANSWER: Certain weapons are not considered "dangerous weapons", thus *pepper spray* may be carried open or concealed unless specifically prohibited in local government buildings. A *common pocketknife* may be lawfully concealed if the blade is entirely closed within the knife body.   North Carolina case law treats *Tasers* as a type of *stun gun* and NCGS 14-269(a) specifically **prohibits concealment** of stun guns or "weapons of like kind." Of course, any weapon openly carried cannot be displayed in a *threatening manner* unless in lawful self-defense.

QUESTION: How do "open carry" laws work in North Carolina?
ANSWER: Open carry law refers to the fact that all weapons and all firearms may normally be openly carried as long as the area is not *posted* to prohibit them, such is not done in a *threatening* manner, and the open carry is not in an area *prohibited* by law.

QUESTION: Are there any weapons that can be carried concealed without the CWL?
ANSWER: Yes. As previously stated, *pepper spray* or a *common pocket knife* in the closed position. If you have a CWL – add to that list a "handgun", but nothing else.

QUESTION: Are these laws consistent in all cities across the State, or are different cities allowed to vary it?
ANSWER: The general rule under N.C.G.S. § 14-409.1, is that local governments are prohibited from regulating "firearms" with a few exceptions. Local governments may set limited prohibitions on carrying *concealed handguns* at and around the premises of local *government buildings.* Further, local

governments may also enact prohibitions on carrying *concealed handguns* at municipal or county *recreational facilities* (defined specifically as athletic fields, swimming pools, gymnasiums and similar facilities used for athletic events). However, any such prohibitions at recreational facilities must be *posted* and must still allow a CWL holder to place their handgun within a trunk, glove box, or other closed compartment of a locked motor vehicle.

QUESTION: But, open carry of rifles, shotguns, and all other weapons are legal as long as openly carried?

ANSWER: Yes. Other than the exceptions previously mentioned, and also N.C.G.S. §§ 153A-129 & 160A-189 allows local governments to "regulate the *display* of *firearms* on the public roads, sidewalks, alleys, or other public property. Currently, the city of **Chapel Hill** prohibits open carry of *handguns* with an overall length **less than six inches** in public places. However, open carry of rifles or shotguns, or other weapons other than a handgun would still be lawful.

QUESTION: If stopping at a hotel, restaurant, gas station, or store – and leaving the vehicle – are there any restrictions where or how your *firearms* are left in the vehicle?

ANSWER: Remember, North Carolina is an "open carry/open possession" state. If left in a vehicle they must either be kept in the open, or if concealed must be locked in the trunk or in a locked compartment within the trunk (or luggage area in a SUV or hatchback). A CWL would vary this only in that a *handgun* could also be kept in any closed compartment or closed container within the vehicle. Likewise, a CWL holder could store the handgun in the vehicle while on a State owned/leased parking areas, or carry concealed at a parade, or in a funeral procession.

QUESTION: How about at a camp ground, or overnight trailer park? Any differences?

ANSWER: No restrictions on open carry other than as already mentioned. Concealed carry is legal with a CWL. However, carry of anything might be unlawful on federally owned lands, and certainly it is illegal to have a loaded firearm, or even any ammunition in parks and property owned by the *U.S. Army Corps of Engineers* except where specifically permitted for lawful hunting.

QUESTION: What places are prohibited with a CWL?

ANSWER: You may not carry *on or about your person* on any educational property; the grounds of any state owned building or courthouse; any law enforcement building, correctional facility, any building that houses state or federal government employees; at any demonstration or protest; on any private premises that have a conspicuous notice *posted* that prevents such. However, with a CWL, you may keep a firearm in a closed compartment or container within a locked vehicle, locked in the trunk, or in a locked container securely affixed to your vehicle – while on the grounds of any school property or school sponsored event, or the grounds of any state government building or courthouse.

QUESTION: What about concealed carry per a CWL in a bar, or other places?

ANSWER: A CWL holder may lawfully carry concealed in bars, places charging admission, parades, funeral processions, and the grounds and waters of state owned parks – so long as they are **not posted** as having firearm prohibitions.

QUESTION: Without the CWL – are there any places you can legally carried concealed?

ANSWER: Yes. At your home, business, or residence – including your room at a hotel, motel, or even inside a tent (subject to any park rules/prohibitions). Guests are not covered – only persons actually residing or employed therein. The immediate grounds are also covered – but **not** any areas that are *shared* by others such as ***common areas***, shared parking lots, etc.

QUESTION: Same question as to the "*common areas*" of a **condo** where the condo owner owns an undivided interest in the whole of the property?

ANSWER: There is no case law on this, and at this point the likely safe answer is "no", although it would be a total *test case*.

QUESTION: Where would it be illegal to have open carry of a firearm or weapon without a CWL?

ANSWER: It is unlawful to possess a firearm or other "*dangerous weapon*" on any educational property or at any state buildings and property, in your car, parking areas, or otherwise. Likewise, unless you have a CWL, it is unlawful to have any firearm in a State Park (other than hunting and fishing reservations), any establishment serving alcohol, at parades, or at funeral processions.

SELF DEFENSE IN NORTH CAROLINA:

QUESTION: Under what circumstances could you lawfully display (without firing) a firearm or other weapon if you believed you might have to use it in self-defense?

ANSWER: **Display** of a firearm is generally prohibited as it is considered a *threat of using deadly force*, and likewise prohibited is any other *threat of using deadly force* unless responding to a *"felonious assault"* (ie: A *"felonious assault"* creates a substantial risk of death or some serious bodily injury).

QUESTION: Does North Carolina have a *"retreat rule"*?

ANSWER: Prior North Carolina law held that **retreat** was required before engaging in the use of **deadly force**, or even the **threat of a deadly weapon** if retreat could be done without increasing the risk to yourself. However, there has never been any duty to retreat **inside** your home or residence. Recent changes in the law also allow you to **"Stand Your Ground"**, and use **deadly force**, if all the following conditions are met: you are in a place you have a lawful right to be; you were not the **aggressor**, and it is reasonable to believe that there is an imminent threat of a *felonious assault* to yourself or another. (ie: *imminent death or great bodily harm*).

QUESTION: What is the law on the use of non-deadly force?

ANSWER: If you are not facing a *felonious assault*, you have the right to meet force with force (i.e. a fist for a fist), but may not use or threaten to use deadly or otherwise excessive force (i.e. a gun for a fist). Put bluntly, you have the right to **display** a firearm in self-defense only if you reasonably believe a *felonious assault* is imminent.

QUESTION: Under what circumstances may one actually use deadly force to defend himself?

ANSWER: North Carolina defines *"deadly force"* as *"force likely to cause death or great bodily harm."* State v. Clay, 256 S.E.2d 176, 182 (N.C. 1979). Thus any time you use (discharge or use as a blunt object), or even **threaten to** *use* a firearm, you are using deadly force and therefore must be under reasonable belief of an *imminent felonious assault*.

QUESTION: And, what about non-deadly force?

ANSWER: You always have somewhat broader permission to use ***non-deadly force***, as you always have the right to repel force by force and give blow for blow, even in a non-felonious assault. However, you may not escalate the situation through use of a firearm or other weapon. Use of ***pepper spray*** would not likely be considered *excessive force*, and would thus be permissible if you were under an imminent threat of a physical assault. However, *stun guns and Tasers* should be avoided, as they might be considered "***deadly force***" in North Carolina, depending on their usage. [State v. Rivera, 716 S.E.2d 859, 862 (N.C.App. 2011)]. Be aware that North Carolina self-defense law is concerned with *excessive force*, and therefore you should always consider not exceeding the degree of force you're responding to (i.e. unwanted touching vs. being punched, etc.).

QUESTION: What about the "***castle doctrine***"?

ANSWER: The ***castle doctrine*** in its most basic form is that you have no duty to retreat before using deadly force so long as you are: (1) in your home **or** its ***curtilage***, whether a permanent or temporary residence (which would thus include a hotel room and even a tent); (2) inside a motor vehicle you are occupying (a ***motorcycle*** would qualify, but not a ***moped***); or (3) your workplace, whether permanent or temporary and regardless of building type or mobility.

QUESTION: What is meant by "***curtilage***"?

ANSWER: "*Curtilage*" is the yard around a dwelling house as well as the area occupied by barns, cribs, and other outbuildings. State v. Browning, 221 S.E.2d 375, 377 (N.C. 1976).

QUESTION: Are there any "***presumptions***" when using deadly force in defending yourself in such places?

ANSWER: Yes. N.C.G.S. § 14-51.2, creates a presumption that a lawful occupant of a residence, motor vehicle, or workplace, who uses deadly force, is ***presumed*** to have held a *reasonable fear of imminent death or serious bodily harm* so long as: (1) the intruder against whom the defensive force is used was in the process of *"unlawfully and forcibly"* entering, the intruder had already unlawfully and forcibly entered, or the intruder was removing or attempting to remove another person from therein against his will; and (2) the defender knew or had reason to believe that this unlawful and forcible entry or act was occurring or had occurred.   However, it is important to note that this presumption is always rebuttable and further there is no presumption if: (a) the person against whom force is used is lawfully present or is a lawful resident and there is no injunction or other court order against their presence, (b) the person is a child, grandchild, or is in lawful custody of the person against whom force is to be used, (c) the person using defensive force is themselves engaged in or attempting to escape from a criminal offense involving physical force or violence, (d) the person against whom force is used is a law enforcement officer or bail bondsman in lawful performance of his or her duties and they properly identified themselves as such, or (e) the person against whom force is used has discontinued all efforts to unlawfully and forcefully enter and has exited.

QUESTION: What does *"unlawfully and forcibly"* mean?
ANSWER: This is relatively new in North Carolina and the Courts have not yet clearly defined what constitutes "forcible" entry. Surely, kicking in a door, picking a lock, or breaking a window would qualify, but anything less or not otherwise clearly "forcible" falls into a legal gray area, and a possible *test case.*

Locke T. Clifford, Esq. is board certified in both State and Federal criminal law, and has been practicing for over forty years. He served in the U.S. Army J.A.G. office in Vietnam, then as a State prosecutor, and since then as a criminal defense lawyer. He has tried more than 150 jury trials in both State and Federal Court, and is regularly listed in Super Lawyers, Best Lawyers, and Business North Carolina's Legal Elite. He has handled numerous trials and appeals involving firearms and self-defense issues, and also handles petitions for restoration of rights. He was one of the first group of individuals to receive a CCW license in the State. *Daniel A. Harris, Esq.* is an attorney admitted to both State and Federal courts in the State. He is a distinguished writer and researcher, and has handled numerous criminal cases at both the State and Federal level. He is a longtime member of the NRA, and comes from a family of firearm owners and instructors. He also handles restoration and expunction matters for clients. Both Locke and Dan practice at the firm of Clifford, Clendenin & O'Hale, LLP, located at 415 West Friendly Avenue, Greensboro, North Carolina 27401.   Phone: 336-574-2788.   The firm website is www.ccolawyers.com, and an email address is: Clifford@cliffordlawoffice.com.

THE LAW OF THE STATE OF SOUTH CAROLINA:
By: Stephen Fulton Shaw, Ph.D., with Jon H. Gutmacher

QUESTION: What does the CWL cover in South Carolina?
ANSWER: The CWL covers open or concealed carry of "***concealable weapons***" which are those ***handguns*** not over 12 inches in length. What else constitutes a "*concealable weapon*" is not further defined, and is a grey area. Thus, you can certainly carry a handgun on your person concealed in your vehicle, or anywhere else on or about your person except prohibited and posted places, and those prohibited by federal law.

QUESTION: Without a CWL, are there any restrictions in weapons?
ANSWER: Only a CWL holder may carry a handgun, although there are specific exceptions. Without a CWL you may carry any longgun openly except in a posted area or one prohibited by law, and you may carry open or concealed pepper spray with container not over 50 cc, or knife with blade 2 inches or less.

QUESTION: What are the exceptions for a non-CWL with a handgun?
ANSWER: You may carry a handgun open or concealed loaded or unloaded as follows:

1.   licensed hunters or fishermen engaged in lawful hunting or fishing or while going to or fro in a vehicle or on foot.

2.   persons in their home or real property, or with prior permission of the owner or person in legal control.

3.   owner or persons in legal possession of a "fixed place" of business, and employees who have a CWL, and prior permission, except where alcohol is served.

4.   Persons engaged in firearms related activity at a gun store or gun range at that location, unless posted.

5.   Open or concealed transport of a handgun from a lawful place in a vehicle to any other lawful place it is allowed. However, if a

"concealable weapon" is taken to a hotel or other type accommodation for which a fee is paid, the accommodations tax must be paid first. In other words, if you're checking in and haven't paid – don't carry any weapons in until you've paid.

6.   On a motorcycle inside a closed saddlebag or similar closed container attached to the motorcycle, either on a permanent or temporary basis.

7.   In a vehicle any **handgun** must be kept in a closed: console, glove compartment, trunk, or container in the luggage compartment secured by an integral fastener. Luggage compartment means the area behind but not under the rearmost seat in a van, hatchback, station wagon, or SUV. In a truck it means behind the rearmost seat, but never under the front seat.

QUESTION: What about school property, and government buildings?
ANSWER: Neither a CWL or non-CWL may possess firearms or most other weapons on the grounds of a school (including colleges), property owned or controlled by such, grounds of the Capitol, or any government owned building, except with express prior permission. This includes *public highway rest stops*!!!
"Grounds" do not include any public roads open full time to public traffic that run through or adjacent to the grounds or properties. However, a CWL holder may keep weapons on such property if stored inside their attended or locked vehicle secured as previously described in subparagraph 7; and a CWL holder may also carry at interstate highway rest stops. There is an exception for a knife with a blade under 2 inches, which is not prohibited on school grounds and at schools.

QUESTION: Can a CWL holder carry at a bar or restaurant that serves alcohol?
ANSWER: No.   Moreover, it is unlawful for anyone to be under the influence and use any firearm.

QUESTION: Can anyone carry pepper spray?
ANSWER: Pepper spray is lawful open or concealed if the container does not exceed 50 cc.

QUESTION: Any other places that are prohibited for firearms and weapons?
ANSWER: Any place that is posted for no weapons or no firearms is prohibited. Signs must conform to State law, and must be at all entrances. This applies to everyone including CWL holders. Furthermore, even without posting, a CWL holder may not carry concealed in a residence or dwelling of another without prior approval from the owner or person in legal control.

QUESTION: Any place a CWL cannot lawfully carry a *concealable weapon*?
ANSWER: The following places are unlawful:
(1) any law enforcement office or facility;
(2) detention facility, prison, or jail or any other correctional facility or office;
(3) courthouse or courtroom;
(4) polling place on election days;
(5) office of or the business meeting of the governing body any local government entity
(6) school or college athletic event not related to firearms;
(7) daycare facility or pre-school facility;
(8) place where the carrying of firearms is prohibited by federal law;
(9) church or other religious sanctuary unless with express permission
(10) any medical office, clinic, hospital or facility unless with express permission.

QUESTION: How can I carry a handgun on local transportation?
ANSWER: Concealed with a CWL. Without a CWL you may not possess a handgun.

SELF DEFENSE IN SOUTH CAROLINA:

QUESTION: Under what circumstances could you lawfully display (ie: threaten, without firing) a firearm if you believed you might have to use it in self defense?
ANSWER: Only if you reasonably believe that you, or someone else is in immanent danger of death or serious bodily injury.

QUESTION: Under what circumstances may you actually use non-deadly force to defend yourself?

ANSWER:. Non-deadly force is permissible to the extent such is reasonable to repel or defeat non-deadly force. Also, in defense of habitation, the force reasonably necessary to remove trespasser.

QUESTION: Same question as to the use of deadly force?
ANSWER: Deadly force may be used only if you reasonably believe that you, or another person is in immanent danger of death or serious bodily injury. *Display* of a firearm is the use of deadly force, and cannot be used unless you have a reasonable fear of death or great bodily harm.

QUESTION: Is there ever a duty to retreat?
ANSWER: There is no duty to retreat if you have legal right to be in your location, you are not the aggressor, and you are not engaged in any illegal activity.

QUESTION: Are there any presumptions that allow the use of deadly force?
ANSWER: There is a statutory presumption that person in a dwelling, residence, or occupied conveyance has a reasonable fear of **imminent** peril of death or great bodily injury to himself or another person when using deadly force that is intended or likely to cause death or great bodily injury to another person if the person against whom the deadly force is used is in the process of unlawfully and forcefully entering, or has unlawfully and forcibly entered a dwelling, residence, or occupied vehicle, or if he removes or is attempting to remove another person against his will from the dwelling, residence, or occupied vehicle; and the defending person knows or has reason to believe that an unlawful and forcible entry or unlawful and forcible act is occurring or has occurred.

Dr. Stephen Fulton Shaw is a practicing attorney in both South Carolina and Florida. He holds a J.D. and a Ph.D. from the University of Florida with a Masters and Bachelors in Business from Florida State. He served for several years on staff with U.S. Rep. Cliff Stearns who led the charge for a national right to carry law since 1995, and has handled a variety of civil and criminal gun issues, as well as numerous other cases in both state and federal court. He is also the author of the book "*South Carolina Gun Law*" which was just released in its revised Second Edition, and extensively covers both federal and South Carolina laws. Steve organizes the Annual South Carolina Gun Law Seminar for attorneys and judges, and is often retained to draft NFA gun trusts. His office is located at 27 S Main St, Travelers Rest, South Carolina, 29690,

Phone: 864-834-4404, and website is located at www.steveshawlaw.com. His book may be purchased online at www.scgunlaw.com for $24.95 plus shipping.

CHAPTER TWELVE

SELF DEFENSE & THE LAWFUL USE OF FORCE

<u>SELF DEFENSE OVERVIEW:</u>
Your rights to defense of self, family, and property all have different rules. Understanding the rules are important if you are a responsible individual. If not, understanding the rules are still important to avoid criminal prosecution, or civil liability.

One thing I must say is a word on the practicality of using self-defense. The criminal always has the advantage, because he is not afraid to use his weapon illegally. Moreover, you may fall into the trap of trying to decide if your use of the weapon is legal, or not. If you miss, or not. If you get sued, prosecuted, or not. All of these things, and more will be going through your mind, and all are unfortunately to your disadvantage from a standpoint of survival. However, they are the law, and must be followed to whatever extent you reasonably can.

When people ask me when they can use a firearm, I tell them that from a practical, and not necessarily legal standpoint -- the only time anyone should know you have a weapon, or ever see the weapon -- is when you're ready to use it, sure you can use it, and can legally pull the trigger.

Why?

For one thing, it gives you the advantage of surprise. This split second advantage is often the difference between who is lying dead on the ground -- you or him. If you chose not to fire the weapon, and hope that by displaying it the other person will desist in his felonious conduct (you should never display a deadly weapon to stop anything but a "*forcible felony*") -- good luck. At least you still have a momentary advantage.

But whatever the situation -- as soon as the weapon is displayed, or you threaten to draw it, whether you are justified or not -- you have probably escalated the situation. There is no real way of turning back once it comes out. The situation tends to intensify, rather than get better -- unless the guy runs, backs down, or surrenders.

The real question then becomes whether the other person is willing to push his luck -- or whether you are willing to take another life to protect your own, to protect the life of your loved ones, or in certain instances, to protect your property. Don't think you can just wound him, or shoot the knife out of his hand. It doesn't work that way. Modern thinking in the instructional area of self-defense is to keep shooting until your opponent falls to the ground, incapacitated. Moreover, until the assailant falls, it is almost impossible to determine if you've even hit him. Until that happens, and the attacker is disarmed, he's still a very lethal threat, and one shot is rarely enough to stop an attack -- even if it's enough to eventually kill him. An attacker who dies in a hospital three hours after you shoot him, still has two hours and fifty-nine minutes to kill you, and your family before he dies. If you think I'm kidding you -- don't! It happens all too often. Ask any police officer. In fact, that scenario was confirmed by the United States Supreme Court in the recent case of *Plumhoff v. Rickard*, 134 S.Ct. 2012 (2014). In that case the Supreme Court noted that police are trained to shoot continuously until a threat is completely stopped (ie: a deadly force situation), and completely approved that procedure as being justified, and not excessive force.

Now obviously, if you get into one of these predicaments, and misjudge the situation, you will either be dead, or be prosecuted. Neither alternative seems very fair, and it rarely is. However, these are some of the facts of real life, and let me assure you that no honest, responsible citizen wants to carry a weapon or firearm if they had a choice. Unfortunately, it's just come to that point if you want to survive. On the other hand, you must somehow manage to keep your cool, and act responsibly. Certainly, in this type of circumstance -- that will be a very difficult, if not an impossible task.

On this happy note we start the most important chapter in my book -- your current rights to self-defense under Florida law. The first part of this is understanding some basic definitions and concepts which are essential to having the slightest idea of what your rights or liabilities are. Here goes:

FORCIBLE FELONY:

Before you learn anything else, you need to know those specific crimes that constitute a "*forcible felony*". They are each listed in F.S. 776.08. Knowing them is very important because it defines when you can use, or even **threaten** to use *deadly force* in self-defense, and when you can't. Of course, a "*deadly weapon*" is one that by use or design is **likely** to cause death or great bodily harm. A "*deadly weapon*" doesn't need to meet the typical classification of what you'd think a weapon would be. Thus, the courts have held that where there is proof a person intended to use an object (broom stick; blow gun; cinder block; screwdriver; lawn mower blade; box cutter; beer bottle; BB gun; etc.) as a "*deadly weapon*", and the object was capable of inflicting such harm, a jury is entitled to find that the object is a "*deadly weapon*". However, because of its legal definition, a *firearm* – no matter how it is used – will always be considered to be a "*deadly weapon*". Thus, under Florida law -- the only time you can use a firearm, or any other deadly weapon in self-defense is when it is used to stop or prevent a " *forcible felony*."

The list of *forcible felonies* in Florida is as follows:

1. Treason
2. murder
3. manslaughter
4. sexual battery
5. robbery, including carjacking & home invasions
6. burglary
7. arson
8. kidnaping
9. aggravated assault
10. aggravated battery
11. aircraft piracy
12. unlawful throwing/placing or discharging of a bomb or destructive device
13. aggravated stalking
14. unlawful discharge/placing/throw destructive devices any other felony (not misdemeanor) which involves the use, or threat of physical force or violence against any person (not animals -- persons!)

Now, the list of forcible felonies may seem all very clear on paper, but I can assure you that it's not as simple as you may think. You still cannot just shoot someone for the heck of it, even if they are committing a forcible felony. Your use of deadly force must still be **"reasonable"**, or a jury could decide you were using "*excessive force*". If that happens, you face possible manslaughter or aggravated battery charges. To help you along on this rather varying system of what is legal or not, we'll move on to the specific statutes that define the parameters of lawful self-defense, but before we do, I think you should also be aware of a few more important definitions:

THREAT:
A "*threat*" is a communicated intent to inflict physical or other harm on any person or on property. <u>United States v. Stock</u>, 728 F.3d 287 (3^d Cir. 2013) . It can be purely verbal, made by overt conduct, or a combination of the two.

A *threat* is a serious statement expressing an intention to injure any person which under the circumstances would cause apprehension in a reasonable person as distinguished from mere idle or careless talk, exaggeration or something said in a joking manner. *United States v. Stacy*, 2014 U.S. App. LEXIS 8123 (10th Cir. 2014).

Not all threats are illegal. Many threats may be lawful where made to stop or prevent the unlawful conduct of another. Threats may be completely verbal, completely overt conduct, or a combination of the two. However, changes in Florida law in 2014 indicate that any threat of using "*deadly force*" in a "*non-deadly force*" situation is no longer permissible. More on that later. However, last, but not least – a threat may be "*conditional*". In other words:

"If you take a step closer – I'll blow your brains out!"

In that situation, it could be a "bare threat" if no firearm was on the person making the threat. Other actions could raise it to an "*assault*". But, either way, the law says that the conditional nature of a threat is evidence going to the question of whether the person threatened had a *well founded fear* that violence was imminent. If they did have such a well founded fear, and your conduct was unlawful, then the threat likely becomes an "*assault*", or at least raises a jury question on that issue. *Bell v. Anderson,* 414 So. 2d 550 (Fla. 1DCA 1982). That being said, we move on to the next obvious definition: "*assault*".

ASSAULT:

An assault is an intentional, **unlawful** threat done by word or act, to do violence to another person, coupled with the apparent ability to do so, and by doing some act that creates a well-founded ("reasonable") fear in the other person that the violence is "*imminent*" (ie: "immediate"). To make an assault "*aggravated*" -- the assault must be committed with a *deadly weapon*, without any intent to kill, or must be done with an intent to commit a felony. F.S. 784.021. Thus, the key elements of an assault are:

a. An intentional threat
b. That is unlawful
c. To do violence to another
d. By doing some act
e. Which creates a well founded fear in the other
f. That violence is imminent.

Just like threats, I'll go into more depth about assault and aggravated assaults later in this chapter. However, an *"aggravated assault"* is the criminal charge most often associated with a self defense situation that's gone wrong. In other words – a situation where the person who thought they were using lawful self defense was the person who got arrested, and charged with a crime. For that reason, understanding exactly what an *assault* is – is critical. On the other hand, a pure verbal threat without any overt act that demonstrates that violence is "imminent" is only a *"threat"*, and not an *"assault"*. <u>Tiger v. Marcus</u>, 37 So.3d 986 (Fla. 4DCA 2010).

<u>DEADLY WEAPON:</u>

A "**weapon**" is defined as an instrument of attack or defense in combat. <u>State v. Houck</u>, 652 So.2d 359 (Fla. 1995). On the other hand, a "*deadly weapon*" is one that is **likely** to produce death or great bodily harm depending on its designed use, or the way it is used. If you're wondering whether a firearm is always a deadly weapon – as I previously mentioned -- the answer is "yes", even where unloaded. However, it's use may not always constitute the use of *"deadly force"* because *"deadly force"* and *"deadly weapons"* are two completely different concepts in the law! More about that later. Furthermore, a baseball bat, or any other instrument capable of inflicting death, or great bodily harm can also be a *deadly weapon* -- depending on its use, or intended use. For instance, a stone could be a deadly weapon depending on size, and circumstances of its use. Same thing for an ice pick, or screwdriver. Obviously, it all depends on the item, and many times, how it is used or threatened to be used.

You should also know that the terms *"deadly weapon"* and *"dangerous weapon"* are synonymous. They mean the exact same thing. <u>Jones v. State</u>, 885 So2d 466 (Fla. 4DCA 2004). Yet, as I said before – there is a <u>material difference</u> between a deadly weapon and deadly force. Two entirely different legal concepts.

<u>MARTIAL ARTS CONSIDERATIONS:</u>

An interesting issue about *"deadly weapons"* arises if you are specially trained in the *martial arts*. For now, Florida case law has determined that while the use of bare hands or feet would **not** ordinarily be considered the use of a *"deadly weapon"* – the cases have also indicated the result might be different if there was proof of special training in the martial arts. Likewise, the cases indicate that if the person were wearing a heavy shoe or boot – the shoe or boot could be found to be a *"deadly weapon"* depending on its use. Of course, even if hands and feet are not "deadly weapons" – they may still inflict an injury or injuries sufficient to qualify as the use of *"deadly force"*.

IMMINENT:
     The next important definition is a word used all the time in self-defense statutes, to wit: "*imminent*". What does it mean?

     It means something that is about to happen on an <u>immediate</u> basis. Not an hour from now, not a month from now, but usually within seconds, and if not -- it is so immediate that there is no way to reasonably avoid it. Before an *aggravated assault* can take place there must be a well founded fear of imminent violence perceived by the alleged victim. <u>McClenithan v. State</u>, 855 So.2d 675 (Fla. 2DCA 9/03).

     "*Imminent*" is also used to define many situations where *deadly force* can be used, or threatened. In those situations the danger must also appear imminent. From reading the case law I think the correct definition of "*imminent*" most closely resembles "*an immediate threat that is unavoidable unless something intercedes to stop it*"

REASONABLE BELIEF ("reasonably believes"):
     What you *reasonably believe* the facts to be, and/or what you need to do to protect yourself, family, or property -- means just that. It must be objectively and subjectively <u>reasonable</u> under the particular circumstances, as they "reasonably" appeared to you at the time, even if you were mistaken.

     "**Subjectively**" means what you think. "**Objectively**" means how others will analyze your actions later on based upon reason. In other words, if you make a mistake, it must be a mistake that a "*reasonable person*" could also have made knowing the same facts as you did at the time of the incident. This is not an easy definition since the reasonableness of your actions will be judged by others, rather than yourself, at a point in time well after the event has transpired. This after-the-fact analysis needs a real good lawyer, and sympathetic jury to assure your legal survival. A sympathetic police officer, and prosecutor wouldn't hurt, either.

     So remember, that while you may have a personal belief that your neighbor, Herb, is from the Andromeda Star System, and is preparing an invasion of earth -- it is doubtful that the rest of your neighbors, judges, lawyers, and juries will go along with this. Thus, when you read the words of wisdom enacted by your Legislature that have limited your once God-given right to self-defense, try to remember that you must act within the terms of normal reality -- rather than the reality you'd like things to be.

The classic real example of this was when some elderly woman heard noise outside her house during the daylight hours, and decided there was a criminal outside who was going to burglarize her house and attack her. When she heard the guy make some noise immediately outside her front door, she grabbed a shotgun and shot it through the door. It killed him dead. Unfortunately for both, it was her milkman, and all he was doing was leaving her some milk. Yeah, it was reasonable to her -- she was scared of everything that moved. Shows you what watching T.V. can do to you. However, it had nothing to do with objective reasonability -- and she was convicted of manslaughter.

Just about the same thing happened in another state where some poor Japanese kid got shot during Halloween by an over-reactive homeowner. The homeowner's fears were real. That's what happens when you watch the news everyday, and start to take it too seriously. You can really lose perspective.

The homeowner had a good jury, and great lawyer in that case, and got off. But he still stood to lose everything if he was sued civilly. Mistakes happen, huh?

A great quote on this subject is found in a Florida appellate court case decided in 1958, *Harris v. State,* 104 So.2d 739, 744 (Fla. 2DCA 1958). It succinctly states the philosophy of today's court in easy to understand terms:

> *"Men do not hold their lives at the mercy of unreasonable fears or excessive caution of others . . . ."*

DEADLY FORCE:

Deadly force, like a deadly weapon, is force **likely** to cause death or great bodily harm. It doesn't legally matter whether either of these result from your actions -- it is legally enough that such might have caused, and was **likely** to cause death or great bodily harm. "*Great bodily harm*" can be a permanent or incapacitating injury, a non-trivial scar, or any other injury of a serious nature. A nosebleed is not a serious injury. A broken arm is.

Use of a firearm, baseball bat, metal pipe, ax handle, knife, etc. -- all are likely to be classified to involve the use of *deadly force*. Intentional "*display*" of these items, combined with the *threat* of imminent violence, may constitute the felony of *aggravated assault*, or at least the first degree misdemeanor of *improper exhibition of a dangerous weapon*, unless there is a legal justification. Legal justifications are not necessarily what you'd like them to be, or think them to be. That's one of the problems.

From a legal standpoint only the **discharge** of a firearm always constitutes the use of *"deadly force"*. Whereas **pointing** a gun to ward off an attack is, as a matter of law, not greater than the use of *"non-deadly force"*. <u>Rivero v. State</u>, 871 So.2d 953 (Fla. 3DCA 2004). Thus, pointing a gun, without more, is always the use of *"non-deadly force"*. On the other hand, it's still usually a jury issue on whether it constitutes *aggravated assault*, and there is also an open question whether it is the *"use"* of any *"force"*, at all.

Remember, that lawfulness of the use of force is determined on whether your subjective belief was **"objectively reasonable"** under the *"reasonable man"* standard, even if you were mistaken. Thus, an objectively reasonable mistake should still be lawful self defense – as long as you can convince everyone else it was reasonable. Still, mistakes usually result in arrests – and then sorting it out in a court of law.

<u>NON-DEADLY FORCE:</u>

OK, we've been discussing some concepts that relate to the use of *deadly force*, but what about *non-deadly force*? Actually, this area will give you considerably more leeway in what you can or cannot do. The problem, as with any use of force, is that it can <u>escalate</u> whatever situation you're in.   In other words, anytime you use, or threaten to use force, the likelihood is that the other party will use equal or greater force against you. Sooner or later this may get way out of proportion to the incident. Here's how it works:

A person is justified in using or threatening force, **except** *deadly force*, against another person, when and to the extent he reasonably believes that such force is necessary to defend himself or another from the other's <u>imminent</u> use of <u>unlawful</u> force. F.S. 776.012. This use of *non-deadly force* will normally apply to misdemeanors, and non-violent felonies that fall short of a *"forcible felony"*.

A person may use or threaten the use of *non-deadly force* to stop the commission of a misdemeanor or non-violent felony upon himself, or property which he has an ownership or possessory interest in, or a legal duty to protect. F.S. 776.031. **"Legal duty to protect"** does not usually extend to a neighbor protecting a neighbor's property.

However, unless you're a security guard hired to protect the property, or an employee on the premises, I think you better just call the police. There should be an exception where a neighbor or friend has actually agreed to protect his neighbor's property – but I haven't found any Florida case law on this. However, an **employee** does have an equal right to protect his employer's property as he is an "agent", and the law says he or she "*stands in the shoes of his employer*". In other words – if the employer could do it, the employee should be able to, as well.

QUESTION: Is that a good idea?

ANSWER: Very hard to say! What if you get hurt – who's gonna pay your off time, medicals, and rehabilitation? Whose gonna hire you if you become permanently disabled? If you think Workmen's Compensation will do it – you'd better read that statute, first. You're not that well protected!

BREACH OF THE PEACE:

Under Florida case law, a person also has the right to use *non-deadly force* to stop a misdemeanor " ***breach of the peace***" that occurs in their presence. A " *breach of the peace*" is a tricky phrase, can get real technical, and is asking for a problem. Stopping one should ordinarily be reserved for police officers if you have any kind of a choice. A good definition would be: ***"acts or words likely to produce immediate violence on the part of others"***. A *breach of the peace* includes all violations of the public peace, order or decorum, such as to make an affray; threaten to beat, wound, or kill another, or commit violence against a person or property; fighting words that tend to immediately incite others to violence; appearing in a state of gross intoxication in a public place; DUI, recklessly flourishing a loaded pistol in a public place; and the like. In other words, it includes not only violent acts, but acts and words **likely** to produce **immediate** violence in others, or cause public tragedy. There is also case law both in and outside Florida that states a ***trespass*** is a *breach of the peace*, and permits the reasonable use of *non-deadly force* to terminate it. However, remember a ***trespass*** rarely occurs under Florida law unless a person is first **warned** to leave, and then refuses. Moreover, the amount of force you use must be reasonable – otherwise you might be using "***excessive force***", and in the case of a *trespass*, there is no right to use **any force** until after a warning is given, and the trespasser refuses to leave.

Unless you're the actual victim, I'm not sure I'd want to try stopping a breach of the peace as it usually winds-up as a really nasty fight, or worse. Plus, while you have a common law right to make a *citizen's arrest* in some instances – you are not a police officer, and attempt's to make a citizen's arrest usually result in even more problems, and in Florida are usually limited to actual felonies. But, at least you have a legal basis to take action if you decide to try to terminate a breach of the peace.

CITIZEN'S ARREST:

I really hate to add this section – because except in rare circumstances where specifically authorized by statute – making a ***citizen's arrest*** is really risky. However, it is an essential piece of information required in understanding all aspects of self-defense and the lawful protection of property. Because of that, here goes:

In Florida, a citizen has the right to make an arrest of another person when that other person commits a felony in their presence, or where a felony is actually committed, **and** the citizen has "*probable cause*" to believe, and does believe – the other actually committed the felony. *Phoenix v. State*, 455 So.2d 1024 (Fla. 1984). There is also case law that has extended the right of a citizen to make an arrest for a misdemeanor "*breach of the peace*" committed in their presence – but there is controversy, and contrary case law on this issue – and thus, it is legally unsafe to make a *citizen's arrest* on anything but a felony, at this time, with a few exceptions we will soon discuss.

In order to make a *citizen's arrest* no particular words need be spoken, however, it should be communicated to the other person that you are taking them in custody until police arrive – or words that make it clear they are not free to leave. You then have a duty to contact law enforcement as quickly as possible. We will discuss this in a later section on escape. You should also know that in any non-violent crime short of a *forcible felony*, the use of physical force is generally **not permitted** in making a citizen's arrest **unless** the other person first resists.

While there is controversy on making a *citizen's arrest* on a misdemeanor – there are several statutes that do make it lawful in certain instances. These include: Florida Statutes 810.08 (2)(c) & 810.092(c) – which allow an owner or person authorized by the owner to take into custody and detain any trespasser who has been warned to leave, and refuses – "*in a reasonable manner, for a reasonable length of time*". These statutes also require that law enforcement be called as soon as practical thereafter.

Likewise, F.S. 812.015(3), authorizes a merchant, farmer, law enforcement officer, or transit agent, to take a person into custody when such person has "*probable cause*" to believe a retail theft, farm theft, transit fare evasion, trespass, or unlawful or attempted use of any anti-shoplifting or inventory control device has occurred – and in retail and farm theft – that the property may be recovered by taking the offender in custody. In such instances the detention must be done in a reasonable manner and for a reasonable length of time. In case of a farmer – it can only be on the farm property. And, a law enforcement officer must be called to the scene immediately thereafter.

One word of warning on any *citizen arrest* involving misdemeanors not specifically permitted by the statutes just previously mentioned: Many law enforcement officers and departments don't like you playing police officer! Likewise, many of them don't know what their authority is to take someone you've arrested into custody unless it is a felony! There are some exceptions they should know because they are actually listed in **<u>F.S.</u> 901.15** that allows them to arrest for certain crimes not committed in their presence such as: criminal mischief, battery, domestic violence, and child abuse. But, beyond that – you will probably get nothing more than the officer just taking a report, and then letting the suspect go. After that, it's up to the State Attorney's Office to determine if they want to bother prosecuting.

And last, but not least – a person wrongfully arrested by a citizen has a right to use reasonable force to stop or prevent the arrest, and can also **sue you** civilly!   Likewise, if you make a mistake on your right to arrest, and use any force in making the arrest – you have probably committed a *battery*. Thus, you may be the one who gets arrested, and beat-up, to boot. Nice, huh?

<u>EXAMPLES OF NON-DEADLY FORCE:</u>
Before I give any examples of non-deadly force, I think a good quote in understanding the concept comes from the case of <u>*Garramone v. State*</u>, 636 So. 2d 869 (Fla. 4DCA 1994);

> *"it is the nature of the force, and not the end result that must be evaluated."*

In other words, if I hit someone with a pillow, and so startle them that they fall backwards, hit their head on the concrete and die – even though they died – I have only used *non-deadly force*. On the other hand, if what I did was a criminal act vs. playing around, then I still might be facing a *manslaughter* charge because a death did occur. Same thing with **waving** a firearm. Waving it around is not causing any harm, nor can waving it without discharging it cause injury to anything. On the other hand – it might still be considered a threat, and even an assault – and if it is an assault – it is an assault with a deadly weapon, hence an "***aggravated assault***".   (I'll explain the legal definitions later in this chapter). People have actually been convicted for *aggravated assault* on such facts.

So, you want some examples of the legal use of *non-deadly force*? Well – why not?

A *trespasser* who refuses to leave your premises after being asked to leave where it's clear they're not changing their mind; a person who attacks you with fists; someone tries to steal something from you short of a robbery or burglary; a person who is committing a criminal mischief on your property; a person who deliberately and unlawfully blocks or prevents you from the use of your property; a person who is so disorderly as to be committing a breach of the peace in your presence and who will not desist; a person you have lawfully arrested (very "iffy" unless a forcible felony) who resists your lawful arrest. If the criminal conduct involves only a trespass to real property that is not the dwelling house -- then you must be a person who has a legal right or duty to protect it. If you don't -- then go call the police because your legislature seems to have screwed-up this law, too. It used to be that anyone could protect the property of anyone else, but this is not the law today **unless** it is a *forcible felony*. I guess that's just part of where being a good neighbor has gone to.

QUESTION: How about the use of pepper spray, a stun gun, or a Taser. These are "non-deadly force", right?

ANSWER: They are certainly *non-deadly force*, but in some situations could still be considered as " *excessive force*" which we'll be discussing soon. If the crime about to be perpetrated upon you involves physical violence -- it's my opinion that you should have an absolute right to use a *non-deadly weapon* to prevent harm to yourself, rather than having to battle it out with your hands. If it involves a trespass, or property damage, I personally still feel the same way, but believe it becomes more "iffy", only because *excessive force* is usually a question of fact, and in a non-violent misdemeanor, or even a non-violent felony, you generally must first try to resolve it without using physical force. Therefore, my opinion is of little use if somebody else disagrees -- especially if they're a judge or jury.   I personally think *pepper spray* is the safest use of "*non-deadly force*" short of a simple push. Most law enforcement agencies list the use of pepper spray as appropriate for "*passive resistance*" situations. That should equate with an individual unlawfully trespassing who refuses to leave after being warned, and given a reasonable opportunity to comply. It should also apply to anyone threatening imminent unlawful physical violence.

QUESTION: Is there anything else other than *pepper spray*, a *Taser*, or a *non-lethal stun gun*, that is *non-deadly force*?

ANSWER: Well, knives and firearms are almost always *deadly weapons*, as are nun-chuks and brass knuckles. There are some risky exceptions. Anything else depends on how it's being used. I mean, a full swing with a baseball bat is the use of deadly force -- but using it as a pole, to push someone away should not be. Fists, and kicking are normally not deadly weapons, although they can constitute the use of deadly force depending on the injury. The flat part of a shovel, or the flat part of a machete might not be a deadly weapon, but then again, it might be real hard convincing a jury on that. The machete would be a real tough sell -- because most people think of it as a deadly weapon, rather than as a tool. Obviously, in the hands of someone skilled, it can be used in a non-deadly manner. But, I think I'd rather pass on that particular trial. Brass knuckles usually are considered deadly weapons. Anyway, you've got the idea.

QUESTION: What about **waving a firearm** in warning without firing it?

ANSWER: Very risky! While it is definitely the use of *non-deadly force* so long as it is not discharged, it is still a "*deadly weapon*", and probably the "**threat**" of using **deadly force**. Likewise, there is a question whether it is an "imminent" threat, a "conditional" threat, mere display, a simple warning, or just becoming prepared. I'll go into that later since the concept deserves a separate explanation. However, unless it's a clear-cut self defense issue where you had a clear right to use *deadly force*, or the other person is definitely in the commission of a *forcible felony* – it could be considered as excessive, and cause your arrest for *aggravated assault*, or misdemeanor "*improper exhibition*". Therefore, I recommend against it unless you are reasonably in fear of your life, or if needed to stop a *forcible felony*. Likewise, if the assailant is a good liar, he may just blame you for starting things – and if the cops believe him – you'll be arrested for *aggravated assault*. I've seen that happen many times over!

QUESTION: Do I have to **retreat** before using, or threatening to use **non-deadly force**?

ANSWER: Not if you have a reasonable fear of imminent **physical attack**.
               In such situations it is lawful to use or threaten the use of *"non-
               deadly"* force as long as you're not the initial aggressor, have a
               reasonable belief that another person is, or is about to use
               unlawful force against you, and the amount of *non-deadly force*
               you use is reasonable. However, if you are only *protecting real
               or personal property* (other than a dwelling), due to changes in
               the law in 2014, you must first ***retreat*** before using or even
               threatening to use *non-deadly force* if you are not a member of the
               household, member of the immediate family, or do not have a
               "duty" to protect the specific property. So, if you want to play it
               totally safe – sometimes retreat, or backing down is prudent.

INITIAL AGGRESSOR:
        In Florida, as in most states, the *"initial aggressor"* is normally the person
whose **unlawful** conduct **causes** a confrontation. Words or actions that are only
insulting, aggravating, or even threatening – are normally **not** sufficient to make
a person an *"aggressor"* unless the threat is such that it raises a reasonable
apprehension in the other person of imminent criminal violence. *See*, Gibbs v.
State, 789 So. 2d 443 (Fla. 4DCA 2001).   However, if the *initial aggressor*
makes it clear he or she wants no more of the conflict, and the other person
continues a physical attack – the person continuing the conflict becomes the
"aggressor" at that point in time. F.S. 776.041(2)(b).

RETREAT RULE:
        The *"retreat rule"* which was all but eliminated by the Legislature in
2005, has reared its ugly head once more in certain circumstances by changes in
2014 to Florida's self defense laws. For those of you who don't remember it,
here's an explanation from *Redondo v. State*, 380 So. 2d 1107 (Fla 3DCA 1980):

> *"Florida, in accord with a strong minority of jurisdictions throughout the country,
> has imposed an additional requirement that the defender against such a violent attack
> has a duty to avoid the difficulty and retreat from the affray, before using deadly
> force, if he can do so consistent with his own safety without exposing himself to death
> or great bodily harm. The policy reason behind this retreat rule is to insure more
> fully that human life will not be taken by a person who is unlawfully attacked except
> as a last resort to save himself from imminent death or great bodily harm."*

        The ***retreat rule***, where applicable, makes anyone who does not abide by
it a *"mutual combatant"*, and criminally liable for any use of unlawful force.
Under the 2014 changes to the statutes, that now likely also applies to any
"threats" of using deadly force. Of course, if there is no opportunity to retreat,

or if ***retreat*** would still expose you to imminent death or great bodily harm – retreat is not necessary. The case law makes it clear that *retreat* is not necessary where it would be "futile". <u>*Dorsey v. State*</u>, 74 So.3d 521 (Fla. 4DCA 2011). Likewise, the "***castle doctrine***" holds that retreat is not necessary if you are within your own home, dwelling, or business premises. For the most part, the ***retreat rule*** will only apply in Florida in lawful "***deadly force***" situations if you are (1) engaged in ***criminal conduct*** at the time the need for self defense arises, or (2) you are not in a "***place where you have a right to be***", or (3) in protecting property in *non-deadly force* situations where you are not a member or the family, household, nor have a duty to protect the property.

As I will explain later in more detail, the most likely interpretation of the 2014 changes are you can't use, or even threaten to use *deadly force* in a non-deadly force situation – period! You can't fire a ***warning shot*** in a non-deadly force situation – period! You can't intentionally ***display*** a firearm in a non-deadly force situation – period! For now, unless an appellate court holds otherwise, or the law is changed by the Legislature – these are the **only** safe ways to interpret the revised sections at this time (November 2014) – and that is how I will be explaining it, henceforth.

<u>JUSTIFIABLE USE, OR THREAT OF DEADLY FORCE:</u>
So, the bastard deserves to get shot. At least that's the way you feel. The real question is: how will the police and State Attorney feel about this course of conduct? What if it goes to a jury, and you're facing a mandatory prison sentence? This is the <u>real</u> crux of the problem! The law basically states that *deadly force*, or the ***threat*** of using ***deadly force*** shall be used <u>only</u> if you **reasonably believe** that such force is **necessary** to prevent the **imminent** commission of a *forcible felony*, or prevent <u>imminent</u> death or great bodily harm to yourself or another. If you'd like to see how this really works in a court of law, here's part of the Standard Jury Instruction that's read in a self-defense case. It hasn't changed that much from the previous instructions other than sections eliminate the retreat rule, although it has not yet been updated to encompass the legislative changes made in 2014 in House Bill 89 (HB 89):

"In deciding whether the defendant was justified in the use of force likely to cause death or great bodily harm, you must judge him by the circumstances by which he was surrounded at the time the force was used. The danger facing the defendant need not have been actual; however, to justify the use of force likely to cause death or great bodily harm, the appearance of danger must have been so real that a reasonably cautious and prudent person under the same circumstances would have believed that the danger could be avoided only through the use of that force. Based upon appearances, the defendant must have actually believed that the danger was real." SJI 3.04(d).

No matter what the instruction is – get a good jury with a good lawyer -- you win. Get a bad jury and you've got real serious problems. And we are not just talking criminal law here, because people are getting sued all the time for the excessive use of force -- which, by the way, is normally **not** covered by your Homeowners Insurance Policy. (Gads! How did that ever happen? More on that later).

Moreover, if you are the ***initial aggressor***, or if you are in the process of perpetrating a crime -- you may not have any right to use *deadly force*, or any force, even in self-defense, since you are the initial wrongdoer. Also, if you were not the initial wrongdoer, but the aggressor changes his mind and breaks-off the illegal act/attack, your continuing the attack may now make **you** the "*aggressor*" in the eyes of the law. Beware! Just because he started the thing, doesn't necessarily give you the right to finish it if he surrenders or withdraws.

On the other hand, if *deadly force* is reasonable and necessary, *excessive force* should generally not be an issue because of the method you chose, because *deadly force* is the "**most**" force you can use!   However, if you've incapacitated your assailant, he surrenders, or runs, or you're using dad's surplus WWII flame-thrower, I think there might be some real serious problems with your pulling the trigger.

Why?

Well . . . under those conditions there is an excellent possibility that you and your family are out of any imminent danger, and/or the *forcible felony* has ended. If that occurs it is rare you would have a "reasonable" fear of an "*imminent*" anything. Such a situation occurred in *State v. Heckman*, 993 So.2d 1004 (Fla. 2DCA 2007), where the appellate court held that the presumptions did not apply to protect a homeowner who had shot a burglar, because the burglar was outside, and retreating from the residence at the time he was shot. Thus, the homeowner was successfully prosecuted for *aggravated battery* – a crime that carries a *twenty-five year mandatory* minimum sentence because a firearm was discharged, and the victim was also shot. F.S. 775.087.   Likewise, the test of "***necessary***" is that it is reasonable to believe that the *forcible felony* will be completed **unless** *deadly force* is used. *Russell v. State,* 54 So. 360 (Fla. 1911).

QUESTION: Hey, you're really getting me nervous. You mean that if I use a firearm to defend myself, and make a mistake in the law, I may get arrested?

ANSWER: Unfortunately, that's always a possibility, unless you have a responding police officer who also believes in your God-given Right to self-defense. On the other hand, you will be alive. Your wife will be alive. Your kids will be alive. The other alternative (lying dead on the ground) sure leaves a lot to be desired. Make sure you have "*self defense insurance*". You gotta be nuts not to have it these days – plus it's cheap!

EXCESSIVE FORCE:

As usual, the use or threat of *non-deadly force*, and the lawful use or threat of *deadly force*, are limited to that amount you **reasonably** believe is **necessary** to prevent or terminate the other persons criminal conduct, or to reasonably protect yourself from harm. If you exceed this imaginary "*reasonable*" amount, your excess of force becomes "*unreasonable*" because it's "*unnecessary*", and becomes "*excessive force*" and a criminal act to that extent, even if the initial use of force was otherwise legal. For that reason, I normally carry a *Taser* or *pepper spray*, as well as a firearm. Most encounters will not justify the use, or even the threat of deadly force – and having a "*non-deadly*" weapon available may be very useful. **Pepper spray** may be the best of "non-deadly" ideas as it is more universally accepted as minimal force, and a two ounce can usually gets at least ten separate sprays in case you miss the first time, or have multiple attackers – plus it's real good on an attacking dog.

On the other hand, if your use of force would legally be limited to the use of *non-deadly force* – and you instead use "*deadly force*" – you may have just committed an aggravated battery or even manslaughter. In fact, even the **threat** of using *deadly force* where only *non-deadly force* is permissible might constitute an **aggravated assault**, or **improper exhibition** charge when combined with the **display** of a *deadly weapon*. The question of whether a defender's belief that he or she acted "*reasonably*", or that it was reasonable to believe his or her actions were "*necessary*" – is normally a question for a jury. Likewise, if the use of *non-deadly force* would be legal, but you **displayed a deadly weapon** as a method of warding off an attack, or otherwise stopping a misdemeanor – the perception of responding police may be that you acted unlawfully – even if there was legal justification for what you did. Plus, it is something that would likely be unlawful due to the 2014 changes in the statutes. Again, this area will be discussed later in a separate section because of its complexity, and the fact that it is usually a jury question whether such a response is reasonable.

QUESTION: I don't understand. If all I do is display my firearm to ward off an attack – isn't that non-deadly force?

ANSWER: Yes – but with the 2014 changes to the statutes, the court will likely say the nature of the threat is a *threat of using deadly force* – which is only allowed in a deadly force situation. Likewise, even under previous law, it was a jury issue whether such a display is reasonable, or excessive, conditional, or a present threat, etc. If *"excessive"* – it could constitute an *"aggravated assault"*. If the firearm were shown holstered – you have a much better argument, but the law still isn't clear on the point. Thus, I do not recommend you show a firearm or other deadly weapon to ward off an attack unless you have a reasonable belief that a *forcible felony* is about to occur, or you have a reasonable belief of imminent death or great bodily harm.

QUESTION: But, what if I see a *felony* taking place or is about to take place – that is **not** a *"forcible felony"*?

ANSWER: I hate to say it – but with the 2014 legislative changes on *threats* you really can't do it. Only *non-deadly force*, or the *threat of non-deadly force* is now lawfully permitted.

QUESTION: Isn't that kind of stupid?

ANSWER: Probably yes, as there are many situations where the mere display of a firearm immediately stops unlawful or potentially unlawful conduct, and many other states say it is totally lawful to display a firearm to stop **any** type of imminent criminal conduct, even a misdemeanor. In such instances, the **safest** legal way to display is not touching the firearm or making any verbal threat, but just pulling away your shirt, or whatever to expose it. I've personally seen this work, and also heard several first hand accounts about it. My personal opinion is that as long as display (probably without pointing) is not "unreasonable" it should be lawful. That was Florida law prior to the amendments in 2014. *Quaggin v. State*, 752 So. 2d 19, 25 (Fla. 5DCA 2000). However, that is **not** the law today, and unless the courts make a different interpretation, or the Legislature changes it, you must act accordingly.

CHARTS EXPLAINING 2014 USE OR THREAT OF FORCE:
       Well . . . consider this your free "cheat sheet" on everything you need to know about the use or threat of force under current Florida law (August 2014),

and hopefully they will make it much easier to understand the rest of the book. The first applies to the use or threat of non-deadly force. The second to where the threat or use of deadly force is permissible. All other sections of this book are based on them, and will be explained in detail as we move on:

Use or Threat of "Non-Deadly" Force:
Allowed without retreat (ie: Stand Your Ground):
  1. To stop or prevent the imminent commission of a physical attack that is a misdemeanor or non-forcible felony. *776.012; or*
  2. Protection of a "dwelling" *776.031; or*
  3. Protection of real or personal property (other than a "dwelling") except as modified below: *776.031*

Retreat will be necessary in (3) where:
You must first apply the "***retreat rule***" unless you are a member of the household, a member of the immediate family, or have a "duty" to protect the property in question.

Warning: All of the above still requires that the threat of non-deadly force actually employed must be reasonable and necessary.

Use or Threat of Deadly Force:
Use or threat of deadly force – all sections of Chapter 776:
To stop or prevent the unlawful and imminent commission of death or great bodily harm upon yourself or another, or to stop or prevent the imminent commission of a forcible felony.

Retreat required:
If you are not at a "***place where you have a right to be***" – or – you are were "***engaged in criminal activity***" at the time the need for defensive force arose.

Warning: The use or threat of deadly force in any of the foregoing instances must be both reasonable and necessary.

HISTORICAL BASIS OF THE USE OF FORCE:

Something that really helps in understanding the lawfulness of the use of force is done by examining its historical basis – or in more legal terms – examining what's called the " ***common law***". The best description I've found comes from an Oklahoma appellate case cited as: *Whitechurch v. State*, 657 P.2d 654 (Ok. App. 1983). While it's not exactly current Florida law – it does give you insight. Here's the quote:

"Historically, the right to use force in preventing crimes was limited to situations where the threatened act would have constituted a felony or breach of the peace. Consequently, the threatened commission of a nonviolent misdemeanor, such as petty larceny, provided no basis for the use of preventive force. However, in the 19th century, this common law distinction between the prevention of felonies and misdemeanors began to erode, and it became the general rule that '[O]ne who reasonably believes that a felony, or a misdemeanor amounting to a breach of the peace, is being committed, or is about to be committed, in his presence may use reasonable force to terminate or prevent it."

A PREFACE ON THE " STAND YOUR GROUND" LAWS:

In April 2005 the Florida Legislature made some substantial changes to Chapter 776 of the Florida Statutes, and passed what has come to be known as the " ***Stand Your Ground***" law. The law had been relatively untouched until the Legislature made some unfortunate changes in 2014. However, before we get into the 2014 changes, here's a partial synopsis of the original legislation written by the Senate Committee on Criminal Justice back in 2005:

"The bill permits a person to use force, including deadly force, without fear of criminal prosecution or civil action for damages, against a person who unlawfully and forcibly enters the person's dwelling, residence, or occupied vehicle. Additionally, the bill abrogates the common law duty to retreat when attacked before using deadly force that is reasonably necessary to prevent imminent death or great bodily harm.

"The bill creates a presumption that a defender in his or her home, in a place of temporary lodging, as a guest in the home or temporary lodging of another, or in a vehicle has a reasonable fear of imminent death or great bodily harm when the intruder is in the process of unlawfully and forcibly entering or enters. It also creates a presumption that the intruder intends to commit an unlawful act involving force or violence. These presumptions protect the defender from civil and criminal prosecution for unlawful use of force or deadly force in self-defense.

You might have noticed that the original legislation didn't mention anything about retreat applying to the use of *"non-deadly"* force. That's because in Florida, as in almost every other state in the country, there is no duty to retreat when using *non-deadly force*. *Keith v. State,* 17 Fla. L. Weekly D 2815 (Fla. 1DCA 1992). That's somewhat changed in certain situations due to the new 2014 legislation. However, at least you now know what the Legislature was trying to do back in 2005, and you'll also see what's happened since then, both in the courts and the legislature. On that note, here's my analysis of the sections of the law, one-by-one:

CHANGES TO 776.012(1) – NON-DEADLY FORCE:

*(1) A person is justified in using **or threatening** to use force, except deadly force, against another when and to the extent that the person reasonably believes that such conduct is necessary to defend himself or herself or another against the other's*

> *imminent use of unlawful force. A person who uses **or threatens** to use force in accordance with this subsection does not have a duty to retreat before using **or threatening to use** such force.* <u>*F.S.*</u> *776.012(1)(changes in bold)*

Subsection (1) of Section 776.012 pertains solely to "*non-deadly*" force. It permits a person to use – or threaten to use – non-deadly force to the extent that the person <u>reasonably believes</u> such conduct is <u>necessary</u> to defend himself or another against another's <u>imminent</u> use of unlawful force. With the exception of adding "*threats*" into the language – it is unchanged from prior Florida law. As you will soon see, what distinguishes it from other sections of the self defense laws is that using or threatening to use *non-deadly force* against a physical attack does **NOT** require you to be "***in a place where you have a right to be***", nor is there a requirement that you are not in the commission of any "***criminal conduct***". Thus, you have no duty to *retreat* before using or threatening to use "*non-deadly force*".

In fact, under the immunity parts of the statute, your use of non-deadly force, or the threat of using it should insulate you from any arrest or criminal charge related to it – so long as you are not the "**aggressor**", and as long as any use of force was not excessive. However, this section does **not** apply to **defense of property**. It only applies to stopping a *physical attack*. The use of *non-deadly force* related to the defense of property (other than a dwelling) has a few different rules. We will discuss that in a later section.

<u>CHANGES TO 776.012(2) – DEADLY FORCE & THREATS:</u>

The law of self defense has always followed a somewhat simple formula in Florida consisting of these predicates: Before using "***deadly force***" you must have a **reasonable** belief that the use of such force was **necessary** to stop or prevent **imminent** death or great bodily harm to yourself or another person; or prevent the **imminent** commission of a *forcible felony*.

Prior to 2005 – there was also an additional requirement, aptly called the "***retreat rule***", which I previously discussed. The *retreat rule* held that you had to retreat before using *deadly force* if you could retreat with safety, unless you were attacked in your home or business. In those home and business situations – we applied the "***castle doctrine***" where basically, you had no duty to retreat. The 2005 "***Stand Your Ground***" law changed all that, and said you didn't have to retreat, and could "***Stand Your Ground***" as long as all the other predicates of reasonableness existed. The 2014 amendments added "***threats***" of using *deadly force* into the law, and some other additions. Here's the current subsection:

776.012(2) A person is justified in using or threatening to use deadly force if he or she reasonably believes that using or threatening to use such force is necessary to prevent imminent death or great bodily harm to himself or herself or another or to prevent the imminent commission of a forcible felony. A person who uses or threatens to use deadly force in accordance with this subsection does not have a duty to retreat and has the right to stand his or her ground if the person using or threatening to use the deadly force is not engaged in a criminal activity and is in a place where he or she has a right to be.

Subsection (2) of Section 776.012 pertains to the *use* or *threat* of *deadly force*. It is a section the Legislature didn't think through, and will most certainly cause problems for anyone using self defense. Because the language is crystal clear – it only authorizes the use or the threat of using *"deadly force"* in a situation that would ***allow*** deadly force – ie – *death or great bodily harm, or to stop or prevent a forcible felony*. Otherwise, in a *non-deadly force* situation, neither is permissible, and a violation of this prohibition may have the following result:

A.   It will probably cost you your *immunity* unless you first **retreat** (unless retreat would not eliminate imminent danger to yourself, there was no opportunity to retreat, or retreat would be futile. In this sense, *"futile"* may be applied in the sense that retreat could reasonably negate your efforts to stop someone else's illegal conduct. This would also implicate certain constitutional arguments. A true *test case*).

B.   It might be considered *"**excessive force**"*, depending on the facts. If so, any "excessive" actions could be considered as criminal conduct. However, like the *"futility"* issue in the previous possibility – a number of constitutional issues come into question.

C.   It might make your actions an *assault, aggravated assault*, or *improper exhibition*.

How it will work out in actual practice will depend on how the courts interpret it. However, since a reported case will not likely come up before the year 2016 – we all will be guessing until then. Whereas, the law prior to the 2014 amendments was that a *threat of deadly force* was lawful as long as reasonable, and did not involve a *warning shot*. My ***personal opinion*** is that the law either needs to be changed back to that, or changed such that display, without pointing, is not unlawful if not *objectively unreasonable*, and is not more than *"improper exhibition"* if the display was a *"conditional threat"* where the defender had a subjectively reasonable basis to believe it was necessary to ward off a physical attack, or stop any felony. Just my personal "two cents" worth.

However, the 2014 Legislature also amended this subsection of the statute to coincide with additional requirements that previously only pertained to F.S. 776.013 shown in (e) and (f) below, which in my opinion, was another really bad mistake. Thus, before you can *"**Stand Your Ground**"* and use (or even threaten to use) *deadly force* pursuant to F.S. 790.012, the following predicates must exist:

a.   You have a reasonable belief,

b.   That the use or threat of *deadly force* is necessary,

c.   To prevent imminent death or great bodily harm to yourself or another,

d.   or to stop or prevent the imminent commission of a *forcible felony*, **and**

e.   you are *"**in a place where you have a right to be**"*, **and**

f.   you are not involved in any ***criminal activity*** at the time the self defense arises.

If either of the last two requirements in the list are not met – then you fall back to pre-2005 self defense law – and have to apply the *"**retreat rule**"* before the use or *threat* of using *deadly force* is lawful. Thus, smoking a joint, driving DUI, possessing drugs or unprescribed medications, trespassing, etc. – all require you to **retreat** before using or even threatening to use *"deadly force"*. State v. Hill, 95 So.3d 434 (Fla. 4DCA 2012).

F.S. 776.013 – RESIDENCE, DWELLING & OCCUPIED VEHICLES:
Florida Statute 776.013 is titled *"**Home protection; Use or threatened use of deadly force; presumption of fear of death or great bodily harm.**"* It first appeared in 2005, and is primarily geared to allow the use or threat of *deadly force* in situations involving a dwelling, residence, or occupied conveyance. Each one of those will be explained shortly. Like the other self defense sections, in 2014 it added *"**threats**"* into the use of *deadly force*; eliminated the wording in subsection (3) that previously covered *"other"* self defense situations, and instead made any defense of a dwelling, residence, or occupied vehicle dependent upon either F.S. 776.012 or F.S. 776.031.

Although subsection (3) states the entire section is governed by 776.012 or 776.031 it still encompasses several distinct *"deadly force"* situations where the *"**Stand Your Ground**"* rule applies, and **no retreat** is necessary. In each of those situations 776.013 also creates some extremely important ***legal presumptions*** which are binding on the courts, and law enforcement. The first set of situations have the effect of allowing the use or threat of using deadly force against a person who "***unlawfully and forcibly***" enters or attempts to enter a "***dwelling, residence, or occupied vehicle***"; or against a person who removes or attempts to remove another person against their will from such a location. These presumptions form sort of a "***safe haven***" for the use of *deadly force*, in that these are the situations most protected by the statutes – and would be very difficult to prosecute successfully.

The **first presumption** in 776.013(1) is:

It is lawful to use or threaten to use *deadly force* where (1) an intruder **unlawfully** and **forcefully** enters, or forcefully tries to enter a dwelling, residence, or occupied vehicle; or (2) the intruder has removed or is attempting to remove another person against their will from such place or occupied vehicle.

In such situations, as long as the defending person using or threatening to use *deadly force* realizes this unlawful and forceful act is happening, he or she is conclusively presumed to have a "***reasonable fear***" of "***imminent***" death or great bodily harm to themselves or others:

> *"776.013(1) A person is presumed to have held a reasonable fear of imminent peril of death or great bodily harm to himself or herself or another when using or threatening to use defensive force that is intended or likely to cause death or great bodily harm to another if:*
>
> *(a)   The person against whom the defensive force was used or threatened was in the process of unlawfully and forcefully entering, or had unlawfully and forcibly entered, a dwelling, residence, or occupied vehicle, or if that person had removed or was attempting to remove another against that person's will from the dwelling, residence, or occupied vehicle; and*
>
> *(b)   The person who uses or threatens to use defensive force knew or had reason to believe that an unlawful and forcible entry or unlawful and forcible act was occurring or had occurred."*

The **second presumption** is in 776.013(4), and states:

> *"(4) A person who unlawfully and by force enters or attempts to enter a person's dwelling, residence, or occupied vehicle is presumed to be doing so with the intent to commit an unlawful act involving force or violence."*

This second presumption appears to be independent of the first, and not dependent on any requirements but those set forth in its own subsection. In other words, no matter what the situation, if a person unlawfully uses force to enter, or unlawfully uses force in attempting to enter a dwelling, residence, or occupied vehicle – there is an absolute presumption that person is doing so with the intent to commit a crime of violence therein. Since breaking into any of these would be a "***burglary***" – any break "**into**" them would also be a "***forcible felony***" since the definition of a "*forcible felony*" includes all ***burglaries.*** Of course, an attempt to break into them, without any "entry" would be at least an "***attempted burglary***", and both F.S.776.012 and F.S. 776.031 allow the use of *deadly force* to stop the imminent commission of a *forcible felony* (ie: its attempt **or** its completion) if the use of *deadly force* appears **reasonable** and **necessary**. However, unless the perpetrator is using *unlawful force* in his attempt to gain entry, there are no "***legal presumptions***" to assist your self defense claim.

QUESTION: Why is that important? Don't the first set of presumptions already do the same thing as subsection (4), but even better?

ANSWER: Yes, and they do somewhat overlap, however, subsection (4) has important independent legal significance – because there are a couple of ways you could lose the presumptions, such as your being engaged in unrelated ***criminal conduct*** (smoking a joint, etc.), or using the residence or vehicle "*to further criminal activity*" – even so you would still have an absolute presumption per subsection (4) that the other guy was committing or trying to commit a *forcible felony*! That's something that could be real important in your defense.

<u>DEFINITIONS IN 776.013:</u>

Since the presumptions in 776.013 only apply to a *dwelling, residence, or occupied vehicle* – it's important to know exactly how those words are defined in the statute. The statute redefines a " **dwelling**" as a building or conveyance of any kind, temporary or permanent, mobile or immobile, including an attached porch, so long as (1) there is a roof over it, and (2) it is designed to be occupied by people lodging there at night. It includes a tent. Obviously, it should also include a house trailer or recreational vehicle, and case law should extend the definition to include attached carports.

A " **residence**" is defined as a dwelling where a person resides either temporarily, permanently, or is visiting as an invited guest. This will include a motel room, hotel room, or even a friend's home.

A " **vehicle**" means a "**conveyance**" of any kind, motorized or not, which is designed to transport people or property. ***Bicycles*** are excluded as they are not legally defined as a "*conveyance*", and this may also apply to mopeds, and smaller non-motored boats where sleeping space is not provided as manufactured, as these may likewise escape the legal definition of "*conveyance*". On the other hand, a **motorcycle** is a conveyance. However, you need to remember that a **vehicle** does not receive the protections of either of these two presumptions unless it is also occupied by one or more human beings. Having your dog, Fido, dressed in a wig behind the driver's seat will not do.

The word "*forcibly*", although not defined in the statute, should mean any use of force, even if slight, according to the case law. Thus, in *Cappetta v. State*, 162 So.2d 309 (Fla. 3DCA 1964), the appellate court in discussing a " breaking" in a burglary case held that even the "slight" force of pushing open a closed and unlocked door was an "*act of physical force.*" Thus, climbing thru an open window or walking thru an open door would **not** constitute "*forcibly*", while pushing a window, or door open – should. Still, there is no case law on this issue directly involving self defense.

WHAT CAN DISSOLVE THE PRESUMPTIONS?:
As I briefly mentioned before, certain situations can dissolve the legal **presumptions** per 776.013(2). When that happens, the use of self defense is still permissible if lawful under either F.S. 776.012 (defense of persons); or F.S. 776.031 (defense of property). That being said, here are the issues that will dissolve the presumptions:

(2)   *The presumption set forth in subsection (1) does not apply if:*

(a) The person against whom the defensive force is used or threatened has the right to be in or is a lawful resident of the dwelling, residence, or vehicle, such as an owner, lessee, or titleholder, and there is not an injunction for protection from domestic violence or a written pretrial supervision order of no contact against that person; or

(b) The person or persons sought to be removed is a child or grandchild, or is otherwise in the lawful custody or under the lawful guardianship of, the person against whom the defensive force is used or threatened; or

(c) The person who uses or threatens to use defensive force is engaged in a **criminal activity** *or is* **using** *the dwelling, residence, or occupied vehicle to further a criminal activity; or*

(d) The person against whom the defensive force is used or threatened is a **law enforcement officer***, as defined in s. 943.10(14), who enters or attempts to enter a dwelling, residence, or vehicle in the performance of his or her official duties and the officer identified himself or herself in accordance with any applicable law*

or the person using or threatening to use force knew or reasonably should have known that the person entering or attempting to enter was a law enforcement officer.

Interestingly, while it would rarely happen in defense of a dwelling, residence, or occupied vehicle, the presumptions will **still apply** even if you are not in *"a place where you have a right to be"* so long as you are **not** otherwise engaged in *criminal conduct* or using the dwelling, residence, or vehicle for such. In such an instance, assuming you reasonably wanted to use or threaten to use deadly force you – you would not lose the presumptions, although you would still have to **retreat** if you could do so without putting yourself at risk, or if retreat would be futile. Only if you were involved in *"criminal conduct"*, or using the vehicle, dwelling, or residence to *"further criminal conduct"* would the presumption in subsection (1) disappear. Likewise, the other disqualifiers I just listed in subsections (a) thru (d) could also make the presumption in subsection (1) disappear.

QUESTION: Wait a minute! I thought the presumptions disappeared if I was not *"at a place where I have a right to be"*?

ANSWER: No. There is no such requirement. The presumptions in subsection (1) would only disappear if you were engaged in *criminal conduct*, personally using the vehicle or residence to further *criminal activity*, or the other disqualifiers listed in a-d. *"Place where you have a right to be"* is in sections 776.012 and 776.031. That deals with *"retreat"* – not the presumptions. Plus, the presumption in subsection (4) never disappears.

QUESTION: Can you give me an example?

ANSWER: Well . . . say you mistakenly wandered unto a road that's private property. You don't realize it until too late. You're not at a *"place where you have a right to be"*, but you're not trespassing or committing any crime, either. A robber comes up to the car, and you use *deadly force* if he uses any force trying to break, or get inside. All the *presumptions* still apply. Likewise, in that situation if he had a gun – safe retreat would not be feasible as any attempt at flight would likely get you shot in the back. So, the *"retreat rule"* would be satisfied.

QUESTION: But, I thought that if I didn't have the presumptions – I can't use, or threaten to use deadly force, right?

ANSWER: No. You can still use or threaten to use *deadly force* if it is otherwise permissible under either F.S. 776.012 or F.S. 776.031. But if you're either not at a "***place where you have a right to be***", or are personally engaged in "***criminal conduct***", or are using the residence or vehicle to further ***criminal conduct*** – you must first apply the "***retreat rule***", and retreat if it can be done in safety.

TWO OTHER IMPORTANT DEFINITIONS:
Burglary:
There are two other very important definitions to know about. The first is the word "***burglary***". The term " *burglary*" means entering or remaining in a dwelling, a structure, or a conveyance with the intent to commit an offense therein, unless the premises are at the time open to the public. A burglary is always a "*forcible felony*". A *forcible felony* allows you to use, or at least threaten to use "*deadly force*". Of course – the actual use of *deadly force* must be *reasonable and necessary* to be lawful, although the reasonable and necessary elements automatically kick in whenever you are acting within F.S. 776.013, due to the "***presumptions***". A burglary does not require a "breaking" or "force" in entering. It just requires an **unlawful entry** with the intention to commit another different crime inside *other than* just a *trespass*. Thus, reaching into the open window or bed of a truck or passenger car to commit a battery, or steal something would be a "*burglary*". The crime the invader intends to carry out inside need not be carried out, or even begin – it is the *mere entry* with the intent to do some further illegal act (other than a *trespass*) that makes it a *forcible felony*. F.S. 810.02.

CURTILAGE:
The term "***curtilage***" is the *fenced area* that surrounds a dwelling or residence. The fence may be any type of material such as chain link, wood slat, cement block, barbed wire, posts, and likely even a solid hedge – and it may even have an ungated opening wide enough for a boat or car to get thru. However, it is limited to those areas typically used in connection with the main residential structure such as a backyard, side yard, and parking areas. In such instances, the fence must be at least **three feet** in height. F.S. 810.011(7). Likewise, the fence must surround the **entire area** considered to be "curtilage". If it is only partially fenced so that one or more sides are open and unprotected by a fence or building – then it is not "*curtilage*".

Curtilage has also been held to include a carport attached to the dwelling that has a roof over it; an adjacent cement slab in rear of home with a ceiling supported by posts; and an attached porch with a roof. These fall within the definition of curtilage per the case law regardless of whether they are fenced, or not.

In Florida, the case law has long held that an unlawful entry into "curtilage" with the intent to commit a crime therein (other than a trespass) is a burglary. F.S. 810.011(1). Case law has also held that where there was an unlawful and **forceful** entry into curtilage (such as opening a closed gate), a person defending the curtilage falls within the protections and presumptions of F.S. 776.013. State v. Vino, 100 So.3d 716 (Fla. 3DCA 2012). Thus, in the Vino case – the use of deadly force was "presumed" to be lawful.

POSSIBLE FUTURE COURT INTERPRETATION:
Before we move on to the next topic – let me say that the 2014 changes in the statutes were not, in my opinion, well thought out, and will cause substantial problems with the use of *non-deadly force*. There is a slight ray of hope in that attorneys and the courts may notice that the definition of threat of deadly force in F.S. 776.013(1) is **very different** than the very limited, and non-definitive wording in either F.S. 776.012 or F.S. 776.031, to wit:

776.013(1): ". . . when using or threatening to use defensive force *that is intended or likely to cause death or great bodily harm to another*." [ie: "threatening" is limited to situations where it is intended or will likely cause actual death or great bodily harm – ie – a *"warning shot"*, or something similar].

776.012(2): A person is justified in using or threatening to use deadly force . . . ." [ie: no definition or limitation on "*threatening*"]

That may mean that the Legislature really intended the definition of "*threatening*" to only apply to conduct that was intended, or actually could result in some type of physical harm. Likewise, it is difficult to comprehend why the Legislature included a reference to F.S. 776.031 in subsection (3) of F.S. 776.013 – because F.S. 776.031 has nothing to do with dwellings, and has almost no relevance to occupied vehicles. Could it be argued that the inclusion was because the Legislature wanted a common interpretation of "threats" to be only those "*intended or likely to cause death or great bodily harm to another*"???

Again, that would make much more sense because the 2014 changes of not allowing a **reasonable** *threat* of deadly force except in a "*deadly force*" situation is completely absent from the *common law*, just like how impractical any requirement of "***retreat***" is in a *non-deadly force* situation where you're trying to prevent a crime, simply because you either are engaged in some type of unrelated criminal conduct, not a resident or household member in a property crime, or made a threat such as you would: "***kick their teeth in if they didn't drop that TV set***". It just makes no practical sense.

QUESTION: Why would that last example be a threat of deadly force?

ANSWER: Because "*kicking in your teeth*" threatens "*great bodily harm*". It's not just knives and guns out there!

So, if the Legislature really intended to make a change in the *common law*, you would think they would have specified that in the preamble to HB89 (the law from which all these changes were derived). *Pages v. Tapia*, 134 So. 3d 536 (Fla. 3DCA 2014). They certainly had the opportunity, and the preamble was one of the longer ones I've seen. But, I realize this is getting complicated, and quite frankly, it's something for lawyers and judges to figure out sometime in the future – not for gun owners.

For now, the rest of us need to act on the 2014 changes in a manner that assures us we are not arrested due to a legal mistake. You never want to be a "*test case*" for the law. It's never a great place to be when you're talking about criminal penalties – especially those that carry mandatory prison sentences like we have in Florida.

On the other hand, hopefully most of us are will already be in a "***place we have a right to be***", and not engaged in "***criminal conduct***" when the need for force occurs. Therefore, the only thing that we will have to deal with that makes no sense – is when using a "*threat*" of *deadly force* makes sense and is reasonable – or when we're trying to stop a non-forcible felony property crime on somebody else's property per F.S. 776.031, but legally have to ***retreat*** because we are not "***at a place where we have a right to be***" . . . or we're just not sure what kind of situation we're facing, or will be facing. In those instances the Legislature has put us at a <u>serious disadvantage</u> because they've made what was once a fairly straight forward area – very complicated. And complicated – means you have a high likelihood of getting confused, making a mistake, or wasting precious time that puts you at a major disadvantage in defending yourself or your property.

QUESTION: I'm a little confused.   Can't I still use the *threat* of deadly force in a *non-deadly force* situation if I first retreat?

ANSWER: I don't think so.   Since prior law would never allow deadly force in a non-deadly situation, even with retreat – the interpretation should not change just because "*threaten*" was added.

IMMUNITY UNDER F.S. 776.032 & F.S. 776.013:

Anyway, aside from the limitations mentioned in the last section, and since section (1) of 776.013 creates a **conclusive presumption** that an attacker who unlawfully uses "*force*" to gain, or who (with the use of "force") attempts to gain entry into your dwelling, residence, or occupied vehicle is doing so with the intent to injure you or another person, and likewise, since the statute creates a *conclusive presumption* that under these circumstances you also have a legitimate and reasonable fear of *imminent death or great bodily harm* to yourself or another – you should be   "*immune*" from prosecution according to the immunity statute, F.S. 776.032(1).

Subsection (1) of that section states:

> F.S. 776.032(1) "A person who uses or threatens to use force as permitted in s. 776.012, s. 776.013, or s. 776.031 is justified in such conduct and is immune from criminal prosecution and civil action for the use or threatened use of such force by the person, personal representative, or heirs of the person against whom the force was used or threatened, unless the person against whom force was used or threatened is a law enforcement officer . . . . As used in this subsection, the term "criminal prosecution" includes arresting, detaining in custody, and charging or prosecuting the defendant."

Now, don't take the "*immunity*" literally.   Immunity is a legal issue that is subject to proof, and hence controversy.   As of right now, the law says you have the **burden of proof** by a preponderance of the evidence in any pre-trial immunity hearing.   This burden is currently being challenged before the Florida Supreme Court in *Bretherick v. State*, 2014 Fla. LEXIS 1339 (Fla., Apr. 15, 2014), where the defense is asserting that the burden of proof in an immunity hearing should be on the State, just like in all other immunity type cases.   While I strongly agree with the defense – the outcome of the case is totally up for grabs, and will likely not be answered until mid to late 2015.   Thus, if the material facts involved in your use of self defense are in dispute (and they often are), you might still be arrested and prosecuted –   although the presumptions in 776.013 are designed to substantially lessen your chances of this happening.

QUESTION: What are the presumptions in the other self defense sections?

ANSWER: There are none. Only situations involving dwellings, residences, or occupied vehicles get any *"presumptions"*.

DO THE PRESUMPTIONS APPLY TO GUESTS:

A question often asked is who can claim the *presumptions* in F.S. 776.013 in using, or threatening to use deadly force? As far as subsection (1) goes the answer is they apply to guests, residents, lawful occupants, and those who have a present right or permission to enter the dwelling, residence, or occupied vehicle. It's also possible that the *presumptions* extend to others defending such a structure or vehicle – although if so, they might first have to follow the *"retreat rule"*. However, as far as subsection (4) is concerned – that should apply without restriction, but the breadth of its application is yet to be determined.

SOME QUESTIONS & ANSWERS ON 776.013:

Alright! I realize I've already given you a splitting headache with all this stuff. Please accept my apologies, and thank the 2014 Legislature for that. It was much easier before. However, in order to clarify some questions that may have popped into your already overworked brain, let's try the ol' question and answer method of clarification:

QUESTION: F.S. 776.013 says the subsection (1) presumptions don't apply if a person being removed against their will is a grandchild. You mean if grandpa decides he wants to kidnap my kid, I can't stop him?

ANSWER: No – you can stop him, and maybe you can even use deadly force, but if you do, then the subsection (1) presumptions in 776.013 do not apply, and your use of force would depend on F.S. 776.012. If you act *"reasonably"* pursuant to that section you should still have *"immunity"* because you have the right to use or threaten deadly force to stop an actual *forcible felony* no matter who is involved. On the other hand, grandma is probably gonna be really bent-out-of-shape if you shoot grandpa. Totally forget about getting invited over for Thanksgiving dinner!

QUESTION: What if it's my landlord, he kicks in the door and he threatens to shoot me unless I pay the rent?

ANSWER: I think I'd pay the rent. However, since he is the "owner" or "titleholder" to the property, once again the subsection (1) *presumptions* of F.S. 776.013 do not apply. On the other hand, he is committing a *forcible felony*, and you likely have the right to use *deadly force* if necessary. If so, the "*immunity*" in F.S. 776.032(1) should apply. Get a receipt for the rent before pulling the trigger.

QUESTION: What if I'm smoking a joint at home when somebody tries to break in?

ANSWER: Well, you shouldn't be smoking a joint because it's unlawful and stupid, and will likely be a federal felony if you also possess a firearm. Moreover, since you are acting illegally by smoking the joint, the subsection (1) *presumptions* will disappear – although you will likely still have "*immunity*"if you acted reasonably because your actions may still fall under F.S. 776.012 . However, you will first have to follow the "***retreat rule***" due to your criminal behavior. *State v. Hill*, 37 Fla. L.Weekly D1952 (Fla. 4DCA 2012).

<u>PLACE WHERE YOU HAVE "A RIGHT TO BE"</u>:

The phrase that seems to come up again-and-again in F.S. 776.013, and since the year 2014 in all the other self defense statutes is being "***in a place where you have a right to be***". If you're not in such a place, and you're using or threatening "*deadly force*" – the "***retreat rule***" is back. If you're only using or threatening the use of "*non-deadly force*" – there is no requirement of being "*in a place where you have a right to be*", nor do you have an issue if you are engaged in "*criminal conduct*", so long as you are not an "*aggressor*" or "*mutual combatant*".   So, assuming we want to play it safe on the meaning and application of this legal phrase – where are these places you "*have a right to be*"?

My best guess is arrived at by figuring out all the places you "**don't**" have a right to be in. That would seem to make the most sense, and follow the intent of the law. These "forbidden places" should include anywhere you would need permission to be where you don't have it; anywhere you've been told to keep off by the owner or a person with authority (ie: trespass); any place where you would be violating the law by being there; any place of nuisance such as a crack house or house of prostitution. What's left is probably where you have a "***right to be***". Again, no case law on this so far, and only my best guess. However, if you want to play it even safer, go to my second guess.

My <u>second guess</u> is a lot more restrictive on where you can be without worrying about the retreat rule, and would seem to defeat the broad purpose of the law. However, sometimes playing it safer is better. In that respect, you have a "right" to be on your own property, property lawfully in your possession, property you have a legal duty to protect, property you have actual permission to be on, and all public property such as roads, parks, etc., where the law does not restrict your presence. For example, if a park closes at night, and you are still there – you no longer have a "right to be" there. Step two feet outside of the park – and you'd be legal. Trying to figure this out in the middle of a self-defense situation would be no easy task which is another reason I don't think the Legislature intended this, and a reason why I don't think the courts will be so restrictive. Still, this is just my opinion, for now, and a "*test case*" scenario.

Thus, if you want to take no chances until the courts sort this mess out, here's my absolutely "safe" list of what constitutes a "***place where you have a right to be***":

a.   Your dwelling or residence (ie: where you live), even if it is only temporary. (eg: motel, hotel, rental, home, tent). This includes everyone who resides there with you, and all invited guests.

b.   Other places you lease, rent, or pay money to belong to and are current on, or have an invitation (eg: club, golf course, pool, health club, restaurant for dinner, mall, movie theater, etc.).

c.   Public places that are then open to the public (roads, streets, side walks, parks, etc.).

d.   Your occupied vehicle, and all invited passengers.

Unanswered in all these situations is what happens to the "guest" status when a person with superior authority orders them to leave the premises, or they commit a *forcible felony* or other crime in the dwelling, residence or occupied vehicle against a person with superior authority. Based on prior case law, I strongly assume they lose any protected status.

BUSINESS & NON-OWNED PREMISES:
There is nothing in any of the amended sections of the law that excludes business premises. If you're on the property of your employer you have the right

to defend it as if it were yours, and you qualify for being "**in a place where you have a right to be**" under 776.013. The case law says this happens even if you're there for non-business purposes. Same thing if you are on duty as a security guard. F.S. 776.031. Of course, if you are using or threatening to use *deadly force* you must first reasonably believe that such force is necessary to prevent the imminent commission of a *forcible felony*, or prevent imminent death or great bodily harm. In other words, if you fit these circumstances you should have immunity under the new law, and not need to retreat.

DEFENSE OF (OTHER) PROPERTY PER 776.031:

While F.S. 776.012 covers defense of persons, and F.S. 776.013 covers dwellings, residences, and occupied vehicles – F.S.776.031 covers most everything else. The title is "***Use or Threatened Use of Force in Defense of Property***". The section is worded as follows:

776.031 Use or threatened use of force in defense of property.—

(1) A person is justified in using or threatening to use force, except deadly force, against another when and to the extent that the person reasonably believes that such conduct is necessary to prevent or terminate the other's trespass on, or other tortious or criminal interference with, either real property other than a dwelling or personal property, lawfully in his or her possession or in the possession of another who is a member of his or her immediate family or household or of a person whose property he or she has a legal duty to protect. A person who uses or threatens to use force in accordance with this subsection does not have a duty to retreat before using or threatening to use such force.

*(2) A person is justified in using or threatening to use deadly force only if he or she reasonably believes that such conduct is necessary to prevent the imminent commission of a forcible felony. A person who uses or threatens to use deadly force in accordance with this subsection does not have a duty to retreat and has the right to stand his or her ground if the person using or threatening to use the deadly force is not engaged in a **criminal activity** and is in a **place where he or she has a right to be.** [bold added for emphasis]*

If you read the first section on use or threat of *non-deadly force* quickly -- you probably noticed there's no language about being in a "*place where you have a right to be*". But, it's still there in that you must have a ***duty to protect*** the property, have some right to possession, or be a member of the household or family in order to escape the "***retreat rule***". Thus, it is still there even for ***non-deadly force*** if you aren't one of the people who have a right to defend the property. How you defend property if you first have to retreat before you can even make a threat beats me. Likewise, there's no way I'm going to get involved in such a situation without a firearm – so I think the whole thing is kind of self defeating. It sounds like the most you can do if you don't have some legal connection to the property is threaten to call 911. Maybe that's what the Legislature wanted?

On the other hand, the second section on *"deadly force"* has the typical exclusions. In order to lawfully use or threaten to use deadly force you must not only be *"in a place where you have a right to be"*, but you must also not be engaged in *"criminal conduct".* If either exclusion applies to you when the defensive situation arises you must first **retreat** before using or threatening to use deadly force, if you can do so with safety, or unless retreat would be *futile.* Again, in the sense of stopping a crime vs. saving myself from physical harm – I'm not sure what *"futile"* means. Probably, the crime will be committed or completed unless the threat or use of deadly force is both *reasonable and necessary.*

Likewise, this particular section does not allow the use or threat of *deadly force* unless we're talking about stopping the imminent commission of a *"forcible felony"*. Anything **less** than a *"forcible felony"* does **NOT** allow the use or threat of deadly force if all you are trying to do is protect personal property, or real property that does not consist of a dwelling. So, even felony grand theft of personal property from a store by someone other than an employee or security guard would not allow the use or threat of *deadly force* – because it isn't a *"forcible felony"*.

QUESTION: Why would an employee or security guard cause a difference?

ANSWER: It wouldn't – unless they first ordered the culprit to stop, and there was some type of a struggle, or threat by the perpetrator. In that case it becomes a *"robbery"* – which is a *"forcible felony."* Otherwise, only *non-deadly force* would be permitted by a civilian. (a police officer has more power)

If you're starting to think: "Boy, this is really getting confusing!" – I totally agree with you. However, the simple way to remember is:

SIMPLIFIED "DEADLY FORCE" RULE:

If you have a reasonable belief of imminent death or great bodily harm to yourself, or another – or – a reasonable belief that a "forcible felony" is taking place, or is imminent – you normally have the right to "Stand Your Ground", and use or threaten to use deadly force, as long as such is reasonable and necessary under the circumstances.

However, if you are involved in some kind of "<u>criminal activity</u>" when the situation arises, or are not "<u>in a place where you have a right to be</u>" – the law says you must retreat, if such can be done with safety before using, or threatening to use deadly force.

If all you are doing is protecting real or personal property that is not a dwelling, residence, or occupied vehicle – you can't use or threaten deadly force unless a "forcible felony" is involved, and the use or threat of deadly force appears reasonable and necessary. *(Also, OK to stop or prevent imminent death or great bodily harm – but that would be under 776.012)* Plus, if you are not a lawful occupant, member of the immediate family, or don't have a duty to protect the property – you have a duty to retreat before using or threatening deadly force. Same thing if you were engaged in criminal activity before you took defensive action, or if you are not at a "place where you have a right to be".

QUESTION: Don't <u>F.S.</u> 776.012(2) and <u>F.S.</u> 776.031(2) overlap when it comes to stopping or preventing the imminent commission of a forcible felony?

ANSWER: It sure seems that way.   If so, your attorney should get to choose which, or both, of these sections he or she wants to defend your actions under, as they are likely independent of each other in that limited situation.   *Hill v. State,* 39 Fla. L. Weekly D1464 (Fla. 4DCA 2014)(*en banc*).

<u>"NON-DEADLY" FORCE IN DEFENSE OF PROPERTY PER 776.031:</u>
Like I mentioned before, the first section of <u>F.S.</u> 776.031 on the use or threat of "*non-deadly force*" actually has limitations on its use! Sad, but true! Thus, before you can use, or even threaten to use non-deadly force to defend property under <u>F.S.</u> 776.031 – you must have a **legal right** to protect it or be an "*immediate member of the family*", or "*member of the household*" of a person having that right. Otherwise, you have no right to defend it, and would also have to apply the "***retreat rule***" before using or even threatening to use "*non-deadly*" force.

QUESTION: Do you mean if I see somebody stealing my neighbor's lawn mower from his driveway – I can't do anything?

ANSWER: Well . . . you can call 911.   You can use your cell phone to take a photo of the culprit.   But, unless your neighbor and you had an actual verbal or written agreement where you had authority to protect his property – you cannot use or threaten to use **any** force in stopping the culprit – before retreating. How the hell this would work is beyond me, but that is now the law! Of course, if you do have his or her official "OK" – then you could use or threaten to use non-deadly force without retreat. Likewise, same thing if you're a member of the owner's immediate family, or a member of his or her household.

QUESTION: Couldn't I use *non-deadly force* per 776.012?

ANSWER: No. 776.012 applies only to **physical attack**, and **forcible felonies**. Not *"property"* crimes.

QUESTION: How about *non-deadly force* under 776.031, because retreat would be *"futile"*? In other words – if I *retreat* the crime is committed?

ANSWER: Well . . . sounds right to me, but how would you know unless you first told him you were calling 911, and backed up a few steps? Plus, we still don't have an appellate court case saying what *"futile"* is for these circumstances. However, if you take my suggestion, yell you've called 911, take several steps back for whatever reason the Legislature was fantasizing about, and if he ignores you and still insists on taking the lawnmower – now you can use or threaten non-deadly force if you want to take the chance of being shot, stabbed, or beaten. Rots o ruck!

QUESTION: What about if the thief took it from my neighbor's garage? Couldn't I use or threaten *"deadly force"* in that example?

ANSWER: Well . . . now we're talking about a *"dwelling"*, and we're under 776.012 – not 776.031. Since the thief "entered" the garage to take it – it's a *"**burglary**"* and thus a *"forcible felony"*. However, are you at a *"**place where you have a right to be**"* when this happens? If not, do you have specific permission to defend the property, or are you an immediate family member? If not, you must first *"**retreat**"* before doing so – and – if you are actually thinking of using deadly force vs. just "threatening" to use it – *deadly force* will never be lawful to stop a *non-violent felony*, or even a *non-violent forcible felony*. Likewise, if the perpetrator comes running out of the house with a ten year old 19" TV – do you honestly think anyone will believe that shooting him was either "reasonable" or "necessary"? It may be "necessary" to stop the crime – but in no way will it ever be "reasonable"! Hence, you will be charged with *aggravated assault* or *aggravated battery* even though the other guy just committed a burglary and *forcible felony*. Good work! Maybe you can get adjoining cells?

QUESTION: What about the "***presumptions***" in 776.013? Won't they protect me?

ANSWER: What protections? The thief did not use "***force***" in entering the garage – hence none of the *presumptions* apply. The garage door was open in our example.

QUESTION: What if it was a shed, but the shed was locked, and the thief broke in?

ANSWER: Then we have a "**burglary**" again, because any entry into a structure or conveyance with the intent to commit a crime is a "***burglary***" – and every burglary is a "*forcible felony*". But – since it is not a dwelling, it is now under F.S. 776.031 – and we again jump the question whether you have any right to get involved – and if not – you must **retreat** before even threatening to use deadly force – and since you only have a non-violent (forcible) felony, while you should be able to point your gun – you'd better not pull the trigger, or else there's an excellent chance you just engaged in "*excessive force*", and (once again) would be guilty of an *aggravated assault* or *aggravated battery* because of it. Both of which carry mandatory prison sentences!

QUESTION: What if I owned the shed?

ANSWER: Well – it's a *forcible felony*, and you certainly don't have to retreat. Plus, you can threaten the use of deadly force short of a *warning shot*, and should have no problem with display – but the issue of actually **using** *deadly force* still falls into that elusive "*reasonable and necessary*" category. Unless you're attacked, or the perpetrator is about to take something valuable – I think you will have a problem with the "reasonable" portion of the case. That's a jury issue – and I'd rather avoid anything close to that, right or wrong.

That being said, let's get back to self-defense, and the use of deadly force:

DEADLY FORCE -- USE TO PREVENT ESCAPE:

A citizens right to prevent an escape is not as broad as a police officers. It is a dangerous area to get into since a mistake can lead to criminal, and civil repercussions. Also – taking a criminal into custody can be a very dangerous. However, the law states you can use any reasonable force that you reasonably believe is necessary to prevent the escape of a person who is under arrest, and was in your custody. <u>F.S.</u> 776.07. If it is anything less than a *forcible felony* – *deadly force* is out! Even with a forcible felony, *deadly force* may not be permissible, depending on the facts and the crime. Also, I will presume you made a "lawful" **citizen's arrest**! If it was unlawful – you're likely acting illegally, and the person you've illegally arrested or tried to arrest may lawfully resist, and use such force as is reasonably necessary to do so!

However, I would **not** suggest that it's a reasonable use of force to shoot somebody who is trying to escape from a *non-violent felony* or any misdemeanor. Nor can you use force on someone who surrenders. And remember, that once the culprit is running away, you are rarely in physical danger, nor is there much of *"imminent"* anything! If you shoot him, and a jury decides that was the use of "*excessive force*", you've just committed an aggravated battery, or manslaughter.

QUESTION: So, when could I use deadly force involving an escape?

ANSWER: Unless you're a police officer, it's a tough question, and likely best to avoid. But I believe it's justified anytime it's a forcible rape, armed robbery, homicide, arson of an occupied dwelling, non-parental kidnaping, or bombing, (or the attempt), and the guy refuses to stop after a warning. These situations are <u>so serious</u> that society will rarely fault you. As to anything else -- it's gonna depend, and probably won't fly. Play it on the side of caution, and only in the most extreme cases would I normally take the chance!

QUESTION: How about *non-deadly force,* like a *Taser, stun gun, pepper spray,* or something similar?

ANSWER: If it involves a *forcible felony* – you might wind-up getting shot or stabbed. I would only get involved in something like that if I had a firearm. Whether I'd fire it or not would depend on whether I thought I was in imminent danger, or the situation were such that I had no doubt in my mind it was absolutely necessary. A mistake is not worth the chance of a mandatory prison sentence. If it was a non-violent **felony**, and you're willing to take the chance, I personally feel use, or threat of using a "*non-deadly*" weapon would be a "legally" better method, although not necessary a "safer" method, as someone committing even a non-violent felony is often armed with a deadly weapon. Still, if you do decide to take the chance, I'd personally avoid a *stun gun* since it requires very close contact — and I don't want to get hurt.

If it's a misdemeanor, I really don't know, and would probably advise to stay away from it altogether and not get involved trying to stop the escape – just because of the civil liability side, no matter what the law is. However, if you are being physically attacked – I believe you are **always** within your rights to use *pepper spray, a stun gun, or a Taser* in a reasonable manner.

LESS THAN LETHAL AMMUNITION:

Law enforcement and correctional officers were granted an exception from the definition of "deadly force" where they use "*less-than-lethal munition*" in good faith, and within the scope of their duties. This is a 1999 amendment to F.S. 776.06. *Less than lethal ammunition* is defined as a projectile that is designed to stun, temporarily incapacitate, or cause temporary discomfort to a person without penetrating the person's body. Thus, the good faith use of such ammunition by an officer will be considered the use of "*non-deadly force*", and an officer using such ammunition in good faith during the performance of his or her duties is not liable for that use, civilly or criminally. This statute does **not** apply to a citizen's use of such ammunition, as the section says that it is the use of "*deadly force*" for anyone **but** law enforcement.

USE OF FORCE BY LAW ENFORCEMENT:

Law enforcement officers need never retreat in the lawful pursuit of their duties. They have no retreat rule – ever. Moreover, they may use any *non-deadly force* they reasonably believe is necessary to defend themselves from bodily harm when taking a person into custody. This is the "*reasonable man*" standard. F.S. 776.05. The degree of force must be both reasonable and necessary, or it may constitute the use of "*excessive force*". However, the use of any force is technically illegal and excessive where the arrest or custody would be unlawful. F.S. 776.051(2). A citizen may **not** resist an illegal arrest with force. If the arrest is unlawful – your remedy is to raise that in the court system. Therefore, the words "Yes, sir", and "No, sir" are recommended in all encounters with law enforcement.

A law enforcement officer may use ***deadly force*** to arrest a fleeing felon or person who escapes from his custody **only** where the officer reasonably believes the prisoner or fleeing felon poses an immediate threat of death or serious physical harm to the officer or others; or reasonably believes the fleeing felon committed a forcible felony involving the infliction or threatened infliction of death or serious bodily harm to the officer or others. In such instances a ***warning*** must be given before using *deadly force*, **if** the making of such a warning is feasible, and will not expose the officer to immediate danger. [F.S. 776.05(3) & F.S. 776.07]. *Tennessee v. Garner*, 471 U.S. 1 (1985). While the statutes are worded in terms that could be interpreted as allowing deadly force any time it was "reasonable" – constitutional limitations have been placed on what is, or what is not "reasonable". Thus, in the case of *Graham v. Connor*, 490 US 386 (1989), the U.S. Supreme Court held that the actions of law enforcement officers are limited to only using force that is "reasonable" pursuant to the *Fourth Amendment* of the Constitution. That means that the use of *deadly force* to stop a non-violent felony, or any misdemeanor – will always be considered unreasonable unless the suspect uses or attempts to use deadly force against the officer, or attempts to secure the officer's weapon. Likewise, under Florida law, the discharge of a firearm in the direction of a fleeing suspect is always considered the use of "*deadly force*", even by a law enforcement officer. F.S. 776.06 (Except for less-than-lethal ammunition.)

TRAP & SPRING GUNS:

A " ***trap gun***", also called a ***"spring gun"*** – is a loaded, unmanned firearm aimed at a particular area, which is usually set off by either a string, wire, or spring mechanism attached to a door, window, or other place where an intruder may enter. When the intruder enters the gun fires, and normally wounds or kills the individual. Problem is – very illegal!

Since the firearm is not manned – it does not know if an "unlawful entry" has occurred, if its use is "reasonable" or "necessary", or even if it's your kid coming in from college when he forgot his key. If it goes off, and kills or wounds someone – generally the charge is manslaughter, or aggravated battery. *Falco v. State,* 407 So.2d 203 (Fla. 1981).

CRIMES & PENALTIES FOR USING EXCESSIVE FORCE:

Uh, oh! Here comes the real bad news! What happens when you screw-up, make a mistake, or are just an unfortunate victim of circumstances. The name of the game is punishment. You and your legislators are screaming for penalties and jail time, but everybody forgot to put some protections in for those of us who are using self-defense, and who mistakenly go over the line, however slight. A person who is justified in using force, but strays over the line somewhat, or just makes a mistake in judgment – should not ordinarily be facing the penalties that exist today, but even with the changes made in 2014 by the Legislature – he or she does. Here's the scoop.

MANSLAUGHTER:

Manslaughter is the killing of another human being by *culpable negligence*, without lawful justification. It also occurs when there is a use of excessive force. F.S. 782.11. Manslaughter is a second degree felony which is ordinarily punishable by up to fifteen years in the prison system.

Since this legal definition of manslaughter may be somewhat confusing, let me explain it a bit simpler by breaking it into its components. Basically, I meant that manslaughter happens one of two principal ways. Method one is called *"culpable negligence"*. *Culpable negligence* is more than simple negligence, it is conduct so gross and flagrant that it amounts to a reckless disregard of human life, or is conduct done with such a want of care as to raise the presumption of a conscious indifference to the consequences. It must be of such a nature that the defendant knew, or reasonably should have known that the act or <u>inaction</u> was likely to result in death or great bodily injury to another.

The second way it occurs is where you misjudge the law or the facts involved in self-defense or legal justification. If you do, and you also wind-up killing someone -- the crime is manslaughter. One way this happens is if you do have the legal right (ie: "justification") to use force, but in doing so you **"unnecessarily"** kill another. What do I mean by "unnecessarily"?

Well, that is kind of self-explanatory. It means that you acted in a manner **disproportionate** to the act, or took a life where there was no reasonable necessity for doing so. I use the word "<u>reasonable</u>" necessity, because deciding what is reasonable doesn't always mean you were right. You may have been wrong to use the degree of force you did, but if this your belief was objectively reasonable under the circumstances -- you would still be legal, and should not be subject to prosecution. However, if it was not objectively reasonable under the facts known to you, and thereby your use of force exceeded the amount of force that was reasonable or could have been reasonable – and a death resulted – it's manslaughter.

By the way, although you may think a mandatory prison sentence is required for manslaughter, you're wrong. Manslaughter is **not** considered "murder", and although it is a "*forcible felony*", it is **not** one of the listed forcible felonies that requires a mandatory sentence for use, carry, or discharge of a firearm in F.S. 775.087. *Murray v. State*, 491 So. 2d 1120, 1123 (Fla. 1986); F.S. 775.087. However, if you use any weapon or firearm in the commission of a manslaughter, it does increase its severity from a second, to a first degree felony. Thus, a term of imprisonment up to thirty years is possible! F.S. 775.082.

AGGRAVATED ASSAULT:

The most common case for self defense situations that have gone wrong is ***aggravated assault***. Aggravated assault is a third degree felony that carries a three (3) year mandatory minimum prison sentence if a firearm or destructive device was involved. F.S. 775.087(2). By mandatory prison sentence -- we mean that if convicted, you've got to serve the full mandatory prison portion, even if the judge doesn't feel you deserve it. He just has no choice, although there was a slight change in the 2014 legislative session which I will go over soon.

So, what is an *aggravated assault*? Well, to understand, you first have to know the definition of an assault.

An "*assault*" is an intentional, **unlawful** threat done by word or act, to do violence to another person, coupled with the apparent ability to do so, and by doing some act that creates a well-founded ("reasonable") fear in the other person that the violence is "imminent" (ie: "immediate"). To make an assault "*aggravated*" -- the assault must be committed with a ***deadly weapon***, without any intent to kill, **or** must be done with an intent to commit a felony. F.S. 784.021. Thus, an *aggravated assault* may be committed with a gun, knife, or any other variety of "*deadly weapons*".

To further clarify it, an "***assault***" is an intentional threat:

a.   That is unlawful
b.   To do violence against another person(s)
c.   By doing some act
d.   Which act creates a reasonable fear in the other person that violence is imminent.

Some cases illustrate these elements. Thus, in _Butler v. State,_ 632 So.2d 684 (Fla. 5DCA 1994), the appellate court held that a threat to do violence in the future lacks the essential element of "_imminent_" – and therefore falls short of an assault. It's only a " _conditional threat_". Another case made it clear that the **intent** of the defendant as to the "threat to do violence" element is crucial, rather than the reaction of the victim. _Benitez v. State_, 901 So.2d 935 (Fla. 4DCA 2005). Of course, reaction of the alleged victim is still essential on another element – "reasonable fear of imminent violence". Thus, holding a gun without pointing it may, or may not constitute a threat depending on whether there was some overt act in aid of a threat. _Turner v. State_, 771 So.2d 1286 (Fla. 4DCA 2000). It's usually a jury question. However, where the defendant only had a knife, made no indication of any attempt to throw it, and there was a vehicle and distance between his victim, the appellate court held that the threat was not yet imminent as it was "two steps removed". _Sullivan v. State,_ 898 So.2d 105 (Fla. 2DCA 2005). My opinion is that this was a lucky decision for the defendant, and if a firearm had been involved the decision probably would have gone the other way. Another case held that a mere verbal threat generally requires an additional "overt act" to elevate it to an assault. _O.D. v. State_, 614 So.2d 23 (Fla. 2DCA 1993).

So, how does an aggravated assault typically happen in a self-defense context?

Well, let's say your neighbor's kid keeps running over your lawn with his truck at high speed. This is dangerous. This is a breach of the peace. This is a trespass. This is criminal mischief. This stinks! Every time you call the cops -- they arrive twenty minutes after all is done and over, and they can never catch the kid. Plus, they can't arrest him for a misdemeanor not done in their presence. That's the law, and it really stinks! It also needs to be corrected.

You're frustrated as hell. You're also rightfully worried that your dog, kid, wife, etc. -- will eventually get run-over by this nut. You're probably right.

Rather than email me for innovative legal advice, you decide to save a buck, confront the stupid bastard, and make an impression he won't forget. Surely, who could blame you? Being an avid movie-goer, you reason: "If Clint Eastwood can do it – so can I!"

The magic day arrives, and as junior begins to zero-in at high-speed, you raise your mighty 12 gauge in his direction, and utter the magic words of your silver screen hero: "_Well, Punk. Are you feeling lucky?_"

Apparently not, because suddenly, an amazing change in attitude is noticed, and junior turns his truck in the opposite direction as fast as he can. However, since he hates your guts, he calls the cops. Maybe he calls daddy or mommy -- who can't understand why anyone would point a gun at dear, darling junior -- but the end result is always the same -- you're charged with *aggravated assault*!

Unless you find an understanding prosecutor, a super jury, a really good attorney, or a combination of all the above -- you're likely going to jail for three years!

Incredible, isn't it? I mean, we all know who should be going to jail -- and it sure aien't you -- but that's the way it goes. Moreover, even if you get the charge reduced -- you stand a very good chance of losing your right to own and possess firearms ever again!

ROAD RAGE PROBLEMS WITH AGGRAVATED ASSAULT:

Another typical example of how you can get yourself into big trouble is good ol' road rage. But before starting, let me personally thank all of you who carry a gun in your vehicle, and think that by displaying it to the nut who is tailgating you – you are acting properly. If it were not for that attitude, my yearly net as a criminal trial attorney before I retired, would have been significantly lowered. Always remember – display of a firearm in Florida makes it a **jury question** whether the display was "*aggravated assault*", *improper exhibition*, or just lawful self defense!

Something else to know about road rage incidents that I've learned and seen over the years: In a road rage incident the person who is instigating the situation is **trying** to get you to lose your cool, and play into their "**get even with the world**" fantasy. Once you do – assuming you both aren't killed in a traffic accident, or don't kill some poor innocent bystander – they will blame you for everything! They will work it so **you** look like the bad guy, especially if you display a firearm! Count on it! They will call 911, and tell the dispatcher you pulled a gun on them for no reason! I've had lots of cases just like that – and in every one it was the same. So, be forewarned! In a road rage incident – do **not** play into the game! Call 911 immediately, report what's happening, ask for a unit to respond immediately, and tell them you "*need help*!" If nothing else – you're now the "victim" vs. the other guy. If the dispatcher asks you if the other party is armed – always respond "*I think so*". Don't say "no" unless you're absolutely certain of it. Many times the other guy **is** armed – and you should always assume that possibility exists. If the dispatcher asks if you saw a weapon

– be honest! Lies and exaggerations have a way of coming back, and biting you! However, stick to your assertion that they *"must be armed"* based upon their conduct! Nobody would do crazy stuff like the other guy is doing unless they also had a weapon to back it up!

QUESTION: So, what if they show a gun, or I really think they have one? Could I then display a firearm?

ANSWER: Maybe – but I would advise against it unless they tried to run you off the road. I think that showing yours might escalate it. Instead, I would call 911 pronto – and tell them what's going on, and that you need help "now"! Remember what I said about displaying a firearm in a road rage situation! In almost every possible situation – don't do it! Remember, calling 911 gets you a **recorded statement** of what's going on, and what you're thinking. Also, if the cops don't respond to help you – it also shows a jury you **tried** to avoid a conflict by asking for help. Don't go telling the dispatcher you have a gun and *"will use it if you have to"*. That always goes the wrong way for you later on.

That advice – by the way – was worth the price of this entire book!

Anyway, you should know that *display* of a firearm in a road rage incident, even if the other driver is the "real nut" – is likely to get you arrested for *aggravated assault*. As I warned before, aggravated assault carries a three (3) year mandatory minimum prison sentence if you get convicted Bye, Bye! Have a nice stay!

Now, you'll probably say – *"I was in fear of my life!"* Maybe you'll even say: *"I wasn't really trying to threaten him! I was just trying to scare him away so he'd stop!"* Interesting response, and a fairly standard argument – and I actually agree with you! Unfortunately, as I've said before – this is usually a **jury question**, and there is no case law in Florida that has settled the issue whether merely holding a gun skyward is a "threat", a "conditional threat", "just being ready if something happens", or a lawful response to unlawful conduct by another. Sure, the *Turner* case I discussed a few paragraphs ago might also apply, but what if the court says your pulling the gun out in anger was the *"overt act"*? Likewise, can you really convince everyone else that you had a *"reasonable fear of imminent death or great bodily harm"*? If you can't – it's likely an "aggravated assault", or at least a jury question.

The argument from the defense side is that holding a gun without pointing it is at worst a *"conditional threat"* that doesn't constitute *aggravated assault* because the threat of violence isn't *"imminent"*, there's no real intent to use it, only the intent to **avoid** any further conflict, altogether. The other argument is that it wasn't really a "threat" at all, but only a "warning" that if necessary, you could protect yourself if things got worse, or that you were in reasonable fear that things were going to get worse, and just **"wanted to be ready"** if it got to that point. And, believe it or not – there are a number of cases in other jurisdictions that support all these theories. So, assuming the police, prosecutor, or jury buys it – you're a free man or woman. Assuming it didn't go that way – you've got very big problems, and are going to be praying real hard that some appellate court will extend the *Turner* case, or my other theories to your situation. If not, you've got a three year mandatory stay in the slam to think about it. Likewise, you have the problem with the 2014 changes to the self defense laws that say you can't even *"threaten"* someone with *deadly force* except to stop a *forcible felony*, or prevent *imminent death or great bodily harm!*

Sure, there are other scenarios. There's always a chance at a misdemeanor charge of getting a *"improper exhibition"* under F.S. 790.10. Get a good lawyer, sympathetic prosecutor – and anything is possible. Many times with a good lawyer, and believable defense, a prosecutor can (rightly) be convinced that the misdemeanor is the better way to do things. Other times, you can plea to the felony – but the prosecutor will agree to do it **without** the mandatory minimum. The mandatory prison sentence can be waived – but only a prosecutor can do that. *State v. Kelly,* 138 So.3d 1169 (Fla. 3DCA 2014). A judge cannot waive the mandatory minimum unless the State Attorney also agrees.

One quick word of advice here – assuming things go wrong and you have to take a plea. If you are offered a plea you should always plea *"no contest"* vs. **"guilty"** if you have any choice! There is a huge legal difference in the ramifications between the two, both civil and criminal. A plea of *"no contest"* means you don't necessarily agree with the charge, but think a plea is in your best interest, and therefore accept the legal consequences. A plea of *"guilty"* means you admit to full criminal responsibility. Big difference!

However, I can tell you that going to trial is a really brave act since an adverse verdict kicks in the mandatory minimum prison sentence without much exception! At that point – if convicted – you're probably going to be more than willing to pay whatever the "test case" price is for an appeal on whether holding a gun skyward is a threat or something else.

Anyway, back to road rage – and here's the really bad part – almost every case I ever took in forty years of practice – had the other driver **swearing** you pointed the gun at him or her regardless of whether this really happened! Likewise, as I said before – they will swear that **you** started everything! *Pointing* a gun is usually considered an *"imminent"* threat, and hence you face a charge of *"aggravated assault"*! Even if you pointed it skyward just as a warning – most of the time they'll swear you pointed it directly at them!

Remember, that people who tailgate and deliberately cut you off are not really the highest quality human beings we have out there. Many times they have a problem which they'd like to resolve at your expense. Getting even with you, the world, or themselves – even if that means lying under oath, and seeing you rot in prison over something they caused – is a **satisfying** thing for these folks. On a psychological level – it means they actually did "get even" with world. Plus, they're usually really good liars. So, I'm warning you to beware of these situations. They are tough cases to win, and often the only way to legally survive them is to work out some kind of plea negotiation.

QUESTION: So, what's the answer?

ANSWER: Well, I thought I made that crystal clear, but if not – here it is again: **Don't go showing your firearm in a road rage situation! Don't!**

Leave it in the console or glove compartment. Pull over or slow down, dial 911 or *FHP, and let the fuzz know what's going on. I know that means you've backed down – but macho is never the smart thing to do in this day and age, and quite frankly – prison sucks! If the nut approaches you after you've stopped your vehicle, that's another completely different situation, and maybe you really will need your firearm. That's something I can't answer without lots of additional facts. But the safe way to avoid arrest, and falling into this terrible trap is not to get in the situation in the first place. Stay out of harm's way. Call 911 early! Nobody should want to be arrested to prove their point, and being prosecuted, rightly or wrongly, is not an experience anybody should ever look forward to.

DASH CAMERAS AND ROAD RAGE:

Another quick word of advice: Get a **dash camera**! For less than sixty bucks you can get one on Amazon – and have a digital record of what happened on the road. (I've seen them as low as $9.95, plus shipping). Better yet, get two. One for the front, and one aimed rearward. That way it picks up the tail-gaiting nut cases. The digital video is stored on a micro flash card, and can be used to prove you really didn't do anything wrong. I bought one right after I handled a road rage case years ago – when a truck driver was behind a twelve minute road rage incident. The whole thing was captured on his dash camera – and proved my client was innocent! The truck driver watched the entire incident unfold, and when FHP stopped and arrested my client – he turned over the flash card to the responding troopers. Without it – my client would have gone to prison, as the other guy was a damned good liar!

CHANGE CONCERNING AGGRAVATED ASSAULT:

Is there no justice? Probably not -- but that's your fault for not pushing the Legislature to protect you more. The 2005 "**Stand Your Ground**" law was a good start, but fell short in many areas. The legislative changes in 2014 were also a disappointment by falling far short of what was really needed, and also causing some really serious problems with the law. However, here's the good news – somewhat:

In 2014 the Legislature amended F.S. 775.087(6) to allow the **possibility** that a person convicted of *aggravated assault* with a firearm or destructive device could be excused from the mandatory portion of a prison sentence if the trial court makes written findings that:

> "*(1) the defendant had a good faith belief that the aggravated assault was justifiable pursuant to chapter 776, (2) the aggravated assault was not committed in the course of committing another criminal offense, (3) the defendant does not pose a threat to public safety, and (4) the totality of the circumstances involved in the offense do not justify the imposition of such sentence.*"

Obviously, this is not normally a great place to start from as a defendant because it assumes you have either plead guilty, or have been found guilty after a trial. Moreover, it has a certain "backfire" issue built into it since it could be used as a bargaining tool by the prosecution to get a harsher plea negotiation where instead of offering to "waive" the mandatory prison sentence for a plea – the prosecutor instead agrees they will not "oppose" your making a motion to the judge to forego the mandatory portion of the sentence, and just leaves that up to the judge, for better or worse. However – at least it gives you a shot (no pun intended) of getting around the mandatory – which is better than nothing.

QUESTION: Didn't you say before only the prosecutor could waive the mandatory sentence?

ANSWER: Yes – but as this section says, the Legislature made a small exception in *aggravated assault* cases only where the trial court makes the findings I outlined above. It will be your burden to prove these predicates if such a situation arises by a preponderance of the evidence. Rots o ruck!

QUESTION: What would you have done differently?

ANSWER: As I've said in previous editions, here's my suggested version:

A NEEDED SELF DEFENSE STATUTE:

> *"No person who is convicted or found guilty of aggravated assault, shall be subject to a mandatory minimum prison sentence where such person establishes by a preponderance of the evidence that the threat of using deadly force or threat of using a firearm was made upon the actual belief, even if mistaken, that (1) the other person was engaged in the imminent commission or attempt to commit a felony or other crime involving imminent physical violence, (2) that at such time said person using or threatening to use deadly force or a firearm was not engaged in any criminal activity related to the need of using self defense, and (3) that said person did not discharge any firearm unless they had a right to use deadly force pursuant to F.S. 776.012; F.S. 776.013, or F.S. 776.031."*

A statute so worded would avoid mandatory sentences in almost all situations where it would be unfair, and would thereby allow a sentence to be imposed within the applicable sentencing guidelines. In fact, in many other states this is known as *"imperfect self defense"*, and requires the reduction of the charge to something less onerous.

EXCUSABLE HOMICIDE:

Excusable homicide is not a crime. It is a defense. You can't be convicted of manslaughter or murder if the homicide is legally excusable.

QUESTION: You mean there are actually times when I can kill somebody, and legally get away with it?

ANSWER: Well, the answer is that "accidents happen", and as tragic as it may be, if a death results from an accident that falls short of culpable negligence -- it's not considered murder or manslaughter, as the conduct is legally excusable.

QUESTION: Why?

ANSWER: Probably because our Constitution has a requirement that the punishment must not be disproportionate to the act being punished, and convicting somebody of murder or manslaughter for a total accident, or simple negligence, is a bit too much for most courts. That doesn't mean that that's the end of it, because I can guarantee you that somebody is gonna get sued in civil court -- and the suit will be for "big time" damages. But, at least there shouldn't be (the key here is "shouldn't be") any criminal charge for a homicide.

If you'd like some examples of **excusable homicide**, I'll pick a few from the law books that actually happened. The classic case is two kids cleaning, or looking at a loaded weapon. It drops, and somehow goes off. Another scenario is a hunting accident where culpable negligence is not involved. However, the definition of *excusable homicide* is much broader than this, and can act as a total, or as a partial defense (which could allow a homicide to be downgraded to a lesser charge). In order to understand this, you need to know the legal definition of " excusable homicide. The definition follows:

<u>Homicide is excusable when:</u>
(1)   *Committed by accident and misfortune in doing any lawful act by lawful means with usual ordinary caution, and without any unlawful intent; or*

(2)   *When done by accident or misfortune in the heat of passion, upon any sudden and sufficient provocation; or*

(3)   *When done upon a sudden combat, without any dangerous weapon being used, and not done in a cruel or unusual manner.*

Subsection (1) we've already discussed. Subsections (2) and (3) are actually pretty similar in execution. They both involve situations where a fight or heavy duty verbal argument is (usually) occurring. In subsection (2) the death must be accidental upon a sudden and sufficient provocation. In subsection (3) it is upon a sudden combat, without any dangerous weapon being used, and not done in a cruel or unusual manner. Thus, the third section protects a person who becomes involved in a fight which accidentally leads to the death of the other party, if the other conditions are met.

There aren't a lot of examples of these cases around. In fact, most of the court decisions explain why the facts do <u>not</u> constitute an *excusable homicide*. However, I will give you some additional examples that have managed to be decided. Please remember, that if you change the facts in these cases only slightly, the result could be just the opposite of what occurred.

Typical, are two people in a normal fist-fight, and a normal blow causes an unexpected death to the other. Another example is one man pushing another in a verbal dispute, and the other man suffering a heart attack, and dying. Last, but not least, is one man pushing another, with the other falling, and unexpectedly landing on an object that killed him.

Obviously, these cases could be decided differently if you change the facts only slightly. For instance, if you knew the other guy had a bad heart -- you might have a real problem. So too, if you saw that pointed object on the ground, and gave him a push in the right direction. And, if you were a karate expert looking for a vital spot that could cause such a result? Anyway, I think you get the point -- and the point is: Don't get involved in these things in the first place.

INSURANCE ISSUES:

One thing many folks don't think about until it's too late concerns insurance. If you haven't already guessed – when using self defense, you're probably not covered by your insurance policy. Your homeowners insurance does not cover it because your act is generally not one of "*negligence*" -- but instead is an "*intentional*" act which is normally <u>excluded</u> in almost all insurance policies. This probably won't apply if the weapon goes off <u>accidentally</u> in a struggle, because an accident would imply "negligence" or an " unintentional act". Either of those should be within your coverage, even under an automobile policy.

Now, you may say that a jury would never award damages against you for defending your life or property -- but in a 1989 in a Florida Supreme Court case, <u>State Farm v. Marshall,</u> the Supreme Court affirmed a $575,000.00 verdict in favor of a person who broke into the Defendant's home and attacked him. In its Opinion, the Court not only upheld the jury verdict, but also held that the Homeowners policy did <u>not</u> cover any part of this since the act of intentional self-defense was involved.

Incredible! How the heck a jury could ever do something like that is beyond me – but it happened! Because of that, you'd better be aware that if it happened once, it can happen again. Anything is possible in the law!

So, what can you do about it? You can obtain *"self defense insurance"* to protect you for any acts of self defense. How extensive and inclusive each plan is varies greatly – and some of these plans have the right to first "review" your claim to determine how much they will pay, or if they will even pay a dime. Others pay only a portion of the retainer to your chosen attorney, and a portion of the bond premium. Still others say they pay "everything" but the bond premium – and some plans are in between all of these, or have a maximum "cap" on what they will pay. You need to be careful in your selection, and should also try to obtain a "sample policy" ahead of time to really determine what you are getting.

The ideal policy would be one that covers your entire bond amount (none do), the entire attorney fee (few do, and some provide their own attorneys – the rest normally cover a portion of the retainer, or reimburse only **after**, and **if** you win your case), investigators to investigate the incident on an immediate basis (few do), depositions of witnesses (few do), expert witness fees (likely only *CCW Safe*), appeals and appeal bond (none).

BOND AND BAIL ISSUES:

Another thing you need to understand is about bond premiums. A *bond premium* is the amount you pay to the bondsman or bonding company for them just to issue a bail bond. In Florida – that's a standard ten per cent of the total bond amount. This is **not** the amount of the bond! Even if your self defense insurance pays all or part of the bond premium – most companies that issue bail bonds require some type of *"collateral"* to guarantee that if you flee, or do something else (like miss a court date) that puts the bond in jeopardy – they can get the face amount of their bond back if the court forfeits the bond. That usually means somebody has put up their car, boat, or home as collateral (depending on the amount of the bond) before any bond will be issued. So, even if you have purchased bail bond protection as part of your insurance plan – it's likely you'll still rot in jail until somebody can come up with enough collateral to cover whatever the amount of the bond is. Just something you need to know.

LIST OF SELF DEFENSE "INSURANCE" PLANS:

Here's a list of the self defense insurers I've found on the web. You'll have to go to their website to really find out what they cover, and how. Most have various plans depending on what you are willing to spend. I'd advise getting a "sample policy" before you purchase – and quite frankly – it might even be worth it to buy a couple of these policies to make sure you have everything covered. That's entirely up to you. Here goes, and these are not in any particular order, and there may be others out there.

1. **CCW Safe**. "On paper", the most extensive. One plan.
2. **Second Call Defense**. Lots of plans. NRA sponsored.
3. **U.S. Concealed Carry** (USCCA). Lots of plans.
4. **Carry Defense**. Plans that cover different protection.
5. **Armed Citizens Legal Defense Network**. Single plan.
6. **U.S. Law Shield**. Single plan with minor add-ons.
7. **Patriot Legal Protection** (CHLLP). Single plan.

DEFENSES TO CIVIL LIABILITY:

OK. What if you do get sued? What are your defenses? Well, it's a complete defense to any civil action for damages if the party on whose behalf damages are claimed was injured while a participant in the commission or attempted commission of a *forcible felony* (not the escape from). F.S. 776.085.

Likewise, under F.S. 776.032, a person who uses or threatens to use self defense (deadly or non-deadly) in conformity with sections 776.012; 776.013; or 776.031, is immune from a civil suit for damages unless the person the force was used against was a law enforcement officer who was acting in the performance of his/her official duties. If the court finds you were immune, then the court awards you all reasonable attorney fees, all expenses involved in defending the suit, and any lost income. Moreover, in any such suit where you claim the person was injured due to the lawful use of self defense, you are entitled to a pre-trial evidentiary hearing on the immunity issue. If you win, the suit is dismissed. *Professional Roofing & Sales v. Flemmings*, 138 So. 3d 524 (Fla. 3DCA 2014). Of course, if the folks suing you have no cash – collection will be the proverbial situation of trying to squeeze water out of a stone.

QUESTION: What about a situation where I accidently shoot a bystander, but I used lawful self defense?

ANSWER: If you used lawful self defense there is no criminal responsibility if a bystander is injured, or killed. *Tucker v. State*, 972 So. 2d 1062 (Fla. 4DCA 2008). However, if there was any negligence involved – you may be civilly liable. Remember – if you have self defense insurance – it will only cover the legal defense of a civil case – not any money damages awarded. However, your homeowners policy may still cover you since the injury was an "accident" vs. "intentional". Therefore, any time a bystander is injured – you should timely notify your homeowner insurance carrier per your policy requirements to make sure you are covered.

QUESTION: How about if my employee shoots someone who's trying to steal goods, injure the employee, or injure a customer – even where it's against company policy for the employee to do so, or have a firearm?

ANSWER: The law says that the employer is responsible in each of those situations. <u>Trabulsy v. Publix Super Market</u>, 138 So. 3d 553 (Fla. 5DCA 2014)

QUESTION: What if somebody steals my gun, and uses it in a crime?

ANSWER: You are **not** responsible for the unlawful actions of another person unless you deliberately gave them the weapon, or permission to use it, knowing they might use it unlawfully. Thus, the theft of a firearm would not result in civil liability to its owner. <u>*Reider v. Dorsey*</u>, 98 So. 3d 1223 (Fla. 4DCA 2012).

DAMAGE CAUSED BY YOUR KIDS:

Believe it or not there's a statute, <u>F.S.</u> 741.24, that makes the parents of any child liable for the damage caused by that child. The only requirements are that the child lives with the parent(s), is under the age of 18 years, and that the child maliciously or willfully destroys or steals property. Damages are limited to the actual loss, and any court costs. There are other theories of liability that might be usable. Negligent supervision. Negligent entrustment of a weapon or firearm. Etc.

If you wonder why I put this here – it's because I thought it was important to know that if your kid is shooting up the neighbor's place – you might want to know that besides your kid being arrested – you can get sued. On the other hand, if you live next to the Beverly Hillbillies – you now know you can legally get even!

SELF-DEFENSE EXAMPLES – GOOD & BAD:

Situation Number One -- Typical Road Rage:

I know we just discussed this, but I've gotta repeat: the worst place to display a weapon is in the heat of a traffic jam, or somebody cutting you off. Tempers seem to flare, and as some jerk cuts you off, tailgates you, or whatever — you're doing it right back only plays into his little game. Eventually, unless you disengage, it sometimes escalates to the point of you taking out your handgun, and displaying it — usually without pointing it. You've shown him that you're armed — and not to push his luck.

Whether justified or not -- this is usually a ***very bad decision***! You should have used the cellular, backed-off, and realized this guy was a low-life, hateful, egg-sucking, moron. Now, because you displayed a firearm — you're now the moron! What's worse is that the jerk now has the opportunity to "really" get even with you and the world, will call 911, and will totally lie about what happened.

He'll say **you** pointed the gun at him, and that he was in fear of being shot. I've seen this happen time and time again! Before I retired from courtroom practice, I handled a minimum of at least one case a year exactly like this. Moreover, once he says that to the police — he's stuck himself to the story, or he may get in trouble for making a false police report. He'll also leave out the fact that he almost killed you several times with his car, and that your gun was pointed skyward. In fact, he'll probably get **immense satisfaction** from your unjustified arrest, and prosecution. If you're real lucky, he may realize somewhere down the line that you don't deserve a three year mandatory sentence, and may tell the truth — or may tell the prosecutor that he doesn't mind if they "*plea bargain*" the case to something less. However, no matter what he says at that point – you're screwed! Plus, there's a good chance that you may just have lost your right to ever own or possess a firearm again!

So remember, rarely will you be in a position that displaying a firearm in a vehicle is anything but a really bad move. Only if you ***reasonably believe*** you're about to be highjacked, or robbed is this advisable. I guess if he was trying to ram you, and you weren't trying to ram back, the same would apply. But otherwise, remember that you can normally pull over, and let him go by. If you can avoid it, you should. And, assuming you're involved in such a situation, I highly recommend that you call 911 or *FHP, and let the police know what's going on, **before** it gets worse! Whatever you do, don't lie to the police — even if you have to admit that you were involved in some improper driving. Better to admit you gave the other guy the "***finger***" than to have the police think you're the instigator, and a liar.

Situation Number Two -- "What's that gonna do against this?":

Remember what I told you about escalation? It tends to get worse and not better. Typical scenario is you get in a verbal confrontation with someone, and rather than walk away — you take out your *pepper spray*. The next thing you know — the guy has his gun out saying: "*What's that gonna do against this?*" Very serious situation. An apology, or back-off is usually the safer method of conduct, even if you were in the right, and do have to swallow your pride. When the guy is gone, call the cops, and thank God you're alive.

Likewise, be very careful what kind of weapon you display, if you display anything. Displaying anything but pepper spray, a Taser, or a non-lethal stun gun will normally be the **threat** of *"deadly force"*. Displaying a weapon such as an *ASP baton* may be considered an *aggravated assault* unless you are clearly using lawful self-defense – because it's gonna be defined as a *"**deadly weapon**"*. Likewise, the display will normally be considered a "threat" of using *deadly force* even though the display itself is *"non-deadly force"*. The 2014 revisions to the statute only allow a threat of using deadly force in a deadly force situation! You could lose your immunity in such a situation – even though you're just trying to bluff your way out of a bad situation! Other weapons that can be classified as *"deadly weapons"* may also put you in the same kind of trouble.

Backing off – is always the better move – even if you were in the right. Avoiding jail, avoiding court appearances, avoiding attorney fees are certainly worth the trade-off.

Situation Number Three -- "Get the hell off my property":

This usually is justified, but nobody believes you. You have a trespasser, or somebody on your property who doesn't belong there. You take your gun with you for "just in case". This is totally legal when you're on your property. You never point the thing at him, but you make darn sure he knows it's there. He, being the wonderful person that he is, makes that 911 call telling the police that you pointed the gun at him, and threatened to blow him away unless he left your property. The police arrest you.

Sometimes this guy honestly believes you pointed the gun at him., even though you didn't. I've seen it happen many times. Sometimes it's a pure crock of you-know-what. Sometimes you over-reacted. But many times, you were probably well within your rights. Whatever, you now have a problem if he didn't tell the complete truth. If he did, then the police shouldn't be arresting you because you do nothing wrong by going armed on your own property. I mean . . . if your intuition was right . . . what are you gonna do? Ask the armed robber to wait while you go and get your gun? On the other hand, let's hope you didn't threaten to shoot him if he didn't leave. This would not be a real good move unless he was in the commission of a forcible felony.

I guess the answer is that you just need to use good judgment even when the pressure is on. That's why I always say *"**the bad guy always has the** *advantage*". Personally, if I were in this situation, I'd try to hide the gun in a pocket, or under a jacket so the other person didn't know it was there. That way, I'd have the element of surprise if I needed it, and be totally legal. I'd also have my cellular with me, and call 911 right there if the guy refused. In this day and age, I advise people that the cellular phone is your best defense against anything. Use it at the beginning of any potential conflict. Make sure it's programed to call 911, and also *FHP, perhaps, as an alternate when you're on the highways. My cell phone allows me to call the number hands-free by just telling the phone to "dial 911".

Situation Number Four -- South Florida Armed and Ready:

Well, I've given you all the bad scenarios -- here's the other one that I've heard over-and-over that always works out for the best. It happens in driveways, in shopping malls, and in gas stations. Nobody reports it to the police because they're scared as heck that they'll get arrested. It goes something like this:

You pull into a gas station late at night. Suddenly, a car pulls up next to you, and three or four very scary looking dudes appear ready to do you in some very serious fashion. You calmly display your handgun, pointed upwards — and they drive away just as suddenly as they came. You wipe away the sweat, and thank God for the handgun. You think about calling the police, and then think better of it. Very typical. You probably did the right thing in display, and avoided a possible robbery or car jacking. But the decision on not calling 911 can be a mistake if someone else sees it, doesn't know all the facts, and calls it in. Likewise, with the 2014 changes in the law – who the heck knows? Maybe you don't want to call it in.

There are other cases I see — but these are the most common. I hope the examples can be of some help, but every situation is different. There are no set answers for anything, and like everything else, there is always the danger that the cops could be called against you, even if you were totally legal. When that happens, if you haven't also called 911 – the police will likely tend to believe the other guy over you. Same goes for a jury. You really have to weigh each situation against life and death, and hope your decision was the right one.

A SUMMARY ON SELF-DEFENSE LAW:

In summation of this chapter I repeat the same old major warning as before. Was your action reasonable? Was it necessary? Maybe to you it was -- but what will a police officer, prosecutor, or jury say later? Hmmmm! That's the problem! That's why these laws are dangerous to the average citizen. Moreover, if you are only permitted to use or threaten *non-deadly force*, and in somebody's opinion exceeded that by displaying and/or threatening the use of a deadly weapon, or engaging in the use of *deadly force* -- you may be charged with of *aggravated assault,* even if you don't fire a shot, shoot an arrow, or throw that hatchet.

So, to summarize this section, when can you use or threaten to use *deadly force*? Hmmm, tough question. The answer? Well, truthfully -- whenever you're not prosecuted for it.

And when will that be, you ask?

Probably, if it's a life or death situation, or it looks like it. Probably, if somebody is already displaying or using a *firearm*, or *deadly weapon* against you. Almost certainly, if someone breaks into your home, residence, or occupied vehicle (car, boat, aircraft, motorcycle). Probably in any kidnap or abduction situation by a stranger. And probably, if there is a robbery of yourself or business involving the display of a firearm or other deadly weapon by one of the perpetrators, or – where it is reasonable to believe they may be armed. (ie: almost every robbery – even if no weapon is displayed).

These are classic cases of where people are usually not prosecuted -- and also where the *"immunity"* in the *"Stand Your Ground"* law will kick in. There are others – but, as I said before: There are no guarantees!

WHAT TO DO AFTER THE POLICE ARRIVE:

I've done a lot of speaking engagements since I first wrote this book, and everybody seems to ask me the following question:

"What should I do if I've shot someone in self-defense?"

Well, first of all -- call me, or another qualified criminal attorney before you make any **detailed** statement to the police. However, if it happened outside don't drag the body inside the house like everyone tells you to. That's the **worst** thing you could possibly do. With modern crime scene technology, you'll already be branded a liar, and it will go downhill from there. Don't disturb the scene, to whatever extent that is possible. Don't get rid of, or destroy evidence. That will also go against you.

Next, remember that *"anything you say can, and will, be used against you."* While many attorneys tell their clients not to say anything, I go along with a modified version of that. I think it's extremely important that the police realize that the body on the floor in the pool of blood is NOT the victim! **You're the victim!** In order to make sure the officer knows this, something akin to the following statement is extremely pertinent:

> *"Officer, I was attacked by this man, and thought he was armed. I was in fear for my life, and was forced to shot him in self-defense."*

Once you've said this, and you're sure he's heard it -- you don't generally want to go into any **specifics** until after you've spoken to a really good lawyer who knows this stuff. Specifics can get you into <u>deep trouble</u>, even if your act was one hundred per cent perfectly legal. I've seen this happen again and again, where the citizen thought they couldn't say anything that could cause them trouble – but got arrested, instead.

Why?

Well, obviously, you're nervous as hell, and fourteen million different thoughts are racing through your head, all at the same time. If ever you're gonna screw something up, get it twisted and out of place, or leave out an important detail -- this is it! Moreover, even though you know what happened, you haven't gotten your thoughts together, yet -- and you don't know how to say what happened in the "right way".

Now, I don't mean that by the "right way" you've made something up. That's not the way I do business. On the other hand, you can say the same thing ten different ways -- and only one of them is gonna walk you out of that courtroom. That's why you want to speak to your lawyer. So he can go over the entire thing with you, and make sure you know what to say -- and more importantly -- what not to say.

Yes, you want to make sure the police know that it was self-defense; that you were in fear of your life; that he was the attacker, and that he was armed -- or you thought he was. But, saying anything beyond these generalizations is often *legally dangerous*, and anything you say (other than wanting an attorney) could seriously screw your defense up. Likewise, you need to know that if you want the cops to stop questioning you **must actually say**: "*I don't want to speak to you anymore until I have the opportunity to speak to an attorney!*" This can be said at any time, even if you've answered some questions. Practice the following:

"Officer, I'd really like to answer your questions, but I'm really nervous right now. I want to speak to an attorney before I say anything else."

QUESTION: Can't my silence be used against me?

ANSWER: No. If you say you *"want an attorney"* all questioning must stop, and your refusal to answer further questions cannot be used in court. Plus, you can say this at any point, even if you have had some conversations with the police. However, police do have a right to ask for certain *basic personal information* for "**booking**" purposes such as your *name, date of birth, address, phone number, and social security number.* These can be given without waiving your right to silence or right to an attorney. Just don't stray!

QUESTION: Is there ever a good time to tell everything that happened?

ANSWER: Well . . . if you were injured – tell them and **show them**. Ask, and try to have them take a photo of your injury. If there was a point of break-in, or area where force was used by the culprit – show them. However, as a general rule, beyond this, the more you say – the more problems you may have caused for yourself and your attorney.

QUESTION: Why?

ANSWER: Because if you forget something, and try to add it in later, or at your trial – the police will say you *"made it up"* because you didn't tell them that in your original statement. Happens all the time. Plus – you will not remember *everything*! I can guarantee that! Some really important things will be mis-remembered. Some will be totally forgotten until you calm down a day or two later. Some will be out of sequence. You need time to **calm down**, and to talk to someone who can advise you what to say, how to say it, and what not to say!

In fact, while I advise you speak to the attorney you want to handle your case as soon as possible – if you're really desperate – for five hundred bucks via credit card and Paypal, I'll listen to your situation over the phone, make suggestions, and give you instant legal advice what to say, do, or not do.

GOOD COP – BAD COP:

When the police arrive – those law enforcement officers who are on your side will not push getting specifics from you, and will almost lead you into saying it was self-defense, you were in fear for your life, and you want to talk to your lawyer before you say anything else. However, if they want **details** -- beware! Tell them that you'll be glad to talk to them once you've had a chance to calm down, and have spoken to your lawyer!. If they're on your side -- that will normally satisfy them. If it doesn't satisfy them, they're probably looking to make an arrest -- and that's certainly not on your side. If they try pushing you as to *"why you don't want to talk to them"*, remind them that you're really nervous, need time to calm down, and time to speak to an attorney -- and then remind them that even police officers are normally given a 24 to 48 hour period **before** they can be questioned about a shooting they're involved in so that they can calm down, get the facts straight in their mind, and have a chance to talk to their F.O.P. representative, and attorney before responding to an investigator.

Remember "Gutmacher's famous truism #1" about arrests: *"**If they're gonna arrest you -- they're gonna arrest you!**"*

Giving them a detailed story isn't going to change anything! If they've decided to arrest you your detailed story will **not** change their mind! You'll still wind-up in a cell, and will have created a ***real problem*** for you and your attorney, even if all you did was leave some stuff out. If you got stuff wrong, besides – big problems! So, if you follow my advice, at least you won't have screwed it up for yourself later on.

WHEN GIVING DETAILS MIGHT HELP:

Like I said before, there is a slight modifier to all of this due to the "*Stand Your Ground*" law. Again, you don't want to go into other details before talking to an attorney, but if there was a break-in or attempted break-in – and you know the intruder broke a window, door latch, left fingerprints, etc. – it would be wise to *show the police* that place. If asked – you may also respond the intruder was not a member of your household or invited guest. If you were injured – show them, and make sure you ask they photo your injuries! Very important! Beyond that – stick to my previous advise. Remember, with the immunity law the less you say, probably the better – because once the police have evidence that an intruder had forcefully entered, or forcefully tried to enter a residence, dwelling, or occupied vehicle – your actions in using deadly force are ***presumed legal***! At that point, you can only screw it up by adding information. Unless the police have evidence this **didn't** happen, they can't legally arrest you! That means that the more you say, the more chances you have of blowing it. The same thing holds true if the self defense situation did not involve a dwelling, residence, or occupied vehicle. So – be very, very careful what you say – and don't let your mouth run! Say you *want an attorney*!

HIRING AN ATTORNEY:
        Next, if you're going to hire an attorney – make sure the attorney is a gun owner, and actually believes in your right to self-defense. There are a lot of attorneys out there who really aren't into this stuff, and the last thing you want is somebody who is philosophically anti-gun, no matter how good they're supposed to be. Make sure your attorney belongs to the NRA, Gun Owners of America, Unified Sportsmen, Florida Carry, or similar organization, or at least has a CWL. If they don't – he or she is probably not the right person for this particular type case.

        Likewise, try to set an appointment with a good attorney as soon as possible. The longer you wait – the more difficult his or her job becomes. Plus, an attorney may be able to influence the State's decision to prosecute if hired soon enough. Usually there is a ten to twenty day window before the State Attorney decides how, or if they will file a criminal charge. Having your attorney try to influence that decision can be critical. However, you should know that different attorneys charge widely different fees. The amount of the fee doesn't guarantee you're getting the best attorney – but – trying to save money by getting someone "cheap" is not a great idea, either.

        Why?

        Because unless an attorney is quoting a sufficient amount of money to cover the time he or she really needs to spend on your case – your case isn't gonna get the attention it needs! They still need to pay the rent, secretaries, the mortgage, and everything else. If the quote was too low – they're gonna spend the time on someone else's case to make up those bucks! Just a fact of life. Average cost of an *aggravated assault* case today starts around **fifteen grand**, and up, plus expenses – assuming you're trying for something better than just a plea to a mandatory prison sentence.

911 – USE IT, AND GET COPIES OF THEM:
        The best thing you can ever do if you think you're being attacked, broken into, or about to be attacked, etc. -- is call 911. Tell them you're frightened! Tell them you think the guy may be armed (even if you're not sure -- it's certainly not a lie in this day and age). Tell them to hurry up and send somebody!

All this is being recorded! It's gonna be used as evidence in your favor! If the police don't get there in a few minutes, call 911 again! It's gonna be recorded again! The jury is going to wonder what the heck the police were doing while you're panicking out trying to defend home and family. Moreover, when the police do get there they already know that **you** are the victim! They're going out there to rescue **you**! The dead son-of-a-bitch on the floor in the congealing pool of blood is the "bad guy" -- you're just the poor victim who luckily managed to save himself . . . and in the process, you performed a valuable civic service. Now, they have one less criminal on the street! Good job!

So, thank heaven for 911 -- if you use it.

One word of warning. These calls are **routinely erased** by law enforcement after a certain period of time, the least being 30 days, and the most being one year. It varies from department to department. You need to get a copy of the tapes before they've been destroyed, and should personally obtain them, or have someone obtain the copies for you before it's too late. I would not wait for your attorney to try unless you've hired him or her within two weeks of the incident, and also provided them funds to obtain the tapes! Likewise, if you're doing the asking -- ask for **all** the 911 tapes that were received in the case – and **"all"** channels, and police communications related to the case. Otherwise, you'll be missing some important portions. They will only give you what you specifically ask for. Nothing more.

The usual method is calling up the ***communications division***, and finding out the procedure they require. Many times it's a certified letter return receipt requested to the Chief of Police, Sheriff's legal department, or Supervisor of Communications. If done by letter, call a few days later and make sure they got it! If you can fax or email it – that's OK as long as you have proof it was received, and you follow-up by phone to verify it was received. Several times in my career, were it not for the follow-up phone call – the recordings would have been lost! The charge is generally less than fifty bucks, and is well worth the trouble. Remember, once it's destroyed — it's too late -- it's gone forever!

CELLULAR PHONES — YOUR BEST DEFENSE:
Of course, if you're on the road, the same thing goes for cellular phones. When in a vehicle, or anywhere where a regular phone is not handy -- they are your best defense against the nut-cases that inherit our streets and highways. If someone is doing strange things, dial 911 just so you have a record of your fear -- in case it really happens.

If you're lucky, they may send a unit to check it out before it happens. If not, at least we know who the victim is, and who the bad guy is. Very important factors in analyzing who gets sued, who gets arrested, or both.

On the other hand, please don't say that "*I'm gonna shoot him if he tries anything*" -- even if you intend to. That's just asking for trouble. You want to make sure that they know you're scared. If you aren't, then there's something wrong with you, no matter how controlled you may be. Moreover, you certainly don't want to give the 911 operator the impression that you're gonna blow this guy away no matter what happens. That just sounds like you're looking for trouble, and want to perform a "legal execution".

That's not what you want to do, in fact, **if** you advise you're armed, you really want to give the impression that you'll only use your weapon as a "***last resort***". Try remembering that.

OTHER THINGS YOU SHOULD DO:
As an attorney who's handled lots of these cases, one of the most unfortunate things I've noticed over the years is when important evidence was not collected – and later on when that's realized – it's too late to obtain. We've discussed that somewhat in the last section, but you need to know about some other things that always seem to be missing.

First, you should have good ***digital*** photos of any injuries you or anyone else may have suffered, and any damage to the home or other property. These should be taken from all angles and distances with a common reference point. Make sure you check the photos immediately afterwards for clarity – blurred photos, and poor lighting are no good! Make sure you have them dated, and know what each one represents. More photos are better than too few. Have them transferred to a disk in .jpg format as soon as possible – even if you need to take them to a professional. Make **copies** on your computer so you have **backups**.

Keep any physical evidence in clear plastic bags, and seal them. Label and date them. Torn clothing, bloody clothing, broken whatevers – all may become critical later on. Don't erase any phone or text messages on your phone if they might have any relevance to the case. Let your attorney decide what is important to save, or not.

If you shared any ***text messages*** or cell calls with the assailant, or anyone important to the case – also get a copy of the actual text messages from your provider. You likely only have **thirty days** to get them. Likewise, get copies of all cell phone logs, incoming and outgoing that may show how often you were being called, or whatever. Also – like I said before, if you received any phone messages – do not erase them until you are absolutely sure they've been transferred to at least two back-up disks that are clear. Remember, that if an edited copy of an original recording is needed – it is always better for an expert to work from the original, and not from a copy!

If you don't have an investigator working on the case immediately – try to get witnesses to write down what they saw in as much detail as possible, or tape record their statements if they are willing. This includes yourself! You will find that in just a couple of days – unless they are directly involved – much of what occurred is already forgotten, being forgotten, or mis-remembered. Plus, as time goes by – witnesses become less and less likely to want to assist. Don't push a reluctant witness for a statement. Those always turn-out against you. Better to have a trained investigator get those. And remember – time is of the essence!

GETTING STOPPED BY THE POLICE:
What are your rights when the police stop you? Do you have to tell them you've got a gun on you, etc.? Interesting questions.

In Florida you currently have no legal obligation to tell a police officer you have a gun or weapon on you, or in your vehicle unless you are taken into custody. However, if you lie about it, and he finds out, you will probably have a very displeased police officer, and a heap of trouble. My personal rule of thumb is to *never volunteer* that information **unless** the officer is about to look into the glove compartment, console, etc. where he will obviously find it, or your driver's license or other identifications are by your weapon, and you'll need to reach for them when the officer is approaching, or is already near you. You NEVER want your hand anywhere near a firearm when being stopped by the police! Other than that — keeping your mouth shut on the issue is probably the best approach.

However, if asked — you need to make a decision on whether to answer the question directly — or not. You could legally, and truthfully say: *"**Officer, I have absolutely nothing illegal, or that you need to worry about**."* However, this might not be an appropriate response in all situations. Moreover, if this doesn't satisfy him, I do **not** suggest lying.

I think the best approach on being specifically asked is usually to say something that **"legalizes"** your position — ie — *"**Officer, I have a legal firearm**"* *'securely encased' in my vehicle."*   Or — *"Officer,   I have a Concealed Weapons License in my wallet. I also have a 'legally concealed' firearm in my console. Would you like to see my Concealed Weapons License?"*

On the other hand, if the officer discovers or is informed that you have a weapon or firearm — he or she has the **absolute right** to temporarily take it into custody during the encounter to protect himself/herself from harm. There is case law on the issue, and it is totally legal. The officer may even unload the weapon, and place it in his unit until the encounter is over. Another annoying thing they can do is run a *"weapons check"* on it to see if it's stolen. I hate that – especially if you have a valid CWL. It seems totally unreasonable. However, it is also supported by the case law.

After the encounter — unless you're being arrested, you're supposed to get the firearm or weapon back. Probably unloaded with the cartridges separate from the firearm — until you or he leaves. Again — totally legal. Police don't want to get shot — that makes perfect sense to me. Likewise, if you're in a vehicle, the smartest thing to do is *place both your hands at the top of the steering wheel* as the officer approaches. This way he can see your hands, and knows you're not hiding anything. Don't go reaching for your license and registration as he or she approaches. Don't exit the vehicle, and then suddenly realize you left your wallet inside, and make a quick turn to get it. I saw a video where some poor guy actually got shot over that! It makes cops real nervous since they can't see what you're doing, and they're dealing with too many "crazies" these days.

Maybe you're reaching for a gun? Maybe you're reaching for a weapon? They don't know who the hell you are, or if you just robbed the 7-11 across town! It's just better to ask for permission once they've arrived, before you reach for anything.

Whatever the situation, I would **rehearse** the suggestions I've made just in case they ever happen. If you've actually verbalized them several times, it won't be as awkward when the situation actually materializes. Otherwise, you'll probably screw it up. *Murphy's Law* in action!

Whatever you do, remember a very important point in how to handle yourself: Police officers are creatures of "respect", and quite frankly, they deserve your respect. If they perceive your response as "disrespectful" — you're probably in for trouble. Therefore, don't argue! Don't challenge his or her authority (that's what lawyers are for). Don't threaten to *"fight it in court"*, "get a lawyer", or make a complaint with the police agency. Even if you're right, even if your "rights" are being violated — saying anything like that is sure to get you in *more* trouble. Those are things you discuss with a lawyer, and do **afterwards** -- assuming they're advisable.

Use the words "**yes, sir**" and "**no, sir**" a lot. If you're unlucky enough to get an officer who likes to make trouble, or give a hard time — trouble it will be, no matter what you say or do – and you need to try to minimize it. So, use your best judgment under the circumstances. If you have to give up some of your constitutional rights to avoid jail — maybe that isn't the worst choice. I've handled lots of false arrest cases, and I don't think anything is worth going to jail for, no matter what damages you might get awarded later on. You'll obviously have to make your own decision on this. On the other hand — let me tell you — jail sucks, no matter how short the visit is.

USE OF FORCE AGAINST ANIMALS:

We all know, or think we know, what our rights of self defense are against another person. But, what are your rights when it comes to an attack or trespass by an animal?

I guess the starting point begins with F.S. 828.12 which is titled "*Cruelty to Animals*". That section makes it a crime to "*unnecessarily kill*" or cause an animal "*unnecessary pain or suffering*". The key word here is "*unnecessary*". What does unnecessary mean? Well, that's a long question, and to answer it I think I'll first explore some Florida statutes.

Let's begin with Chapter 767 of the Florida Statutes which discusses dogs. Read it, and you find out that one defense to killing a dog is that the dog was killing or had been killing any domestic animal or livestock. (F.S. 767.03). If you read further in F.S. 828.24, you find out that if you must kill any animal, it must be done by a "*humane method*". According to another statute, a humane method is any method whereby the animal is rapidly and effectively rendered insensitive to pain, and includes a gunshot with proper caliber and placement.

So, how do we apply these statutes, and is there any case law out there on the subject that further defines it? Well, there's no case law in Florida on these exact areas, but other states have had more than their fair share. Typical example is what can you do when someone else's dog, cat, chicken, etc. wanders on your property? The answer is basically "not much". You could capture the animal, and inform the owner so he/she can pick it up. You could try to shoo it away. I guess you could even turn the water hose on the critter if you didn't intentionally injure it. But, the case law makes it clear that just because an animal wanders onto your property – no matter how annoying you find it – it is usually a minor matter that does not justify any injury to the animal.

Why not?

Well, the damage to you is relatively minor. It's got to be fairly serious before the law starts thinking that killing an animal is *"necessary"*. Furthermore, if worse comes to worse, you can always sue the owner for any damage caused. Even if it's a dog chasing your precious cat – unless there is a real threat to the cat's life that can't be avoided without killing or injuring the dog – the remedy is calling the authorities, capturing the dog or animal for the owner or authorities, or trying to scare it away. In these cases killing or injury is *"unnecessary"* – hence, *'cruelty to animals"*. That is, it could have been handled by another method with far less serious consequences to the animal. Same thing if the dog is chasing a wild animal. All that amounts to is a "nuisance".

Now, remember the statute, F.S. 767.03? It said you could kill any dog that was killing, or had been killing another domestic animal or livestock. But, don't take that section literally! Although it certainly applies if you shoot the critter in the act, still you couldn't track the dog to the owners property, and kill it. That would get you in big trouble. Likewise, there's quite a few cases that indicate that once the attack is completed, and the attacking animal is wandering away – you generally don't have a right to kill or injure it because – there are other reasonable alternatives.

Of course, they'll be some exceptions. One exception that is described in various appellate decisions occurs when the same animal has attacked (and killed or seriously injured) your domestic animals more than once, you've been unsuccessful in stopping it by other means, and you've notified the owner who hasn't restrained his critter from further attacks. In those case the courts usually indicate it's a jury question whether shooting the dog/cat/hog – was reasonable and necessary. (Sounds a lot like self defense law, doesn't it?)

What about when the animal is attacking you, or another human being?

Well, that's a more serious issue! Usually, during an actual attack you will be legal using *deadly force*. Animal bites are often very serious – and even if not – they are very painful. However, from a legal standpoint – it's always going to be a question of was it *"unnecessary"*? Was it *"reasonable"*? Could you escape with safety? Could you take safe refuge somewhere? Was there a reasonable way to avoid a dangerous and immediate confrontation? If not, you may certainly protect yourself and others, and I think law enforcement would likely see it your way. Still, it could wind-up as a jury question if there was doubt.

From a personal standpoint – I usually have ***pepper spray*** with me when I walk my dogs. That way, if they or I are attacked, I have a non-lethal, very reasonable method of defense that almost nobody will question if another animal threatens me, or my pets. That doesn't mean I pepper spray every dog that approaches us. That would just be plain stupid! But, you can tell an aggressive animal – and almost all dogs are supposed to be **leashed** when off their own property. So – *pepper spray* on an obviously aggressive dog as a deterrent is normally not a big deal. If *pepper spray* doesn't deter it – then you probably need a firearm, or one hell of a club. On the other hand, if I had to use pepper spray on an animal, I'd probably call 911 – advise them that an **unleashed** animal had approached me seemingly ready to attack (or attacking), and I used *pepper spray* to save myself or my animal. "***Unleashed***" is the key word here!

Next question – could you ***pursue*** a vicious or rabid dog? Again, a very "iffy" issue. The issue there is whether the danger is real, and was there also an immediate danger to others if you didn't act? If calling the authorities would work just as well, that may be a real fact to consider. If failing to take immediate action means the critter(s) will escape, and continue their rampage – it makes your response obviously more reasonable and necessary. Again, a possible jury issue if you were charged. However, you'd better have a gun if you're following a rabid animal, as it will probably turn on you, and attack once it realizes it's being tracked. Hopefully, you're a good shot.

That raises another interesting issue. What happens if the animal is on a "*protected*" list? We're not talking about "*cruelty to animals*" here – we're talking pure game protection laws.

The few cases where this happened involved bears killing sheep, or moose and horse herds wiping out valuable grazing areas. As a general rule the courts are very unsympathetic to the citizen where human life isn't at stake. Protected animals stay protected, and only state or federal authorities are permitted to remove or destroy them. How does that apply to your favorite dog or cat being attacked by a gator? From a "*cruelty to animals*" standpoint – my personal opinion is that it would be legal since you're saving a life. Again – just my opinion, because there is no case law. If it was a bear, I'd really try a warning shot first, if I had a chance, because more intelligent animals will frequently flee. As to a Florida panther – I'm really not sure, because Florida's Constitution might allow a defense – however, the case law from other states and the federal courts would likely be on the side of the panther. On the other hand – if it's a human being that's about to be attacked by the critter – fire away – as long as you don't have any other reasonable recourse. The one case I came upon made it a jury question whether there really was a necessity, or whether the defendant just wanted an excuse to shoot a bear. In other words – if there's a reasonable alternative – you've got to take it.

I wish there were some Florida cases here to give you a more definite answer – but I think the parameters are clear. You can't shoot or injure an animal just because it's a nuisance. It's got to be a real and immediate threat to something substantial. Even then, there are possible exceptions. But, if a large dog or other animal is about to attack me, or another human being. Deadly force is normally more than reasonable. Hope that helps.

NANOSECONDS TO REACT:

Over the years, I've come to believe that one of the most instructive portions of this book comes from this section, where I've quoted from actual homicide cases – all in situations that could happen to anyone. Even though I am retired from active trial practice I still read lots of cases, every day of the week. Many of these cases are frightening. They don't involve self-defense. They involve people who just didn't have the ability to use self-defense. People who didn't have time to defend themselves, didn't know how, or didn't have the weapons or knowledge to defend themselves. These people, for the most part — are now dead. They are murder victims, and worse. The excerpts I've taken from just a few of these cases are not for the weak of heart — but it's instructional. Maybe, they will not have died totally in vain if you read it, and learn something from it. Again, it's not a pretty sight. It's sad — and if you shed a tear, it's OK. I do, every time I read them.

Heynard v. State, 689 So. 2d 239 (Fla. 1996):

Around 10 p.m. on January 30, Lynette Tschida went to the Winn Dixie store in Eustis. She saw Henyard and a younger man sitting on a bench near the entrance of the store. When she left, Henyard and his companion got up from the bench; one of them walked ahead of her and the other behind her. As she approached her car, the one ahead of her went to the end of the bumper, turned around, and stood. Ms. Tschida quickly got into the car and locked the doors. As she drove away, she saw Henyard and the younger man walking back towards the store.

Ms. Lewis noticed a few people sitting on a bench near the doors as she and her daughters entered the store. When Ms. Lewis left the store, she went to her car and put her daughters in the front passenger seat. As she walked behind the car to the driver's side, Ms. Lewis noticed Alfonza Smalls coming towards her. As Smalls approached, he pulled up his shirt and revealed a gun in his waistband. Smalls ordered Ms. Lewis and her daughters into the back seat of the car, and then called to Henyard. Henyard drove the Lewis car out of town as Smalls gave him directions. The Lewis girls were crying and upset, and Smalls repeatedly demanded that Ms. Lewis "shut the girls up." As they continued to drive out of town, Ms. Lewis beseeched Jesus for help, to which Henyard replied, "this ain't Jesus, this is Satan." Later, Henyard stopped the car at a deserted location and ordered Ms. Lewis out of the car. Henyard raped Ms. Lewis on the trunk of the car while her daughters remained in the back seat. Ms. Lewis attempted to reach for the gun that was lying nearby on the trunk. Smalls grabbed the gun from her and shouted, "you're not going to get the gun, bitch." Smalls also raped Ms. Lewis on the trunk of the car. Henyard then ordered her to sit on the ground near the edge of the road. When she hesitated, Henyard pushed her to the ground and shot her in the leg. Henyard shot her at close range three more times, wounding her in the neck, mouth, and the middle of the forehead between her eyes. Henyard and Smalls rolled Ms. Lewis's unconscious body off to the side of the road, and got back into the car. The last thing Ms. Lewis remembers before losing consciousness is a gun aimed at her face. Miraculously, Ms. Lewis survived and, upon regaining consciousness a few hours later, made her way to a nearby house for help. The occupants called the police and Ms. Lewis, who was covered in blood, collapsed on the front porch and waited for the officers to arrive. As Henyard and Smalls drove the Lewis girls away from the scene where theMr mother had been shot and abandoned. Jasmine and Jamilya continued to cry and plead: "I want my Mommy," "Mommy," "Mommy." Shortly thereafter, Henyard stopped the car on the side of the road, got out, and lifted Jasmine out of the back seat while Jamilya got out on her own. The Lewis girls were then taken into a grassy area along the roadside where they were each killed by a single bullet fired into the head. Henyard and Smalls threw the bodies of Jasmine and Jamilya Lewis over a nearby fence into some underbrush.

The moral to this case is what police experts will tell you: In any attempted abduction, you stand a better chance doing anything but getting in the car. Most criminals who are out to rob you, are normally not going to abduct you. Abductions are usually reserved for murderers. Cooperation only places you in a remote area where help is impossible. Better to be shot where somebody may call an ambulance — than dead in the middle of a field ten miles from nowhere. If you're alone — break and run. If you're armed — use your weapon once you're free of being grabbed, and possibly disarmed. Too many police officers have lost their lives because they tried to grapple with dangerous offenders — rather than break away, and distance themselves first.

Remember, you won't be of any help to anyone if you're disarmed, bound, gagged, stuffed in a trunk, and then murdered. Likewise, even if your children are in the car, and you have to abandon them – they stand a better chance of survival and rescue if you do not surrender! I know that is a hard choice to make – but if you go with the kidnapper – the likelihood is that **all** of you will be killed. If you escape, you can get help, and also give vital information that can identify the vehicle, and your attacker. Police get **very serious** when there is an abduction, and concentrate all their resources in a hurry! Likewise, if you escape – the abductor often may release any remaining hostages to aid in their getaway.

James v. State, 695 So. 2d 1229 (Fla. 1997):

Pearson stated that when the two met, James was on his way to visit Tim Dick, the victim's son, and his girlfriend, Nichole, who also lived nearby. They stopped and talked for about ten minutes and Pearson watched James ingest about ten "hits" of LSD on paper. James told Pearson he had been drinking at Todd Van Fossen's party, but he appeared sober to Pearson. After briefly visiting Tim Dick and Nichole where he drank some gin, James returned to his room at Betty Dick's house. When he entered the house, James noticed that Betty Dick's four grandchildren were asleep in the living room. One of the children, Wendi, awoke briefly when James arrived. She observed that he was laughing and appeared drunk. James went to the kitchen, made himself a sandwich and retired to his room. Eventually, he returned to the living room where he grabbed Betty Dick's eight-year-old granddaughter, Toni Neuner, by the neck and strangled her, hearing the bones pop in her neck. Believing Toni was dead, he removed her clothes and had vaginal and anal intercourse with her in his room. Toni never screamed or resisted. After raping Toni, he threw her behind his bed. James then went to Betty Dick's bedroom where he intended to have sexual intercourse with her. He hit Betty in the back of the head with a pewter candlestick. She woke up and started screaming, "Why, Eddie, why?" Betty's screaming brought Wendi Neuner to the doorway of her grandmother's bedroom where she saw James stabbing Betty with a small knife. When James saw Wendi he grabbed her, tied her up, and placed her in the bathroom. Thinking that Betty was not dead, James went to the kitchen, grabbed a butcher knife and returned to Betty's room and stabbed her in the back. James removed Betty Dick's pajama bottoms, but did not sexually batter her. Covered with blood, James took a shower in the bathroom where Wendi remained tied up and then threw together some clothes and belongings. He returned to Betty's room and took her purse and jewelry bag before driving away in her car. James drove across the country, stopping periodically to sell jewelry for money.

What do you say about this one? First — if she had a gun, she could have used it. Nothing else would have worked. Other than that, if you associate with people who use drugs and abuse alcohol, disaster may occur. Be forewarned!

Campbell v. State, 679 So.2d 720 (Fla. 1996):

Campbell rang the doorbell to the Bosler home at 2:15 p.m. on December 22, 1986, and when Billy Bosler answered the door, Campbell stabbed him a number of times. Billy's adult daughter, Sue Zann Bosler, heard the commotion and came to her father's aid, and Campbell stabbed her. Billy died, Sue Zann lived. Sue Zann's testimony about the murder began with her describing what happened when she came out of her bedroom at the parsonage, which was the home of her father, mother, and sister:

Q. You're indicating that your dad was in the doorway, a man was stabbing him?
A: Yes.

Q. What, if anything, did you do?
A. By the time I got, I was walking out towards him to help him. He was being stabbed so many times that he was collapsing to the floor.

Q. And what did you do as you approached this scene?
A. As I approached the scene I went forward to help and I must have screamed because he turned around and he was going to stab me in the front.

Q. When you say he, Sue Zann, who are you talking about?
A. The man who was stabbing my father.

Q. You turned around and he goes to stab you in the front?
A. Yes.

Q. What do you do?
A. I turned to the right like this and he stabbed me three times in the back.

Q. Where on your back did he stab you?
A. Once in my shoulder, the knife went approximately four inches into my flesh, once below my shoulder in the back and three inches in and right by my spine approximately two inches.

Q. After you were struck those three times, what did you do?
A. I was knocked to the floor on my knees.

Q. Okay. Did he continue stabbing you?
A. No.

Q. What was your father doing?
A. He was trying to get up on his knee to try to help me.

Q. When you last saw him, he was on his knees in the hallway?
A. He was trying to get on his knees.

Q. So he was trying to lift himself up?
A. Yes.

Q. Was he able to do that?
A. No.

Q. Did he start to crawl toward you?
A. No, he couldn't.

Q. And you're stabbed over here?
A. Yes.

Q. Your father starts to move towards you or tries to get up?
A. He is trying to still get up.

Q. What happens to him next?
A. After I was stabbed to the floor, dad was trying to get up and the man turned around and start stabbing dad in the back many times.

You know the answer to this last case, and so do I. Sue Zann needed a firearm, and needed to use it **before** she did anything else. *Nanoseconds to react*! Even if you never use a firearm – having one loaded and available in the home is an absolute necessity of survival if someone breaks in. The cops just won't get there in time!

In fact, private citizens legally use firearms in self-defense 800,000 to two and one half million times a year according to a study by Professor Gary Kleck, a noted criminologist at the Florida State University. In 80 or 90 percent of these cases no shots are fired — because the criminal flees! According to the study, at least half a million cases of lawful self-defense happen a year where the crime is stopped! My studies have confirmed the "no shots fired" scenario. Criminals don't expect you to be armed – and when you are – most try to flee. Another reason I don't like the 2014 changes to the display laws.

So, next time your legislators – especially those in Congress, try taking away your firearms or firearm rights — tell them to get real. Only criminals benefit by firearm regulations! It protects them from honest citizens like you and I. They don't obey the laws, and don't really care about them. That's why we call them "criminals".

MANDATORY SENTENCES FOR FIREARM OFFENSES:
Be careful when you vote for a candidate who promises to pass more laws for mandatory sentences. Remember that every time such a law passes you are taking the discretion out of the sentencing, and basically saying you don't trust the judge or the jury to do the right thing. To me, that's a sacrifice of the liberty your forefathers died for over the generations.

Why?

Well, because we already have so many laws that we've passed the area of sensibility, and are turning a once free society into a totalitarian state where almost anything you do can constitute a crime. If anything, we need to back-off on some of the laws we already have. So, get ready for the bad news — mandatory sentences of draconian proportions. Sheer fright — for anyone with any degree of insight or commonsense. The Legislature doesn't trust judges or juries – and unfortunately doesn't understand how things really work in the courtrooms. With little exception, mandatory prison sentences have almost no discretion built into them, even when justice calls for it. Make a mistake on a self-defense issue — and you are literally fighting for your life before the court. Here goes:

F.S. 775.087(2) & F.S. 775.087(3) requires a judge to impose a " mandatory minimum" prison sentence on any of the following crimes, or their attempt, where a firearm or destructive device was actually possessed by the person being sentenced:

> *Murder, sexual battery, robbery, burglary, arson, aggravated assault, aggravated battery, kidnaping, escape, aircraft piracy, aggravated child abuse, aggravated stalking, drug trafficking, unlawful throwing/placing/discharge of a destructive device, possession of firearm by convicted felon.*

Use of the firearm or device is not necessary – it's actual possession is all that is required. A *"mandatory minimum"* sentence means that if found guilty — the judge has no discretion to impose a lower sentence, even if he or she thinks the mandatory sentence is totally unfair under the particular circumstances!

CHART OF MANDATORY FIREARM SENTENCES:

3 years	aggravated assault; possession of firearm by convicted felon; burglary of conveyance
10 years	firearm/destructive device possessed in any listed felony except aggravated assault; possession by felon; burglary of conveyance
15 years	possessed semi-automatic firearm with high capacity detachable box magazine (ie: capable of holding more than 20 centerfire cartridges); or machine gun, during any of the listed felonies or their attempt
20 years	discharged a firearm or destructive device during any of listed felonies or their attempt
25 - life	same as previous, and as a result death or great bodily harm was inflicted on any person

FIRING A WARNING SHOT:

Remember, if a firearm is discharged unlawfully — then the mandatory sentence is twenty (20) years in prison. This applies even to *aggravated assault*! So, if you fire a *"warning shot"* in a less than *"deadly force"* self-defense situation, and get prosecuted -- you're facing a mandatory twenty year sentence unless you take a favorable plea bargain, or are found *"not guilty"*! If a person suffers death or great bodily harm on any of these — the mandatory sentence is a minimum of twenty-five (25) years to a maximum of life. If you possessed a **machine gun**, or firearm equipped with a *"high capacity"* detachable box magazine that is "capable" of holding **more** than 20 centerfire cartridges — and commit one of the enumerated felonies — you have a fifteen (15) year mandatory minimum sentence. <u>F.S.</u> 775.087(3)(e)(1).

QUESTION: What are all the problems, you talk about?

ANSWER: First, if you misjudge a self-defense situation, and have threatened to use *deadly force* – there's a decent chance you've committed an *"aggravated assault"*. Three year minimum mandatory unless you get real lucky with a plea negotiation. Kiss the wife and kids goodbye unless you've got a sympathetic detective working the case, and a pro-self defense prosecutor, to boot. Even if you were just bluffing, and trying to diffuse the situation – the firing of an unjustified *warning shot* means you're now facing a twenty (20) year mandatory prison sentence. Kiss the wife and kids goodbye. Also kiss any grandchildren goodbye. If you hit the bastard, and wound him — twenty five years to life. Probably a good point to consider suicide.

One thing you should notice immediately from this is — firing a ***warning shot*** is not a very good idea — even if it <u>is</u> a very good idea. What I mean by this is that sometimes — firing a warning shot is the act that saves <u>both your lives</u> — yours, and the stupid bastard's who was about to attack you. But, the Legislature doesn't want to know about that. If firing a *warning shot* is reasonable, and did not cause damage to persons or property – I don't feel it should be labeled as the use of *"deadly force"*, and certainly shouldn't carry an additional mandatory sentence. I know that will never pass – but I also know of too many instances where it really was the deciding factor in saving lives or preventing a felony. However, the is a slight ray of hope in only *aggravated assault* cases where no warning shot is involved. That is the 2014 amendment in <u>F.S.</u> 775.087(6):

> *"Notwithstanding s. 27.366, the sentencing court shall not impose the mandatory minimum sentence required by subsection (2) or subsection (3) for a conviction for aggravated assault if the court makes written findings that:*
>
> *(a) The defendant had a good faith belief that the aggravated assault was justifiable pursuant to chapter 776,*
>
> *(b) The aggravated assault was not committed in the course of committing another criminal offense,*
>
> *(c) The defendant does not pose a threat to public safety, and*
>
> *(d) The totality of the circumstances involved in the offense do not justify the imposition of such sentence.*

Personally, as I've stated earlier in this chapter, I don't think most folks will be able to take advantage of this statutory subsection. Because of that, I think it falls far short of what is needed, and should be amended again – hopefully to something that resembles my earlier suggestion of a needed self defense statute. Only time, and the demands of gun owners like you and I – will tell.

THE AFTERMATH OF MANDATORY SENTENCING:

My personal belief has always been that as a general rule, mandatory laws for first offenders are absolutely awful! They're fine if the guy is really a criminal — but for the marginal case, or the case of mistaken judgment — it's tragic! The judge normally has no discretion. The mandatory sentence must be imposed! And if the other side are a bunch of good actors, or are just out to get even with you or the world – you're gonna pay the price, guilty or not! Sad stuff!

But, what makes it really sad is that the person who just tried to break into your home, or runs when you catch him in the act will probably tell the cops that he was just walking across your lawn, or was ringing the bell on your house, when for no reason you came after him with a gun. You were a *"crazy man"*. All he was doing was cutting across the lawn, or trying to locate a friend, and instead – you pulled a gun on him saying he was trying to break in your house. If this is a neighbor you've been having a problem with, I almost guarantee this is what he'll say — and sometimes the police aren't real concerned about who really did what -- they just want that felony arrest, and let the system *"sort it out"*.

Swell! Nice work by law enforcement! Instead of arresting the real culprit – they've got you! You're suddenly facing three years in prison, thought you were acting legally, and never did anything unlawful before in your life. The prosecutor offers you a deal. No jail — just probation. Are you gonna take it?

You bet you are! When you look into the eyes of your wife and kids — they'll be no doubt what you're going to have to do. Innocent or not — the odds are usually with the State. If the alleged "victim" is a good liar, and really wants to get you — it's even worse. He may even bring some of his buddies in to lie. Like I've said, I seen it all the time over my career. Many times the State is not concerned about what the real truth is. Likewise, if the prosecutor is unsure who's really telling the truth, and has doubts about the case — the best he or she will usually do is offer you probation and/or a reduced charge in return for a plea bargain. Go to trial -- you face the maximum sentence!

And hey, what if you fired a *warning shot*? Now, you're facing twenty years! Are you really thinking you're willing to take the chance of a jury trial if instead, they offer you a deal with two years in prison? Even if you go to trial, and win — how much has it cost you in money, stress, lost wages, and sleepless nights? Have you lost your job? Will you lose it? Have you had to mortgage the house to pay the legal fees? Has the wife left you after two years of trials and appeals? Very heavy duty stuff – make no mistake about it.

MORE EXAMPLES & JURY PARDONS:

Situation number two — also quite common. You have an absolute right to keep and carry a firearm anywhere on your property. You hear something outside, grab your firearm just in case, and walk outside. Your nosey, antagonistic neighbor sees you, asks you *"What are you doing with a gun?"* You tell them to mind their own damn business — and they call up the police saying you threatened them with a gun. And the police, who probably don't have much choice at that point, are forced to arrest you unless you can convince them otherwise.

Doesn't happen?

It sure does! One neighbor trying to *"get even"* with another. The fact that you'll go to jail for something you didn't do — is not even a real concern. Life in America! God Bless this Country!

Want another example more on the lines of a real criminal? Fine! Here's the typical example:

Some stupid kid drops off a friend who commits a residential burglary. The kid waits for his buddy not knowing what he is about to do, but soon finds out when he sees him break in the house. The kid has a firearm legally in the glove compartment, and now knowing what is happening, still waits for his buddy to come out. He hears a police car coming, and when his buddy gets in the car they try to escape, but are caught. This kid is just an *"accessory"*, but he faces a ten year minimum prison sentence for having possession of the gun. For a career criminal — very good. For somebody in between — perhaps a total injustice. Hard to say — it depends. But again, there's the problem. Judges don't have discretion. The sentence is mandatory. If you fall **one inch** within the statutory definition of the crime, no matter what the degree of your involvement — you are in deep trouble. The fact that a jury has the right to come back with any verdict they want isn't real comforting when you know the Florida Supreme Court has **<u>forbidden</u>** juries from being told what the possible sentence is that might be imposed, and has forbidden lawyers from telling the jury that they have the inherent right under the law to "***jury pardon***" a defendant no matter what the evidence is, or to come back with a guilty verdict on a **less serious** charge as part of this pardon power.

A last example?   OK

It usually happens in some type of domestic situation. Boyfriend/girlfriend. Ex-husband/ex-wife. Kids, whatever. For example: A kid calls up his Dad who is divorced from mom – says some guy his mom is dating just threatened to beat him up if he didn't shut up. "*Dad, please come over, quick!*" Dad comes over immediately. The new boyfriend is inside. Dad is upset, bangs on the door, mom doesn't want him inside, and tells him to just "*go away*". Dad decides he "*needs to find out*" what's going on, has an old key, comes inside, anyway – and just happens to have a gun on him – "just in case".

Guess what?

Armed burglary! Either his ex-wife or the boyfriend could have shot him dead – legally! Fear of imminent death or great bodily harm was ***presumed***! Assuming he isn't shot – and they just call the cops – he's now looking at a mandatory ten year prison sentence! I'm not saying he might or might not deserve some jail – but ten years?

So, juries that used to do the "*right thing*" when attorneys were allowed to tell them they had a choice, and tell them what the possible sentences were have now been severely hampered. They aren't allowed to tell the jury about the power they actually possess! To me – that's just disgraceful, and we need a constitutional amendment to correct that.

Same problem with judges. The Legislature doesn't trust them to be fair -- so they've imposed mandatory sentences, and also a mathematical set of *Sentencing Guidelines* which a judge must normally follow. This is where we are currently at. I think it's a damn shame because I've seen how it operates, first hand.

A NEEDED CONSTITUTIONAL AMENDMENT:

As much as I dislike amendments to the Florida Constitution, what we need is a constitutional amendment that would guarantee that a jury be told about any mandatory penalty that might be imposed. If that happened, and they were also told they had a "***jury pardon***" power where they could acquit, or come back with a lesser crime in situations where they felt they should exercise that discretion. That way, any unfair mandatory sentencing law would be counter-balanced by the common sense of the jury. Until that happens — or unless the Legislature gives us some real relief from mandatory sentences in self defense situations – we're still in a lot of trouble.

PLACE WHERE YOU HAVE A RIGHT TO BE – ADDENDUM:

An interesting question came up after the book was completed, and this was the only spot to add it. What if you had a weapon or firearm legally with a CWP, but the location (like Disney) had a "No Weapons" policy? Are you still at a *place where you have a right to be*"? My answer is "yes", on the same basis I spoke about in "trespass" issues. First, you are not committing any criminal conduct. Second, until and unless you are told to leave, you are still an invitee on the premises. However, if you are told to leave, you must. You should still have a "right to be" on the property while you were leaving. Again, my opinion as no case law.

CHAPTER THIRTEEN

SCENARIOS & COMMENTS ON SELF DEFENSE

Over the years there are certain select types of instances that tend to repeat themselves, over and over again. This chapter is a short collection of these miscellaneous scenarios, some real appellate case examples, and some additional advice and explanations. Hopefully, you'll find this helpful. However the scenarios are purely my opinions, thus the actual result could turn out to be very different:

CAR OR BOAT BREAK-IN:
In a situation where a perpetrator is trying to break into your car or boat – until the culprit succeeds in some type of **entry** into the vehicle, however slight – it is only an "**attempted**" burglary. That is not yet a "*forcible felony*". However, even with the 2014 changes in the law – you should still be able to "**threaten**" the use of deadly force – although **using** deadly force would normally be excessive.

QUESTION: Why? How could I legally threaten to use "*deadly force*" where it's not yet a "*forcible felony*"?

ANSWER: Well . . . both F.S. 776.012 and F.S. 776.031 say you can use or threaten to use deadly force to "***prevent***" the imminent commission of a *forcible felony*. (if such is reasonable and necessary). Thus, a *threat of deadly force*, short of a warning shot – should be lawful. On the other hand, use of actual *deadly force* in such a situation has rarely been sustained.

On the other hand, if the perpetrator actually ***enters*** the vehicle, even slightly, the *burglary* is complete – and becomes a "***forcible felony***". F.S. 810.02. As in the previous example – unless the perpetrator is armed with a deadly weapon, or tries to attack you – while your **threat** of using deadly force (short of a warning shot) should be totally lawful, the actual **use** of *deadly force* would still rarely be reasonable. If he simply flees – shooting at him should be the unlawful use of "***excessive force***", and extremely illegal. If the perpetrator reasonably appears to be a threat to you after actual committing a "*burglary*", and advances on you in a threatening manner – a ***warning shot*** is probably legal, but is still a question of *"reasonableness"*, and therefore normally way too risky due to the twenty (20) year mandatory penalty. A loud verbal warning, and some backing up (retreat) would be a good idea whenever possible, with *deadly force* being used **only** if the advance continued, and it was reasonable to believe you were about to be attacked. Likewise, if he was armed with a *deadly weapon* – the use of *deadly force* is almost always lawful, and if advancing – always necessary if you care to survive.

But, let's use the last portion of the last example, and say the perpetrator sees you while trying to break into the vehicle, but not yet having *"entered"*. Instead of running or surrendering, he actually advances on you in what you reasonably perceive as the anticipation of a physical attack. Has the status changed?

Sure! In such a case it is now reasonable to believe that the perpetrator not only attacking you, but is doing so *"in furtherance"* of the commission of the felony, otherwise he would have fled at your approach, or surrendered. So, you still have a right to use, or threaten *deadly force* as long as you reasonably believe his attack is in aid of his desire to complete the burglary, or cause you death or great bodily harm in the process.

QUESTION: Why?

ANSWER: Because the law says that if it is reasonable to believe the perpetrator is assaulting you, even without a weapon, **and** that assault is to **further** his commission of a felony (ie: the 'burglary') – then he is also committing an *"aggravated assault"*, as an "aggravated assault" is defined to include an assault *"with the intent to commit a felony"* even if no *deadly weapon* is involved! F.S. 784.021(1)(b). Thus, if he was trying to break into something, and then assaults you when you try to stop it, versus trying to escape – you can reasonably assume his attack is now an *"aggravated assault"*! With rare exception, there is likely no way to avoid his attack other than the use of *deadly force*, unless you want to take the chance of making just a threat, using non-deadly force, or even more risky – a *warning shot*.

In such a situation, if I had a weapon displayed (which would be legal to stop or prevent a *forcible felony*, **or** the *attempted commission* of one), and the perpetrator was advancing on me – you can bet the only reason he'd be doing so would be to take away my weapon, and then use it on me. Because of that, my advice is that immediate *deadly force* would be prudent to save your life. However, whenever possible, a **very loud** *warning* that you will use your firearm if he "***comes any closer***" would be a good idea. Likewise, while *retreat* is not legally required (unless you are not in "*a place where you have a right to be*", or are otherwise engaged in the commission of any "*criminal conduct*") – **any** type of retreat, even if only a **few steps** is better than none if you have to argue it before a jury.

TWENTY-ONE FOOT RULE:

QUESTION: What about this "***21 foot rule***" I've heard about?

ANSWER: The "***21 foot rule***" is really a study originated by Dennis Tueller, and later repeated by the *Tempe, Arizona Police Department* to measure reaction time. What they found were a number of very important things. First, it takes around 1.2 seconds before a trained officer even begins to react to a dangerous threat situation. Then he still has to draw his firearm, aim, and press the trigger. Just pressing the trigger takes .31 seconds, and an additional .6 second average to stop pressing the trigger if the officer realized the threat had abated, with the average time from realizing a threat exists to drawing and firing (by a well trained individual) is **2 seconds** overall. So – best case scenario – if he already had his gun out and ready, the optimum time it would take to fire the weapon is just over one-and-one half (1.5 seconds)!

They also found that the average officer could not stop a trigger press once it started, and normally got off **two to three shots** before they even realized a threat situation had ended. On top of that they determined that the average individual running at you with a knife from a stand-still will reach you within 1.5 seconds – which equated to **21 feet**. Hence, the "***21 foot rule***". *Fredericks v. State*, 675 So.2d 989, 990 (Fla. 1DCA 1996).

Of course – I'm not a great believer in getting involved in situations where deadly force might be needed. Those can result in both legal issues that result in your arrest, or perhaps serious injury or death to yourself or an innocent bystander. However, in our last example – a police officer or prosecutor would be hard pressed to make an arrest or file charges. That's another reason for the **"loud shouted warning"**, and some retreat! If there's a witness around – they'll hear it, and maybe see it. Even if not, you can testify you tried to avoid it. That will go a long way with any police officer or prosecutor – and an even longer way with a jury.

However, rather than take chances – my personal suggestion in these situations is to: Call 911, stay inside your home, and yell out the window that the police are *"on their way"*. Do not try to confront the suspect as you do not know if he is armed, or if he has any companions hidden who could ambush you. Do not expose yourself to possible gunfire. Most of the time the culprit will flee when they noticed they've been discovered. If they don't – they're probably **very** dangerous, high to boot, and armed to the teeth! Your car isn't worth risking your life.

WARNING!   If someone is only **looking** into your vehicle while on your property it is probably only a *"trespass"*, at least until they make some actual attempt to break into the vehicle. A definite misdemeanor. Plus, except in fenced and posted areas, before something becomes a *"trespass"* – the trespasser normally needs to be **warned** to leave before it becomes a crime!

BURGLARY OF CARPORT OR OTHER STRUCTURE:
A burglary of a carport or other structure (and the items therein) is *a forcible felony* – but remember, a " *burglary*" requires an actual **entry** or partial entry into the structure before it escalates from an "*attempt*" – and it requires the culprit's intent to commit a separate crime within the structure – usually a theft. Thus, an " *attempt*" to commit a burglary is **not** a "*forcible felony*". Still, an attempted entry into a dwelling, residence, or **occupied** vehicle done with "*force*" would activate the presumptions in F.S. 776.013, and allow the use of deadly force by anyone **inside** where the perpetrator was also **inside** any of those places, or was actually attempting to enter. Once they're outside, or have stopped the entry process, or have otherwise broken off their attempt, and are trying to flee – the presumptions end, and your right to use *deadly force* has also likely ended.

Furthermore, since only a dwelling, residence, or occupied vehicle has the protections of the presumptions in C. 776.013 – your actions in the use of force will be judged from the "*reasonable man*" standpoint. If you use *excessive force* – there could be a problem.

While a roofed carport attached to your home is considered part of your dwelling under the law (same for an attached **roofed** porch) – since no "*force*" is usually involved in such an entry – again – you lose the presumptions in C. 776.013 – and are solely under the '*reasonable man*" concept. Still, once the culprit enters the carport – the burglary is complete – and it is a *"**forcible felony**"* (assuming it is reasonable to believe he was attempting to commit a separate crime therein <u>other than</u> a mere *trespass*).

If the culprit entered a fully fenced yard around your dwelling, this is called " ***curtilage***", and is also considered part of your dwelling. Thus, the crime is a *"forcible felony"* once the culprit enters the fenced area – and you may or may not be entitled to the presumptions in C. 776.013 – depending on whether *"force"* was used in entering the property, such as the opening of a gate. Of course, the issue of *"how much force"* is *"force"* has not been resolved by the courts in a self-defense case, and it is possible more "force" than just opening a gate could be required. However, case law involving burglaries does support my interpretation. (ie: Opening a door or unlocked window is a *"breaking"* for the older form of burglary that required both a *"breaking"* and an *"entry"* vs. just an *"entry"*)

However, if you ever discover the person entered simply due to a mistake, or under a claim of right such as the guy from FPL trying to read your meter – *any* use of force becomes unlawful from that point on! Likewise, if all they did was open an unlocked gate – it's not always unusual for folks to do that in the service or delivery business. A court might say your actions were not "reasonable", or as I've already hinted to – maybe *"force"* requires something more where it is not uncommon for non-residents to enter such areas on their own, and unannounced.

As I've mentioned before, it is my **personal opinion** that in responding to any situation that is an actual felony – your possession of a firearm in hand "should" be completely legal. Anything else is kind of suicidal if you are suddenly attacked. However, due to the 2014 changes in the law regarding *"threats"* – that is no longer the law **unless** you are responding to a *"forcible felony"* or its *"attempt"*, or have a *"reasonable belief"* of such. If that is the case, then I believe it is perfectly lawful to having your firearm out, and ready – although " ***pointed***" raises more of a reasonableness question.

QUESTION: Why? What's the difference with pointed?

ANSWER: It's more of a threat, and possible *aggravated assault* if you're wrong, or the perpetrator is a really good liar. Likewise, if I'm on my home or business property and am carrying a firearm or other weapon – I'm totally legal under <u>F.S.</u> 790.25 unless I get involved in an *"improper exhibition"*. So, just carrying and openly displaying a firearm at such places should be protected unless a *"threat"* is added to the situation. ***"Pointing"*** – is normally a *"threat"* in Florida, although it is a jury question.

HOME INVASION - BURGLARY OF RESIDENCE:
Somebody is trying to break into your home:

This is a crime absolutely protected by section 776.013 of the ***"Stand Your Ground"*** law. So long as the invader is not someone who has a right to be there, a family member, or police in the exercise of their lawful duties – you have the right to use *deadly force* if any *"force"* was used in entering, or trying to enter, and you don't fall in any of the exceptions. Whether you use such force – is another question only you will be able to answer. Under any circumstance, you should not be arrested or prosecuted as long as the invader was not outside the home trying to escape, or you're stupid enough to make it sound like you "executed" him for the heck of it.

TRESPASS TO PROPERTY:
Someone comes on your home or business property, and refuses to leave:

1.   The refusal to leave the property of another when told to leave by a person with authority to do so is a ***trespass***. Unless the offender is armed with a firearm or other deadly weapon, a trespass is a misdemeanor. If armed with a deadly weapon – a felony – but NOT a *forcible felony*.

2.   Any owner or authorized person may take a trespasser into custody and detain them until police arrive. The detention must be done in a reasonable manner for a reasonable period of time, and may not involve force or violence unless the trespasser physically resists. Remember, a person does not ordinarily become a "trespasser" until **after** they've been warned to leave, and refuse. Likewise, while the law allows **"reasonable force"** to be used to remove a trespasser from your property if they refuse – if you exceed what is reasonable for the circumstances – you will likely be guilty of a criminal battery for the use of *"excessive force"*. It is **not** generally lawful to hold someone just to complete a *"**Trespass Warning**"* unless the person was actually trespassing vs. merely being warned to leave. If they voluntarily leave, and have not been previously warned to stay away – it is not a trespass, and you have no legal right to interfere with their leaving.

ASSAULTS ON YOUR PERSON:
You are approached by a person or persons who want to engage you in a fight:

1. An *"assault"* occurs when another person makes an intentional, **unlawful** threat to do imminent violence, combined with some deliberate outward act, that places you in reasonable fear of imminent violence. *Assault* is a misdemeanor unless made with a *deadly weapon*. *Assault* with a *deadly weapon* is " *aggravated assault*" – a *forcible felony*. Likewise, a *battery* occurs when you are intentionally, and unlawfully struck or touched by another without your express or implied permission. *Battery* is also a misdemeanor unless you are severely injured, or a *deadly weapon* is used. The use of a *deadly weapon*, or severe injury (ie: "great bodily harm") elevates the crime to an *aggravated battery* – a *forcible felony*.

2. Where it is reasonable to believe that the assault is in aid (ie: *"in furtherance of"*) of the commission of a robbery or other *forcible felony*, or where it is objectively reasonable to believe that the assault will result in death or great bodily harm to yourself (ie: not a nosebleed, not cuts and bruises – but something really serious) – *deadly force* is normally justified. If you want to play it smart – the words *"absolutely sure"* should be substituted for the word *"reasonable"*, even if that exceeds what the law requires. Likewise, sometimes, in such a situation – display of a weapon will stop the attack. If the *display* was in reasonable anticipation of imminent attack – display alone should be lawful – even a deadly weapon. However, I have seen cases where citizens were prosecuted for such display – especially where the assailant is a good liar. Plus, I almost never suggest a *"warning shot"* even where it would be legal – because a warning shot will always be considered the use of *deadly force*, will open you up to the possibility of a twenty year mandatory minimum sentence if you are prosecuted – and will be **closely examined** by both police and prosecutors no matter what the situation was. In an unfriendly jurisdiction – it would likely be tested by an arrest and prosecution.

So – if you think a *warning shot* would work – maybe the situation isn't as bad as you think it is. Quite frankly – sometimes from a legal standpoint – you're better off shooting the rotten S.O.B. rather than firing a warning shot. Sad! But, that's the state of the law.

3.   If you are obviously frail, obviously beyond 65 years of age, have a bad heart, or have warned the individuals that you have such a condition – and they persist – the reasonableness of your being able to use a deadly weapon **increases substantially** as you have a much greater reason to fear *"great bodily harm"*. Likewise, other factors can play into reasonableness of using a deadly weapon such as: number of attackers, specific threats made by the attackers ("we're gonna kill you!"), relative size and strength of those involved, whether they are armed, whether they reasonably appear to be violent gang members, whether the victim is a woman, pregnant, etc. All of this factors into the *"great bodily harm"* issue. However, before I ever chose to display a weapon – even a non-deadly one – I would do everything in my power to avoid the situation – even apologize or retreat when I was totally in the right. I've done that several times. Only if you are absolutely sure you will be robbed, raped, kidnaped, dead, lose an eye – or wind-up in the hospital – would I draw a weapon, or fire it. I also highly recommend carrying a *non-deadly weapon* besides a firearm – as their use is legally much safer both from a standpoint of avoiding a felony charge – and being thought of as within the realm of *"reasonable force"* in response to a misdemeanor, or non-violent felony. I always carry a *Taser* for that reason – even if I have a handgun. *Pepper spray* is also an excellent option, and very good on animals. Plus, <u>F.S.</u> 790.053 says I can legally **openly carry** pepper spray or a Taser, etc., in my hand. (so long as I don't violate another section, <u>F.S.</u> 790.10 – *"improper exhibition"*). Thus, walking into a dark parking lot already prepared with one of these in hand – can be a great idea.

<u>ROBBERY & ATTEMPTED ROBBERY:</u>
<u>You are approached by a person who demands money or your car:</u>

Assuming this is not your landlord coming after you for late rent – then if you can safely draw your weapon, and the culprit is armed or you reasonably believe he may be armed (which should be a "given" in almost every attempted robbery), the law would allow you to threaten or use *deadly force*. Big problem here is: does he have a partner waiting in the shadows who can also shoot you? Will he get a shot off before you do – or after? Will you both die? Is it better just to give him the money or keys – and hope for the best? Unless it's an *abduction situation* – that's not a question I can answer, and you'll have to use your best judgment. However, a robbery or attempted robbery are two of the most dangerous situations you can face, and the law should be totally on your side no matter what you do. If it also appears likely that you will be abducted in the process – statistics indicate you, and all those abducted with you will be soon be homicide victims if you comply. Don't get in the car, even if you have to leave a family member or companion! Your escape may actually save their life. Your compliance will likely get all of you killed. Better to take the chance of trying to escape, and possibly being shot in an area where there may be help, than ten miles out in the woods where there is zero chance of survival. Once you get in that car, and your hands are taped – you are usually dead, as is everyone taken with you!

DISCREET DISPLAY:
Discreet display where you believe a crime is about to occur:

I have been in this situation, and heard of many situations where discreet display of a firearm has stopped a potential crime - usually a robbery – before it occurs. In these situations, discretely holding open a jacket or shirt to reveal a firearm without touching it – has resulted in the 'bad guy" turning around, and walking the other way – or just driving off. The problem with these instances is that if you make a mistake, and it wasn't really a robbery – you could be in deep trouble.

Why?

Because in a mistaken situation where the other guy wasn't really going to commit a crime – you probably will be reported to the police, and in many of those instances I've seen where the other person actually believes you **pointed** the gun at them, even when it was purely mere display! I've seen that in at least twenty variations over the years. Assuming, the police respond – I will make an exception to my usual advice: In such a situation it is **absolutely necessary** to for you to advise any responding police officer that you thought you were about to be robbed, and (if true) never pointed the firearm. If you don't do that it will be hell to pay later. Likewise, if your belief was reasonable, even if you were mistaken, it is normally a complete defense to any charge. Therefore, this **one type** of situation that is the **exception** to the usual rule. In such a case it is important that the police know your story, what you did, what you didn't do, and why you did it.

I'll make one other observation here from my reading of cases: Discrete display is the safest when you **do not touch the firearm**! If you only pull back a jacket, lift up a shirt, or whatever to merely display the firearm – these have been the cases where the court is most reluctant to call your actions unlawful – and my belief is that handled properly – a jury would feel the same way. *Tiger* *v. Marcus,* 37 So.3d 986 (Fla. 4DCA 2010); *Bell v. State,* 670 So.2d 123 (Fla. 2DCA 1996). However, anytime you handle the firearm, even in a holster pointed skyward – it becomes a jury question whether or not it was an *aggravated assault.* *Stewart v. State,* 872 So.2d 865 (Fla. 2DCA 1996). I think that's ludicrous, and legally incorrect – but it is currently the law. To me, where used in a self defense situation – that's clearly a *conditional threat,* an attempt to withdraw from any further conflict, a warning, or a combination of all three. Not – an *"assault".*

However, and hopefully not to beat this issue to death by repetition: It is not unlawful to point a firearm at someone **engaged** in a *forcible felony,* or its *attempt.* On the other hand – firing it would be entirely another thing. An excellent quote about this comes from the case of *Chesnut v. State,* 516 So. 2d 1144 (Fla. 5DCA 1987), where the appellate court stated:

> *" It is not unlawful to threaten a burglar to require him to leave, or to threaten an assaulter to require him to desist, or to threaten a thief, as here, to require him to return the stolen property. "*

Unfortunately, Mr. Chesnut went a bit further when he put a gun to a thief's head, and threatened to shoot him, unless he told him where he hid the stolen items. When he didn't – Mr. Chesnut pulled the trigger. As you probably guessed – the appellate court agreed this went somewhat, and perhaps way over the line of what was reasonable – and was a definite act of excessive force. Still . . . a really great quote!

DISPLAY IN OTHER SITUATIONS:
F.S. 790.053 forbids open carry of firearms. *"Open carry"* is not a **momentary display** of a lawful firearm by an individual with a valid CWL. Such is lawful in Florida if not done in threatening manner so long as you have the CWL. F.S. 790.053(1). Likewise, F.S. 790.053 does not forbid open carry of any other weapon except an *"electric weapon or device".* It then goes on to specifically authorize open carry of a *self defense chemical spray,* and any *nonlethal stun gun, dart firing stun gun,* or electrical weapon or device designed solely for defensive purposes. That should mean *Tasers, stun guns, and pepper sprays* since these are considered defensive weapons by almost everyone. On the other hand, unless you're on your home or business property, or fall within the exceptions set out in section F.S. 790.25 of the Florida Statutes – it's usually against the law to openly display a firearm except in lawful self defense, or lawful defense of property. The qualifier here is: Is intentional display lawful in self defense situations that are less than a forcible felony, or an attempt at one?

The answer, which I've been trying to pound into your brain for over seventy pages is: "Hell, no!" "Don't do it!"

USE OF HOLLOW POINT AMMUNITION:

I constantly get emails from people asking me if they'll get in trouble because they used certain ammo that has a "reputation" for causing severe injuries. I'm asked if using these types of ammunition can cause problems if they are prosecuted when using self defense. My answer is: "it shouldn't".

Why?

Well, almost all modern self-defense ammunition is based on a *hollow-point,* although modern developments are beginning to use different type tips and core fillers to help the uniform expansion of the bullet, and also help it penetrate outer obstacles intact, like thick clothing, glass, etc. Since you're using "*deadly force*", and trying your best to incapacitate your assailant immediately – so you can survive – you'd think the most powerful and efficient ammo you can find would be the correct way to go. I mean – it is "**deadly**" force! It's supposed to kill the assailant – or otherwise instantly disable him – otherwise YOU may die! If that happens – why the hell defend yourself in the first place?

Likewise, many law enforcement agencies are using hollow point +P, or P+P, for their ammo – which is really heavy duty. Same basic idea – the officer survives – the bad guy gets what he deserves. However, there's always a chance a prosecutor may try to use the type of ammo you use against you if the court lets him or her get away with it. Legally, this should never happen as it is misleading to the jury, and highly prejudicial to your case. Thus, one Florida appellate court has already held it is reversible error for a prosecutor to argue that hollow point bullets are only for killing. *Kolp v. State,* 932 So.2d 1283 (Fla. 4DCA 2006). Your attorney should be making a pre-trial motion to keep this type of argument out of the case. As long as the ammo is legal – it should not matter what you use – only how you used it.

On the other hand, ammo that has a name like "*safety shot*", or "*Extreme Defense*" sounds much better than "Black Talon" to citizens who have no idea about guns or ammo. Sometimes – it's all about perception, no matter what the law says!

REASONS AGAINST MISDEMEANOR DISPLAY:

I've decided to add this last section as a word of **strong warning**, because I've run across way too many citizens who thought it was perfectly OK to display a firearm to stop a misdemeanor or non-forcible felony situation. And I know I've already covered this several times – but with the changes in 2014 – you can't! On the other hand, in other states where display is legal to stop a misdemeanor – it sometimes ended in tragedy – legal or not. So, just for the heck of it, let's explore the reasons for and against:

If you display a firearm or other deadly weapon where you can't use it – what happens if the other guy still attacks you? What happens if he tries to take it away? What happens if you were mistaken about the situation, and the other person was doing something entirely innocent which you misinterpreted? What happens if you were equally responsible for the incident, or were involved in a "mutual combat" situation under the law? What happens if he lies – and is better at it than you?

What usually happens is that you're in a whole mess of very serious trouble! And worse, what sometimes happens is that in the heat of the moment when you have it out – you accidentally, or intentionally fire it – shove it in his chest – or use it as a club – or he grabs it, and it fires!

If you fire it intentionally – you've used "*deadly force*" to stop a misdemeanor, or non-violent felony. Very bad move! Go directly to jail! If you strike him with it – it's normally excessive force, and likely an **"*aggravated battery*"**, even if the injury is slight – because you've used a firearm in a battery – which is **always** a "deadly weapon". Of course – a battery with a "*deadly weapon*" is an "***aggravated battery***" thus elevating even a simple battery to a second degree felony! Not real good! Also, if you were wrong about being legally able to defend yourself – throw in an additional aggravated assault. If you're lucky – maybe you'll only be charged with a misdemeanor "***improper exhibition***" under F.S. 790.10. However, any of these possibilities are absolutely insane! It's just not worth it – and will almost always result in your arrest. **So, don't do it!**

How about if I just verbally threaten the use of a firearm or baseball bat if someone is committing a crime less than a forcible felony?

Well . . . either you haven't read anything I've said so far, or you're just joking. The 2014 changes to F.S. 776.012 and F.S. 776.031 say you can only **"threaten"** the use of deadly force in a deadly force situation. A felony that is not also a *"forcible felony"* is **NOT** one of those! A misdemeanor certainly isn't! So, do I recommend you have it displayed? Do I recommend you have it pointed? Do I recommend you even let the culprit know you're armed?

Hell, no! Not unless the Legislature changes the law back to where a ***threat*** of using deadly force is OK in any situation where it is reasonable, or at least to stop a felony, or imminent physical attack. Or . . . better yet . . . just use the exact wording in <u>F.S.</u> 776.013 and apply it to <u>F.S.</u> 776.012 and 776.031:

> *"or threatening to use defensive force that is intended or likely to cause death or great bodily harm to another."*

ONE OTHER COMMENT:
Well . . . I've read and reread this chapter, over and over – and no matter how many times I read it – there are still things I could add to it. The problem here – for all of us – is the lack of Florida case law, and the fact that when you use a standard of *"reasonableness"* – you just don't know how "reasonable" will be defined by others at a later time – especially if they're anti-gun, pacifist, or whatever. Same thing with when a *threat* is lawful or not. It just leaves too many unknowns in how you should react legally to all these possible situations. That's why I think a statute allowing ***"imperfect self defense"*** is needed in Florida, just like they already have in other states. Where only a *"threat"* of using force is involved, such a statute would trump any mandatory sentence. You can't just sock somebody who's never been in trouble in their life with a mandatory minimum sentence because they made an honest error in judgment. Likewise, it makes no sense to restrict someone from not being able to threaten deadly force to stop at least felony conduct as long as such is reasonable, there is no discharge of a *warning shot*, and they are not the initial aggressor. That's my opinion.

However, here are some other thoughts to ponder – especially if you somehow get on a jury where these issues come into play – or even have a chance to discuss it with friends or family, or a legislator you happen to know.

WOMEN:
I think that a woman really is in a different position than a man in many self defense situations – as long as her antagonist is a male – or more so, several males. Women are often victimized by men – sexually, violently, or both. If a woman is driving, and some guy tries to force her off the road, tailgates her at highway speeds, or whatever – it's not quite the same thing as it happening to a guy.

Why?

Because as a practical matter – victimizing a woman in this way isn't the norm. For most guys, it shows they're either completely out of control – or have something more sinister in mind. It is a response that is normally unacceptable even when the woman is in the wrong. Most men - even young men – are brought up to be able to walk away from this kind of thing! Sure – there are exceptions – but this is the general rule of conduct in our society. So, when a woman is surrounded by a group of guys, grabbed by a male in a remote setting, or is a victim in a road rage situation – especially if the other driver is trying to force her off the road, bump her, or box her in – she has some major additional issues as to what this nut-job has in mind – and the display, or even use, of a deadly weapon would seem to be a lot more reasonable than the same situation between just two guys having a real bad day with each other. Another reason I do not like the 2014 changes to the self defense statutes.

TAKING THE CONCEPT FURTHER INTO THEORY:

OK – let's go a little dangerous here (maybe really dangerous), and move into **pure theory** of what the limits are, or are not, as to **display** in attempting lawful self defense. Please – **do not** consider this current Florida law! It is not! It is pure theory, and is based upon what I believe logic requires versus what the law might actually be. Likewise, this is an area that is more of a long-time observation than legal advice – because we still have that elusive standard of what the hell is really "reasonable" – unless you're the poor slob it's happening to – at the moment it happens. However, in this sense – the definition of "reasonableness" that **should** be required in the courts – or at least argued by attorneys appears in Quaggin v. State, 752 So.2d 19, 25 (Fla. 5DCA 2000):

> If your actions are not clearly *unreasonable* – then legally, you are acting *reasonably.*

While this is not currently the wording used in the jury instructions, Quaggin establishes it is most certainly the law! Therefore, it is something every defense attorney should be arguing! Likewise, we come to the next question: Since all sections of Chapter 776 say that a person is justified in using or threatening to use force (except deadly force) to the extent he or she reasonably believes such conduct is necessary to defend themself against imminent harm – aren't we talking about the amount of force actually **used on** the attacker, or **at** the attacker (ie: a punch, discharge of a weapon, etc.) versus mere **display** or pointing something that **MIGHT** be used against them at some future point if they persist in unlawful conduct?

So . . . how can *"pure display"* ever be the excessive *"**use**"* of anything, and certainly not of *"**force**"*? Because from a logical standpoint – a mere *"**conditional threat**"* to stop potentially criminal conduct should never be *"excessive"* unless the Legislature wants to create a new standard that punishes the *degree of a threat* – vs. – the *degree of an attack*, or the actual resulting physical damage or harm.

What I mean by this is: If I display a firearm, knife, bazooka, baseball bat, blowgun, or even a broom – I've used almost the exact same amount of *"force"* as to all of these as far as their *display* goes – but I still haven't used any *"force"* on or against the other individual. *"**Force**"* should mean I've **touched** them in some way, or caused them to be touched – or probably if I **tried** to do so, and missed, or deliberately gave them that impression. So – how can mere display be excessive? And more importantly – how can it not be "reasonable" – or likewise – how could that be *"unreasonable"* – as long as I had an objectively reasonable believe that the other person was committing an unlawful act against myself or my property, or where I had a reasonable belief that I might lawfully need to defend myself on an imminent basis? And . . . what possibly is *"imminent"* about *display* where left in a holster, in a belt, or pointed at the ground or skyward? That I might shoot a bird or a groundhog?

I mean . . . let's take another example to the absurd: You are walking down the street, and are holding a wet sponge because you just cleaned a neighbor's kitchen. You're a hell of a nice guy or gal! Two thugs (male or female – take your pick) come walking down the street from the other direction, and yell at you that they're gonna beat your a_s! You stop. You point the sponge directly at them, you wave it violently around in the air, and tell them if they take a step further – you will shove the sponge up in a place for which they will ever remember! Both die of laughter – and you are prosecuted.

Same example – this time as you're walking down the street you are holding a hatchet – because you've just chopped down your dad's old cherry tree. They are thirty feet away, and once again threaten you. You hold up the hatchet, swing it around – and remind them you have just hacked down a cherry tree with one mighty blow – can throw a silver dollar across the Potomac – and never lie. They immediately decide to vote for you for as our next president. However, have you actually used any more *"force"* against them – than with the sponge?

Same example – but this time with knife . . . or a bow . . . or a gun. And – the same question: Have you used any more *"force"* in any of these situations

AGAINST the person?

My belief is: **You have not!** And if you haven't – maybe the question of *"reasonable"* or *"necessary"* isn't what weapon you used – *deadly* or *non-deadly* – but whether you had a right to use ANYTHING – merely to try to stop an attack before it begins – or stop an unlawful act against you or your property?

Unfortunately, with the changes in Chapter 776 in 2014, these questions now seem to be foreclosed – because the current question isn't just whether you are acting *"reasonably"* – it is also simply whether any *"threat"* was made (*conditional* or not), and if the *threat* involved a *"deadly weapon."* Because, if that's the case, it can only be made to stop or prevent a *forcible felony*, or *death or great bodily harm.*

ZIMMERMAN CASE:

Most gun owners were probably shocked by the Zimmerman case – because from a legal standpoint it had nothing to do with *"standing your ground"*, and from a technical standpoint, while he may have placed himself in unnecessary danger, and caused Trayvon Martin to misapprehend his situation – he didn't do anything illegal – even under post 2014 legal standards! So, why was he prosecuted?

The answer was pure politics! It was obviously a bit more complicated than that, and I certainly explained that on a daily basis in my blog while the case was going on. But, when you realize it cost the then State Attorney and Chief of Police their jobs because they refused to make an arrest or prosecute – you get the idea.

However, the one thing the case conclusively demonstrated was that the alleged *"immunity"* in Chapter 776 is largely an illusion except in defense of a residence or occupied conveyance. Why?

Because Florida's appellate courts have consistently held, contrary to all the established case law on immunity situations – that a defendant (not the prosecution) has the burden of proving *immunity* by a preponderance of the evidence – and thereby **gutted** the effectiveness of the statutory protection. Thus, unless the Florida Supreme Court reverses its position – gun owners need to be very careful when they rely on any statutory "immunity" – because in large part – it exists in name only – and not in application.

IF YOU REALLY LIKED THIS BOOK:

OK . . . here comes the shameless plug for the book, and three important questions:

Do you think the book provided invaluable information?
Do you think every gun owner should really read this book?
Do you think this book may save you from an arrest or jail?

If you answered all those questions in the affirmative – I'd be grateful if you'd spread the word about the book, and how important it really is. Likewise, if you can convince your local gun store, or firearms instructor to carry it – that would also be appreciated.

It's not that I need the money – although that certainly doesn't hurt – but it's something far more important – because there is NO OTHER PLACE you can find this information! Nowhere! Letting a friend know that – might save their life – or keep them out of a mandatory jail sentence. Be a friend – spread the word.

CONCLUSION:

Well, that's it for the book. Hopefully, you've learned something. Hopefully, you'll never have to experience any of the situations I've outlined in it. Hopefully, by reading the book you will have the knowledge to avoid any of these situations, or at worst, you'll know how to handle them, and what to do. That's why the book was written in the first place. Good luck, and God bless.

INDEX

NOTES